ARE SKILLS THE ANSWER?

*The Political Economy of Skill Creation
in Advanced Industrial Countries*

COLIN CROUCH
DAVID FINEGOLD
MARI SAKO

OXFORD
UNIVERSITY PRESS

OXFORD
UNIVERSITY PRESS

Great Clarendon Street, Oxford OX2 6DP

Oxford University Press is a department of the University of Oxford.
It furthers the University's objective of excellence in research, scholarship
and education by publishing worldwide in

Oxford New York

Athens Auckland Bangkok Bogotá Buenos Aires Calcutta
Cape Town Chennai Dar es Salaam Delhi Florence Hong Kong Istanbul
Karachi Kuala Lumpur Madrid Melbourne Mexico City Mumbai
Nairobi Paris São Paulo Shanghai Singapore Taipei Tokyo Toronto Warsaw
with associated companies in Berlin Ibadan

Oxford is a registered trade mark of Oxford University Press
in the UK and in certain other countries

Published in the United States
by Oxford University Press Inc., New York

First published 1999
First published in paperback 2001

British Library Cataloguing in Publication Data
Data available

Library of Congress Cataloging in Publication Data
Crouch, Colin.
Are skills the answer? : the political economy of skill creation
in advanced industrial countries / Colin Crouch, David Finegold, and
Mari Sako.
p. cm.
Includes bibliographical references (p.) and index.
1. Occupational training. 2. Occupational training—Government
policy. 3. Vocational education. 4. Vocational education—
Government policy. 5. Vocational evaluation. 6. Labor supply—
Effect of education on. 7. Economic development—Effect of
education on. 8. Skilled labor—Government policy. I. Finegold,
David. II. Sako, Mari. III. Title.
HD5715.C76 1999
331.25'92—dc21   98–8569
ISBN 0–19–829438–7
ISBN 0–19–924111–2 (pbk.)

1 3 5 7 9 10 8 6 4 2

Typeset by Graphicraft Ltd., Hong Kong
Printed in Great Britain
on acid-free paper by
Biddles Ltd., Guildford & King's Lynn

CONTENTS

PREFACE

This study focuses on the problems confronting institutions for the creation of occupational skills in seven advanced industrial countries (AICs). We hope that it will contribute to two different areas of debate in contemporary political economy. The first concerns the diversity of institutional forms taken by modern capitalism, and the difficulties currently surrounding the survival of that diversity. Most discussions of this theme (for example, Albert 1991; Crouch and Streeck 1997; Hollingsworth, Schmitter, and Streeck 1994) analyse economic institutions and governance in general. Here we try to be more specific and illustrate the general theoretical debates by considering one specific topic. Skill creation is a useful area for such concentration, since it brings together public policy ambitions and the market economy.

The second focus is on vocational education and training (VET) in its own right. Our concern here is with those levels of the VET system dealing with foundation and intermediate, not the higher levels of academic, training. This does not mean that we are limiting our attention to manual skills; the distinction between manual and non-manual is in any case one which is breaking down. Therefore, when we speak of 'skills', this is not to be understood to mean only 'skilled manual' work. Similarly, the term 'vocational' education is intended to be equally applicable to the preparation of banking staffs and bricklayers. In at least Germany and the USA several intermediate vocational skills are offered in parts of the higher education system. What we do leave out of consideration is the university provision of advanced professional and academic skills at masters and doctoral level, including MBAs. These last are of considerable vocational importance for key managerial and professional roles, but our principal interest is in the use of VET policy to advance and safeguard the economic position of the mass of the working population. The importance of this theme for general economic welfare and employment opportunities is today recognized by policymakers in both government and business. It is widely viewed as essential that the advanced countries secure competitive advantage in a global economy by moving into product markets requiring highly skilled and highly productive workforces if standards of living are to advance. We in no way wish to undermine this consensus, and share the universal view of its importance. Our analysis, however, draws attention to certain problematic aspects of relying too heavily on improvements in the supply of skills to solve economic and social problems.

First, the employment-generating power of improvements in skill levels is limited. The internationally traded sectors which use truly advanced skills are small in size and number and become even less labour intensive as their skill levels increase. Employment policy cannot depend fully on education policies.

Second, while the acquisition of skills has become a major public need and a fundamental issue for governments, we are increasingly dependent for their provision on the private sphere of the individual firm which, by definition, is not set up to meet general needs. Left to themselves, firms will engage in a large amount of vocational training, but it will be targeted on selected groups of employees. There are no inherent tendencies for firms' market-driven search for improved skills also to supply a strategy for skill maximization for a society as a whole. In particular there is a danger that, as governments gradually privatize expertise in this field and defer to the private sector's priorities, they will lose the capacity to sustain collective, public concerns.

Third, this process leads in turn to government action being restricted to residual care for the unemployed, which then limits even further the capacity of public agencies to contribute at the leading edge of advanced-skills policy.

Fourth, government action without extensive co-operation with firms is ill-informed and becomes rapidly outdated; but moving too far to accept firms' own agendas incapacitates public policy. Truly co-operative, expert forums are needed. Neo-corporatist institutions have historically often proved to be the most effective means of doing this, but at a time when these institutions are needed more than ever, they are experiencing difficulties in developing adequate sensitivity to company needs. This is partly because the pace of change is now so fast; partly because firms increasingly want skills defined in terms of their individual company culture or techniques, where they are reluctant to allow even representative business associations to be involved in their affairs.

We do not, however, limit ourselves to negative comments. Although our book is not concerned with elaborating detailed policy proposals, we draw attention to the points where reform is needed and identify possible paths forward and needs for progress in a number of areas.

First, skills policy cannot provide an entire employment policy. Policies to improve the job chances of low-productivity workers through deregulation have generated employment, but expose individuals in these jobs to insecurity and harsh working conditions. There must therefore be reconsideration of the former role of public-service employment as a provider of secure employment with a living, though modest, wage for low-productivity workers.

Second, the task of helping the unemployed find work must be separated from that of pursuing national strategies for advanced-level skills, or the public agencies involved in the latter will lose credibility.

Third, public agencies need to find new ways of working with the business sector that neither repeat the former remoteness of government departments nor continue the present trend of relinquishing policy leadership to firms. An essential aspect of this will be the acquisition of expertise and authority by public agencies, through such means as supporting the development of skills standards, improving the certification of employers as trainers, and identifying benchmarks for high-skill enterprises.

In its early stages our work benefited greatly from generous financial assistance from the Centre for Economic Performance at the London School of Economics and Political Science, and from assistance with the substantive research from Lucy Matthew, then a research assistant at the Centre. The usual disclaimers apply: neither the Centre nor Ms Matthew necessarily share the views expressed, and neither is responsible for any errors we have made.

We are also grateful for advice and assistance given by fellow researchers in various countries, in particular Birger Viklund and colleagues at the Arbetslivs-centrum, Stockholm, Mirella Baglioni and Marino Regini in Milan; and Uschi Backes-Gellner and Peter Sadowski in Trier.

Parts of Chapter 1 have appeared in C. Crouch, 'Skills-Based Full Employ-ment: The Latest Philosopher's Stone', *British Journal of Industrial Relations*, 35 (1997), 367–84. Parts of Chapter 2 have appeared in C. Crouch, 'Labour Market Regulations, Social Policy and Job Creation', in J. Gual (ed.), *Job Creation: What Labour Market Do We Need?* (Cheltenham: Elgar, 1998). Earlier versions of part of Chapter 8 appeared in D. Finegold and D. Levine, 'Institutional Incentives for Employee Training', *Journal of Education and Work* (1997).

LIST OF FIGURE AND TABLES

ABBREVIATIONS

AIC   Advanced industrial countries
ALMP   Active labour market policy
AMS   Arbetsmarknadstyrelsen (Sweden, the Labour Market Board)
AMU   Arbetsmarknadsutbildningen (Sweden, the Labour Market Training
          Board)
BIBB   Bundesinstitut für Berufsbildung (Germany, Federal Institute for
          Occupational Training)
CAP   Certificat d'aptitude professionelle (France)
CBI   Confederation of British Industry (UK)
CEREQ   Centre d'Étude et de Recherches sur les Qualifications (France)
CNC   Computer-numerical control
CPS   Current Population Survey (USA)
CSS   Community and Social Services
EMU   European Monetary Union
EU   European Union
GCSE   General Certificate of Secondary Education (UK)
GNVQ   General National Vocational Qualification (UK)
IALS   International Adult Literacy Survey
IIP   Investors in People (UK)
ITB   Industrial Training Board (UK)
LEA   Local Education Authority (UK)
LEC   Local Enterprise Company (Scotland)
IOE   International Organization of Employers
LO   Landesorganisationen (Sweden, the National Organization [of trade
          unions])
MSC   Manpower Services Commission (UK)
NAB   National Alliance of Business (USA)
NCEE   National Center on Education and the Economy (USA)
NCVQ   National Council for Vocational Qualifications (UK)
NIC   Newly industrializing country
NIESR   National Institute for Economic and Social Research (UK)
NVQ   National Vocational Qualification (UK)
OECD   Organization for Economic Co-operation and Development
PIC   Private Industry Council (USA)
SAF   Svenska Arbetsgivarföreningen (Swedish Employers Union)
SAP   Socialdemokratiska Arbetarpartitet (Sweden, Social Democratic
          Labour Party)
SIPP   Survey of Income Program Participation (USA)
SMEA   Small and Medium-Sized Enterprises Agency (Japan)
SOU   (Sweden, government publications agency)

TEC	Training and Enterprise Council (England and Wales)
TNC	Transnational corporations
TUC	Trades Union Congress (UK)
TVEI	Technical and Vocational Education Initiative (UK)
VET	Vocational education and training
YTS	Youth Training Scheme (UK)

1

The Dispiriting Search for the Learning Society

Britain lives by the skill of its people. A well trained work force is an essential condition of our economic survival.

> (*Training for Jobs*, White Paper issued jointly by Department of Employment and
> Department of Education and Science, UK government, 1984)

In the emerging global economy, everything is mobile: capital, factories, even entire industries. The only resource that's really rooted in a nation—and the ultimate source of all its wealth—is its people. The only way America can compete and win in the 21st century is to have the best-educated, best-trained workforce in the world.

> (*Putting People First*, Bill Clinton and Al Gore, book produced for their
> presidential election campaign, 1992)

In all advanced industrial countries debates about education and vocational skills have acquired a distinctive prominence and urgency. Everywhere the argument is broadly the same, and at a very general level is shared by all shades of political opinion and by business and labour leaders. The acquisition of knowledge and skills is increasingly seen as both the main challenge and the central opportunity for achieving a return to full employment in a post-Keynesian economy. We are commonly described as living in a 'learning society' filled with 'knowledge workers', a description that stresses the centrality not only of knowledge but of rapid changes in knowledge, requiring learning as a permanent process, in the economic life of the future.

This is considered a challenge because it is feared that people without appropriate knowledge and skills will be unable to find work in that future. There are two main reasons for this. First, most though by no means all the jobs that have been destroyed through technological progress in recent years have been low-skilled ones, and the educational levels demanded for most occupations seem to be rising; in nearly all societies unemployment is highest among those with low levels of education. Second, it is generally assumed in the existing advanced countries that the challenges posed by the rise of new low-cost producers in other parts of the world can be met only if labour in the advanced countries has high levels of skill which will differentiate it from the capacities of workers in the newly industrializing countries (NICs)—with the implication that those people in the advanced countries who do not acquire high levels of skill will be left at the mercy of global labour competition.

More positively, knowledge and skills are seen as presenting opportunities: individuals who acquire advanced levels of education are more likely to secure prosperous futures for themselves. At its most ambitious this perspective refers to an attractive and not completely unrealistic utopia: a vision of a world (or at least some individual societies) almost without unskilled, low-productivity people, in which all mindless and physically damaging jobs are carried out by robots; all members of the workforce have a source of occupational pride in their skills and knowledge; income differentials are compressed through the market-compatible device of overcoming the scarcity of high skill. In such a society the number of citizens who could not attain a high skill level would be so small that the rest of the community would be able to subsidize the wages earned by their low-productivity labour, ensuring that their standard of living would not fall too far behind that of the rest. Also, were low-productivity personal services to become scarcer than popular taste wanted, people would be willing to pay for their restoration and would value the capacity to practise them (for example, through provision of caring services within public or charitable employment). Such a utopia would be compatible with many of the aspirations of both the political left (seeking a reduction of material inequalities) and right (seeking to achieve any social goals through market-compatible means).

While this vision is utopian, it is a utopia towards which there has been real progress, especially during the first three post-war decades, the period the French call *les trente glorieuses*. In Sweden a combination of active labour-market policy, centralized collective bargaining, strong export activity, and public service growth virtually abolished both unemployment and unskilled work. The Federal Republic of Germany reduced the proportion of the workforce without a recognized skill to a very small proportion through a significant expansion of higher education and an almost universal apprenticeship system, and again a high level of export activity. More generally throughout the industrial world, two particular forms of low-skilled work—back-breaking rural labour and domestic service jobs which combined personal subservience with hard work and long hours—declined massively between 1950 and 1980.

Some aspects of the onward march toward a high-skill society then seemed to have been checked. The growth of public service employment—which in most countries is both the biggest single source of highly educated employment and the main means whereby workers with low skills can find work with reasonable employment conditions—hit a ceiling. This was caused by a combination of declining confidence in the capacity of government and the political problems of high taxation at a time when it was becoming easier for companies to move operations across national borders to avoid high-cost regimes. Further, improvements in productivity gradually made it more difficult to generate employment at former rates, a problem that first hit mass-production industry but later spread to many routine activities in various services sectors. This created particular difficulties in parts of the world (for example southern Europe) encountering this new wave of productivity growth while still undergoing the secular decline of agricultural employment.

But some developments favourable to the utopia have continued apace. The globalization of many productive activities has produced an increasing shift to high-skill production in the advanced countries as technological advance mainly replaces unskilled work.[1] Also, populations in the advanced countries seem willing to take more and more advantage of educational opportunities in order to improve their employment chances. There is a constant upward shift in the skill profile of the working population.

Two large main clouds remain over utopia. In many countries and sectors, new, secure jobs making use of advanced skills are not expanding fast enough to absorb those liberated from low-skilled agricultural, factory, and menial service work. This happens partly because in a post-Keynesian economy with free capital markets governments have to pursue tight-money, restrictive policies, and firms are cautious about taking on new staff who must be trained. Alternatively, there is a return to menial work and poor working conditions, for example in the USA and the UK, as governments deregulate protected sectors and corporations rely on the newly found flexibility of contingent workers to sustain their comparative advantage. There are clear limits on who can enter utopia. The fact that many succeed in the competition for attractive employment makes it particularly tough for those who fail, whether because they are outsiders in the sense of being unemployed, or because they remain in poor, marginal jobs which are available to them only because they accept low wages and highly insecure and uncongenial conditions: a distinct dystopia for some while others continue to move towards the knowledge society.

One consequence has been a widening of income differentials in many countries, but especially in those like the UK and the USA, where the relatively low levels of worker protection, including the low level of entitlements for displaced workers, made possible a new growth of low-skilled employment—thereby limiting the level of unemployment. Since the USA at least has also seen considerable growth in high-skill employment, there has been a pattern of bipolar growth: skilled manual and routine non-manual forms of employment are 'hollowed out' by the twin processes of the upward shift in skills promoted by competitive pressures and the growth of insecure, low-productivity work for those left over who have to find their place in the workforce by becoming disposable and cheap to employ. A sign of this trend in the USA has been the dramatic increase in the earnings gap between corporate chief executives, who have seen unprecedented growth in rewards in the last decade, much of it through stock options, and the average worker, whose earnings have held stable or declined in real terms, despite sustained high levels of corporate profitability (OECD 1996a).

Acceptance of this situation has increasingly become the dominant strategy in the advanced countries. It advocates the deregulation of labour markets and temporary reduction of living standards to ensure avoidance of unemployment among those who fail to improve their productivity, while giving incentives to

---

[1] This is the process usually known as the Hekscher/Ohlin effect, following the work of the Swedish economists who first identified it (Ohlin 1967).

people to acquire education so that they might improve it. In its most extreme form this turns its back on the attempt at moving towards the skill utopia; it is no one's business to be concerned with such general moves; individuals must look after themselves as best they can; too bad for those who fail. In practice it is difficult for democratic governments, even of a neo-liberal kind, explicitly to endorse such a view. They may stress the importance of people being willing to take any work (for a wage appropriate to the labour demand–supply conditions) rather than remain unemployed, but will combine this with encouragement of increasing uptake of educational opportunities which should in the long run reduce to a minimum the number of people in such a situation. It is in this form that the project for continuing the onward march to the knowledge society is adopted by the political right: if individuals invest in their own education, then social expenditure to help them can be reduced; the high-income groups that constitute the right's core constituency among high-income groups is largely unaffected; and meanwhile managerial authority in the workplace will be restored under conditions of weak labour markets.

An alternative approach stresses the role of certain kinds of collective action in promoting the knowledge society: the competitive level of the economy could be improved by action to encourage the movement of people out of those sectors which compete directly with low-skilled producers in the newly industrializing countries (NICs) and thus to increase the proportion of the workforce in high-skilled sectors.[2] Although the rise of the NICs is initially experienced as a threat to employment, it becomes an opportunity for improving skills levels (upskilling) in the existing advanced countries. This view is mainly associated with the organized labour movements, since it is their members and supporters who gain from avoiding direct competition with the NICs—though problems are created for unions if the workforce moves into levels and types of employment which are not usually unionized. Alongside encouragement of these sectoral shifts, educational improvement, especially education that is considered to have some vocational relevance, is seen as a successor to Keynesian demand management and the welfare state. During the 1970s Keynesian policies lost their capacity to avoid inflation as it seemed to become clear that in democratic and pluralistic societies they were vulnerable to a ratchet effect: there were strong pressures to increase public spending during recessions, but equally strong ones to prevent the downward adjustments necessary during periods of high growth if demand management was to be inflation-neutral. While reductions in taxation and increases in public expenditure are still used by governments to stimulate demand at certain junctures, nowhere today can one find the commitment to using demand management to guarantee near-full employment that characterized the first three post-war decades in many countries.

---

[2] This might also be associated with an argument saying that, as the society becomes wealthier, it can afford to employ more people in the social services, but the main stress is on upskilling for competitiveness.

Governments have also had additional motives for wanting to reduce the expenditure on the welfare state which had provided the main instrument of this demand management. Occupational and social changes have reduced the proportions of electorates which have fixed political loyalties; increasingly voters are likely to support a party in a particular election on the basis of the promises that it can make to them. At the same time, a perceived declining effectiveness of governments within the less predictable cycles of a global and post-Keynesian economy makes people less likely to see governments 'doing something for us' in terms of positive policy delivery. Instead, voters are likely to want parties to promise to let them have more money themselves to make their own spending decisions. Governments might increase the wealth available to people in two ways: by improving growth within the economy, and by cutting taxes. Economic growth is difficult, uncertain, rather long-term, and not necessarily amenable to public policy; tax cuts can be delivered quickly and directly by governments. General elections have therefore increasingly become auctions with parties attempting to outbid each other with offers of tax cuts. Political parties of all kinds are therefore interested in any policies which will reduce the obligations on governments themselves to make provisions, as such policies are likely to make tax cuts possible. This logic accounts for much of the attractiveness of the arguments of neo-liberalism even to parties whose whole history and political stance is one of opposition to that doctrine.

For many political parties the encouragement of education seems to provide a means of ridding themselves of certain welfare commitments while at the same time offering government some opportunities for constructive and positive action. If people are educated they can probably fend for themselves in the economy without needing much support from the state. If individuals themselves can be persuaded to undertake the necessary educational expenditures as a form of personal investment, so much the better. Even if not, they might at least be prepared to exempt education from their general suspicion of public spending, because it is expenditure that seems clearly targeted on individuals and is an investment with the potential for increasing economic growth in the future.

An improvement in educational standards and levels has therefore become a major preoccupation of contemporary politics. The concern is almost solely with education that will be occupationally useful rather than as a civilizing mission or a broadening of minds—though that does not necessarily mean that narrowly vocational courses as such are always favoured. The advancement of the learning society is a solid part of virtually all attempts to construct a political consensus for the 'post-post-war' period.

In many respects we accept the main arguments of this consensus. We are however worried that, in the attempt to find grounds for optimism, policy-makers are clutching at the idea of the learning society with insufficient attention to its limitations and to ways in which its pursuit presents awkward choices rather than a smooth consensus. The purpose of this book is to explore these difficult choices as they have emerged in the recent experience of leading industrial nations.

LIMITATIONS AND AWKWARD CHOICES ON THE ROAD TO UTOPIA

The goal of the learning society presents itself initially as a set of clear and simple messages. For individuals it is: 'get educated to as high a level as you are able'. For firms: 'keep working to improve the knowledge base of your activities in order to stay ahead of low-cost competition'. For governments: 'improve the quality of educational facilities and ensure that as high a percentage as possible of your population participates, and you will maintain your standard of living and avoid mass unemployment'.

However, in the short run the fact that the educationally successful tend to be occupationally successful is the result of a competitive process; if everyone becomes educationally successful according to some criterion, then the criteria of success shift to a higher level. Improving the educational level of a potential workforce does not immediately create new jobs, as the USA experienced in the 1970s with the emergence of the 'over-educated American' (Freeman 1976). More recently several European countries (for example, France, Italy, Spain) have seen higher levels of unemployment among the graduates of their expanding higher education systems (Jobert 1995; Capecchi 1993; Iannelli 1998; Prieto and Homs 1995). In France there has been increasing concern that the rapidly improving educational level of the young French population is being used by employers simply as a signalling device to identify which are the best qualified of a cohort of potential recruits to take an existing array of jobs, and not as an opportunity to increase the number of jobs requiring higher ability (Béduwé and Espinasse 1995; Bourdon 1995; Büchtemann and Verdier 1998). This produces the paradoxical, and in the long run unstable, situation whereby young people find prolonged education increasingly unsatisfactory but increasingly demand it (Goux and Maurin 1998). It is ironically also possible for a general increase in educational achievement through policies of equality of opportunity to have the unintended consequence of increasing the role of parental background in job placement (ibid.). This can happen because parents from higher-class backgrounds are better placed to use contacts, personal know-how, and other characteristics unrelated to their children's own educational achievements but of renewed importance at a time of intensified competitive struggle.

Improving education can be an individual solution because it assists one in the competitive process. But by definition that very characteristic means that it cannot be a general or a collective one. It can be general from the perspective of a single country provided other countries are not doing the same, though as all advanced industrial countries (AICs) and increasing numbers of newly industrializing ones (NICs) pursue the same path, the competition for positions requiring high skilled levels is re-created on a global basis.[3]

[3] In the case of some high skills in particularly innovative areas it might be possible for supply to create its own demand, as highly trained people establish their own firms to develop ideas emerging from their own training, providing employment for others as they do so.

Further, although the tendency towards an upskilling of employment seems real enough, there are certain problems about turning this into a general policy. First, part of the upskilling is simply a response to the improved educational level of the population; if education standards are generally rising, the educational level of the persons engaged in any particular occupation will be seen to rise. It does not necessarily follow from this that the skill level of the work has risen—though it is always possible and often likely that employers will be able to make productive use of the increased capacities among their workforce. Second, when a real upskilling takes place within a particular occupation, one consequence is usually a reduction in the quantity of manpower needed for that occupation.[4] This imparts a quality of, at best, 'two steps forward, one step back' to any attempt at improving employment opportunities by means of educational advances. Third, when companies truly empower front-line workers they remove the need for the control function performed by traditional middle managers and are thus able to eliminate several layers from their organization (Lawler, Mohrman, and Ledford 1995). Finally, by no means all new employment opportunities require high skills; new jobs that require low or even reduced skills might be smaller in number than those that require higher skills, but they are usually easier to create and more readily address the situation of the hard to employ. If one were to be given a large sum of money and told to use it to create some employment for the young unemployed as quickly as possible, it would be better to open outlets for selling imported T-shirts than to launch a software laboratory.

A further problem is that, while the pursuit of a high level of vocational skills for a society is a collective goal, it is increasingly found that the principal sources of these skills are often individual firms, and governments increasingly have to defer to firms for judgements about what skills should be provided and through what means (Streeck 1989). Research on learning suggests that individuals learn most effectively, not in traditional classrooms, but in real work settings that have been structured to encourage development (for example, McCall 1997). This is one of the major changes caused by the move from the Fordist mass-production economy, the move which itself creates the main opportunities for the learning society. The most innovative corporations today, such as Intel and Hewlett Packard, are those which try to shape a distinctive whole-firm strategy, with organization and human resource practices designed to attract and retain the most talented individuals and provide them with continuous opportunities to develop their own and the organization's capabilities (Finegold 1998b). This point is often intensified in the case of services, which account for an increasing proportion of economic output, since there is not the same distinction between production process and product as in agriculture or manufacturing: the presentation and

---

[4] This will not happen if the improved productivity resulting from upskilling leads to such improvements in export performance and output growth that the manpower demanded need not decline. Even then, not all nations' exports can rise in this way as it is relative cost competitiveness that matters, so there is a nation-to-nation equivalent of the zero-sum characteristic of the upskilling solution.

personal attitude of the employee delivering a service is often part of the product. There is evidence that, in current competitive conditions, even within the manufacturing sector itself sales and marketing functions have become more important to corporate success than production (Regini 1996*a*). A firm may therefore not only have an interest in developing the attitudes and capabilities of such employees, but want to associate itself with particular styles of service that cannot be easily developed by short-term employees. These factors make it increasingly important that skills suit the specific needs of companies. There are therefore limits to what governments or any other collective actors can do alone to engineer appropriate improvements in vocational training.

Business firms are equipped to maximize not collective objectives, but their own profitability. In doing this they will certainly provide training and retraining for large numbers of employees; there is, however, no reason why company decisions and market forces will maximize the level of vocational ability for a whole society except through a largely serendipitous fallout. There is therefore a dilemma: achievement of a collective goal depends on actions by private actors who have no necessary incentive to achieve that goal.

THE PARADOX OF COLLECTIVE ACTION AND WORKFORCE SKILL

Posed in this way, the special problems of vocational education and training (VET) become an example of something far more general among contemporary advanced industrial societies: the problems we confront increasingly require collective solutions; but the core biases of political and economic action increasingly reject collective action. On the one hand the growing scale of what mankind can do through its capacity to mobilize technology, labour, and finance increases the circle of those affected, for both good and ill, by economic actions, far beyond the scope of those who are party to contracts within the area concerned. On the other hand, there has in recent years developed a drastic loss of faith in the capacity of collectivities to express their will through institutions other than private firms. Environmental issues raise this collective action problem most severely of all, but they are evident in the area of VET as well.

This study is intended to show both how VET policy needs to be understood within the broader context of different forms of capitalism, and how this specific area helps throw light on the relative merits of different economic policy regimes which are usually debated only in general terms. It is not our objective to provide detailed descriptions of educational and training systems—these can be found elsewhere—but, through the recent experience of such systems, we look at the problems of certain different broad types of institutions for making general policy within capitalist economies: states, interest associations, local business networks, and certain kinds of firm. As indicated in the Preface, we are concerned with preparation for most manual and non-manual work skills in the contemporary economy, other than those which are normally provided for in institutions of higher education. For each type of institutional solution we exam-ine the record of certain national examples which have in the past been widely regarded as embodying best practice in this area (for example, Germany for col-lective employer organizations), together with one or two other cases that seem to have been particularly problematic.

Before examining each institutional case in detail, it is necessary to develop elements of the above argument more fully.

At the heart of the paradox, that policy-makers increasingly look to individual profit-maximizing firms for solutions to collective problems, lies a second one: the same processes that are taking the decisive actions 'down' into individual companies are also taking them 'up' into global levels. In a world of rapidly changing and highly competitive markets, considerable reliance is placed on indi-vidual firms finding new niches; there is little confidence that public policy of a general kind, such as that associated with Keynesian economics, can make a contribution. Trust in firms' ability to achieve their goals is strengthened by the growing size and reach of transnational corporations (TNCs), that operate in an increasingly integrated fashion across national boundaries (Adler 1997). Even those companies that are not TNCs themselves are able to make strategic alliances and build a web of supplier and customer partnerships for certain shared purposes, making possible action on a global scale. Achieving a capacity for collective action at a cross-national public level is slow and painful, as the stilted progress of west-ern European integration shows. Private collective action by firms, in contrast, can be achieved quickly and flexibly. The apparent move down from national government policy to the firm is often also a move up to the global level. Both the firm and the global economy are levels which escape the reach of traditional public collective action at the national, regional, or local level. While, therefore, this book concentrates on the single theme of vocational education and the devel-opment of work skills, it addresses this subject as an aspect of a far more gen-eral contemporary issue. One might similarly study the ways in which attempts by various national populations to choose particular patterns of working hours or retirement ages can also be inhibited by requirements to satisfy firms' global expectations.

For this argument it is useful to distinguish between four types of inter-nationalization in the operation of firms (ibid.). In two stages—exporting and international investment—firms typically have a global reach in the sale and marketing of their products and in locating some aspects of their production, but keep their main base in a country of origin where they retain core facilities, have large sunk costs and tend habitually to look for their main source of managerial talent and skilled labour. Other companies, in the multinational or TNC or global stage of organizational development, are more genuinely 'footloose' and can move around the global economy at will, with no particular commitment to an indi-vidual country or region (Bartlett and Ghoshal 1992). During the earlier period of nationally based capitalism, firms were often concerned for the general qual-ity of the resources of labour or social infrastructure within what they regarded as 'their' home country. This was so, not because they felt particularly patriotic, but because they were more or less tied to their national base and, if not satisfied with what they found there, would have to work to improve it. The process is an excellent example of the Hirschmanian (1970) use of voice in the absence of easy opportunities to exit. They could therefore be called upon by governments or associations of firms to participate in collective national projects. In contrast, a truly footloose global firm which fails to find, say, adequate skilled labour in one country, may feel no need to contribute to the enlargement of its stock, but will move to a country where it is already to be found. The number of firms in this category is still small; most multinationals still have an identifiable national base. Nevertheless, their numbers are likely to increase as globalization proceeds, and many more national firms are already outsourcing an increasing percentage of their output to foreign suppliers. Thus, governments and others are increasingly likely to find that, having vested most of their hopes for initiatives in achieving the learning society in the corporate sector, that sector will not be particularly interested in responding.

Large countries still retain some market power; for example, China is able to insist that inward-investing firms use a certain proportion of domestic content and help upgrade local skills. However, the extensions of free trade consequent on agreements within the European Union, NAFTA, the World Trade Organization, and other arrangements frequently involve limitations on the imposition of requirements of this kind.

Meanwhile, labour is far less mobile (Reich 1992). Even if all political constraints on migration were removed, only a minority of individuals could easily move around the world in pursuit of employment opportunities. Such movement is concentrated at opposite poles of the skill spectrum: most mobile of all are the very highly educated and skilled, whose services may be sought on international labour markets.[5] However, global firms are finding that even their core managerial staff cannot be moved around the world at will; these people often have partners with their own careers, and they care about their children's education.

Also mobile are the poor and desperate with neither existing stakes nor future prospects to keep them tied to their home country. There are potentially very large numbers of people of this kind and they would be the most likely core of any mass international labour force. However, large-scale movements of this labour produce other collective problems: ethnic tensions increase; some parts of the world would become heavily crowded while others become deserted. Governments of the advanced world, whatever their political composition, are increasing

---

[5] More than half of all the engineering Ph.D.s in the USA, for example, are now awarded to foreign (predominantly Asian) nationals, who are attracted by the country's world-class universities. Indeed, a child born in Taiwan is now statistically more likely to obtain a science or engineering Ph.D. in the USA than is an American citizen (North 1995). The international students who graduate from US programmes are often fought over by TNCs which see them as ideally equipped to return to their home countries to become managers who can bridge the gap between American and Asian cultures.

the barriers to global labour mobility even as they reduce those to global trade. Apart from some movement at the margins, nation states remain as entities, as human collectivities; and the majority of people will find their fates and futures tied to one or other such collectivity. This means an inevitable collective component in their attempt to confront economic opportunities.

In some respects there is 'an end to geography'. Information technology has enormously expanded the capacity for detailed communication within and between organizations. The growth of TNCs has brought examples of global product development, where firms in a number of countries provide different components of a complex product, like an aeroplane; or disaggregated services, such as the processing of European airline ticketing in India, or the location in Ireland of a customer call centre to deal with enquiries to some US insurance companies. But the ending of geography for large employers only intensifies its importance for relatively immobile employees, as the economic and social infrastructural characteristics of one's 'place' become all important in determining one's occupational chances. National and local governments, especially in a world where imperial expansion is no longer a possibility, are also unable to change their geographical location. They remain bound to their national populations and, at least in democracies, cannot abandon the task of framing some kind of strategy for securing employment chances for them in the global economy. But can governments and communities do anything other than hope that firms will provide solutions to their need for higher skills? Can they do anything other than ensure that their populations are attractive for reasons of low cost?

No significant current approach returns a completely negative answer to these questions, but the ruling economic ideology of our period, neo-liberalism, is one that offers a very restricted range of possibilities. It is suspicious of collective actions, especially state or associational actions, on the grounds that these interfere with market forces which it sees as the sole guarantors of efficiency. It therefore seeks to minimize the areas of legitimate collective action to such carefully defined areas as national defence and a few basic social services. Outside these areas, it suggests no viable role for government other than the limiting case of collective action to prevent collective action: that is, policies for deregulation or for turning departments of government into analogues of firms, acting in the market and therefore no longer possessing the capacity for collective decision-making that distinguishes public from market actors.

The current dominance of neo-liberal ideas can be partly attributed to the major change that has taken place in the balance of power within the global labour market. This has both an economic and a political component. The way in which the increase in foreign direct investment has surpassed the increase in international trade has greatly enhanced the mobility of capital, whereas that of labour remains in practice very limited. Although overall there has been an upskilling of the world's workforces, a large number of tasks that used to require workers trained in and working within the existing advanced countries can, through new technical methods of work and of control, be carried out by people in countries typified by low wages, poor working conditions, and low levels of democratic rights. Business interests are therefore often using this situation to oppose much regulation of labour markets: collective bargaining, rights to consultation, minimum wages, regulation of working hours, health and safety legislation, and the social security costs of employment. The deregulatory thrust therefore strikes with particular strength at employment regulation.

This economic context contrasts with the dominant experience of the initial post-war decades. In the early years it was possible to use Keynesian or similar methods of demand stimulation to take up the slack of economies and labour markets that had been disrupted by war. Fordist production techniques spread from the USA to continental Europe, acting similarly to Keynesian demand management by creating a demand for relatively low-skilled jobs which enabled their possessors to purchase mass-production goods; this in turn further stimulated activity and therefore employment in those industries. After the first few years of reconstruction, there were major shortages of labour, while the capacity of capital to use the productive human resources of Asia, eastern Europe, or other parts of the world was inhibited by economic backwardness, the dependence of much of the population on subsistence agriculture, or political impediments to capitalist development. At the political level there was, even in countries with weak labour movements, a perceived need by political élites to prevent the alienation of the working population. The social upheavals of the 1930s remained a recent memory, while the Soviet Union and the Eastern bloc seemed for a time to offer an alternative form of economic organization if capitalism betrayed the population. In this economic and political context there was widespread agreement that government and other forms of collective authority should be used to limit the disruptions to stability that might be caused by unchecked market fluctuations. This context has now changed. The Soviet alternative has collapsed, while activity in the consumer goods market has shown itself capable of raising the living conditions of the majority of people in the advanced countries to high levels of choice and affluence.

In addition to—and to some extent autonomously from—these changes, which have advanced the political power of policies based on unobstructed markets and produced the rise of neo-liberalism, governments and other collective agents (primarily organizations representing economic interests) are beset with a lack of confidence in their capacity to act unless the action takes the limiting-case, neo-liberal form of action to deregulate. This lack of confidence has three primary sources, all of which converge in an overwhelming bias in public policy towards neo-liberal or free-market approaches by political forces of both right and left.

First is the continuing reaction to the inflationary crises of the 1970s, associated primarily with the two oil shocks but seen as also having domestic causes. Government intervention in the economy to sustain employment levels when the natural rate of unemployment was rising in most countries was widely regarded as having perpetuated and exacerbated the inflationary crisis, while the protective actions of collective wage bargainers—employers' associations and trade unions

—had a similar effect. A labour market 'burdened' by Keynesian policies and by collective organization proved to be particularly sticky in making downward adjustments. This has produced a policy preference for generally 'cleaning out' institutions: reducing the role of the state, reducing the role of organizations, generally lowering the scope for all non-market behaviour where labour is concerned. This mainly affects collective bargaining, but in turn has an impact on other areas where institutions have played a role in the labour market.

Even if at times a Keynesian demand expansion approach might have been a rational solution to overcapacity and failing consumer confidence for a nation state, it was strongly discouraged by the increasingly hegemonic role of global financial markets. These markets, which had become increasingly powerful as a result of both deregulation and the enhanced global capacity imparted to players in them by new technology, placed a strong priority on maintaining stable currency values. This meant that individual governments attempting a Keynesian deficit-spending approach, with the accompanying devaluation of the currency, would confront a crisis of international confidence. This was the fate of both French and Swedish governments during the 1980s. In any case, the increased synchronization of national economic cycles and growing dependence of nearly all economies on foreign trade has made it difficult for individual countries to expand in isolation.

Second, and more generally, there has been a widespread triumph of the belief that deregulation offers the best hopes for economic success. This is partly associated with a further belief in the beneficial long-term effects of the growth of trade and the futility of protectionism, an important argument against the hopeless closed-border policies of the kind that eventually destroyed the economies of eastern Europe and the USSR by insulating them from both external challenge and innovation. Given the lure of protectionism at a time of intensified competition and accompanying job insecurity, the advocates of deregulatory policies rightly feel a particularly strong need to maintain a vigil against all potentially protectionist forces; this then leads to a general hostility to all measures of government action or actions by business associations.

Third, these years of declining capacity of public policy have also been a period in which individual firms—in certain sectors—have thrived and demonstrated great vitality. In some instances this has been a particular property of small firms, which are often best placed to take advantage of new initiatives in science and technology, or new ideas for business and personal services. As some of the most successful of these firms grow—for example, Microsoft and Intel—they have worked hard to retain the nimbleness and lean corporate structures of smaller organizations. In other cases, already giant corporations have taken initiatives to forge the global alliances referred to above in order to take advantage of opportunities presented by the changing geography of competition. Whereas governments can produce an international level of co-operation only after long, and painful, frequently and typically open, debate, firms can move quickly and secretly to such deals.

Governments and associational networks have been obliged both to defer to the superior capacity for flexible response of either small or large firms in such situations, and to imitate corporate methods in their own practices—which in turn weakens further their confidence to speak authoritatively to firms. As noted, government services either have been privatized or have at least been required to remodel themselves to operate as though they were firms, abandoning any pretence at a role of co-ordinating, or of taking advantage of their central position and collective responsibilities to show leadership (for example, Osborne and Gaebler 1992). Associations of firms have been under a similar pressure to become sellers of services to members, again abandoning leadership roles. Firms have then shown growing restlessness against constraints of either governments or, indeed, their own associations.

Finally, the declining power of the labour movement which has taken place in most though not all advanced societies has weakened the pressure on governments from those political forces wanting labour regulation at precisely the time when those seeking the opposite have been becoming stronger. Union decline results mainly from the changes in employment patterns, with the shift away from manufacturing and, much more recently, public-service employment, unionism's two heartlands. However, as Scandinavian evidence shows, it is not impossible for unions to recruit members in the new services sectors or among administrative and managerial staffs, and it is possible that with time more will learn how to do this and recover; there are already signs of this in the Netherlands (Visser and Hemerijck 1997). These sectors are particularly important for the future of the labour movement, as it remains significantly more difficult for employers to relocate these jobs on a global basis.

It is largely in France and the USA that there has been widespread refusal of recognition of unions in manufacturing itself. Even here, some of the new intensive working practices which place considerable reliance on certain key groups of employees, such as 'lean production' (Womack *et al.* 1990), can be used as leverage by unions. The declining power of organized labour, though real, should not be assumed to be a continuing and ineluctable phenomenon.

THE AMBIGUOUS IMPORTANCE OF LABOUR MARKET POLICY AND VET

It is against this background that policy-makers have to resolve current collective problems in creating vocational skills. Similar arguments apply whether the challenge to employment is seen as coming from the growth of international competition or the development of technology. Workforce skill, it is argued, is one of the resources that can still give the old industrial world some competitive advantages in the globalized economy. Low-cost labour in NICs is already being equipped with excellent technology, but it will take some time before it can attain high levels of skill; in large countries like India or China, however, only a small élite of highly educated individuals represents millions of new graduates available to international companies. According to international achievement tests, other newly industrialized economies such as Singapore and South Korea, and probably now Taiwan, have already achieved parity with or surpassed the general educational levels found in the West, further strengthening the argument for the urgency of improving skills in the industrialized world (IAEA 1997).

The threat to jobs from 'robotization' and the spread of microtechnology is similarly perceived as capable of resolution by highly skilled and educated populations who can succeed in the new areas of work opened up by the technology itself. Expressed in this way the issue of skill formation, although in many respects something essentially individual, is perceived as a highly collective good. A particular community (city, region, country, or whatever) is seen as having a shared need in acquiring a particular characteristic, namely, a high level of workforce skill. This collectivism is at a peak when the goal is expressed in terms of the need to maximize the skill potential of every possible member of the community concerned.

Paradoxically, this logic might be seen as extending to that most individualistic form of work, self-employment. After a very long period of decline associated with economic modernization, self-employment has in recent years begun to increase, most strikingly in the UK and USA, but to some extent more generally. Self-employment is not a single category of work; it can refer to entrepreneurial founders of small firms; to practitioners of the liberal professions; to people who are really employed by a corporation but who are kept in a fictional self-employed category by the employer in order to avoid social security and health and safety legislation; or to some marginal people who are essentially unemployed but sell things or do odd jobs in order to scratch a living. The recent increase has included all of these, with perhaps a large proportion of the third and fourth categories. We should anticipate further increases. Corporations are likely increasingly to reduce their own direct employees to those with core competences and to contract out other activities; and to try to 'flexibilize' their workforces through the use of precarious contracts. At the same time, governments are likely to make eligibility rules for claiming unemployment benefit tougher, leading workless people to seek various forms of money-earning opportunities.

If self-employment of various kinds is likely to grow, it is important that vocational education is not conceived solely in terms of those in normal employment. Of the categories listed, only the second (the liberal professions) have obvious and essential sources of vocational education. It might, however, be thought equally important and in the general interest that people setting up new firms should be competent in both business organization and the substance of their intended businesses. Poorly equipped entrepreneurs are more likely to fail then well-prepared ones, and failed businesses impose losses on creditors, employees, and customers. VET for the third category, those in forms of self-employment tied to one *de facto* 'employer', are unlikely to receive training from that source.

The fourth group is often beyond the reach of training activities, though some important exceptions are developing. Some of the organizations specializing in hiring out temporary workers are not operating at the lowest levels of the labour market but are coming to be important providers of skilled occupations which are needed only occasionally by particular firms. These organizations may then take very seriously their responsibilities for maintaining the skills of the workers on their registers, and firms come to them for the quality of their staff. An important example would be Manpower Inc., which operates in several countries, often recognizing trade unions among its staff too. In the USA Manpower is now the biggest single employer, with over 500,000 people on its books.

More generally, if the vocational preparation of contingent workers is seen as an aspect of public educational responsibility, rather than just being left for individuals to sort out for themselves in the market, there is likely to be an all-round improvement in competences.

As we have noted above, in the short run this collectivism is deceptive. Initially, improving the educational level of a population only enables individuals to compete against each other for a fixed number of jobs. VET policies are collective employment policies only if an improvement in the quality of labour supply creates an increase in the demand for trained labour. This would happen if employers, noting an improvement in the quality of the young people available in the labour market, decided that they could start producing new goods or services and therefore to increase employment opportunities. It is this hope that has inspired much of the recent belief in the job-creating possibilities of educational advance—though it clearly involves a number of heroic assumptions, not least because one of the main consequences of an improvement in the skill of labour should be a rise in its productivity and hence a reduction in the amount of labour that is required to produce a given output of goods or services.

Even at the level of the individual the ostensibly obvious rationale of seeking to improve employment prospects through educational advance can be deceptive. Having taken the advice to improve their qualifications, each young person discovers that nearly everyone else has been doing the same, and, like everyone else, will become discouraged, even angry, if prolonging education seems to be bringing neither new work opportunities to his or her area of residence, nor any relative advantage in competing for existing jobs. Resources of time, money, and effort are to some extent being used wastefully, just as there is waste whenever each shop in a street erects big neon signs in order to be the most visible shop in the street. In their attempt to link education more closely to economic advance politicians, employers, and others have placed overwhelming stress on the instrumental, vocational value of education and have tended to downgrade the old liberal concept that education was a valuable possession in its own right—a consumption as well as an investment good. Such a strong change of emphasis might have been a mistake, rendering people culturally impoverished as well as incapable of finding attractive work.

The distinction between short- and long-term perspectives is fundamental here. The long term starts at the point where the supply of certain kinds of labour begins to determine production possibilities. This assumes the availability of a critical mass of persons educated at certain levels which either makes it possible for existing firms to make major changes in their activities, consciously applying research and development to take advantage of the improved skills situation, or encourages new (or inward-investing) firms in high-skill areas to start operations. Most political formulations of the role of skills and training in facing the challenges of international competition imply this putative long-term effect of an increase in the skills base. Such a model is defective if it claims that the supply of skilled labour is the main constraint on its demand. If systems of corporate governance and finance and the pressures of global competition exercise independent pressures on the demand for skills—as is very likely—equilibrium might still not be reached. There might continue to be an oversupply of skills and an indefinite continuation of the short-term problem of credentials being used solely for zero-sum competition. The short-term disequilibrium case is, therefore, not just a special, transitional problem.

The short term is that indefinite period before any benign long-term effects can be perceived. Here labour demand is not driven by its supply. During the short-term period, an improvement in the supply of skills might enable firms to carry out their existing tasks more efficiently, but is unlikely to cause them to make major innovative shifts. In practice it may well be that such a clear dividing line cannot be observed, as long-term incremental changes begin to occur during the short-term period. However, the contrast between the two end states is important as different groups involved have different interests within them.

Within the short term, there is as we have just seen no reason why individuals (whether in their roles as workers, voters, young persons entering the labour market, or the parents of these latter) should share a general interest in an increase in either vocational training or general education, since the main immediate consequence of such an increase is only to increase competition for skilled jobs. People already possessing skills, or confident of their ability to acquire them under pre-expansion policies, should in fact oppose a general increase in the educational level, as it both intensifies competition for jobs to which they might otherwise have had easy access, and exercises downward pressure on the economic return to skills. People with low skills do share the general interest in an increase in skills, as they are helped by educational expansion to enter the competition. All individuals, irrespective of their existing educational level, have an interest in improving their own chances of acquiring skills, but not those of others. They have a motive to participate in education, but not necessarily to support a general improvement. Once we turn to the long term these problems no longer exist; everyone can share an interest in a move of the whole economy to higher levels of skill, which would if successfully achieved mean an increase in opportunities for skilled work for large numbers of people.

Trade unions face the same contradictions. The most immediate questions that they can influence concern within-firm or within-industry measures for upskilling existing employees. This will be valuable, but it might be argued that such policies increase the gaps between insiders and outsiders, as those already in work increase their value to employers relative to those seeking employment. With the exception of those trade unions (such as many in the USA) which represent small segments of the workforce and have little interest in the macroeconomics of the labour market, unions have no interest in allowing a weak general labour market to develop among outsiders. Therefore, in the long term they share the general interest in upskilling as much of the workforce as possible. However, in the short term they do not in fact share that interest, since it serves, as noted, to increase competition among labour. Nevertheless, these contradictions do not matter very much to unions. With the exception of countries with effective scope for the participation of organized labour in policy formation, in the short term unions can only affect skills through bargaining over company training for new recruits and existing employees. Here their concern will be to ensure that the work categories they represent are receiving a good share of firms' in-service training resources. This typically amounts to an attempt to ensure that such training is not concentrated on managerial and other senior, usually non-unionized, categories. Any work they might do to affect general government or employer policy could have any real effect only in the long term, when these conflicts of interest within the employee population cease to be operative.

Employers face a different equation. They do have an interest in a rise in the general VET level even during the short term, because this improves the quality of the potential supply of labour, increases their choice and efficiency, and exerts a downward pressure on wages and salaries. They also share the general interest in the long term, since they would gain competitive advantage in moving to more highly skilled markets. However, whether they have an interest in themselves contributing to this outcome is subject to different calculations. For well-known reasons (see Crouch 1995 for a summary), employers have a low incentive to provide initial training—unless they are bound by strong collective associations, or are large oligopolies dominating their local labour markets. In reality, as we shall see in subsequent chapters, these exceptions cover many firms. However, the kind of firm assumed to be standard in most economic theory— the average, middle-sized firm in a competitive market—is not in one of these situations. If it is faced with a skill shortage in the short term it is more likely to pay premium wages to attract workers from elsewhere than to improve training: this achieves more quickly the results wanted and is easier to reverse once the shortage is resolved.

The employers' dilemma therefore is that, while they unambiguously share a general interest in higher skills, they are reluctant to do anything about it. There might seem to be an easy resolution of this: let the state improve both the general and the vocational education capacity. But this is not so simple, and some of the factors discussed above which have induced a loss of confidence in economic policy-making by governments come into play here. The rapid changes characteristic of contemporary technologies require an almost constant interaction between the development of products and training in the production process. There is also the increasing priority on the role of the individual company discussed earlier; there are severe limits to what governments can do alone within VET policy, and they must therefore try to involve employers.

Companies may thus be in the contradictory position of demanding action on VET, complaining that government and other education providers are out of touch with their needs, but be unwilling to help (for the usual reasons that inhibit their participation in collective action). It may well be that they are not particularly able to help, as many companies are not expert in skill development. Most small and medium-sized firms have never been able to afford internal training experts and there is a trend for larger firms to reduce their personnel or human resources departments as part of their general strategy of concentrating on core competencies (Prahalad and Hamel 1994). Less strategic downsizing efforts have also left many firms with a net loss of internal competence on skill issues (Finegold 1998a).

It is also necessary to distinguish between firms in different market and institutional contexts. Backes-Gellner (1996: 52) sees firms having to make a trade-off between the 'risk of being short' and having too few trained workers at their disposal and the 'risk of having excess' and having too many such workers for their needs. Firms' position on this dilemma will be affected by whether they are in mass-production or flexible specialization production regimes (ibid.: 80–1). Testing this theory against empirical data drawn principally from Germany and the UK, but also from France and Luxembourg, she is able to demonstrate the utility of this distinction in research findings, use of which will be made in subsequent chapters of this study.

Therefore, while the long-term goal of a high-skill economy offers a resolution to a number of conflicts and problems, it is an end state that it is not easy to reach. A common response to this situation has been for governments to engage in general expansions of education and VET arrangements without necessarily knowing how this will be related to the long-term aspiration. This is, after all, compatible with the long-term goal even if it might not actually help its achievement. It meets employers' short-term needs for slacker labour markets while simultaneously and perhaps deceptively satisfying the demands of the existing and potential labour force for improved opportunities as individuals. (Governing parties whose core constituencies include those who benefit from existing rather than expanded educational provision can usually find means of protecting élite educational channels from the new competition.)

Governments will also concentrate on measures aimed at improving the skills of the unemployed. Some neo-liberal economists oppose this, but few neo-liberal governments can take the political risk of doing so. Such measures give hope to those in despair, and remain compatible with the presumed long-term goal of a general upskilling. However, so long as the skill structure remains within the bounds of the short term, all that these measures can do is to intensify competition in the labour market, unjustifiably raise expectations, and increase the insecurity and dissatisfaction of employed and unemployed alike. Even when viewed thus cynically, policies which do little more than recycle unemployment among different individuals can at least reduce long-term unemployment for some and thereby limit the generation of large numbers of people who become unfit for work— albeit at the expense of what might be seen as the lesser evil of increasing the number of people who experience short spells of unemployment.

The approach to public VET policy in many countries therefore has a pattern of the following kind: considerable effort around general educational participation and basic skills provision; many programmes for helping the unemployed (or, more accurately, helping the unemployed compete with others and thereby perhaps increasing the rate of flow through unemployment); attempts to encourage diffusion of best practices; and hesitant, uncertain efforts by various combinations of actors to take action oriented to the coveted long term. There has also been encouragement of voluntary skills standards (for example, in Australia, New Zealand, the UK, and USA), an approach which fits well with a neo-liberal policy as it entails minimal government effort and addresses the problem of labour market information (Finegold and Keltner 1996).

This combination, based on sustaining the consensus on short-term needs, is not well geared to the avowed long-term goal, since this requires measures for getting the skill level of the average company up to the level of the current best. No one is really sure what such a strategy means. A few obvious generally high-skill sectors can be identified: computers, pharmaceuticals, aircraft manufacture, financial services, the health and education sectors. But these cannot employ everyone; the biggest components in terms of numbers employed—health and education—are not easily internationally traded and can make only an indirect contribution to national competitive advantage; and actual numbers employed in a capital-intensive sector like semiconductors are very small. There are limits on the extent to which any one country can learn from the experience of others, since virtually by definition it is not possible for all countries to find the same competitive niches. Although it is in terms of the long-term approach that nearly all policy is enunciated, in practice it is difficult to do anything about it.

Further VET

Until now we have assumed a simple model of VET whereby a worker is equipped with work skills before or soon after joining the labour force (that is, 'initial VET'). But it is increasingly important to take account of the fact that training and retraining are likely to proceed throughout the working lives of at least some members of the workforce ('further VET'). Indeed, in an economy facing rapid technological and organizational change as the contemporary one does, this kind of training is likely to grow in relative importance. Employees need frequent updating of their existing type of skill, and may well need complete reskilling if change leads to either major redesign or actual redundancy of their current employment. Developments in either initial or further VET are also likely to have implications for the other, as the kind of training given to a new entrant will differ if it is considered likely that he or she will have ready access to further training in subsequent years.

Arrangements for further VET may well be very different from those for initial VET. In particular, it is likely that company-level measures will grow in relative importance and collective agencies will retreat, as one leaves the public task of equipping a new young generation for entry into the workforce—one at the interface between the education system and employment—and enters the private tasks of a large number of firms seeking to adjust their staffs to changing market needs. On the one hand, some of the *a priori* disincentives to firms to train have a declining impact. If firms find themselves within product markets where in order to remain competitive it is necessary to adopt new technology and organizational methods requiring an adaptation of employee skills, they face the choice of either doing so or leaving the market. They also know that their competitors face the same challenge and will incur similar retraining costs. They are, however, likely to try also to ensure that the skills they convey are company-specific and therefore not useful to the flexibility of the external labour market.

Although this resolves some of the dilemmas of collective action in VET, it raises certain others. To the extent that the main model of training becomes this extended kind, public policy becomes increasingly dependent on the decisions of firms, and whole areas of VET begin to 'disappear' into the corporation, while remaining no less an object of public concern—a new instance of the fundamental paradox established earlier in this chapter.

Some recent evidence (Finegold 1998*b*) suggests that an increasing number of the most advanced US employers are asking individuals to take ownership over their own careers and, in direct contradiction of human capital theory, are providing them with generous financial support to do so. United Technologies, for example, not only pays the tuition fees (which could amount to $70,000 for an MBA) for all employees who want to take a course in their own time, but also provides 1.5 hours off from work each week and a grant of 100 shares of company stock (equal to about $7,000) to those who complete a degree. This often substantial investment has the paradoxical effect of making some of their most talented employees more externally marketable at a time when the flattening of the organization and repeated downsizings have meant that there are fewer opportunities for promotion available within the firm. The rationale is that, since they are not able to offer employment security, the only sustainable bargain they can offer knowledge workers in return for their commitment to the company is the opportunity continuously to develop their skills, and hence their employability, whether within the organization or outside it.

In Germany, Japan, and the USA there have long been examples of firms assisting existing managers and scientific staff to learn the skills of business ownership before floating them off as independent entrepreneurs running largely autonomous supplier companies. Not much is known about the full extent of this practice or whether there is any tendency for it to increase alongside the general increase in 'hiving-off' and sub-contracting.

INSTITUTIONAL FORMS OF COLLECTIVE ACTION

In a widely noted article, Finegold and Soskice (1988) drew attention to the possibility that individual countries might develop either high- or low-skill equilibria. Obviously, individual firms or districts would produce examples of high- or low-skill activities within any overall system; but, given that systems of education tend to be more or less national in scope, the authors described what they saw as the likely development of central tendencies. Where incentives to individuals and companies to invest in training were low, including poor quality of and limited access to VET provision, firms would become accustomed to occupying market niches where little skill was required of workers. They would therefore impose few demands on the system for an improvement; and forces of both demand and supply would sustain the equilibrium. Conversely, in a system where incentives to all participants and quality of provision were high, employers could rely on a constant source of well-qualified labour that would enable them to occupy high-quality niches, and would in turn make strong demands on the future quality of the system—the high-skill equilibrium. Finegold and Soskice saw the UK as an example of the low-skill equilibrium and Germany as one of its opposite.

The idea of stability implied by the idea of 'equilibrium' was somewhat misleading in the low-skill case, since the onset of intensified competition from low-cost producers in the NICs would render the markets of countries having this equilibrium highly vulnerable to challenge. The underlying message of Finegold and Soskice was that countries which failed to locate themselves on a high-skill equilibrium could find themselves spinning into disequilibrium. Subsequent years have borne out much of their argument, at least in the British case, as policy took a double direction. On the one hand, many initiatives were taken to improve work skills and the British skill equilibrium, while on the other a major attempt was made to lower wage and non-wage labour costs, including legal and collectively bargained guarantees of employee security, in order to enable British firms to compete with the NICs—that is, to follow the logic of the low-skill equilibrium.

More recently there have been grounds for doubting the stability of even high-skill equilibria. The changes discussed in the opening pages of this chapter challenge every form of skill development strategy to be found among the advanced nations. If the institutions that sustain a high-skill equilibrium are challenged, so is that equilibrium. At the very moment when the pursuit of high and improving skills has seemed to represent the best available strategy for the sustained competitive advantages of the advanced economies, the viability of these institutions is being called into question. This is perhaps seen most strongly in Germany, where the powerful business associations which have sustained the distinctive features of German capitalism, including its apprenticeship system, are now being criticized, precisely because they impose 'burdens' such as apprentice training on firms already under considerable pressure to reduce their operating costs.

Subsequent chapters will discuss the problems and challenges of institutional forms of collective action. It should be noted from the outset that our conception of collective or public action is not limited to the state or government. We see the public arena as comprising all those elements of action that either are not or cannot be appropriated by market forces, and which therefore either are neglected or are carried out by some non-market actor or institution. There can be a great diversity of these institutions, ranging from the state to neighbourhoods and families. In practice we shall concentrate on those associated with the main forms of collective action—the state, formal corporatist associations, informal but deeply rooted inter-firm networks—but also, as a kind of limiting case, will examine the scope for action at the level of the individual company. In identifying various actors as being in the collective arena one is not necessarily implying that they are in fact acting for a collective or public good, or performing in a manner superior to the free market. The kind of contribution being made has to be established by research.

The policy debate in this field is therefore a comparison of various alternative forms of economic institutions which are considered to be able to resolve the problem of providing this kind of impure public good. Our study should therefore be seen as a contribution to what has come to be called the 'neo-institutionalist' approach to studying economic institutions. This approach, while sharing many of the rational-choice assumptions of neo-classical economics, does not try to reduce all collective phenomena to mere aggregates of individual actions, but sees institutions as having an irreducible *sui generis* role in determining human action (Mayntz and Scharpf 1995; Powell and DiMaggio 1991; March and Olsen 1989). There are differences among various types of neo-institutionalists. Some remain close to the neo-classical paradigm but seek to correct it at certain points, such as through consideration of the implications on organizations of transaction costs (for example, North 1981; Williamson 1975; 1985). Others would bring institutions into the centre of the frame of analysis of economic life rather than restricting them to the explanation of certain awkward corners (for example, Granovetter 1985; Streeck 1992; specifically within the field of VET, van Lieshout 1997). We would mainly align ourselves with the second group, but it is not part of our task here to engage in the theoretical polemic, except on one central point: neo-institutionalism must not become an aspect of the 'state versus market' debate. This is partly because there are other important non-market institutions in addition to the state at work in the economy; and partly because positing polar oppositions of that kind is unhelpful in understanding a reality where there is virtually always interaction and co-operation between various of these forces.

Hollingsworth, Schmitter, and Streeck (1994) have developed a useful ana-lytical scheme for analysing these institutions, dealing separately with: govern-ment or state action exercised through regulation and policy intervention; formal associations of economic actors, normally behaving in a neo-corporatist way; com-munity networks based on trust and reciprocity rather than formal rules; and the markets and hierarchies of capitalist enterprises themselves. In a similar account Crouch and Streeck (1997) distinguish more between markets and hierarchies and consider the relationship of 'company communities' to hierarchy. They also relate the overall scheme to an analysis of types of capitalism, different nation states being seen as embodying different combinations of these various institu-tional forms, the combinations sometimes changing. We shall use this same set of concepts to form our account of institutions for seeking collective VET goods.

The empirical base for this analysis will be the post-war experience of seven countries: the six largest economies of the advanced capitalist world (France, Germany, Italy, Japan, the UK, the USA) together with Sweden, which has in the past pursued distinctive policies in the labour area. Each of these countries will be located within the concept of a skill equilibrium and within a labour market context: first through an examination of recent VET and labour-market-participation trends (Chapter 2); then through consideration of their changing pattern of participation in international trade (Chapter 3). From this discussion the countries will be seen as having particularly embodied one or more of these institutions (see Table 1.1). But each case has also demonstrated disturbing vul-nerabilities for the future. In the second part of the book these institutions will become the focus of analysis, as the national cases are used to demonstrate advan-tages, weakness, and scope for future change in the institutional forms themselves.

First it is necessary to introduce briefly the range of alternative policy ap-proaches, starting with the extreme form of the neo-liberal argument: that the best role for public policy in the labour market at present is simply to deregulate as much as possible, leaving market forces to find the way forward for recover-ing employment levels. Such an approach is in practice compatible with strat-egies for improving the quality of labour through improved general education, though not with attempts at more discriminating public policy. Its main concern is not with training policy as such, but with a perceived need to reduce the level of employment protection. Internationally this strategy has been argued through a polemic which contrasts European, American, and Japanese labour markets. This begins with the observation that the first of these regions is developing per-sistently higher unemployment levels than the other two; proceeds to the claim that labour market regulation and social security costs in Europe are persistently higher than in the USA or Japan; and then draws the conclusion that a solution to Europe's employment problem rests with the deregulation of its labour mar-kets and dismantling of its welfare states.

This is not necessarily an alternative strategy to the search for upskilling; it can appear in a package alongside measures for the former, as it does in the pol-icies of the Organization for Economic Co-operation and Development (OECD)

TABLE 1.1. *Dominant forms of skills provision: initial VET and further VET*

Direct state	Corporatist networks	Local firm networks	Institutional companies	Free markets
(a) Initial VET				
France			(France)	
	Germany			
Italy		Italy		
	(Japan)	(Japan)	Japan	
Sweden	(Sweden)		(Sweden)	
UK			(UK)	UK
			(USA)	USA
(b) Further VET				
(France)			France	
			Germany	(Germany)
		Italy		Italy
		(Japan)	Japan	
Sweden	(Sweden)		Sweden	
			UK	UK
			USA	USA

Note: Country names in parentheses indicate that this is a minor model within the country in question.

and the European Union (EU). However, it tends to become such an alternative, for two reasons. First, one of the main functions of the deregulation of labour markets is to improve the employment possibilities of low-productivity (and therefore, *ceteris paribus*, low-skilled) labour. If this is where the main opportunities are being developed by public policy, it is difficult simultaneously to stress to young people the need for them to equip themselves with skills if they are to find employment. Second, policies for deregulating labour markets probably mean trying to weaken labour market institutions which are normally seen as valuable aids to enabling firms to accept the risks of generating collective goods. The scope for deregulation strategy therefore needs to be examined before we consider other possible policy instruments. Is it likely that the deregulation of labour markets will by itself resolve the problem of full employment, enabling us to dispense with the problems of a skill strategy? Or, to what extent is a deregulation strategy consistent with simultaneous pursuit of high skills? These questions will be included in the discussion in Chapter 2.

Markets and institutions

The central challenge for the neo-liberal approach is that, viewed in terms of formal theory, work skills frequently have the attributes of impure public goods of a particular kind: those that are non-excludable but rival. Within a perfectly

competitive labour market, firms will provide that level of VET that equips employees with those firm-specific skills necessary to sustain the firm's short-term
position in its product markets. If it goes beyond this to provide marketable skills,
it risks losing workers to employers in the same labour market who are able to
offer a wage premium by not spending money on providing their own training.
This latter phenomenon is often crudely described as 'poaching', though in reality it is as likely to take place through the normal operation of the labour market
as through explicit targeting of trained workers for rival recruitment.

Strictly speaking, skill is excludable. Employers usually pay higher wages for
skilled than for unskilled labour, and, in principle, in a pure market economy
this wage premium should be adequate to induce workers themselves to invest in
acquiring skills that will give them such a premium. Alternatively, if employers
finance training they could in principle indenture trained workers and charge a
transfer fee to firms which wish to buy the workers from them. However, in practice, for reasons that need not be discussed here, both these market solutions to
the provision of training are found in only a very limited range of occupations.
Except where the individual employee paid for his or her own earlier training
and this is recognized in a wage premium, the new employer of skilled labour
does not compensate whomever funded the acquisition of the skill. In the normal case training is a good with positive externalities that render it *de facto* non-
excludable. Skill is however rival in nature, in that it is not in infinite supply,
and if one firm is employing it no one else can. There are likely therefore to be
acute problems of under-provision of skilled labour: firms compete for it, but it
is impossible to prevent access to it by firms that have not played their part in
providing it.

Skill acquisition is also future oriented, and therefore involves risks. As
Schmid has argued (1990: 141–2), there are three ways of countering risks: savings, insurance, and the acquisition of flexibility to limit the specificity of the
future commitment. Where normal investments are concerned, markets have been
able to produce their own institutions for overcoming these problems. Where labour
is concerned this possibility is limited, first by the 'poaching' point already discussed: firms are unable to ensure that the object of their investment (the skilled
employees) will remain with them; and partly because the workers themselves
are very frequently people without either capital or expertise in the use of capital and therefore not able to take advantage of market solutions for discounting
their risks. Public and other institutional agencies are therefore often found providing non-market solutions to these problems. As Schmid (ibid.) argues, there
can be analogies of savings in the form of public incentives to firms and individuals to take the risk of training;[6] collective training funds and the regulation

---

[6] For example, as Soskice (1991a: 393) shows, where adequate performance in school is both
necessary and sufficient to enable young people to gain access to broad-based training and long-term
employment as a skilled worker, they have a strong incentive to take training courses. The existence
of such mechanisms usually requires specific links between schools and businesses that bridge the
uncertainties of the pure labour market.

of entitlements to training can provide the function of insurance; avoidance of over-specialization in training programmes together with frequent retraining can provide flexibility.

The analytical scheme of Hollingsworth, Schmitter, and Streeck (1994) and Crouch and Streeck (1997) can be used to consider the role of institutions in tackling these various problems in the following way.

States   The most obvious answer to the question of collective provision is of course state intervention: the state may undertake the task of providing or at least subsidizing the training that creates skills. Major elements of this will indeed be found in all countries under review, even if it is only the maintenance of a general national education system. However, as will be shown in Chapter 4 with particular reference to French and Swedish evidence—the two countries within our group that would generally be regarded as examples of effective states in this field—there is considerable danger that the state's training agencies will fail to keep up with changes in the production system and with employers' needs. Unless policy takes the form of subsidizing training by employers, there is a problem in the relationship between packages of skill that the individual has acquired in schools and colleges and those in the employing firm. Unless government is working closely with employers, there can be ineffectiveness of manpower planning, and a rapid pace of technological change may lead to obsolescence of equipment in state facilities. Particularly important at present, when company identity is becoming an increasingly prominent component of competitive strategies, the characteristics of certain workplace competences can often only be developed on an employer's own premises (Streeck 1989).

Some of these problems are eased if government subsidizes company activity, perhaps raising a levy from firms to finance the subsidy as has been done in France with some success for over twenty-five years. This can however bring other difficulties. Given the rival nature of work skills, the state is taking on the task of providing resources that will help particular firms. It may be reluctant to do this as it may consider that employers ought to be 'playing their part'. Further, proper use of the subsidy has to be monitored; governments find it difficult to maintain detailed links with large numbers of firms and may therefore concentrate their attentions on the largest, neglecting training in small and medium enterprises. There are therefore likely to be gains in effectiveness if government policy operates in co-operation with associations of employers; this raises the possibility of a different approach.

Corporatist organizations and informal community networks   The ability of associations of firms, occasionally in association with trade unions, to provide collective goods for the operation of businesses that are not simply protectionist cartels conspiring against the public has been discussed in a large literature (for example, Crouch 1993: chs. 1 and 2; Dell'Aringa 1990; Hall 1986; Streeck 1992). The role of these organizations is by no means uncontentious; in particular it needs to be shown under what circumstances they can act as anything other than protectionist cartels, given the analysis of Olson (1982) which demonstrates the difficulty of this. In Chapter 5 we shall consider both the theory and the evidence relevant to the issue. At present we need to note that work skills may be among the goods delivered by associations in various ways. In the most obvious case a business association acquires control over access to a set of functions, with the result that virtually all firms employing workers in a given set of labour markets find it advantageous to join. These functions might include such matters as technical and marketing advice, but they might also involve a share in the administration of some publicly provided resource, so that non-members will be at a disadvantage. These latter examples might more effectively fulfil the monopoly criterion than the provision of individual membership services. The association can use the sanctions at its disposal in these areas to require member firms to contribute to training, whether through carrying out training themselves or by financing its being done elsewhere.

There might however also be more informal cases. A group of small firms located in a community might be able to act like an association by threatening various sanctions of social exclusion towards firms in the area which will not contribute to shared training activities. The issues selected for sanctions in this way can be diffuse, informal, and constantly developing. Streeck (*et al.* 1987; 1992) has described such processes even within what might appear to be the purely formal framework of German employers' collective VET arrangements. Similar analyses have been made in central Italy by Bagnasco (1977; 1986; 1987), Trigilia (1986; 1989), and others. These networks, which raise some questions different from those of corporatist associations, will be considered in Chapter 6.

Markets, hierarchies, and institutional firms   Finally, a pure neo-liberal approach must itself be regarded as a form of institutionalism, even if a limiting case. It tackles the problem by denying the existence of any collective goods component in the provision of skills. Following the distinction made by Becker (1962), firms (a) use those general skills with which young people come equipped from school (or, in the purest market case, with which youths have paid to equip themselves, knowing that without such an investment in their own skills their earnings potential will be reduced), and (b) add to them skills specific to the firm, which they are willing to provide because they are not transferable to other employers. These latter skills are thus rendered excludable. Firms are the only institutions that remain in this model. Given the new prominence of the individual firm discussed above, the implications of this model for the behaviour of both individuals and firms require consideration. We shall turn to this in Chapter 7.

But the neo-liberal model does not exhaust the potentialities of the firm. Market approaches and the role of the firm are often treated as equivalent in the economic literature, as firms are regarded in neo-classical theory simply as market actors. However, there is a more realistic tradition of economics, often associated with the literature on management, which sees firms as comprising two forms

of action: markets and hierarchies (see especially the work of the transaction economics school, for example, Williamson 1975; 1985). This latter recognizes that
many of the transactions of firms, largely those with employees but also increasingly those with supplying companies, do not take the form of pure market
exchanges. Strictly speaking, if the labour contract is seen in market terms, the
idea of managerial authority has to be remodelled as a series of exchanges between
equals, through which it is agreed that certain work tasks shall be performed in
exchange for a certain wage, as does occur in the case of a private contractor
working for a number of clients. But such a reduction ignores very important
differences between the situation of the contractor and that of the employee.

First, the purchaser of the labour services (the employer) is, at least in the short
run, a monopsonist, so the market cannot be a perfectly competitive one. Second,
there is not in practice a series of transactions between work-giver and work-
taker (to use the German names for employer and employee, *Arbeitgeber* and
Arbeitnehmer), but a general understanding that the employee submits him- or
herself to the authority of the employer or its agents (managers), and in practice a considerable amount of effort is devoted by firms to sustaining cultures of
obedience to authority. To negotiate every new piece of business, as happens
in arm's-length or pure market contractor relations, would involve considerable
transaction costs.

There is thus a distinct social order within the firm. Once established, this
can have many components. Firms can simply assert a tough regime of obedience to authority with associated penalties for insubordination (so-called macho-
management); or they can develop an elaborate structure of co-operation and a
company culture, usually associated with encouragement of long service, persuading employees to develop careers within the firms. This is the distinction
established by Walton (1985) between management by exercising control and
management by securing commitment. The latter may be more difficult to achieve,
but it is probably a necessary condition for encouraging initiative taking by
employees; it is difficult, if not impossible, to coerce innovation. Associated with
the commitment approach is the use by firms of internal labour markets, involving the planning of internal career paths for employees whose services they wish
to retain. This will also include the firms' initiatives in the provision of training
and, in particular, retraining. Frequently it is this characteristic of firms which
enables them to minimize the problems of poaching and ostensible disincentives
to train reported by the theoretical literature. Such companies produce within themselves a form of institutional structure going beyond the simple requirements of
market and hierarchy. We shall call them here 'institutional companies'.

A particularly strong form of the institutional company, sufficiently distinctive to be regarded as a sub-type, is what Dore and others, concerned specifically
with Japanese firms, have called the 'community model' (Aoki and Dore 1994;
Sako 1997). Here very elaborate steps are taken to encourage active identity with
the firm, including guarantees of lifelong employment to the core workforce. It
is notable that in these companies shareholders play a very passive role. Both

simple hierarchy and the more complex cases of institutional companies enable firms to provide training in a manner that might obviate the need for certain kinds of public policy. This will also be discussed in Chapter 7.

POLICY CONCLUSIONS

Finally, in Chapter 8 we shall draw together the conclusions that have emerged from the analysis of the adaptability of the various institutional forms to the task of pursuing the learning society. These conclusions are uncomfortable. We in no way propose abandoning the search for the 'learning society'. The logic is sound that tells individuals, firms, and governments that they must strain to maximize the advantage they take of opportunities to improve educational levels and skill standards. Those who allow skill levels to stagnate will be doomed to the inefficient and low-earning niches of the market. The search for appropriate balances between general and vocational education, between encouraging firms and becoming dependent on them, must continue to be at the forefront of policy making and planning. But all these activities fall in the dispiriting class of being 'necessary but insufficient' for the task of guaranteeing high levels of social welfare.

We are very doubtful of two things in particular. First, we do not believe that there is any one institutional and policy mix which, once found, will prove to be the 'right answer'; virtually all policy approaches embody flaws, tendencies to entropy and potential capture by vested interests; all need frequent renewal. Second, and worse still, we do not believe that the search for a high-skill economy can fulfil the hopes so widely vested in it for solving the problem of employment. As we shall see in Chapter 2, the prospects for achieving full employment largely through upskilling are doubtful. This means that policy-makers' hopes for replacing general social policy with education policy are unrealistic.

2

Employment and Employment Skills

Discussion of public policy on vocational training and education is preoccupied with two different questions: Can countries ensure that their working populations are competing internationally at the 'sharp end' of skills? And can VET help solve the problem of mass unemployment? As we shall see at several points of our discussion, attempting to kill these two rather different birds with the same stone creates a number of problems. Nevertheless, it is unavoidable that training policies have to address the general problems of the contemporary labour market. We must therefore relate our analysis to this context. In so doing we must also concern ourselves with the reigning orthodoxy in labour market policy, which sees the main solution to unemployment in deregulation of that market and increasing the disposability of labour. This strategy clashes at certain points with the main prescriptions of a skill-maximization policy.

These different themes come together in the work of the OECD. The OECD has a major role as a technical body providing detailed and sophisticated data based on its privileged access to national and international sources, and any analysis of the labour market is heavily dependent on its publications, in particular on its *Jobs Study* (OECD 1994*a* and *b*). This provides the most comprehensive and widely accepted analysis available of employment growth in the advanced industrial societies since the end of the 1970s. However, it is also a highly political document. The different parts of the OECD have distinct political ideologies. The Economics Directorate, which produced the *Jobs Study*, favours the universal deregulation of labour markets as the central strategy for ending high unemployment, and its empirical analyses tend to be oriented towards that end. Since this clashes at certain points with policies implied by skill-maximization strategies, another goal to which the OECD is committed, there are inevitable contradictions in the Organization's stance—which in the case of the *Jobs Study* was dealt with by treating skills and training in chapters separate from the main analysis. Discussion of the OECD's labour market and VET analysis must therefore deal with these tensions in a critical manner. In this chapter we shall develop our own account of what has been happening in various labour markets in recent years through a critique of this kind.

The approach to employment creation of those who seek a high-skilled route as a kind of replacement of Keynesian strategy is to upskill workforces so that the country concerned can take a larger share of world markets that require such skills. Whether it involves direct government action or action by organizations of firms and others, it is clearly an approach to employment that implies a direct policy towards the labour market and therefore something other than reliance on free market forces. It is therefore most likely to be associated with institutional approaches to economic management rather than neo-liberal ones. Neo-liberals will welcome the idea of firms moving into high-skill areas, and will argue that creation of a competitive environment will provide incentives to firms to do so. They will, however, argue that it would be a mistake for governments and other national institutions to try to force the pace of such a development with explicit policy. They will therefore stress the importance of other approaches, in particular the deregulation of labour markets to make it easier and cheaper for employers to hire and fire.

The OECD *Jobs Study* embodies this latter approach in that its main concern is with the creation of jobs of any kind, mainly by reducing the price of labour (especially the reservation price of unemployed labour), and with reducing employment protection rights so that employers may easily dispose of labour. This leads to a number of contradictions with the Organization's advocacy of a high-skill strategy. For example, Japanese experience is cited as suggesting that investment in training and stability of employment, including low job turnover, may be mutually reinforcing (OECD 1994b: 122, 123), while the rest of the *Study* encourages instability of employment. The training discussion also points out that the countries which secure the highest education enrolment rates among young people after the compulsory school-leaving age are those where vocational education is highly organized, with clearly defined and collectively organized and accepted responsibilities (ibid.: 130); but the rest of the *Study* seeks to undermine all forms of supportive organization in the labour market above the level of the enterprise.

The training discussion is also aware of high youth unemployment in North America, caused partly by the need for so much trial and error in finding suitable work (ibid.: 140), and attributes this in part to the absence of certification of skills in the USA (ibid.: 144). But this is itself a consequence of the autonomy of enterprises and the absence of either public regulation or strong employers' organizations—essential characteristics of what the *Jobs Study* otherwise finds praiseworthy about the US economy. The training discussion might also have noted that this frequent trial and error of young people's labour market experience, which it sees as unfortunate and wasteful, accounts for at least part of the high number of people leaving jobs within a year in the USA—a phenomenon which in general, as will be seen below, the *Study* treats as evidence of a commendable labour market flexibility.

Although we are ourselves sceptical of much of the case for seeking the universal high-skills economy, we also see important weaknesses in the OECD Economic Directorate's approach and suspect that the dominance of neo-liberal ideology among government economists in many countries has affected the one-sided nature of its arguments. For example, although a large amount of sophisticated empirical evidence is deployed in the *Study*, in most instances the results of this are inconclusive, and the authors then often fall back on *a priori* reasoning. Thus, attempts to demonstrate that unemployment compensation affects the job-seeking behaviour of the unemployed (OECD 1994b: 44), or that minimum wages raise the level of unemployment (ibid.: 46 ff.), find very little tangible empirical support. The Organization therefore has recourse to a first-principles argument that there *must* be some effect of the kind predicted (ibid.: 51 ff.). A summary of the cases for and against employment protection displays inconclusive empirical evidence but falls back for a conclusion on the a priori argument that protection of employees' job rights is likely to reduce employment because the anticipated costs of dismissals are an aspect of labour costs and are therefore likely to discourage hiring (ibid.: 73–6).

The *Jobs Study* has particular difficulties when dealing with the case of Japan. The fact that that country, which has continued to experience rapid job growth, also has very long job tenures and has been ranked by some observers as intermediate (rather than low) in its degree of job regulation (for example, Bertola 1990), potentially causes major difficulties for the deregulation thesis. The OECD therefore argues that the Japanese employment system does not really provide job protection (OECD 1994b: 79). The reasoning for this is as follows: because there is little state social security in Japan, it is important to employees that employers offer them job security; therefore, in order to attract labour, employers make such an offer. Because this is seen as a labour market decision by employers and not regulation by the state, it is not regarded as a form of regulation—even though it has the same effect on security for those workers concerned as would a legislated system.

It might be objected on behalf of the OECD's argument that, unlike statutory protection which is likely to be universal, the Japanese system, which necessarily limits secure long-term employment to certain categories of workers, contains its own flexibility via a segmentation of the labour force. Further, these workers are mainly those in large corporations, while other categories of employees are less well protected, including those on special temporary contracts. Overall therefore the Japanese labour market might be seen as one that offers less protection than a universalist scheme typical of a northern European country. Further, even for the core regular employees, the lifetime employment norm gets diluted as one moves from large to medium-sized and smaller firms. These are valid points, but they sit uneasily with the stance of the OECD researchers, who are in general very critical of segmentation as a source of rigidity in labour markets. They rightly regard devices which accord different levels of statutory protection to different categories of workers as creating barriers between insiders and outsiders and as generally impeding the free flow of labour. In particular, they come down hard against the policies of various European governments (for example, France and Spain), which have tried to reconcile continued protection for much of the workforce with the need to reduce high youth unemployment by developing special legal categories of temporary employment (ibid.: 78). The OECD unequivocally prefers policies which remove protection from all workers, as this is more consistent with the pure market model of labour being available as an uninterrupted flow rather than coming in certain defined 'lumps' as in a segmented market.

However, the Japanese employment system, which embodies one of the world's most segmented labour markets, is not subjected to the same criticism. Nor does the *Jobs Study* regard racial inequalities in the US economy as providing the basis of any segmentation in the labour market, despite the existence of a number of studies confirming this finding (Freeman 1994; Gans 1995); nor does it see segmentation in the particular labour market role played by students and elderly people in the USA and elsewhere (see below); nor in the practice of many large firms in many countries of offering very diverse packages of job security to different types and levels of staff. In each case the explanation is the same: from a neo-liberal perspective market distortions can be produced only by governments, and by definition not by the actions of firms acting in free markets (OECD 1994*b*: 79).

Particularly important to our present concerns is the central claim that job growth will correlate inversely with the degree of job regulation or employment protection, since it is this that forms the main rival to the 'institutions for skills thesis'. The *Jobs Study* proposes an interesting variety of measures of the strength of labour market regulation, and finds strong correlations between some of them and measures of employment growth (ibid.: Table 6.9, reproduced here as Table 2.1). However, as can be seen, when the data were recalculated by the *Study* itself after removing the four southern European countries, Greece, Italy, Portugal, and Spain (among which, with the exception of Portugal, western European unemployment is heavily concentrated), a different picture emerges. The *Jobs Study* claims that the correlations are largely unaffected by this, but it is difficult to reconcile this claim with the results it reports. There is now a considerable lack of explanatory power in nearly all the tests, the only measure performing well being the index of job strictness produced originally by the International Organization of Employers (IOE) and subsequently extended by the OECD to include all countries in its coverage. As pointed out by the *Jobs Study* itself (ibid.: 76), the principal differentiating characteristic of this index is that it rated the degree of regulation in the Scandinavian labour markets less stringently than did other measures.

We therefore already have indications of two important subregional effects within Europe: exclusion of the southern European countries makes a considerable difference to the strength of the findings; and there is disagreement over how to interpret the impact of Scandinavian job regulation, the more moderate assessment of the strength of regulation in those countries producing the results more in line with the prediction of neo-classical models.

There is another questionable feature of the OECD's correlations. Although some of the measures used take some account of collective bargaining and other aspects of labour market institutions, the main weight is borne by estimates of the strength of government regulation.[1] Also, the strength of this regulation is

---

[1] Particular use is made of a ranking devised by Bertola (1990). This author had developed a single scale of level of restrictiveness based on a purely qualitative discussion of different components of labour market regulation by Emerson (1988). Emerson had in fact stressed the complex diversity

TABLE 2.1. *OECD evidence on the employment effects of employment regulation*

Employment protection indicators	Employment indicators							
	Total employment			Dependent employment			Incidence of self-employment	
				as a proportion of population of working age				
	Total	Present at work	Present at work, full-time equivalent	Total	Present at work	Present at work, full-time equivalent	Total economy	Non-agricultural sector
	Correlation coefficients calculated for 21 countries							
International Organisation of Employers	−0.67**	−0.74**	−0.67**	−0.63**	−0.68**	−0.67**	0.42*	0.43*
Ranking by Bertola	−0.56**	−0.59**	−0.40*	−0.64**	−0.70**	−0.63**	0.57**	0.53**
Maximum notice and severance pay	−0.54*	−0.62**	−0.45*	−0.64**	−0.76**	−0.70**	0.62**	0.52*
Tables 6.5 and 6.6	−0.43*	−0.44*	−0.29	−0.45*	−0.50*	−0.44*	0.37	0.35
Compromise index	−0.60**	−0.65**	−0.48*	−0.65**	−0.72**	−0.66**	0.55**	0.51*
	Correlation coefficients calculated for 17 countries, excluding 4 countries of Southern Europe							
International Organisation of Employers	−0.49*	−0.64**	−0.61**	−0.36	−0.47*	−0.48*	−0.11	−0.15
Ranking by Bertola	0.36	−0.45*	−0.29	−0.34	−0.46*	−0.35	0.17	−0.01
Maximum notice and severance pay	−0.38	−0.62**	−0.50*	−0.36	−0.60*	−0.53*	0.23	−0.02
Tables 6.5 and 6.6	−0.21	−0.27	−0.17	−0.10	−0.15	−0.08	−0.23	−0.32
Compromise index	−0.42*	−0.55*	−0.43*	−0.36	−0.49*	−0.41*	0.07	−0.10

* = Significant at 10 per cent.

** = Significant at 1 per cent (two–tailed tests).

Note: References within Table 2.1 to Tables 6.5 and 6.6 are to tables in OECD 1994*b*.

Source: OECD 1994*b*, table 6.9.

measured by the mere existence of legislation. Not only is non-statutory regulation given little attention, but it is assumed that all legislation is implemented.

There are grounds for questioning both assumptions of this legalistic methodology. On the first, we have already discussed above the major problem that the
OECD has with Japan. This country has, within its great firms, possibly the most
institutionalized labour markets in the world; but because the factors which reduce
the disposability of labour result from corporate strategy rather than government
regulation, they are disregarded as not really being job regulation.[2] Denmark is
also regarded by the OECD as a low-regulation country because it has little statutory regulation of the terms of hiring and firing. However, as we know from much
research, the Danish labour market is very thoroughly organized by employers'
associations and trade unions which negotiate regulation of the labour market
through binding agreements (Due *et al.* 1994).[3] Denmark also has a very well-
developed welfare state and strongly redistributive taxation; it hardly suits the
neo-liberal ideal of a free-market society any more than does Japan, though in
very different ways.

The second issue, the assumption that regulations are implemented in accordance with the strength of their provisions, leads the OECD to regard the high-
unemployment countries of southern Europe as having the most highly regulated
labour markets. It is of course very difficult to measure the implementation of
law and one sympathizes with the OECD analysts, but it is widely known that
in at least some economic sectors and geographical areas within southern Europe
legislated labour regulation is very widely ignored. This will not be true for the
public sector or for the large corporations whose opinions become represented
in forums like the IOE. It does, however, apply to many small firms; and small
firms have been important producers of employment growth in nearly all countries in recent years.[4] These are also economies with particularly high levels
of self-employment and employment in very small firms, which are not even
formally covered by employment regulation.

It is also likely that, where job regulation is poorly implemented, implying the
existence of considerable 'black' employment, the existence of many jobs will

of labour market regimes, drawing attention for example to the role of private litigation in establishing employment rights in the USA, whereas statute was perhaps more likely to be used in many
European countries. Most of his data used sources from the mid-1980s and therefore, like the IOE
study of 1987, cannot take account of the differential progress of deregulatory policy in various European
countries during the latter 1980s; France and Spain in particular introduced major programmes of
deregulation.

   [2] In fact, the Japanese Ministry of Labour does provide subsidies to employers during recessions
to retain employees and retrain them, rather than lay them off, thus helping to foster the long-term
employment relationship and increase the investments in productivity-enhancing skills (Finegold
et al. 1994*b*).

   [3] Danish implementation of the parental leave directive under the terms of the Social Protocol of
the Maastricht Treaty takes the form of joint administration by the central union and employers'
organizations, not legislation. This was approved by the European Commission because this form
of implementation in Denmark is seen as being as effective as legal regulation.

   [4] There is evidence that the initial euphoria about growth of small firms was based partly on a
failure to distinguish between gross and net employment effects, leading to exaggeration of the gains
(Davis *et al.* 1996).

go unrecorded and some people who are in fact in work will falsely declare themselves to be unemployed. Taken together these data will give the impression of a combination of low levels of employment, high levels of unemployment, and very strict job regulation where in fact employment is higher, unemployment lower, and job regulation less strict. Doubts must be cast over the reliability of any tests of a thesis about the relationship between employment and labour regulation that are dependent on official data from this part of Europe. As Table 2.1 shows, whether or not southern Europe is included has a considerable effect on the strength of correlations found for the OECD's hypotheses, because these countries occupy extreme positions on the measurement scales of both low employment and high regulation.

An alternative approach to the legalistic one, which is also used by the OECD study, is to consider *de facto* labour rigidity by considering the length of employees' tenure with a particular firm. It is argued that employers need the freedom to dispose of employees easily if they are to be willing to hire them. We should therefore find job growth higher in those countries where average job tenure is lower. Recent data on different average lengths of tenure by country are shown in Table 2.2. There is no tendency for job growth over the period 1990–5 to be negatively correlated with average tenure length. It can be argued

TABLE 2.2. *Employment tenures, 1995–1996*

Country	Average stay in a specific firm (years)	% in specific firm for less than one year
Australia	6.4	25.2
Austria	10.0	12.6
Belgium	11.2	11.6
Canada	7.9	22.7
Denmark	7.9	25.1
Finland	10.5	17.6
France	**10.7**	**15.0**
Germany*	**9.7**	**16.1**
Greece	9.9	12.6
Ireland	8.7	17.8
Italy	**11.6**	**9.5**
Japan	**11.3**	**7.6**
Netherlands	8.7	16.3
Portugal	11.0	13.4
Spain	8.9	35.5
Sweden	**10.5**	**14.8**
Switzerland	9.0	15.7
UK	**7.8**	**19.6**
USA	**7.4**	**26.0**

* Unified Germany.
Source: OECD 1997*b*.

that data on overall job tenure do not really tell us about the margins at which employers seek flexibility in their labour forces, since large numbers of employees are included whom employers have no wish to lose. We might perform a better test on the margins by considering only short-term stays, which we might assess by considering the percentage of employees who left their jobs after less than a year. This is also shown in Table 2.2. Again there is no statistical relationship with data on job growth.

These data on tenure are important to the conflict between the deregulationist and the skill-maximization strategies, because at this point the strategies make diametrically opposite recommendations: deregulationists stress the disposability of labour, while institutionalists stress the importance of employers being committed to their labour so that they try to improve employees' deficiencies through training rather than through dismissal. It is a good example of the conflict between Hirschman's (1970) exit and voice modes of dealing with failure and inadequacy. Ease of 'exit', in this case the ability of an employer to dispose of labour, seeks improvement by 'shopping around'. If employers are unable to dispose of workers easily, they will have to use 'voice' mechanisms, that is work to improve the quality of those they have available.

EMPLOYMENT CHANGE OVER TWO DECADES

In the light of these criticisms of the OECD's approach we can now make use of its data to assess employment development in the advanced countries during the period covered by the *Jobs Study* (OECD 1994*a*; 1994*b*), that from 1979 to 1990, with some further updating of our own.

At the most basic level, the *Jobs Study* showed that, during the period 1979–90, there was 1.6% and 1.1% job growth in the USA and Japan respectively, whereas the only western European countries to experience positive employment growth were Norway (0.7%), Germany, and Finland (both 0.6%) (OECD 1994*a*: Table 1.1). However, as the *Study* then acknowledges, these crude figures leave out of account the fact that European populations of working age were growing more slowly than those in Japan and the USA. A more relevant figure is the growth in the number of jobs per capita of the population of working age (conventionally defined as ages 15 to 64). This reveals a less dramatic contrast (ibid.: Table 1.2). The USA still had the fastest rate of job growth, but down to 0.6%; second were Finland and Sweden (0.3%), fourth Japan (0.2%), fifth the UK (0.1%); Denmark, Greece, and Norway had zero growth and all other European countries had negative levels.

These data relate to the major period of economic transformation that took place in the wake of the oil shocks and other inflationary crises of the 1970s. Table 2.3 brings the account up to date by considering what happened during the first half of the 1990s, when there had been a new world-wide recession and major changes in labour market and general economic policy.

TABLE 2.3. *Changes in employment/population ratio, 1990–1996, population aged 15–64*

Country	Males				Females			
	1990	1996	Annual change	Rank order	1990	1996	Annual change	Rank order
Australia	79.7	77.3	−0.40	11	57.5	59.3	0.30	7
Austria	77.7	76.9	−0.13	5	53.5	59.2	0.95	3
Belgium	68.4	67.3	−0.18	8	41.0	45.8	0.80	4
Canada	79.4	74.8	−0.77	14	63.6	62.2	−0.23	16
Denmark	82.5	81.4	−0.18	8	71.5	67.8	−0.62	18
Finland	77.6	65.4	−2.03	19	70.8	58.9	−1.98	20
France	**70.4**	**67.2**	**−0.53**	**13**	**50.6**	**52.1**	**0.25**	**9**
Germany*	**76.4**	**73.4**	**−0.50**	**12**	**52.8**	**54.3**	**0.25**	**9**
Greece	75.8	75.1	−0.12	4	38.5	39.0	0.08	12
Ireland	70.3	68.8	−0.25	10	37.3	43.5	1.03	2
Italy	**73.4**	**66.4**	**−1.17**	**17**	**36.9**	**36.5**	**−0.07**	**15**
Japan	**86.3**	**88.5**	**0.37**	**2**	**59.1**	**60.7**	**0.27**	**8**
Netherlands	76.2	76.6	0.07	3	47.0	55.0	1.33	1
New Zealand	77.6	80.6	0.50	1	59.2	63.8	0.77	5
Norway	82.9	81.9	−0.17	7	71.6	68.9	−0.45	17
Portugal	83.8	76.1	−1.28	18	58.2	58.7	0.08	12
Spain	69.8	63	−1.13	16	32.0	33.4	0.23	11
Sweden	**86.9**	**74.7**	**−2.03**	**18**	**81.8**	**70.6**	**−1.87**	**19**
UK	**83.7**	**77.7**	**−1.00**	**15**	**63.7**	**64.1**	**0.07**	**14**
USA	**83.1**	**82.3**	**−0.13**	**5**	**65.8**	**68.1**	**0.38**	**6**

* The 1990 figure is for former West Germany; the 1996 figure is for united Germany.
Source: OECD 1997*b*.

Among males very few countries experienced net job growth, and they comprise a geographically and institutionally varied group: New Zealand, Japan, and the Netherlands; with only minor decline in a few other, equally diverse countries: Greece, Austria, the USA, Norway, Belgium, and Denmark. Very severe declines were experienced by the other two Nordic countries (Finland and Sweden), all southern European countries (Portugal, Italy, and Spain) except Greece, and the UK. Among women more countries experienced net growth, the leaders being European countries with previous low records of female employment (Netherlands, Ireland, Austria, and Belgium). The severest declines were in the Nordic countries, this time including Denmark and Norway which had had good male records. These countries have had particularly strong past experiences of female employment.

Summarizing the lessons of the data for the two periods, there was most job growth (or least job loss) in the period 1979–90 in the lightly regulated countries and in the Scandinavian countries. The worst performers were the southern European countries and what we might call the 'core continental' European countries. The good performance of the unregulated and the poor performance of the core continental countries is consistent with the deregulationist hypothesis, but the good performance of Scandinavia and the the poor performance of ineffectively regulated southern Europe is not. In contrast, an institutionalist theory would have predicted the Scandinavian and southern European positions but will have been surprised by the American case. In the more recent period, 1990–5, the evidence is again mixed. Parts of Scandinavia have now started to perform as anticipated by neo-liberal theory, but the UK should be performing much better than it did. Also, the performance of the core continental countries (even when one has removed the southern European countries from the category) is far more diverse than justifies the common generalizations of the OECD and others about 'Europe'. More important, certain countries in the group, including some which appear to be highly regulated on any measurement, such as Austria and the Netherlands, performed as well as Japan and the USA and considerably better than the UK (or indeed than France, which had implemented many deregulatory policies in previous years).

Of the countries of interest to this study, Japan was the only one to experience positive male job growth during the more recent period.[5] Italy and Sweden were the only poor performances among women.

In addition to considering job growth we should examine the overall contours of employment. This is also a preferable approach to analysing the state of labour markets as opposed to considering levels of *un*employment. Counts of unemployment are heavily affected by different national rules for defining the unemployed. Unemployment levels are politically sensitive, and definition as being unemployed usually entitles persons to benefits; both factors give people varying incentives to present themselves as unemployed while giving governments incentives both to change definitions of unemployment in a way that reduces the estimate, and to take measures to make registration as unemployed difficult (see King 1995 for a detailed study of the changes over time and the highly political character of policy on benefit entitlement in the UK and the USA). The OECD, commending British policies during the 1980s of 'frequent monitoring' of unemployed people, points out that 'even quite low levels of contact with unemployed people reduce the number of benefit claims' (OECD 1994*b*: 104). And the UK's Youth Training Scheme (YTS) was praised because it restricted access to benefit for young people (ibid.: 105). The role of unemployment registration as a measure of excess supply within the labour market is here completely lost in the policy-maker's concern, for political and cost reasons, to

---

[5] In appraising German performance one must bear in mind that the 1990 figure relates to the old West Germany, while that for 1996 relates to the whole of the new Germany. The mid-ranking per capita job growth levels in that country were therefore achieved amidst the reconstruction crisis in the east, where it is estimated that over four million jobs were lost during the years immediately following the collapse of the former East German regime.

be able to present a lower number of claimants. If governments do this differentially, comparisons between unemployment levels might simply reflect different regimes of counting and of severity of treatment of potential claimants.

Similarly, a person's decision to declare himself or herself to be unemployed might be a claim for benefit rather than a declaration of entry into the labour market, and the varying severity of different benefit regimes will affect claimants' capacity to fudge this distinction.

Further, today's labour markets differ from those of previous decades in that far more married women now perceive themselves as members of the workforce; like men, they are either in paid employment or registered as unemployed. But a third option remains for women: to be regarded as housewives and mothers and not to register as unemployed if they do not have paid jobs. Women's decisions as to how to define themselves will have a major effect on the unemployment rate. Further still, both men and women leaving the labour force in the latter part of their working lives might perceive themselves as retired rather than unemployed, though they might take employment of various kinds if it appears. It is difficult to determine whether or not housewives and retired people are 'in the labour market'. They are unlikely either to describe themselves as unemployed when approached by a labour market survey researcher or to try to register at their local benefit office. They may well, however, respond to a sudden job opportunity or even start looking for work.

Finally, a similar question can arise among younger age groups, where people might 'park' themselves in education courses rather than either become unemployed or take unattractive work; or if pursuing educational courses they might take part-time work to help pay their way through it. Whether they will register as unemployed will depend partly on their self-perception, partly on rules for benefit entitlement which often make it illegal (though not necessarily impossible) for students to register as unemployed.

The economic concepts that inform standard labour market analysis assume that two types of person are 'active' in the labour market: those actually in jobs and those who have registered as unemployed and are hence in principle offering themselves on the market for work. These two groups together comprise the 'supply' of labour. A high rate of unemployment therefore indicates excess supply, carrying with it the strong presumption that a reduction in labour's price would reconcile the imbalance. On that basis depend all currently fashionable recommendations that the cost of labour must be reduced, whether through cutting wages, reducing security levels and other rights, or reducing the non-wage costs of labour. However, registration as unemployed is less a signal of a desire to enter the labour market than a request for social security benefit; the two decisions are related but far from the same. It is possible that government rules do not permit someone to claim benefit, though that person might well remain actively searching for work.

We shall therefore concentrate on a comparison of numbers *in work* rather than on unemployment. We look first at the simplest feature of the labour market: the proportion of the relevant population which is in employment. This relevant population is conventionally defined as those between the ages of 15 and 64. We make two changes to this. First, increasingly large numbers of young people between the ages of 15 and their twenties remain in education. We therefore remove from the population all people in full-time education. (This will lead to the opposite and unavoidable inaccuracy, as increasing numbers of young people in some countries are working part time during their studies, but we shall discuss this in due course.)

We should also remove the artificial constraint of the age 65 cut-off. One problem with the OECD data used in the *Jobs Study* and also in Table 2.3 above is that they measure *all* job growth but as a proportion of the population aged 15–64 only. This would give a statistically exaggerated view of per capita job growth in any countries where there was also a rise in employment among the over 65s; as we shall see in due course, this is a relevant point for the issue of job creation. Retirement ages vary across countries, and various numbers of people work after formal retirement. To gain a more accurate picture we should remove any artificial cut-off age that might exclude some members of the potential working population.

In the following discussion we exclude from consideration the population aged over 80, since work is very unlikely to be continued by people of this age. The population universe is therefore everyone between the age of 15 and 80 who is not in full-time education. Table 2.4 shows the proportion of this population in work in a number of countries, by gender, in about 1990.

Japan topped the list among overall providers of employment, though it is followed by three of the Nordic countries, Portugal, and Switzerland, within the high employment group. The UK and the USA occupy moderately high positions, ahead of the 'core continental' group which is in turn (except for Belgium and Ireland) clearly ahead of the southern European countries. There is support here for the deregulationist thesis, *but* also for those arguments that draw attention to the heterogeneity of 'Europe' and of the difficulty of accommodating a simple deregulationist thesis to a situation that has high employment in Scandinavia and low employment in southern Europe.

If we now consider the genders separately, among men Japan is joined by the two anomalous cases of Portugal and Switzerland as the three high employers, though the USA (but not the UK) also ranks high. Below this there is no discernible pattern of country types within Europe. In fact, all countries are heavily bunched here (with a standard deviation of only 7.92% of the mean). It is female employment which accounts for the greatest absolute differences among countries as well as the most recent rates of growth (standard deviation of 19.19% of the mean). Here all four Nordic countries lead, followed by Japan, Portugal, the UK, the USA, and then the other western European cases. It can certainly be concluded that the core countries of western Europe—including all the original European Community members—have lower female employment levels than either the non-European cases or those (Portugal, Scandinavia, and the UK)

TABLE 2.4. *Proportions of population aged 15–80 in employment, c.1990*

Country	All employment (%) Men %	Men Rank	Women %	Women Rank	All %	All Rank	All in part-time work (%) Men	Women	All	All full-time employment (%) Men %	Men Rank	Women %	Women Rank	All %	All Rank
Austria	74.18	9	46.95	12	60.11	11	4.00	26.90	13.90	71.21	6	34.32	9	51.75	7
Belgium	65.67	18	46.30	13	55.81	15	2.80	29.80	13.60	63.83	16	32.50	11	48.22	14
Denmark	74.89	7	60.42	2	67.62	3	10.40	35.50	21.60	67.10	11	38.97	4	53.01	4
Finland	66.04	17	58.42	3	62.14	9	5.70	11.30	8.40	62.28	17	51.82	1	56.92	3
France	**69.26**	**15**	**48.73**	**10**	**58.85**	**12**	**5.00**	**28.90**	**15.60**	**65.80**	**12**	**34.65**	**8**	**49.67**	**11**
Germany*	**74.63**	**8**	**48.70**	**11**	**61.35**	**10**	**3.60**	**33.80**	**16.30**	**71.94**	**5**	**32.24**	**12**	**51.35**	**10**
Greece	70.99	13	38.15	16	54.26	16	2.80	8.40	4.80	69.00	7	34.95	7	51.66	8
Ireland	69.28	14	35.12	17	52.25	17	5.10	21.70	11.30	65.75	13	27.50	15	46.35	16
Italy	**75.07**	**6**	**38.54**	**15**	**56.49**	**14**	**2.90**	**12.70**	**6.40**	**72.89**	**4**	**33.65**	**10**	**52.87**	**5**
Netherlands	72.62	11	44.68	14	58.50	13	16.80	67.20	37.40	60.42	18	14.66	18	36.62	18
Norway	76.12	5	57.41	4	66.61	5	9.40	46.60	26.50	68.96	8	30.66	14	48.96	12
Portugal	77.69	3	56.41	6	66.65	4	4.20	11.60	7.50	74.43	3	49.87	2	61.65	1
Spain	66.23	16	31.50	18	48.54	18	2.80	16.40	7.50	64.38	15	26.33	16	44.90	17
Sweden	**71.68**	**12**	**66.86**	**1**	**69.26**	**2**	**9.40**	**40.30**	**24.30**	**64.94**	**14**	**39.92**	**3**	**52.43**	**6**
Switzerland	83.03	2	49.73	9	66.19	6	8.60	54.70	28.30	75.89	2	22.53	17	47.46	15
UK	**73.09**	**10**	**55.98**	**7**	**64.49**	**7**	**7.70**	**44.30**	**24.10**	**67.46**	**10**	**31.18**	**13**	**48.95**	**13**
Japan	**88.73**	**1**	**57.38**	**5**	**72.59**	**1**	**10.10**	**34.90**	**20.10**	**79.77**	**1**	**37.35**	**5**	**58.00**	**2**
USA	76.48	4	51.14	8	63.10	8	11.00	27.40	18.60	68.07	9	37.13	6	51.36	9

* Former Federal Republic of Germany.
Source: various ILO and OECD publications.

which are for various reasons outside the core. Southern Europe is, with the exception of Portugal, towards the foot of the table.

With the exception of Greece, all countries with low reported female employment have had prolonged periods of government by political parties (or dictatorships) close to the Catholic Church.[6] With the exception of Portugal, all countries with high female workforce participation lack this experience, diverse though their political and religious composition might be. The Portuguese exception can be explained. During the prolonged period of pro-Catholic dictatorship, Portugal did have a low female participation rate, even lower than that of other Catholic countries. This changed rapidly and suddenly following the Marxist military coup that overthrew the dictatorship in 1975. Laws regulating female employment were then changed drastically in a manner that was never imitated in Spain (or Greece).

The different genders therefore tell different stories. The pattern of male employment lends some support to the deregulation thesis and also suggests little diversity among European nations, though male employment does not explain much of the overall picture: less than 2% more employment in the USA than in Italy or Germany. The female pattern supports a totally different explanation based on disincentives to female employment embodied in Catholic social policies of various kinds. Much writing on female employment has argued that it is the positive policies associated with the Scandinavian countries that explain high female participation rates. The evidence reported here suggests rather the negative thesis that in various ways Catholic social policy might discourage what should otherwise be assumed to be a desire by women to work (see also Esping-Andersen 1996). This evidence is therefore supportive of a deregulationist thesis, but concerning a very particular kind of regulation only.

The position of our seven countries in the list varies very much by gender, Sweden and the UK being notably higher ranking on their capacity to employ women rather than men, with Italy being the other way round.

Full time and part time; young and old

So far we have regarded a job to be a job. Central to a debate between deregulationist and institutionalist approaches to the labour market is a questioning of the types of job likely to be created. There is first a difference between full- and part-time employment. The creation of a full-time job clearly indicates a greater job-creation capacity than a part-time one. In arguing this we do not intend to join the debate over whether the creation of part-time jobs is worthless or somehow exploitative (Blossfeld and Hakim 1997), but merely to make the quantitative point that a difference between the two forms of work must be taken into account. To take an extreme case: Let us assume two economies; in one there is a 1% growth in jobs, all these jobs being of 40 hours a week duration; in the

---

[6] It may well be that the Orthodox Church has had similar implications for Greece, but in the absence of other Orthodox cases we shall have to set that country aside.

second there is a 2% growth in jobs, but they are all for 20 hours a week. An equal amount of work has been created in the two economies, but a simple count of job growth would regard the second as having been twice as effective in job creation.

Do factors of this kind help explain some cross-national differences? The later columns of Table 2.4 show the effect on the data given in the earlier columns of removing from account all part-time work; in other words, they provide a measure of full-time employment.

The effect of this is not surprisingly greater on levels of female employment. In particular the strong 'Catholic effect' disappears; the relationship between level of full-time employment and political domination by Catholic parties that obtained for the overall female employment figure no longer operates. Catholic social policy would therefore seem to have inhibited, not the participation of women *per se* in the labour force, but the possibility of combining work and family roles. It may therefore operate as much at the wider level of child-care provision, etc. as through job regulation in particular. Why this happens would require more detailed research into the family position of full-time and part-time working women —and also an attempt to take account of possible non-reporting of employment in southern Europe.

While the part-time issue is primarily a female one, in some ways the differences in levels of *male* part-time employment are more interesting. When we concentrate solely on proportions of men in full-time work as shown in Table 2.4, there is no effect on Japan's relative ranking (even though its male part-time ratio is high), but the relative rank of the USA sinks to below some core continental countries, though above most Nordic ones. If the USA has a distinctively high capacity to provide work because of its low level of employment regulation, this operates largely through a capacity to provide part-time work, especially among men. The same conclusion cannot be drawn about Japan.

Under what circumstances do men work part time? The number who do so because they have volunteered to become 'house-husbands' is probably very small. There will be some who are disabled, but most significant must be those who can find only part-time jobs, or who are working while they are studying, or who are elderly and do not want to manage a full working day. (Of course, female part-timers will include all these groups too, in addition to the more familiar 'dual burden' working housewives.)

Above we raised the question of the age range over which proportions of the population in employment should be considered. At what ages do people in various countries tend to stop working? Ages of statutory retirement vary, an aspect of the deregulation of the US labour market being the absence of any such age at all. Even where retirement does take place, people sometimes take on new post-retirement jobs. At the other end of the age scale we have assumed that we should remove from consideration among the potentially employed all those persons in full-time education. However, it is possible for someone to be in full-time education and yet also to be in some kind of employment. This too varies

TABLE 2.5. *Educational and employment position of 18-year-olds, 1984 and 1994*

Country	Males				Females			
	% of those employed also in education		% in neither work nor education 1994	% registered unemployed (15–19) 1994	% of those employed also in education		% in neither work nor education 1994	% registered unemployed (15–19) 1994
	1984	1994			1984	1994		
Belgium	7.10	11.50	13.00	32.50	3.20	6.70	13.50	37.50
Denmark	23.90	50.80	4.40	8.50	32.50	63.50	10.60	5.10
France	1.90	15.60	10.70	21.90	5.70	27.60	10.10	34.50
Germany*	5.80	12.00	7.80	5.80	7.30	15.40	8.20	6.80
Greece	5.80	5.10	10.80	20.60	2.10	8.50	20.80	47.60
Ireland	5.90	10.80	16.80	32.80	6.90	23.30	11.90	34.00
Italy	2.10	2.60	15.20	33.00	2.50	2.60	19.70	42.40
Netherlands	23.70	55.10	5.30	16.00	18.80	65.70	4.70	12.00
Portugal	10.20	16.00	7.20	11.30	4.00	15.80	10.20	19.90
Spain	2.00	11.30	17.20	39.80	0.50	17.80	18.10	58.10
UK	14.60	21.90	23.50	20.80	18.10	33.00	25.40	16.10
USA	43.80	46.30	12.00	19.00	42.90	45.60	16.80	16.20

* 1984, former Federal Republic of Germany. 1994, unified Germany.
Source: OECD 1996b.

by country. The OECD's assessments of job growth, and our own assessments above of the total workforce, do nothing to remove from the 'in work' category elderly persons and students in some kind of employment.

Let us first consider the young. Table 2.5 shows the proportions of 18-year-olds in employment who were also in education in 1984 and 1994. (Smaller numbers continued in that situation at least until age 26.) It is notable that in some countries—Denmark, the Netherlands, the USA, to some extent the UK, and (among women only) Ireland—there were particularly high levels of employment among young persons in education; one assumes that most people both in employment and in education are working part time.[7] A further useful statistic is that of young people neither at school nor in work, which may be a more reliable indicator of inactivity than the unemployment rate, also shown in Table 2.5. It is interesting to note the poor performances here of the UK and the USA. It is also possible that the higher rates of crime and some other indicators of social distress in the Anglophone countries are relevant to this situation. For example, about 2% more of the male population of the USA is in prison than of most countries in continental north-western Europe; this almost entirely accounts for the difference in male unemployment rates between the two zones (Freeman 1991).

Table 2.6 enables us further to examine the age and gender profiles of employment. Within the core (age 25–54) male workforce there is only limited variation in the proportion of the population in employment (from 78.4% in Finland to 95.3% in Japan). There are no particular patterns here: 'low regulation' USA and UK are respectively in the upper and lower-middle parts of the range; even with the inclusion of the new Eastern *Länder* the German employment rate is only 1.3% below that in the USA; the Nordic countries are scattered throughout the range, as are the southern countries. Japan on the other hand does seem to hold a rather distinctive high-employment position. There is considerably more diversity in core-age female employment (40.2% in Spain to 80.1% in Sweden), and much more obvious pattern to it: all four Nordic countries, followed by the UK and the USA, head the list; all southern European countries apart from Portugal foot the list, along with Ireland.

Employment among the young (15 to 24) is distorted by educational participation and the different ways in which forms of employment can be combined with education. There is very extensive diversity here (from 25.3% to 69.7% among males and an even bigger 17.7% to 62% among females—in both instances the range running from France to Denmark). Although the Nordic countries are scattered within these lists, there is a tendency for the lightly regulated Anglophone block (except for Canada) to have high participation among the young and southern Europe to have low participation (again with the exception of Portugal).

There is most diversity of all at the upper age range (55 to 64), varying from 32.2% (Belgium) to 80.6% (Japan) among men and from 12% (Belgium again)

---

[7] However, some community college students in the USA hold full-time jobs while trying to pursue their studies.

TABLE 2.6. *Employment and population ratios, various age and gender groups, 1996*

Country	Males						Females					
	Age 15–24	Rank order	Age 25–54	Rank order	Age 55–64	Rank order	Age 15–24	Rank order	Age 25–54	Rank order	Age 55–64	Rank order
Australia	61.6	5	84.9	14	54.4	13	58.0	4	64.4	14	29.9	12
Austria	58.4	7	88.2	7	42.4	16	52.7	8	70.1	7	17.3	19
Belgium	29.4	20	86.3	13	32.2	21	22.6	17	61.2	16	12.0	21
Canada	52.4	11	83.1	18	54.7	12	50.8	9	69.9	8	34.1	9
Denmark	69.7	1	88.5	6	58.4	10	62.0	1	75.8	3	37.0	8
Finland	38.1	15	78.4	21	36.8	20	29.0	16	73.2	4	32.6	11
France	**25.3**	**21**	**86.3**	**12**	**38.6**	**19**	**17.7**	**21**	**67.6**	**12**	**28.6**	**13**
Germany	**53.8**	**10**	**86.6**	**11**	**47.2**	**15**	**48.5**	**11**	**65.1**	**13**	**24.4**	**14**
Greece	33.3	17	89.7	3	58.9	7	20.3	20	49.0	18	23.8	15
Ireland	38.0	16	81.3	19	58.7	8	33.7	14	48.6	19	13.1	20
Italy	**30.1**	**18**	**83.4**	**17**	**42.1**	**17**	**20.6**	**19**	**47.0**	**20**	**19.4**	**16**
Japan	**45.6**	**12**	**95.3**	**1**	**80.6**	**1**	**44.4**	**12**	**63.2**	**15**	**47.5**	**4**
Netherlands	54.4	9	88.7	4	40.7	18	53.9	7	60.5	17	18.0	17
New Zealand	62.1	2	87.7	10	66.1	4	56.9	5	68.0	11	37.9	7
Norway	54.5	8	88.6	5	71.4	3	50.0	10	77.4	2	56.4	2
Portugal	41.7	13	87.7	9	58.6	9	32.1	15	69.6	9	33.2	10
Spain	30.0	19	78.8	20	49.9	14	21.2	18	40.2	21	17.6	18
Sweden	**40.7**	**14**	**83.4**	**16**	**66.0**	**5**	**39.9**	**13**	**80.1**	**1**	**60.7**	**1**
Switzerland	61.9	4	90.9	2	75.3	2	60.3	2	69.2	10	40.5	5
UK	**61.9**	**3**	**84.6**	**15**	**57.0**	**11**	**58.6**	**3**	**70.3**	**6**	**38.8**	**6**
USA	**60.1**	**6**	**87.9**	**8**	**64.7**	**6**	**55.2**	**6**	**72.8**	**5**	**47.9**	**3**

Source: OECD 1997*b*.

to 60.7% (Sweden) among women. The main discernible pattern here is that both male and female workers in continental European countries (central and southern) tend to leave the workforce earlier than in Anglophone or Nordic countries or Japan.

The age spread of employment might be considered relevant to issues of the underlying flexibility and adaptability of labour markets. The more rigid the labour market, the more likely it is that existing employees will have established their place and will prevent access to jobs by newcomers. There will then be a further difference, determined by whether a high rate of employment is sustainable throughout life or whether, as it were, high youth employment has to be purchased at the 'cost' of low employment among older workers. We put 'costs' within inverted commas because a low level of employment among older workers may be variously interpreted. To the extent that the economy gains from having younger, more recently educated people doing its work while people in their declining years enjoy more leisure time on comfortable pensions, there may well be a positive sum in a pattern of high employment among the young and low employment among older age groups. If economies are flexible and adaptable, there should be a premium on youth and recency of educational experience. However, against these points are the negative sums resulting from the loss to the economy of the experience of older workers who in turn are required to reduce their standard of living. Further, as human longevity increases and with it the extension of good health until later ages than in the past, there is a case for *raising* retirement ages. Otherwise a smaller proportion of the population has to contribute more from its earnings to support growing numbers of both non-working elderly people and students. It is difficult to evaluate the balance of this complex exchange. Assessing differences in women's participation requires even more complicated judgements, as it involves evaluations of the relative values of different kinds of social order.

In summary, much of the apparently dramatic differences between US and Japanese employment rates on the one hand and certain European ones on the other result from a greater proportion of part-time male work in the USA (and some European countries), probably mainly concentrated among the elderly and students. Thus, the original OECD comparison offers little guidance to employment opportunities for the core workforce (15–64 years old) and even less about skill-maximization strategies. Among women these factors are also at work, but supplemented by the further differentiation which separates countries which have been strongly influenced by Catholic social policy from others.

To further test the hypothesis that institutional labour markets protect insiders and therefore exclude the young, we can compare unemployment rates for different age groups. An important hypothesis of the deregulationist argument is that employment regulation protects insiders and is therefore likely to result in particularly high unemployment among the young. The OECD draws attention to the fact that youth unemployment is proportionately much higher than adult in its so-called high-protection countries (1994*b*: 79), but fails to note that among

TABLE 2.7. *Ratios of youth to adult unemployment, 1994*

| Country | | Unemployment rates | | | Ratios and rank orders | | | | | |
		(a) 15–19 years	(b) 20–24 years	(c) 25–54 years	a : c	Ranks M	F	b : c	Ranks M	F
Belgium	M	32.50	18.90	6.40	5.08	15		2.95	14	
	F	37.50	22.00	11.20	3.35		14	1.96		10
Denmark	M	8.50	11.50	6.70	1.27	2		1.72	2	
	F	5.10	13.80	9.00	0.57		1	1.53		4
Finland	M	29.80	32.10	17.40	1.71	3		1.84	4	
	F	35.10	27.90	14.50	2.42		6	1.92		9
France	**M**	**21.90**	**24.50**	**9.70**	**2.26**	**6**		**2.53**	**12**	
	F	**34.50**	**31.40**	**13.10**	**2.63**		**8**	**2.40**		**12**
Germany*	**M**	**5.80**	**9.00**	**6.90**	**0.84**	**1**		**1.30**	**1**	
(1993)	**F**	**6.80**	**8.70**	**10.30**	**0.66**		**2**	**0.84**		**1**
Greece	M	20.60	19.50	4.80	4.29	14		4.06	15	
	F	47.60	33.60	10.70	4.45		16	3.14		16
Ireland	M	32.80	24.70	14.40	2.28	7		1.72	2	
(1993)	F	34.00	19.60	14.10	2.41		5	1.39		3
Italy	**M**	**33.00**	**27.80**	**6.00**	**5.50**	**16**		**4.63**	**16**	
	F	**42.40**	**34.60**	**11.70**	**3.62**		**15**	**2.96**		**15**
Japan	**M**	**8.30**	**5.00**	**2.00**	**4.15**	**13**		**2.50**	**11**	
	F	**6.80**	**5.00**	**2.80**	**2.43**		**7**	**1.79**		**7**
Netherlands	M	16.00	12.40	5.60	2.86	11		2.21	7	
	F	12.00	7.80	8.00	1.50		3	0.98		2
Norway	M	12.70	10.70	4.70	2.70	10		2.28	9	
	F	11.00	8.70	3.50	3.14		12	2.49		16
Portugal	M	11.30	12.40	4.80	2.35	8		2.58	12	
	F	19.90	15.10	7.00	2.84		11	2.16		11
Spain	M	39.80	36.40	16.40	2.43	9		2.22	8	
	F	58.10	47.40	28.40	2.05		4	1.67		5
Sweden	**M**	**17.70**	**19.30**	**7.90**	**2.24**	**5**		**2.44**	**10**	
	F	**15.40**	**13.90**	**5.80**	**2.66**		**10**	**2.40**		**12**
UK	**M**	**20.80**	**18.30**	**9.80**	**2.12**	**4**		**1.87**	**5**	
	F	**16.10**	**10.70**	**6.40**	**2.52**		**8**	**1.67**		**5**
USA	**M**	**19.00**	**10.20**	**4.90**	**3.88**	**12**		**2.08**	**6**	
	F	**16.20**	**9.20**	**5.00**	**3.24**		**13**	**1.84**		**8**

* Unified Germany.
Source: OECD 1996*b*.

15–19-year-olds it is also particularly high in the USA and only average among 20–24-year-olds (see Table 2.7). Even more important, these figures are for *registered* unemployment and will therefore reflect different government policies towards registration by different age groups; in appraising the UK's ranking one must recall the point cited above, that that country was singled out for praise by the OECD for finding means of preventing young people from registering as unemployed. Germany's position is particularly interesting here, in that for both genders in the teenage group and among women in their early twenties the youth unemployment rate is actually lower than that for older workers.[8]

In the German case (and the same would probably be shown for Austria and Switzerland if we had their statistics) the answer lies in the capacity of the apprenticeship system to absorb young workers. The German system itself depends for its success on co-operative networks among firms and formal associational structures of the kind that the OECD finds problematic. It also constitutes a leading example of how institutions, which *a priori* neo-liberal reasoning regards as labour market cartels protecting insiders, can in fact embody mechanisms that offset this tendency.

Change within sectors of employment

A further way of breaking down the global data for jobs to determine what kinds of work seem to be created by different kinds of employment regime is to consider different economic sectors. The OECD *Jobs Study* enables us to do this over the period 1979–90. Table 2.8 sets out the essential data in terms of rank orders of countries, enabling us to see considerable diversity of experience.

Agriculture First we should note the concentration of job losses in agriculture among southern European countries, including here France. As noted in Chapter 1, compared with countries like the UK, the USA, and the Netherlands, these countries were still experiencing the secular decline of agriculture when the universal decline of industrial employment began. Countries which had industrialized earlier had been able to absorb surplus agricultural population in the industrial sector. Although this is a major explanation of the particularly severe employment problems of southern Europe (see Esping-Andersen 1996), the OECD, in its search for a single variable (labour-market regulation) according to which differential employment performance can be explained, fails to acknowledge it.

Manufacturing Manufacturing has been in decline as a sector of employment, but it retains its central importance as by far the most important internationally traded sector. It is therefore one in which competitive pressures from NICs with low levels of labour security should be particularly strong. It is also one in which trade unions have had their main strength and where labour regulation originated and has been particularly important. The deregulationist hypothesis should therefore be at its strongest here in accounting for job losses. These should be concentrated in high-regulation countries. The competitive superiority of the

---

[8] The only other ratio below unity is that for Dutch women in their early twenties.

TABLE 2.8. *Growth rates in employment by sectors (annualized percentages), 1979–1990*[#]

Agriculture		Manufacturing		Construction		Trade		Transport and communications	
USA	-1.40	**Japan**	0.10	Finland	1.40	Greece	2.40	Finland	0.70
Netherlands	-1.50	Greece	0.10	UK	0.80	Portugal	1.40	**Sweden**	0.50
UK	-2.00	Denmark	-0.01	USA	0.70	**Italy**	1.10	Denmark	0.40
Greece	-2.20	**Sweden**	-0.80	Spain	-0.10	Spain	1.00	USA	0.20
Belgium	-2.30	**Germany***	-0.90	**Sweden**	-0.10	USA	0.90	Netherlands	0.10
Norway	-2.70	Portugal	-1.20	Norway	-0.40	UK	0.90	**Japan**	0.00
Ireland	-3.20	Finland	-1.50	**Japan**	-0.60	Finland	0.80	Spain	0.00
Japan	-3.30	Ireland	-1.50	Portugal	-0.90	**Japan**	0.30	**France**	-0.10
Sweden	-3.40	Netherlands	-1.50	**Italy**	-1.30	**Sweden**	0.30	**Germany***	-0.30
Denmark	-3.40	USA	-1.50	**Germany***	-1.60	Belgium	0.20	Norway	-0.30
Finland	-3.50	**Italy**	-1.70	**France**	-2.10	Norway	0.10	**Italy**	-0.40
Germany*	-3.90	Spain	-1.80	Belgium	-2.20	Netherlands	-0.10	UK	-0.50
Portugal	-4.30	Belgium	-1.90	Denmark	-2.20	**France**	-0.10	Ireland	-0.70
France	-4.50	**France**	-2.50	Greece	-2.80	Ireland	-0.50	Portugal	-1.00
Italy	-4.70	Norway	-2.80	Netherlands	-3.00	Denmark	-1.00	Belgium	-1.10
Spain	-5.10	UK	-3.20	Ireland	-3.10	**Germany***	-1.00	Greece	-1.30

Financial and business services		Private social, etc.		Government		Personal services	
Italy	5.00	**UK**	5.10	Spain	3.40	**USA**	0.80
UK	4.80	**Italy**	5.10	Finland	2.20	**Japan**	0.30
Finland	4.60	Ireland	3.80	Portugal	2.20	UK	0.10
Greece	4.00	**Japan**	2.70	Norway	1.80	**Sweden**	0.00
Norway	4.00	**Germany***	2.60	Greece	1.20	Greece	-0.10
Spain	4.00	Belgium	2.60	Denmark	1.10	**Germany***	-0.20
Sweden	3.90	USA	2.20	**Sweden**	0.90	Finland	-0.20
USA	3.30	Greece	2.00	**France**	0.70	Belgium	-0.30
Ireland	3.20	**France**	1.40	**Italy**	0.60	**Italy**	-0.30
France	2.60	Netherlands	0.40	Belgium	0.30	Denmark	-0.40
Denmark	2.60	Norway	0.40	USA	0.20	Netherlands	-0.60
Japan	2.00	**Sweden**	0.30	**Germany***	0.20	Norway	-0.60
Belgium	1.90	Portugal	0.20	UK	0.10	Ireland	-0.80
Portugal	1.30	Denmark	-0.20	Netherlands	-0.60	**France**	-1.00
Netherlands	1.10	Finland	-0.20	**Japan**	-0.70	Spain	-1.10
Germany*	0.90	Spain	-1.00	Ireland	-1.30	Portugal	-1.40

[a] Countries ranked in descending order by growth rates.

* Unified Germany.

Source: OECD 1994*a*.

UK and the USA should be clear, with the Nordic countries having the worst records. The core continental cases should come in between. Southern European countries might be growing strongly because some of them are still undergoing industrialization. The fact that (as Table 2.8 shows) only Greece and Japan saw a net increase in manufacturing employment partly confirms these expectations. However, the USA was in mid-table among several European countries; and the UK had the worst record of all. With the exception of Norway the Scandinavian countries were highly placed. Overall the deregulationist thesis does not explain employment change in this key competitive sector.

The relatively strong performance of some Scandinavian countries and the German economy is, however, what would be anticipated by several forms of neo-institutionalist theory, which argue for the importance of organized employer interests and industrial relations, strong mutual commitments between workforce and management, and strong social infrastructure in sustaining high performance. Institutionalists would also claim Japan to be an institutional economy in its externally oriented firms in this sector. Among the countries with which we are mainly concerned in this study, there was actual growth only in Japan, small decline in Sweden and Germany, and much larger decline in the others, particularly France, and most of all, the UK.

Construction   Construction is another sector which showed overall decline. It is an industry in which, if regulation can be evaded, there is considerable scope for highly flexible employment. It should therefore be one in which deregulationist countries have advantages. Indeed, the UK and the USA were among the strongest growers, though they were joined by Finland and Sweden, which ought to have the worst performances. Japan's position was mediocre, and there seems to be little logic in the overall spread of countries. There is only weak support for either deregulationist or institutionalist theses.

Commerce   Far more important for employment growth was the commercial or trade sector (retail and wholesale sales). Here there was clear evidence of superior employment growth among the southern European countries and the larger Anglophone countries. Our characterization of the former as those in which regulation is easily evaded and hence as low-regulation countries (rather than the OECD's conception of them as highly regulated) should be particularly applicable here, where much employment is in small firms. According to our grouping of countries, therefore, this pattern of growth is fully consistent with the deregulationist thesis that employment growth will be positively associated with low levels of labour security. There is little support for institutionalist analyses of the labour market. (According to the OECD's own ranking of the southern European countries as strictly regulated, however, the evidence is contradictory.) Among the countries of interest in this book, Italy was a strongly growing 'southern' case, with strong growth also in the UK and the USA; less in Japan and Sweden; and decline in France and, in particular, Germany.

Transport and communications   Trade's partner within the distributive sector, transport and communications, was a sector in moderate decline. Much employment in this sector is in state enterprises or private near-monopolies; we might therefore expect that countries with strong regulatory systems and public infrastructure would do better at preserving jobs, though probably only in the short term. It may therefore be significant that the Scandinavian countries have done well here, though so has the USA where there were declines in public transport but increases in private transport and telecommunications following deregulation towards the end of the period. There was a static situation in Japan, but decline elsewhere. There is no overall pattern in the remaining countries.

Financial and business services   Financial and business services is a small but rapidly growing sector. It should not be particularly vulnerable to labour market regulation issues as it mainly employs an educated élite workforce which is rarely unionized and relatively untouched by most labour regulation. The UK was prominent in rapid growth in this sector, but the US financial sector grew less strongly and the Japanese was among the slowest. It is possible that deregulation of financial markets, while not directly concerning labour, can have effects on it. In the USA removal of inter-state banking and other government restrictions on the operation of financial institutions led to major consolidation among firms from the late 1980s. This produced widespread reduction in employment alongside a global strengthening of the US industry and major improvements in productivity. Overall the span of countries embodies no particular labour regulation regime patterns and lends support to neither deregulationist nor institutional theories.

Community and social services (private and public)   The OECD data separate private community and social services (CSS) from public. This is somewhat curious as the same was not done for manufacturing or transport and communications, where there is also a good deal of public employment. Also, much of what is 'private' in CSS is provided by charitable trusts and foundations and often financed by state transfers and subsidies to charitable providers; 'private' is not here synonymous with 'subject to market forces'. The UK and Japan, and to a lesser extent the USA, were among the countries in which there was strong growth in private CSS. As would be anticipated in view of their strong public welfare systems, the growth in the Scandinavian countries was among the weakest. This sub-sector therefore conformed to the deregulationist hypothesis, though this was partly so by definition or at any rate by a kind of political elective affinity. We might expect *private* CSS to grow most strongly in deregulationist countries during a period of differential deregulation, partly because labour regulation itself is probably important to the allocation of labour between the two sectors, but also because deregulationist countries are likely to have small state welfare institutions, with a correspondingly greater role being played by the private sector. Also, staff in public welfare are likely to have strongly protected employment conditions even in countries with little overall job regulation; in the latter there is therefore likely to be particularly strong growth of private-service jobs. Certainly, a country that is rapidly privatizing public welfare ought to show a rise in employment in private CSS.

The same reasoning that applied to private CSS should lead us to the opposite conclusion in government employment: employment growth should be inversely related to deregulation. The data reflect the fact that southern European countries were building up their social services during the 1980s (Maravall 1997)—in all cases apart from Italy following the collapse of their dictatorships in the mid-1970s. They and, as might be expected, the strong welfare states of Scandinavia, dominated high growth in this area. Here the OECD's view that southern Europe has strict labour markets is more likely to be true than for the economy in general, since regulation is not easily evaded in public services, and trade unions are likely to be strong in this sector even in countries with overall weak unions. The deregulationist and the core continental countries shared the lower ranks in job creation here. Overall during the period as a whole government and public-service employment was among the positively growing sectors, though moving less rapidly than private CSS, and was therefore a major contributor to the overall pattern of job change. Among the countries on which this study concentrates Sweden, France, and Italy saw moderately strong growth; Japan saw actual decline.

Personal services   Finally, there is the small personal services sector. Households can usually afford to buy labour services of this kind only when there are few constraints on the labour market and when there are wide income differences between those likely to employ such labour and those likely to constitute it. For much of the twentieth century this form of employment declined as inequalities of income were reduced. One would therefore expect to see any growth in this sector limited to deregulated situations where the cost of such labour would be reduced and where above-average growth in the income of the wealthy has created added demand for such services. There should be only decline in institutional labour markets. In line with the historical trend, Table 2.8 shows this sector to have been in moderate decline everywhere except in the USA, Japan, and the UK. This pattern of growth conforms fully to the expectations of the deregulationist thesis; in this sector, which is far outside the scope of the big corporations, Japan is a low-regulation country. The UK and the USA were also countries which saw sharp increases of inequality during the 1980s (OECD 1993). It is surprising to find Sweden the next strongest performer, except that Sweden's long egalitarian trend in incomes was being reversed during the decade (ibid.). There is no particular ordering among other countries.

Summary   Four sectors saw important job growth during the period covered by the OECD study: trade, finance and business services, private community and social services, and public services. Of these the one that best suits the deregulationist thesis is retail and wholesale trade. Finance and business services was the most strongly growing sector of all but, for the reasons mentioned, not very relevant either way to the thesis. Private and public CSS both grew, but with opposite implications for deregulationist and neo-institutionalist theses. Manufacturing was not in general a growing sector, but maintenance of it was more compatible with the expectations of institutionalist hypotheses. On the other hand, another sector that experienced overall decline, personal services, has also shown growth in some places in a manner strongly supportive of the deregulationist thesis.

The structure of sectors of employment

Besides considering change flows, we should also examine the resulting stock, that is, consider the absolute sizes of the different sectors in different countries. By the early 1990s, how did national economies differ in their capacity to provide employment for their populations in different sectors of the economy, and to what extent are the patterns found compatible with the expectations of the deregulationist thesis?

The available data (which are based on a more detailed analysis in Crouch 1999: ch. 4) are summarized in Table 2.9. The contribution of each sector is expressed as a percentage of the population aged between 15 and 80 who are not in full-time education. The rationale for this kind of calculation was given above in relation to Table 2.5. The data for the two genders are expressed as proportions of the whole population, not of each gender separately, so that the relative importance of each gender within a sector can be assessed. For ease of analysis we have reduced the number of sectors to six, following Singelmann's (1978) analysis which seeks to improve on the crude treatment of the services sectors embodied in the normal split between primary, secondary, and tertiary. This does not give such a fine breakdown as the OECD study, in that construction is not separated from manufacturing or transport from commerce. Private and public CSS are also not separated, but as explained above that separation is of dubious value.

Agriculture, mining, and other extractive industries continue to constitute the primary sector (I); manufacturing, public utilities, and construction the secondary (II); trade and transport and communications are combined as a general distributive sector (sector III); financial and business services form sector IV; private and public CSS together constitute sector V; personal services are sector VI. In general, sectors I and VI (the primary sector and personal services) constitute the 'traditional' sectors of the economy, many of the occupations in them predating industrialization, even though of course often transformed in their mode of performance by technological change. Sectors II and III constitute the core of industrial society, being focused on the production of material goods and their

TABLE 2.9. *Proportions of populations aged 15–80 (not in full-time education) employed in various sectors, c.1990**

Country	I Agriculture and mining						II Manufacturing, utilities, and construction					
	Male		Female		Total		Male		Female		Total	
	%	Rank	%	Rank	%	Rank	%	Rank	%	Rank	%	Rank
Austria	2.64	6	2.33	4	4.97	7	17.68	2	5.04	4	22.72	2
Belgium	1.35	14	0.52	12	1.87	15	13.34	9	3.09	11	16.43	11
Denmark	1.35	14	1.20	7	2.55	9	13.33	10	4.98	5	18.31	7
Finland	2.23	8	2.93	1	5.16	5	14.62	5	6.77	2	21.39	4
France	**2.34**	**7**	**1.17**	**8**	**3.51**	**8**	**13.25**	**11**	**4.33**	**9**	**17.58**	**8**
Germany*	**1.57**	**12**	**0.88**	**9**	**2.45**	**10**	**17.00**	**3**	**5.62**	**3**	**22.62**	**3**
Greece	7.71	1	2.70	2	10.41	1	9.99	15	2.76	12	12.75	15
Ireland	7.68	2	0.55	11	8.23	2	13.63	7	2.75	13	16.38	12
Netherlands	1.83	10	0.48	13	2.31	11	12.33	14	2.25	15	14.58	14
Norway	3.64	4	1.34	6	4.98	6	13.36	8	3.45	10	16.81	10
Spain	5.63	3	1.81	5	7.44	3	12.68	12	2.47	14	15.15	13
Sweden	**1.62**	**11**	**0.60**	**10**	**2.22**	**13**	**14.62**	**5**	**4.40**	**8**	**19.02**	**6**
UK	**1.53**	**13**	**0.36**	**15**	**1.89**	**14**	**15.34**	**4**	**4.83**	**6**	**20.17**	**5**
Japan	**3.02**	**5**	**2.44**	**3**	**5.46**	**4**	**17.70**	**1**	**7.83**	**1**	**25.53**	**1**
USA	**1.84**	**9**	**0.46**	**14**	**2.30**	**12**	**12.55**	**13**	**4.41**	**7**	**16.96**	**9**
St. deviation	2.184		0.901		2.627		2.128		1.606		3.485	

TABLE 2.9. (Cont.)

Country	III Commerce, transport, and communications						IV Finance and business services					
	Male		Female		Total		Male		Female		Total	
	%	Rank	%	Rank	%	Rank	%	Rank	%	Rank	%	Rank
Austria	6.77	12	5.70	7	12.47	8	1.99	12	1.96	10	3.95	12
Belgium**	8.61	5	5.16	10	13.77	5	2.59	10	1.92	11	4.51	10
Denmark	9.33	3	5.57	8	14.90	4	3.31	5	2.94	4	6.25	5
Finland**	4.68	15	7.67	2	12.35	9	2.04	11	1.94	13	3.98	11
France	6.37	13	4.47	11	10.84	12	3.12	7	2.85	5	5.97	6
Germany*	5.61	14	6.36	5	11.97	10	3.67	4	2.95	3	6.62	4
Greece	8.54	6	2.79	14	11.33	11	1.83	13	1.29	14	3.12	14
Ireland	7.04	10	3.55	12	10.59	13	1.49	15	1.89	12	3.38	13
Netherlands	8.25	7	2.25	15	10.50	14	4.18	2	2.52	8	6.70	3
Norway	8.72	4	6.90	4	15.62	3	2.85	9	2.44	9	5.29	9
Spain	6.80	11	3.11	13	9.91	15	1.52	14	0.51	15	2.03	15
Sweden	7.36	9	5.40	9	12.76	7	3.04	8	2.74	6	5.78	8
UK	7.93	8	5.72	6	13.65	6	3.78	3	3.62	2	7.40	2
Japan	11.54	1	7.10	3	18.64	2	3.21	6	2.61	7	5.82	7
USA	11.01	2	8.02	1	19.03	1	4.77	1	4.29	1	9.06	1
St. deviation	1.854		1.783		2.801		0.983		0.915		1.840	

TABLE 2.9 (Cont.)

Country	V Community and social services						VI Personal and domestic services					
	Male		Female		Total		Male		Female		Total	
	%	Rank	%	Rank	%	Rank	%	Rank	%	Rank	%	Rank
Austria	5.22	8	6.47	10	11.69	9	2.08	6	3.54	4	5.62	4
Belgium***	8.05	1	10.48	5	18.53	4						
Denmark	7.08	4	14.96	2	22.04	2	2.24	5	2.73	9	4.97	6
Finland***	4.22	13	10.09	7	14.31	8						
France	**4.77**	**11**	**6.49**	**9**	**11.26**	**10**	**4.05**	**1**	**5.61**	**1**	**9.66**	**1**
Germany*	**4.50**	**12**	**5.11**	**12**	**9.61**	**12**	**1.43**	**11**	**3.00**	**7**	**4.43**	**9**
Greece	5.15	9	4.28	14	9.43	13	2.52	4	1.66	13	4.18	10
Ireland	3.55	14	5.21	11	8.76	14	3.40	3	3.61	3	7.01	3
Netherlands	7.32	2	8.30	8	15.62	7	1.73	9	1.90	11	3.63	11
Norway	7.18	3	14.23	3	21.41	3	1.87	7	2.76	8	4.63	8
Spain	1.96	15	2.39	15	4.35	15	3.79	2	3.63	2	7.42	2
Sweden	**6.06**	**6**	**17.37**	**1**	**23.43**	**1**	**1.66**	**10**	**1.85**	**12**	**3.51**	**13**
UK	**5.48**	**7**	**10.18**	**6**	**15.66**	**6**	**1.76**	**8**	**3.40**	**6**	**5.16**	**5**
Japan	**4.91**	**10**	**4.95**	**13**	**9.86**	**11**	**1.41**	**12**	**3.42**	**5**	**4.83**	**7**
USA	**6.55**	**5**	**11.62**	**4**	**18.17**	**5**	**1.34**	**13**	**2.29**	**10**	**3.63**	**11**
St. deviation	1.617		4.384		5.615		0.924		1.047		1.782	

† Proportions are always of total population, not by gender.
* Former Federal Republic of Germany.
** Figures for commerce, etc. sector include hotels and restaurants, which are elsewhere included in the personal services sector.
*** Figures for community and social services include all personal services except hotels and restaurants; no separate data provided for personal services.
Source: Crouch 1999: ch. 4.

distribution. Sectors IV and V (financial, and community and social services) might be regarded as post-industrial, except that many of the business services grouped within IV are activities which can either be sub-contracted by manufacturing firms to specialist consultants or be performed in house by the manufacturing firm.

If we consider the full range of countries and examine the standard deviations for each sector and each gender sector, we can discover which contribute most to diversity in the capacity of different societies to provide employment for their populations. These are shown at the foot of the columns in Table 2.9. Taking the two genders combined, the single most important source of diversity is sector V (CSS), where the extreme contrast is between the Scandinavian and southern European groups. To the extent that this employment is in the public or publicly financed sector, one would expect it to be more successfully sustained in institutionalized economies. The relative rankings of Scandinavia and southern Europe are consistent with this, though the high position of the USA and the low position of Germany are notable. Next in importance comes sector II (manufacturing, construction, and public utilities), where some Scandinavian and southern European countries again appear at opposite ends, though this time the former are accompanied by Japan, Austria, Germany, and the UK, and the latter by some other central western European countries. (The continuing high relative level of UK manufacturing employment despite its heavy decline during the 1980s is a reminder of that country's earlier position as exceptionally highly industrialized.) With the exception of the UK, this is more consistent with institutionalist than with deregulationist hypotheses about international competitiveness. The third most important source of diversity is sector III (distribution and communications), where Japan and the USA lead—though accompanied by some Scandinavian countries. The bottom positions are a mix of southern European and core continental countries. Since this is a sector where one expects the deregulation thesis to be most effective (as it was for growth patterns), the respective positions of Scandinavian and southern European countries are surprising.

If we now disaggregate by gender sector, by far the biggest source of diversity in countries' employment performance is in the proportion of women employed in sector V, the extreme contrasts being between Scandinavia and the USA on the one side and southern Europe and Japan on the other. This is fully consistent with Esping-Andersen's thesis (1996) about the importance of this sector for female employment. We have above discussed the relevance here of a particular, essentially Catholic, form of labour regulation. The second and third biggest sources are males in sectors I and II, but then follow both genders in sector III, with Japan and the USA being major employers in both cases.

The distributive sector appears as that where deregulationist theories of employment carry most weight. It is the sector within which the employment of students and elderly people is concentrated; it is also one within which skill is relatively unimportant and therefore where the contradictions between deregulation and skill-maximizing strategies are less relevant: not only is the sector unimportant to overseas trade, but the supply of student and elderly labour provides, in the former, a supply of 'over-educated' workers, and in the latter, a supply of very experienced people. The whole concept of skill strategies for global competition therefore has little importance here.[9] If it is desired to increase employment with the least possible strain on collective effort for skills, this is a sector in which employment growth is likely to be concentrated.

THE EDUCATIONAL AND SKILL STRUCTURE OF SECTORS

Analysis of the educational and skill structure of sectors finally leads us to a further breakdown of employment that comes close to the core concerns of this study: is job growth, or existing employment strength, concentrated in sectors of high or low skills, and how do different countries compare on this dimension?

Unfortunately it is not easy to make direct comparisons of this kind. The actual skill level of which workers are capable is not known, especially if that skill has been improved by company VET for which no generally valid credentials are given. We therefore have to make do with formal, usually pre-employment, educational achievements which have to serve as unsatisfactory proxies for assessments of skill used. There are two further problems. First, in all countries the level of formal educational achievement has been rising for some decades. This means that younger people are likely to have higher formal levels of achievement than older. Since sectors that have expanded in more recent years will tend to have higher concentrations of younger people than those which had only limited recent recruitment, statistics will give us an exaggerated impression of the differences in skill levels being used in different sectors—especially if firms in some older sectors have devoted considerable in-service training to improve the skill levels of workforces poorly educated in the formal sense. Second, despite recent attempts at facilitating cross-national comparisons of formal educational levels, one can never be certain that a particular level in one country is really equal to the same level in another.

We can tackle the latter problem by ensuring that we restrict our comparisons to relative terms. For example, if a sector has a particularly high concentration of skilled persons in one country in comparison with other sectors in that country, we can regard it as a relatively skilled sector. And if the relative position of that sector in that country seems out of line with the relative position of the same sector in another country, we may regard this as an important difference. What we may not do on the basis of these data is to make statements about employees in a sector in one country being more highly skilled than those in the

---

[9] It is notable that Japan's large distributive sector is not cited as among that country's paragons of economic efficiency, being characterized by multiple layers of wholesaling and the predominance of small family shops.

same sector in another (for comparisons using more appropriate data see Mason and Finegold 1995; Finegold and Wagner 1997; OECD 1996*b*).

Within these limits we can examine differences in the educational levels of persons working in the different identified sectors of employment. Unfortunately it is not possible to get US or Japanese figures on a comparable basis with European cases here. Japanese data on the educational structure of the workforce only count enterprises employing more than ten people and therefore exclude many small businesses, in the distributive sector particularly. US data only cover a sample of production industries, and these may not be representative. However, Table 2.10 (based on Crouch 1999: ch. 4) gathers data from as many European countries as possible. It shows the educational level of those employed within certain sectors of the economy, expressed as a ratio of the overall distribution of persons of that educational level within the economy as a whole.

The sectors divide neatly into three following the progression from traditional to post-industrial: the traditional sectors, agriculture and personal services (I and VI), have the weakest educational profiles; those of industrial society, both the manufacturing and the distributive sectors (II and III), are relatively bottom-weighted; while the post-industrial sectors of business services and community and social services (IV and V) provide more opportunities for the more highly skilled. In some cases (Austria, Spain, Japan, and Norway) the distributive sector employed more people from the highest educational category than did manufacturing; only in Finland and Norway did distribution employ more people from the lowest educational category than manufacturing. The two sectors are overall very similar in their low levels of skills.

In all countries a small but growing group of highly skilled people is concentrated in sector IV. Parts of this sector are externally traded, though since it is small and jobs in it highly rewarded, it is likely that firms can find the labour they need without calling into question national skill provision strategies. A higher proportion of the highly educated is employed in sector V, though this sector can also provide relatively secure employment for the low skilled. It is only very marginally involved in international trade and is under little indirect competitive pressure, though it employs the greater part of the educated workforce of most countries.

If we are seeking the purest expression of the concept of the learning society giving direct competitive advantages in international trade and the employment of large numbers of people, our attention therefore comes to be concentrated on the manufacturing sector, alongside some components of financial and business services. Although it is in decline as an employer of labour, manufacturing is numerically still by far the largest component of any country's internationally traded efforts. It tends to recruit relatively poorly educated workers and is therefore a point of concentration for concerns that skill levels are inadequate. Efforts to improve in-service skills have largely been concentrated here.

TABLE 2.10. *Percentages of persons at various educational levels employed in different economic sectors in relation to percentages employed in economy as a whole, western European countries, c.1990* (NB: the classifications of educational levels vary considerably by country; the lowest and highest levels have been indicated in each case)

	Economic sectors											
	Males						Females					
	I	II	III	IV	V	VI	I	II	III	IV	V	VI
Austria												
1	22.17	−2.09	−5.79	−20.06	−16.42	−6.48	44.65	17.50	−1.28	−11.10	−7.05	17.64
2	−5.50	16.60	14.70	−14.86	−9.80	10.74	−22.40	−12.91	6.17	−22.75	−24.44	−4.63
3	−1.26	−5.93	−2.48	4.72	−2.70	−1.90	−5.15	4.28	3.36	20.25	11.36	−0.97
4	−8.43	−2.74	−0.94	16.59	6.03	−1.82	−9.24	−2.18	−1.73	15.36	7.68	−5.06
5	−6.33	−4.97	−4.50	14.49	23.76	−2.23	−6.90	−5.75	−5.51	−0.83	13.38	−6.01

1 = compulsory schooling only; 5 = university education

	I	II	III	IV	V	VI	I	II	III	IV	V	VI
Belgium*												
1	13.69	5.91	1.95	−11.76	−5.55		20.85	6.10	1.41	−11.09	−5.20	
2	9.02	8.34	10.12	−16.82	−8.91		9.28	3.18	7.24	−13.79	−11.51	
3	−4.93	−1.96	2.55	2.51	−3.61		−12.90	0.51	5.45	14.63	−1.69	
4	−12.45	−8.75	−10.07	11.36	6.90		−9.30	−5.45	−8.61	6.48	18.02	
5	−5.32	−3.53	−4.56	14.71	11.17		−7.93	−4.34	−5.49	3.76	0.39	

1 = primary schooling only; 5 = university education
* No separate data for sector VI; different components found within sectors III and V.

	I	II	III	IV	V	VI	I	II	III	IV	V	VI
Denmark												
1	−10.54	−1.83	2.74	−12.07	−10.55	6.74	30.71	14.40	4.61	−8.17	−2.92	17.23
2	10.28	−0.57	−0.04	−1.83	−2.33	−0.43	−0.52	2.70	3.58	1.94	−1.96	2.87
3	10.04	10.02	7.76	−0.79	−10.60	3.28	−18.30	−5.32	3.49	13.29	−8.99	−9.32
4	−7.91	−5.19	−7.72	4.12	11.26	−7.99	−7.94	−8.30	−8.15	−6.04	14.18	−7.81
5	−1.86	−2.43	−2.75	10.56	12.23	−1.61	−3.87	−3.48	−3.54	−1.02	−0.31	−2.97

1 = no vocational education; 5 = university education

France

1	13.14	8.48	−1.93	−6.45	−7.99	2.18	14.92	6.72	−5.44	−9.71	−6.78	−2.51
2	9.61	−0.48	1.27	−7.59	−6.10	−4.08	28.94	12.02	2.97	−5.85	−3.28	−0.59
3	−8.52	8.55	12.80	−13.02	−1.87	−0.19	−24.20	−15.42	8.41	−5.92	−5.58	−3.73
4	−3.59	−4.83	−1.41	8.24	2.67	−4.88	−7.54	−0.36	3.03	10.29	5.43	−1.78
5	−10.65	−11.72	−10.73	18.82	13.29	6.97	−12.00	−2.96	−8.97	11.19	10.22	8.61

1 = no formal education; 5 = higher education

Greece*

1	7.05	−3.56		−7.54	−5.85	19.67	−2.92	−2.61	−7.13	−4.55
2	27.80	7.08	−4.08	−40.37	−24.80	22.70	8.12	−7.59	−38.49	−28.16
3	−17.82	4.72	10.70	5.73	1.97	−24.40	4.88	16.58	18.05	0.21
4	−5.66	−0.50	2.13	5.09	3.28	−6.05	−1.35	−0.53	5.47	7.89
5	−11.38	−7.74	−5.23	37.09	25.39	−11.80	−8.74	−5.85	22.10	24.61

1 = incomplete; 5 = graduate

* No separate data for sector VI; different components found within sectors III and V.

Italy

1	9.40	0.36	−1.03	−2.15	−1.86	0.13	11.99	−0.88	−1.33	−1.62	−2.20	1.41
2	24.12	6.74	1.73	−16.96	−10.34	4.08	24.11	1.48	−3.20	−13.61	−14.15	10.80
3	−7.61	7.18	7.27	−20.61	−4.72	12.11	−9.05	9.63	3.39	−12.00	−15.11	7.23
4	−18.95	−8.65	−2.20	24.23	3.99	−9.44	−19.83	−4.10	6.57	24.94	17.24	−12.20
5	−6.96	−5.63	−5.77	15.49	12.94	−6.88	−7.23	−6.13	−5.42	2.29	14.22	−7.22

1 = none; 5 = university education

Japan*

1	31.15	5.21	−4.75	−20.41	−8.76	14.90	14.30	−12.00	−14.33	2.07
2	−19.39	−6.48	−0.28	−16.92	−9.97	3.11	3.71	30.10	32.34	15.94
3	−11.76	1.28	5.03	37.32	18.73	−18.01	−18.01	−18.00	−18.01	−18.01

1 = primary education only; 3 = graduates

* No separate data for sector VI; different components found within sectors III and V.

TABLE 2.10. (Cont'd)

| | Economic sectors | | | | | | | | | | | |
| | Males | | | | | | Females | | | | | |
	I	II	III	IV	V	VI	I	II	III	IV	V	VI
Netherlands												
1	3.50	5.87	2.14	-7.07	-6.32	6.98	2.41	4.88	-0.56	-5.03	-5.43	8.09
2	13.12	5.94	5.68	-13.04	-12.40	2.47	25.95	8.71	12.76	-5.04	-9.85	3.72
3	3.38	-0.64	4.29	-1.47	-6.96	-0.12	-7.22	-2.37	2.86	3.55	1.82	-2.81
4	-13.06	-7.19	-7.37	8.57	12.07	-4.05	-14.20	-4.29	-8.13	4.33	12.32	-4.59
5	-6.94	-3.99	-4.73	13.02	13.61	-5.28	-6.94	-6.94	-6.94	2.19	1.14	-4.41

1 = primary education only; 5 = graduates

	I	II	III	IV	V	VI	I	II	III	IV	V	VI
Norway												
1	-0.27	-0.01	0.04	0.44	0.41	3.67	-0.49	-0.08	-0.69	-0.75	-0.27	0.40
2	12.01	5.34	1.47	-13.86	-12.17	-2.90	8.98	9.15	4.74	-10.16	-4.14	4.22
3	0.58	6.06	6.42	-9.09	-17.14	7.15	4.59	2.79	8.86	11.09	-8.78	6.30
4	-12.32	-11.39	-7.93	22.50	28.90	-7.92	-13.08	-11.87	-12.90	-0.18	13.19	-10.90

1 = primary education only; 4 = university education

	I	II	III	IV	V	VI	I	II	III	IV	V	VI
Spain												
1	16.22	-1.02	-4.81	-11.19	-6.02	-5.66	19.24	-4.71	-2.82	-9.00	-6.34	2.70
2	7.91	10.17	5.11	-29.88	-22.46	-2.77	9.46	-4.62	-4.39	-35.73	-28.61	-3.83
3	-15.50	-3.52	4.72	20.06	-7.42	6.15	-19.56	15.44	12.39	33.72	-6.09	4.60
4	-4.46	-2.65	-2.71	6.91	14.12	-0.91	-4.67	-3.19	-2.77	4.34	29.68	-1.58
5	-4.13	-2.95	-2.46	14.13	21.83	3.19	-4.41	-2.95	-2.36	6.69	11.39	-1.87

1 = no formal education; 5 = higher education

	I	II	III	IV	V	VI	I	II	III	IV	V	VI
United Kingdom												
1	15.17	1.14	2.64	-15.50	-11.31	4.09	25.40	13.37	2.90	-12.21	-1.43	12.22
2	-4.45	-8.95	3.07	-2.52	-7.87	-4.05	-0.89	12.48	4.95	24.59	1.52	3.67
3	-3.42	12.52	3.88	0.74	-1.93	4.90	-13.44	-15.20	1.73	-7.19	-15.78	-5.76
4	-4.08	-1.09	-4.06	-1.33	2.07	-3.59	-3.78	-4.46	-4.02	-3.70	12.69	-3.48
5	-3.22	-3.62	-5.52	18.61	19.03	-1.36	-7.29	-6.18	-5.56	-1.49	3.00	-6.65

1 = no qualifications; 5 = university degree

Note: The classifications of educational levels vary considerably by country; the lowest and highest levels have been indicated in each case.
Source: Crouch (1999: ch. 4).

CONCLUSIONS: EMPLOYMENT, SKILLS AND GLOBALIZATION

In most advanced countries there have been strenuous attempts to raise productivity in the export and import-substitution sectors; labour has been replaced by technology; low-skilled labour has been replaced by high-skilled; and inefficient producers have closed down. Niches have been found in globally competitive markets, not by reducing labour standards, but by improving productivity. This has often led to improved standards for those remaining in employment, but a large decline in their numbers. The competitive pressure from global competition has therefore fallen indirectly on those *forced out* of employment in the sectors directly engaged in the competition. Many of these have become unemployed; although the evidence is mixed and heavily contested, there are clear indications that *part* of the rise in unemployment in Europe and elsewhere has been the result of the new competition (Wood 1994: ch. 8). Many others, however, have found employment in services sectors not directly touched by global competition. The process has often been even more roundabout than this implies. Workers do not necessarily move from one sector to another; rather, one generation stays in the old sector while its sons and daughters find employment in the new; or the wives of men made redundant or taking early retirement find the new employment and thereby sustain the family's income.

The growth of non-traded services has in no way been *caused* by globalization. In many cases it has been fortuitous that employment opportunities have opened in these services at a time when employment was contracting in manufacturing; and many of the jobs created have been at high skill levels, especially in community and social services. Although in most countries a majority of these services is either publicly or charitably provided, and employment of this type typically enjoys high levels of security, nevertheless, public employment has not been free from the pressure of globalization. Since an important part of the cost advantage of third-world producers and—perhaps more important—relatively low-cost advanced countries comprises the low taxes and social costs borne by businesses, many advanced countries have tried to improve their competitiveness by reducing their own social expenditure. This eventually has an impact on the employment conditions of public employees in CSS.

Governments have also used reductions in taxation (and therefore in the sums available for expenditure on CSS) as indirect inducements to workers not to press for increased wages and thereby to constrain labour costs. Finally, the ability afforded by globalization to some firms to 'regime shop' may involve governments in competitive reductions in taxation on business and managerial incomes, again with negative consequences for public employment. This can be seen in the evidence reviewed above of the recent collapse of employment in the Nordic countries following the introduction there of neo-liberal policies. Within individual countries sub-national governments may also compete against each other by reducing business taxes in order to attract inward investments; this is particularly important in the USA, where state governments have considerable autonomy over such policy areas.

Increased productivity and intensified competition in sector II alongside this forced decline in sector V are now leading to greater reliance being placed on other services sectors to provide employment opportunities: distribution and communications, business services, and personal and domestic services. This provides part of the explanation for the 'productivity paradox': manufacturing growth has been rapid, but aggregate employment shifts to less productive sectors. These sectors grow through a process that initially had nothing to do with globalization but with changes in patterns of consumer demand, the implications of differential productivity rates in different sectors of the economy (the Baumol effect (Baumol 1967)), and the growing tendency for manufacturing firms to contract out a range of service activities to firms in sector V. This process of job creation has been at varied skills levels: business services, like public services, have provided a large number of professional and managerial positions (though to the extent that this results from contracting out it leads to no net increase in employment, just a shift from sector II to sector IV). Sector III has mainly contributed routine non-manual jobs. Sector VI has provided very few professional and routine non-manual jobs, but more unskilled manual ones. In all cases, again including sector V, most of the employment creation, especially at the lower levels of skill and earnings, has been taken up by women.

In some areas of job growth there has been virtually a trade-off between skills and employment, rather than the positive association that most political rhetoric leads us to expect. For example, the high turnover rates and low wages in the UK and the USA which are associated with rapid job growth in fast food and hotels are linked to poorer levels of service quality and lower levels of training than in Germany—where wages are higher and both turnover rates and job creation lower (Schlesinger and Heskett 1991; Finegold and Levine 1997). In some areas of manufacturing, in particular machine tools, US firms have found their own solution to the training problem by polarizing the skills in the workplace (Finegold *et al.* 1994*a*): computer numerical control (CNC) technology is used to centralize control over most programming, thereby upskilling technicians, set-up men, and programmers to oversee the manufacturing process, while machine operators and assemblers receive little training (ibid.; Jacobs *et al.* 1991; Rogers and Streeck 1991).

Globalization has been only indirectly involved in these main processes, but one of these indirect effects is particularly interesting. The decline in the demand for labour in manufacturing, created *partly* by globalization, leads to a rise in unemployment among low-skilled, low-productivity people. This will be especially the case if the manufacturing sector responds by moving up-market and leaving low-skilled industries or production methods. Employment can be created for the displaced low-productivity workers only if they are inexpensive to employ. This requires not only low wages but also low indirect costs and low levels of security. It is this line of reasoning that has led the OECD and the consensus of economic experts to advocate a *general* deterioration in the regulation of labour markets.

No one expects the actual levels of security and employment terms of higher-paid employees to be adversely affected by the removal of legislated or bargained security arrangements; such employees would continue to benefit through labour market forces. Employers choose which parts of their workforce they would prefer to retain—and on whom they will therefore often be willing to devote further VET—and which they would prefer to keep insecurely and casually engaged. One outcome of this is a segmentation of labour markets.

One form of employment that could result is what might be called the Silicon Valley model, where individuals have very low employment security in the traditional sense, but high individual expectations of continued good job opportunities, because they can change jobs every couple of years or so without having to move their family or disrupt their lives more generally. Further, the shift in emphasis from employment security to *employability* entails a shift in responsibility from the employer ensuring stable employment to the individual employee ensuring continuing employability by acquiring skills and planning his or her own career. As we shall see when we discuss industrial districts in Chapter 6, such a form of employment requires conditions like those found in Silicon Valley: namely, a geographical concentration of a relatively large number of firms in an industry of constant innovation and growth, where the aptitudes of highly skilled workers are well known. An image of this kind clearly informs much political and business thinking about training, as it envisages a solution to many of the classic problems of VET provision with a minimum of institutional effort. The problem is that these concentrations of firms and networks among them constitute a highly specific institutional form, and the conditions necessary for their formation are limited.

In the course of this discussion we have found some evidence to confirm the OECD's account that Japanese and US forms of capitalism are more able to provide employment than many of their European counterparts. We have, however, also found good reason for querying the simple argument that deregulation of the labour market constitutes the main explanation of a gap between Japan and the USA on the one hand and Europe on the other. We have disputed the bracketing of Japan and the USA as two 'deregulationist' cases set against a monolithic Europe. Instead we would identify a number of different labour market regimes, among which it is particularly important to distinguish among sectors and to separate Scandinavian and southern European patterns within Europe. Regarding the countries of southern Europe as the main exemplars of labour protection—an attribution necessary to the deregulation thesis if its equations are to be impressive—is also problematic on two grounds. First, there are legitimate doubts concerning the implementation of legislation there; and second, the forms of labour regulation and other social policy are more influenced by Social Catholic thought than by the Social Democracy which is neo-liberals' prime political target.

The superior employment performance of the USA, and of some European countries, can be largely explained by their particularly high incidences of part-time working, most interestingly male part-time working. There is also evidence that much of this is accounted for by work by students and elderly people. It is far less clear that there is any superiority in US employment among the core job-seeking under-64-year-old population, at least the male proportion of which should be presumed to be seeking full-time work. There may or may not be reasons for seeking to encourage greater numbers of students and elderly people to be in paid employment. However, highly specific changes can be made to social policy and labour regulation provisions to encourage employment among these groups should it be deemed desirable. The OECD's arguments in favour of general rather than specific regulatory relaxation (or change), on the grounds that it is bad to encourage segmented labour forces, fails when it is realized that the principal categories of employment likely to be encouraged by deregulation are themselves highly segmented categories.

To summarize briefly and provisionally the conclusions of this chapter as they relate to our seven countries of principal interest:

(1) The relatively unregulated US market model seems to be associated with high and increasing employment levels but with a question mark over the skill content of some of this employment.

(2) Far less impressive employment results are found in the UK, despite considerable imitation of the US approach.

(3) The segmented, partly corporate-hierarchical Japanese case seems associated with success in both manufacturing (which may be related to skills) and commerce (which may be closer to the US case).

(4) The corporatist German model seems to be associated with the strong presence of, and the high skills probably produced by, the apprenticeship system, largely in manufacturing, but with difficulty of transfer to other sectors.

(5) The French statist model has not been associated with any notable employment success.

(6) The Swedish mix of corporatism and statism has been particularly associated with high levels of female employment, especially within community and social services, but with decline in other sectors and decline in CSS itself once it became fiscally impossible to sustain.

(7) There has been a very uneven pattern of employment growth in Italy, which leads us to consider this as a very disaggregated case.

Both Japan and the USA are significant performers in the distributive sector. Despite the considerable differences between their employment regimes, both are countries where VET activity is concentrated on firms rather than on public institutions. This makes possible a sharp distinction between sectors (like manufacturing) which need very high levels of skill to remain internationally competitive, and those (like distribution) which can provide employment without elaborate training to those coming from lower levels of educational achievement. This implies a *de facto* segmentation or polarization of employment. Both Japan and the USA are countries where labour movements have a weak political influence and where it might therefore be easier to pursue such approaches than those where there is some political constraint on governments to strive to provide good-quality opportunities for all. Perhaps more important, both are countries whose international trade comprises a relatively small share of total GDP compared with European and other smaller countries. Very high quality performance can therefore be limited even further to certain firms within certain sectors. There is, in other words, neither economic nor political need for a skill-maximization strategy.

Such differences among the seven countries in international trade will be pursued in more detail in the next chapter.

3

Skill and Changing Patterns of Trade

What links can be made between the employment patterns discussed in the previous chapter and any role for occupational skills in the improvement of national
economic performance? In particular, is there evidence that the development of
good-quality skills enables countries to secure strong positions in world trade in
sectors which keep them ahead of low-cost competition from newly industrializing countries (NICs)? In this chapter we shall examine available data on the
the existing stock and flow of skills available to economies, make a more detailed
comparison of the quality of skills in different countries, and examine the relationship between skills and economic performance.

Table 3.1 presents data on the educational levels of the labour force in the
countries with which we are primarily concerned, though unfortunately no comparable information is available for Japan. It shows the proportions of the workforce who terminated their education at certain levels. There are problems of
comparability in the use of such data; for example, we do not know whether a
post-secondary education in Sweden amounts to the same level of knowledge,
ability, etc. as that in Italy. We can, however, compare the overall shapes of countries' profiles.

TABLE 3.1. *Percentages of labour force by highest level of education achieved, labour
force aged 25–64, 1994*

| | Lower secondary or lower | | Upper secondary | | Tertiary (all forms) | |
	Men	Women	Men	Women	Men	Women
France	24	29	56	51	19	20
Germany	8	14	54	57	26	18
Italy	62	51	29	37	10	12
Sweden	28	23	45	47	27	29
UK	17	25	59	52	24	23
USA	13	9	51	55	36	36

Source: OECD 1996c.

Four provisional types appear, which we characterize by their dominant mode
of skill provision.

- *Low skill*: Here there is a heavy concentration at the lowest level, tapering
  off at the highest. Today this describes the situation of Italy alone, though
  in the past a greater number of countries would have exhibited this pattern,

especially among women. This is still the common pattern in almost all countries outside the OECD, although some Asian economies (such as Singapore
and Taiwan) have undertaken a dramatic upgrading of the skills of their
workforces.

- *Intermediate skill*: In these cases particularly high proportions (45% or more)
  have medium levels of education, while rather low proportions (10–15%)
  have high levels, and a moderate proportion (20–30%) have low levels. This
  pattern fits all our cases except Germany, Italy, and the USA.
- *Upper-middle skill*: This is another category invented to take account of one
  case: Germany. The distinctive feature here is the very small proportion of
  both men and women who have experienced only low levels of education.
- *High skill*: In no case does the proportion of the workforce who have
  received a higher education qualification actually exceed those who completed at upper secondary level, but a majority of Americans now enter some
  form of tertiary education and the USA has a distinctly higher percentage
  with post-secondary qualifications (over 35% in the table) than in any other
  country, with a concomitant reduction in those with the lowest levels. This
  system therefore stands by itself.

TABLE 3.2. *Percentages of populations by age group with different maximum
educational attainments, 1994*

Age group	Upper secondary and above (including tertiary)				Tertiary (all forms)			
	25–34	35–44	45–54	55–64	25–34	35–44	45–54	55–64
France	84	73	60	41	24	18	16	8
Germany	90	88	84	72	20	27	24	17
Italy	47	41	26	14	8	10	7	4
Sweden	85	78	69	52	27	30	26	17
UK	86	78	69	57	23	24	20	17
USA	86	89	85	76	23	24	20	15

Source: OECD 1996*c*.

The given stock of skills of a population at any one time is the result of
several generations passing through the education system. During the last forty
years, all the education systems featured in this study have undergone major
changes. To understand this process we need details of the educational achievements of different age groups. These data are given for the countries in our group
in Table 3.2 (it should be noted that these data relate to the population as a whole,
not to the workforce only). In terms of completing at least upper secondary level,
these confirm the previous impression of the enduring success of the German
and US systems in getting young people into higher levels of schooling. All
countries, however, have been improving over time (with the possible exception
of the USA), and today there is little difference among them. Italy is, as we would
expect from its above position as a low-weighted country, an exception in still

TABLE 3.3. *Various measures of educational attainment, c.1990, selected countries*

	Still in education at age 18 1989–90 (a)		Giving access to higher education				Other (d)		Total (b + c + d) (e)	
			General (b)		Vocational (c)					
	%	Rank	%	Rank	%	Rank	%	Rank	%	Rank
Austria			13	16	28	8	46	4	87	7
Denmark	67.90	6	32	9	54	2	14	8	100	3
Finland			46	4		14	73	2	119	1
France	**71.00**	**5**	**31**	**10**	**40**	**3**	**6**	**10**	**77**	**12**
Germany	**81.00**	**1**	**24**	**12**		**14**	**93**	**1**	**117**	**2**
Ireland	52.00	9	74	2	7	11	1	11	82	9
Italy			**18**	**14**	**33**	**4**	**13**	**9**	**64**	**14**
Japan			**67**	**3**	**25**	**9**		**14**	**92**	**5**
Netherlands	73.80	3	29	11	31	6	22	6	82	9
Norway	72.90	4	39	6	32	5	18	7	89	6
Portugal			44	5	5	12	1	11	50	16
Spain	50.50	10	34	8	30	7		14	64	14
Sweden	**52.50**	**8**	**20**	**13**	**61**	**1**		**14**	**81**	**11**
Switzerland	76.60	2	17	15		14	70	3	87	7
UK	**37.60**	**11**	**35**	**7**	**16**	**10**	**44**	**5**	**95**	**4**
USA	**57.70**	**7**	**75**	**1**		**14**		**14**	**75**	**13**

Source: OECD 1994*a*.

not having even 50% of its young population completing upper secondary level. It is difficult to compare the numbers for the youngest generation in tertiary education here, as in many countries people over 25 are still working for their first degrees; in particular this accounts for the low German figure for 25–34-year-olds.

The OECD *Jobs Study* produced various data on different indicators of educational achievement (OECD 1994*a*), which are reproduced as a series of ranked lists (Table 3.3), indicating also where our countries fall within a wider group of industrialized nations. In terms of success in retaining young people in education until age 18, the countries in our present study are ranked in descending order as Germany, France, USA, Sweden, and the UK. (The figure for Japan is not comparable and no data are available for Italy.) Rankings for the attainment of school-leaving qualifications show a difference in the relative emphasis on general or vocationally oriented courses and in the relationship of the latter to the main higher-education streams of a country, in addition to absolute numbers. By having relatively high proportions of people qualifying in vocationally

TABLE 3.4. *Percentages of upper secondary students enrolled in different forms of education, 1994*

| | General | Vocational and technical | |
		School-based	Dual
France	47.5	43.6	8.9
Germany	22.5	22.8	54.7
Italy	26.9	73.1	0
Japan	72.2	27.8	0
Sweden	36.6	[63.4]	
UK	42.3	[57.7]	

Note: Swedish and UK data do not distinguish between dual and school-based vocational and technical education.
Source: OECD 1996c.

oriented courses that can lead to higher education, France, Italy, and Sweden (the three countries where VET is primarily carried out in state schools) sustain that link. Italy does so for rather fewer young people than in the other cases. Germany and the UK are weighted towards separate VET strands, and in both cases this gives qualifications to a higher proportion of school-leavers than in the other three countries. This is the mark of an apprenticeship approach, though in Germany this form of education is clearly much more important than in the UK. Japan and the USA are essentially general education models, the former providing qualifications for a high proportion of its young people.

Table 3.4 shows a similar comparision in a slightly different form—the percentage of upper secondary students enrolled in general, school-based vocational, and dual-system vocational upper secondary education and apprenticeships. This again demonstrates the singularity of the German system, with its dual apprenticeship model, and explains the very low numbers of young Germans without upper secondary education. The particularly high proportion of Japanese young people in general education is also notable. The other countries all present more balanced combinations of general and vocational (largely school-based) systems. Unfortunately comparable data are not available for the USA here, since US students tend to take a few vocational courses as part of a general high school diploma, rather than enrolling in separate institutions.

Studies of the effect of employees' initial education on access to employers' internal training procedures usually show that firms' resources are concentrated on those already highly educated or at least in senior positions. The most recent available data on this question (summarized in Table 3.5) suggest that this remains true. Unfortunately Japan was not covered by this survey, but other studies (for example, OECD 1994b) suggest that Japanese corporations train a much higher percentage of the workforce than their US and European competitors. The three most comparable countries (France, Germany, the USA, where the enquiry is based on the previous 12 months) suggest roughly similar overall provision, with French

TABLE 3.5. *Percentages of employed population aged 25–64 receiving job-related training, by highest level of formal education achieved*

		Education				
		Secondary		Tertiary		
	Primary	Lower	Upper	Non-univ.	Univ.	All
During previous 12 months						
France (1994)	8	28	42	72	57	40
Germany (1994)	0	15	28	43	50	33
USA (1995)	7	13	24	36	49	34
During previous six months						
Sweden (1995)	28	31	41	60	60	44
During previous month						
Italy (1994)	0	1	2	n.a.	3	1
UK (1994)	0	3	12	24	24	13

Source: OECD 1996c.

firms possibly being the biggest providers. The very high six-month figure for Sweden makes it clear that this is in fact the country where firms do the most training and also distribute it most equitably among their employees. It is more difficult to relate the one-month statistics of Italy and the UK to the rest, but the Italian in-firm training rate seems particularly low.

A recent cross-national attempt at examining the achievements of different educational systems in imparting specific basic skills (OECD and Statistics Canada 1995) included consideration of the partly related question of participation in adult education. Unfortunately only three of our countries (Germany, Sweden, and the USA) were covered by this, and the others involved (Canada, the Netherlands, Poland, and Switzerland) give us no clues that might be extended to our other four. This study too found such courses to be heavily concentrated among those already possessing high levels of education. There was considerably less inequality in Sweden than in the USA. Unfortunately data on this item were not available for Germany, but those for the dual system of German-speaking Switzerland suggested slightly more inequality than in the USA; thus, while a dual system provides broad access to initial training, this equality is not necessarily continued in further training.

This ambitious study, known as the International Adult Literacy Survey (IALS) (somewhat misleadingly, since it covers considerably more than literacy in the proper sense of the term), also went beyond a comparison of formal certification levels or years in schooling in order to measure actual skills and capabilities imparted by testing individuals in the workplace. Some of the results are summarized in Figure 3.1. In general they suggest a tendency for Sweden to

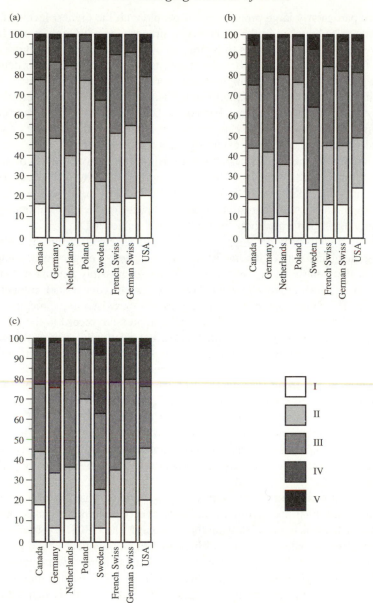

Fig. 3.1 Relative national performances, International Adult Literacy Survey
  a Prose literacy levels
  b Document literacy levels
  c Quantitative literacy levels

Note: Percentages are of adults whose maximum achievements were at each of the five levels
(I is the lowest, V the highest).
Source: OECD and Statistics Canada 1995.

produce particularly large proportions of people with the highest levels of skill; Germans to be bunched in the middle (low proportions with highest and lowest achievements); and Americans to be the opposite of Germans (high proportions at the two extremes). The report also suggested (ibid.: 58) that in all countries except the USA chances of employment increased directly with literacy level; and (ibid.: 63) that German skilled manual workers operated at higher levels of literacy than their US counterparts. Indeed, the USA resembled Poland more closely than any other western country in the survey in terms of the abilities of skilled manual workers (and to some extent of sales and service staff).

An attempt by the IALS to establish a relationship between levels of schooling and literacy achievements (ibid.: 73) suggested that Swedish education did best at providing skills for both its lowest and its most highly educated, while the USA produced the poorest achievement levels for each educational grade. Germany again performed best for middle-level achievers.

This discussion provides support for our original classification of countries. Among the main group of intermediate-weighted cases, we have noted some evidence of particularly strong Swedish performance, possibly leading it therefore to be classified as approaching the German case in educational competences achieved. This latter country is reinforced as an otherwise unique member of an upper-middle weighted group, with the most impressive record in the provision of middle-level, vocationally oriented skills, but relatively weak at the highest levels. Italy is confirmed in its place as a low-skill weighted model, though the country has not appeared in as many comparative studies as Germany, and it is less easy to make strong statements about the quality of its education. The top-weighted position of the USA is reinforced by knowledge of the poor quality of its lower levels of education in contrast with the excellent quality of its higher ones. So much of Japanese VET takes place within companies that it is not possible to include Japan in more than the most limited comparisons. However, besides being a data problem this also constitutes a substantive statement about the Japanese system.

It is very difficult to investigate in what ways and to what extent these diversities of educational preparation actually affect economic performance. Can we observe what use is made of skills in the economy? The OECD has tried (1996b) to give some estimates for shares of high-skilled employment in job growth in various countries, but restricted its concept of high skill to non-manual employment requiring high educational qualifications. It therefore treated highly skilled manual work as by definition low-skilled, tending to rank it below routine non-manual labour. This seems a method of accounting biased in favour of Anglo-American concepts of where skill lies. A distinguishing feature of German and to some extent Swedish approaches to VET has been the development of advanced skills in jobs which remain in the manual sector. Of those of our countries for which data were available (all except Sweden and the UK), during the 1980s Germany was the country to see the largest growth in highly skilled manual jobs, and in fact the USA was the only other country to see growth in these occupations. In the other three they declined, particularly in France and Japan. Germany saw the heaviest decline in low-skilled manual work, with France and Italy also showing declines, while Japan and the USA had increases. Both low- and high-skilled non-manual work grew in all countries, Germany and Italy show- ing somewhat slower advances in developing highly skilled non-manual jobs than the others.

Case studies and other qualitative research

A different approach to trying to understand countries' relative skill positions is to review the state of research on detailed comparisons of skills levels and occupations in specific industries. This work necessarily takes the form of case studies, usually comparing pairs or slightly larger numbers of countries. This makes it possible to achieve finer detail and accuracy, but at the expense of a reduced capacity to draw extensive generalizable conclusions, as only a few industries, even firms, have been studied.

Germany emerged from our quantitative review as being the best equipped eco- nomy to deploy large numbers of workers at middle-ranking (but not advanced) skills with very few workers having low educational standards, this advantage being achieved mainly through the apprenticeship system. This has also been the conclusion of most comparative work, in particular the extensive series of case- study comparisons of matched plants within identical industries in Germany and the UK carried out during the 1980s and early 1990s by a team at the British National Institute for Economic and Social Research (NIESR) under the leader- ship of Prais, Steedman, and Wagner (for example, Mason and Finegold 1995; Finegold and Wagner 1997; Prais 1981; Prais and Wagner 1983; 1988). Among the areas covered were the metalworking industry (Daly, Hitchens, and Wagner 1985); foremen (Prais and Wagner 1988); mechanical fitters, electricians, con- struction workers, office workers, and shop assistants (Prais and Wagner 1985); fitted kitchens (Steedman and Wagner 1987); women's outerwear (Steedman and Wagner 1989). In each case German firms seemed to be able to secure higher value-added niches in markets, especially export markets, because their employees were more productive and could achieve higher quality on the basis of the skills they had acquired in apprenticeship.

There were, however, some more nuanced findings. In a study of microelec- tronics in the engineering industries of both countries Campbell and Warner (1991) continued to find familiar evidence of German superiority: while firms in both countries had incorporated microelectronics into at least some of their products, the British firms tended to be dependent on outside suppliers for related devel- opment and production, whereas in Germany companies had tried to integrate design and production. Also, while firms in both countries reported skill short- ages at graduate level, these had been less significant in Germany, not only because of the existence of a better-qualified intermediate workforce, but because German companies were able to combine skills across design and production. However, the researchers did find that the formality of the German system constrained the further training of craft workers unless it was promotion centred. In the UK training managers seemed to have more discretion to provide informal training outside their formal budgets.

Based on more recent case studies of German metalworking firms, Herrigel (1996) makes the controversial argument that the German education and training system and the types of skills it produces, while well suited to diversified craft production, may now be hindering German firms' ability to adapt to the new competitive conditions. Specifically, he contends that the high degree of specialization among skilled workers and the narrow functional orientation of German managers from different disciplines—for example, manufacturing engineering, product engineering, marketing, purchasing—make it difficult to establish the multifunctional teams on the shop-floor and integrated product teams or concurrent engineering in the product development process that are hallmarks of lean production. The obstacles, he argues, are not only structural, part of the organization of the firm and the VET system, but also part of individual identities, as skilled workers and managers have come to define themselves based on their relatively narrow functional capabilities. Finegold and Wagner's comparison of US and German pump manufacturers (1997) finds some support for Herrigel's argument, showing that the more highly skilled German plants have been slower to adapt the multifunctional work teams found in lean production, but also that the German firms have come up with alternative ways of reorganizing work that may prove equally successful.

Oulton (1996), using quantitative analysis of export statistics rather than a case study, argued that British inferiority in relation to Germany was not general across all industries but limited to certain well-known cases in the engineering industry. Recent research has also examined industries where the UK has strong records of success (for example many branches of chemicals), and where high skill levels seem to be achieved by workers coming through the normally much criticised British skill acquisition routes (Mason and Wagner 1994).

Carr (1992) added Japan and the USA to a comparison, including Britain and Germany, of productivity and skills in vehicle component manufacture. The study focused on change over a ten-year period, and found the gap between the UK and Germany in both productivity and sales per employee narrowing, largely due to manpower cuts in the UK which had removed large numbers of low-productivity workers from employment. A large gap remained, however, between Japan and the three other countries, and the author regards this as the difference that really needs attention rather than the NIESR's Anglo-German contrasts. At the level of formal technical training, Carr's study suggested that the difference was between Germany and the others; at the higher levels Japanese technical skills compared poorly with even those of British engineering graduates in the early stages of their careers, and were well behind those in Germany. However, the subsequent within-company training in Japan was very impressive, based around a team-management organization. Workers at various levels were able to move between jobs to gain experience of different production and technical fields as job security was much greater. Also, salaries were guaranteed to rise irrespective of the kind of work the individual was doing.

In terms of institutional analysis, the key component in Japan is clearly the large corporation, performing in the highly institutionalized way (internal labour markets, strong company cultures, lifetime careers, in-house job designations) typical of Japan rather than of the closer-to-the-market approach to labour markets in the normal British or US company.

A different approach to cross-national comparison was taken by Sako (1994), who compared the experience of Japanese multinational companies setting up plants in Britain and Germany. In Germany the Japanese firms' main problem lay in getting around the rigid qualification system in order to provide more flexible learning and promotion opportunities for semi-skilled workers. In Britain the problem was the unavailability of people comparable to the German *Meister* who could take on both supervisory and technical roles. The Japanese firms in Britain had to choose on the one hand between training supervisors in technical skills and making supervisors out of reluctant technicians, and on the other being content with the British norm of a more centralized technical department supporting the shop-floor. She found only a few making the long-term commitment involved in transposing a Japanese system.

In both countries several Japanese firms were developing tailor-made, off-the-job courses or adopting those developed at the headquarters plant in Japan, to supplement local external courses. Another mode of firm-specific training was to send supervisory and technician workers for short-term training to Japan, which was regarded as a means of communicating to them through direct experience both technical skills, the corporate culture, and how to train, and relate to, subordinates. While using local approaches, the Japanese firms continued to believe in on-the-job training, in-house courses, and internal promotion as the only way to cultivate and retain workers capable of enhancing plant-wide performance.

Productivity and quality performance in both Britain and Germany were found on average to be not as good as at headquarters plants in Japan. Inferior quality was considered to be due to a combination of reasons, including small-scale and batch production, inferior component quality, and lack of awareness and accumulated know-how in maintaining and improving quality. Sako found no significant gap in the productivity and quality performance of Japanese plants in Britain and Germany, despite the fact that workers at the latter were in general better qualified, with supervisors and some blue-collar workers having sufficient engineering knowledge to solve problems, similar to the situation in Japan. She argued that the reason for this might rest partly in the fact that what had mattered for plant performance to date had been the quality of management decisions rather than shop-floor skills. The fact that product design and process technology were largely fixed by Japanese engineers and managers in Japan might have pre-empted a major source of variability in performance between plants based in Britain and Germany.

Also, however, there are some signs that Britain and Germany are being chosen as bases for different kinds of operation. Britain has gained a disproportionate share of Japanese plants manufacturing electronic goods requiring primarily semi-skilled workers; Germany has attracted Japanese operations in a more dispersed range of industries, including rubber and plastics, chemicals, and machinery. Britain's advantages seem to be in relatively low-cost, semi-skilled labour, and Germany's in those sectors where skilled and more expensive labour was required. The sources of cost advantage in the two countries are therefore different.

France emerged from the quantitative study as an intermediate-weighted system, having reached that position following rapid acceleration from a low skill base in previous decades. That its skill ranking remains ambiguous has emerged when researchers have included France in case studies, as the NIESR researchers occasionally did. In work on intermediate skills in France, Britain, and Germany, Steedman, Mason, and Wagner (1991) examined 30 firms in each country, two-thirds of them in batch-production engineering and the remainder in textile spinning (continuous shift work). The study confirmed previous Anglo-German contrasts on the role of foremen, and located French practice as similar to British but in the process of being upgraded. However, Marsden and Ryan (1991) considered that the combination of apprentice pay rules, occupational markets, and lesser segmentation of industries in terms of adult pay had facilitated more direct access to skills training by young workers in Britain than in France. In France the absence of industrial apprenticeships, the lesser influence of wage-for-age rules, the importance of internal labour markets, and a larger degree of segmentation had worked to produce a greater degree of occupational downgrading and concentration of young adults in low-paid industries. There is, however, also more in-firm training for older workers due to the training levy and the internal character of large firms' labour markets.

An important issue in French training debates has been whether the weakness of apprenticeship of the German kind inhibits the development of intermediate skills. In particular a difference often assumed to exist between state-run full-time courses and apprenticeship forms of training is superior socialization to work in the latter, even if high technical standards can be found in the former. This was confirmed in a comparison of the French and German systems (Erbès-Seguin 1990; Erbès-Seguin *et al.* 1990). A study by the French CEREQ group[1] (Campinos-Dubernet and Grando 1988), primarily of the construction industry, systematized the distinctions among France, Germany, and the UK into three different models of training: Germany as training led and industry based; France as training led and school based; Britain as market led and industry based. By a training-led system the authors mean a supply-led one, in which skill-creation institutions provide a supply of skilled workers, use of whom is then made by

---

[1] CEREQ (Centre d'Études et de Recherches sur les Qualifications), which is based in Marseilles, carries out research on training and changes in the workforce in the manner of the NIESR team.

the productive system. A market-led system is instead demand oriented: training will be provided if demand in the product market indicates a need for it.

Steedman (1988) compared the training of mechanical and electrical craftsmen in France and the UK, reaching conclusions somewhat different from the
Anglo-German comparisons which had attributed German superiority to apprenticeship, and suggesting some success for the French state-led system. Whereas
the UK still had an apprenticeship model for engineering workers and electricians, in France this had been abandoned for full-time vocational schools.
Although it differed strongly from the German system, the innovation of the French
vocational baccalaureate was seen as having enabled French production systems
rapidly to move closer to a German one through the institution of a supervisor
holding a vocational baccalaureate working with a team of flexible workers.
Similar conclusions were reached in studies of training in the retail sector (Jarvis
and Prais 1989) and office work (Steedman 1987).

Far fewer comparative studies have included Italian training, which emerged
from our brief quantitative review as the only country among those being studied
here to retain a low-weighted skills base. The CEREQ researchers (Campinos-
Dubernet and Grando 1988) treated Italy as similar to the UK, despite the apparent similarity of the state-led system in the former country to that of France.
They argued that the poorly developed condition of the Italian state education
system and the lack of enforcement of its provisions rendered the Italian case
more like a market-led system. 'Market-led' is here taken to mean that training
supply is strictly proportional to the evolution of the number of people in a given
trade. Also, and in contrast with German work-based training, the work-based
component is not systematically monitored, while off-course components of the
training are not strictly enforced or regulated, and are not subject to obligatory
examination. The quantity and quality of training are heterogeneous and heavily dependent on individual firms and young workers. Even when it is defined,
the apprentice's status is not guaranteed, the distinction between apprentice and
young worker being rather dependent on trade union supervision in the UK and
on personal bond in Italy.

While much of this account would not be disputed by Italian observers, they
would point out that a contrast between state- and market-led systems excludes
the possibility of informal, community-led approaches. Especially in the small
family firms of central Italian industrial districts, skills are often acquired in a
manner that will not be picked up by research based on formal courses and certification. This proposition is, of course, by definition impossible to test by assessments based on formal qualifications, but it cannot be dismissed out of hand.
The inclusion of Italian small firms in comparative direct observation studies of
the NIESR kind would considerably improve knowledge here. Meanwhile the
only other means of indirectly assessing Italian skill levels would be evidence
of Italian achievements in sectors normally requiring medium or advanced
skill levels of a kind that the formal Italian system would seem not to provide.
One indication of such a success comes from the machine tool industry, where

networks of small Italian firms have been more successful at integrating the new computer numerical control (CNC) technology into their equipment than larger European rivals in the UK, France, and Germany (Finegold *et al.* 1994*a*).

The UK and the USA are often seen as being similarly 'market led', but in terms of outcomes of skill profiles the UK is a fairly normal intermediate-led case, while the USA has distinctive performances at the highest educational levels. American firms have been included in some comparative case studies. Carr's 1992 study contained little specific on the USA, which emerged from the comparison as rather similar to the UK (though with its well-known long productivity lead). Daly (1986) undertook a more systematic comparison of Britain and the USA, on the grounds that their shared market-led character-istic might enable the USA to provide a more accessible model for changing the British pattern than the more institutionalized German one. Dominant US features included: flexibility in manning arrangements, with less demarcation between skilled and unskilled activities and few restrictions on entry into craft work; large numbers of management and business graduates; and in general more vocational graduates. There were also a school-based system of VET, in which a much higher percentage of the population received a basic education with a VET component (although generally not leading to well-recognized voca-tional qualifications); and a much higher number of school leavers going on to higher education. Within the school system there was an emphasis on more aca-demic and intermediate skills.

As Daly points out and as we have seen, Britain (like France and Italy) has neither the large proportion of graduates that the USA enjoys nor the high num-ber of workers with intermediate qualifications found in Germany.[2] However, a recent study from the US Economic Policy Institute (Rasell and Mishel, no date) draws attention to an unusual feature of US education. While both enrolments in and expenditure on higher education are the highest in the world, its per capita expenditure on pre-primary, primary, and secondary levels is among the lowest in the OECD. This is consistent with the evidence from the IALS of poor achieve-ment at the lowest levels in the USA, but does not contradict the classification of that country as performing particularly strongly at the highest levels.

INTERIM CONCLUSIONS

This survey of detailed comparative studies of VET, taken in conjunction with the more aggregate quantitative studies summarized earlier, suggests the following provisional appraisal of the seven countries.

(1) France has a school-based system with strong state guidance. It is a sys-tem in the process of rapid improvement, though no studies suggest that

[2] It is perhaps necessary to point out that 'university' education in the USA covers a wider range of levels of study than is normally implied by the term in Europe; it may embrace some intermedi-ate levels as understood in the European context.

it has overtaken Germany in overall achievement. It remains defined as intermediate weighted.

(2) Germany's apprenticeship system is ranked highly by most research, with some doubts about the slowness of its response to change. Its dual system provides a particularly effective link between education and industry. It also succeeds in providing middle-range skills and lifting manual workers out of low-skilled status; it performs less well at the very highest levels.

(3) Italian VET and general education are rarely ranked highly, and it emerged from our quantitative review as the country among those being studied providing the poorest formal educational base for the majority of individuals.

(4) Japan is particularly highly regarded for the high level of general education for the majority, the flexibility of its company-based system, the companies in question being the distinctive, highly institutional ones of the Japanese large corporation model. There is a strong association between this and the efficiency and productivity of Japanese industrial production.

(5) Sweden, like France, has a school-based system with strong state guidance. It performs better than France (indeed, probably best of all the countries) as a system of education providing a high level of general skills for its whole population. It also compares strongly and favourably in the use of an active labour market policy, including aspects of training, as a means of reducing unemployment, but that will be discussed in more detail in Chapter 5. It is difficult to evaluate its detailed VET performance, as it has not featured in many comparative studies that relate training to productivity.

(6) The UK has emerged poorly from detailed comparisons with Germany, but it does have a strong record of high-skill work in a small number of industries, a noted flexibility in adjustment to change, and the level of participation in numbers of enrolments in advanced education has increased considerably in recent years, while the country retains relatively low wastage rates from higher education.

(7) The US school system fares relatively poorly in international comparisons, but this is somewhat compensated for by the high proportion of people who undertake some form of higher education, and by the innovative skill-development activities of many individual firms. This fits what is known about the highly segmented nature of US labour markets and the bunching of employment in very high and also low-skilled activities. As we have characterized it above, it is an upper-weighted system.

The OECD (1996*b*) has recently drawn attention to a certain kind of 'fit' between skills availability and general labour-market policy which unites the UK and US economies and sets them apart from a different pattern found in some western European countries. This so-called Anglo-American system, which was analysed in part in the previous chapter, provides relatively large numbers of potential employees at the two poles of the education range, feeding into a system of differentiated employment conditions and external labour markets. In both countries, the level of statutory labour protection being low, most employment security is provided by employers; they are concerned to provide this for employees whom they want to retain, which mainly means well-educated staff in whom the firm is therefore willing to invest a good deal of training. At the other end of the scale, large numbers of low-skilled workers can be employed and easily disposed of if not needed, with little attention to their training and with frequent recourse to the external labour market.

Set against this stylized Anglo-American case is the opposed and also stylized 'European' model, which is seen as providing a high level of statutory protection and a relatively large supply of potential workers with medium and upper-medium levels of education, in nearly all of whom the firm will both want and be able to invest in training because of generally low levels of labour turnover. European labour markets are seen here as primarily internal. Prospects for the relatively small number of unskilled workers or other outsiders in the labour market then become correspondingly bleak. Having largely failed within a well-organized general and vocational educational system, the unskilled are not attractive to employers. This leads to a combination of relatively low levels of inequality, a small problem of low skills, but high unemployment, and low flexibility and change. This provides a neat mirror-image of the problems of the Anglo-American countries: a skills problem, large labour-market inequalities (for example, income), but relatively low unemployment, and a capacity to adapt to new technologies and working methods.

This dichotomy has some uses. It is, however, as oversimplified in its analysis of skills and training systems as we found it to be in its general discussion of labour markets in the previous chapter. There is considerable difference between the skills profiles of the UK and USA, as the former has reached nowhere near the mass system of higher education which provides the US economy with a large number of generally moderately well-educated people.[3] Failure to recognize this difference between the two countries could have adverse effects for attempts by British policy-makers to treat their country as though it were 'just like the USA', as a far higher proportion of British workers would be placed in a vulnerable market position by application to them of US labour-market principles than can happen to the bulk of the relatively well-educated US workforce.

It is also inaccurate to characterize European labour markets as uniformly 'internal'. As Marsden (1990) has shown, while large firms in France and Italy make considerable use of internal labour markets, this has not generally been true of Germany. German employees have in the past identified primarily with

---

[3] The dramatic improvement in UK higher education participation rates that took place in the last decade (rising from 15% of young people in 1985 to close to a third by 1995) is too recent to have had more than a small impact on the overall volume of educated people in the labour force. Further, in the most recent years there has been a check to and possibly even a slight reversal of the improvement.

their occupation and its structures rather than with individual firms; their relatively high recourse to the external labour market has not, however, had the same implications of weak training incentives often alleged to be the case in the UK and the USA because of the organized structure of German employers and trade unions. We shall consider this further in a later chapter. Japan offers a further contrast again, with highly internal and very segmented labour markets with extremely low levels of unemployment. Simple dualistic contrasts are often misleading in labour-market analysis.

EDUCATIONAL LEVELS AND COMPETITIVE ADVANTAGE

We must now try to relate our characterization of VET regimes to changing patterns of export activity. When the issue is confronted in this way as one of international competitiveness, we need to shift our attention away from the overall occupational structure and concentrate on export sectors to answer the question: In what sectors are countries performing most effectively in international trade? For example, it might be possible to have the workforce in general becoming more educated, but with most of the best educated workers finding employment in community and social services or insurance companies serving an overwhelmingly domestic market, while overseas trade depends on relatively low-skilled people. It might also be possible for a country to produce most of its exported goods with a small number of intermediate and highly skilled workers in highly robotized industries, leaving the main working population employed in sectors sheltered from international competition. Provided the latter do not impose strong wages pressure that affects prices in the traded sector (via prices for private domestic goods and services, or via high taxation to pay for public-sector incomes), this might be a viable solution to the problem of the new global labour market competition.

Unfortunately there are particular difficulties in establishing such an analysis, since in every country evidence on the educational levels of the workforce by industry is collected on a very different basis from that used to classify goods in international trade, and there is no standardization by country. Detailed statistics on countries' international trade performances are published annually in the *United Nations Trade Statistics Yearbook*, but these data have two major defects that limit the effectiveness of this research. First, they cover only trade in physical goods (agricultural produce, manufactured goods, and miscellaneous objects) and exclude the whole important and rapidly growing services sector. Second, although statistics are available for very finely distinguished definitions of goods (for example, self-propelled bulldozers are distinguished from self-propelled excavators), there is rarely information on different quality grades within the same good (for example, to give the most important case, there is only classification of motor cars, irrespective of whether these are very basic models or luxury cars). This is unfortunate, as much theorizing about niche markets has

been concerned with moves up-market within categories of good. We are therefore unable to test some of the central hypotheses of the NIESR literature, that
within particular industries (say kitchen fittings) one country will have a better
trained workforce than another and as a result be able to secure superior niches
in the market.

However, the thesis of upskilling enables us to come at a different aspect of
the issue. According to this thesis, the advanced countries should be shifting, not
just to better levels of skill within industries, but to those industries which require
overall higher levels of skill or formal education.

A study of occupational change in Sweden entitled *Långt kvar till
Kunskapssamhället*—'A Long Way from the Knowledge Society' (Landell and
Victorsson 1991) considered changes in the educational level of employees in
Sweden's main industries and concluded that there had been no evidence at all
of a shift in the country's occupational structure towards high-skilled sectors.
This presented a challenge to the views expressed by all shades of opinion in
Sweden that the country would surely move towards these sectors in order to
sustain its position in the global economy at a time when low-cost producers
were increasingly able to rival the old industrial countries in traditional industries using low or medium skills. Instead, the study found, employment in some
high-skilled industries had actually declined, while some of those that had seen
most employment growth used only low skill levels. Similar research in the USA
concluded that, while the most rapidly growing occupations are in highly skilled
areas (such as software programmers and technicians), the largest growth in jobs
in absolute terms continues to be in relatively low-skilled ones such as security
guards, retail cashiers, and food servers (US Department of Labor Web Page 1997).

The question raised with respect to Sweden can be put in the form of a more
general hypothesis: that international competition will lead firms in the advanced
industrial countries to concentrate their exports increasingly within industries
requiring labour with higher levels of skill.

The available data remain unsatisfactory even for this research strategy since
information on the educational level of workforces is available only for broadly
defined industries, while export activity might take place only in niches of such
industries, which might have different skill ranges from the wider sector. For
example, a given country might have a strong performance in pharmaceuticals
(an industry with a particularly well-educated workforce), but labour-force statistics may go to no further detail than the chemical industry as a whole—still a
highly skilled sector, but not universally at the level of pharmaceuticals. Statements relating trade to skill data have to take the form: 'products n_1 to n_n fall
within larger category N, which has skill characteristic x; therefore we assume
that all n have skill characteristic x'. Such statements are always prone to the
ecological fallacy: product n_n may in practice involve skill characteristic y, even
if category N as a whole is characterized by x. Nothing can be done to resolve
this problem with the available data, but it does considerably restrict the confidence with which conclusions may be drawn from our findings.

The gaps in the education data also raise problems of how we are to determine what we mean in the above hypothesis by 'labour with higher levels of skill'. Since there are no universally applicable measures of actual skill, and since to date the IALS measures have been applied to only a small number of countries and even then not disaggregated by sector, we have to fall back on measures of formal education. In effect, we have to use formal educational achievements as a proxy for skill, and they may not be effective in this regard, as the Italian case in particular seems to demonstrate. The hypothesis therefore has to be reformulated in a weaker form as follows: that international competition will lead firms in the advanced industrial countries to concentrate their exports increasingly within industries requiring labour with higher levels of formal education.

Given the difficulties of treating these data with any great precision, we shall concentrate on simple measures of the proportions of an industry's workforce (a) lacking in formal educational qualifications and (b) possessing tertiary educational qualifications. These are chosen for the very pragmatic reason that, although problems of comparability are not thereby eliminated, they are less severe than if we try to find equivalents among the very heterogeneous set of intermediate qualifications. Even if we were to solve this problem we would still find considerable variation in the extent to which countries report the existence of these qualifications among workers at the level of different industries. The position remains unsatisfactory, but it is not possible to do better with the information available.

The available data are set out in Table 3.6 for all our countries except Italy. There is not necessarily comparability among countries in the indicators used. For example, in Germany no industry-level data are available on workers entirely lacking in educational qualifications, because the figure would be so small. Instead, we have statistics on those who do not have an advanced (*Fach*) vocational qualification. Further, the French data use a particularly restricted concept of higher education, excluding sub-degree qualifications which in other countries are usually regarded as part of the tertiary sector. Our comparisons are therefore in the first instance within individual countries; only then can we compare different national profiles with each other.

Subject to these limitations, we can test for certain associations and changes over time. If a country is using higher education levels to find its niches in world trade, we should expect its exports as a proportion of total world trade to be positively associated with educational level. We should not expect correlations to be particularly strong, since they are dependent on the proportion of total world trade occupied by a particular type of good world-wide. (For example, imagine a world in which two commodities are traded, a low-skilled one comprising 90% of the market and a high-skilled one comprising the other 10%. Even if one country has all of that 10% but a 20% share in the other commodity, it will show up with exports negatively correlated with skill.) However, we can learn something from intra-national changes even within such a framework, and from the relative importance within industries of different skill levels.

TABLE 3.6. *Skills rankings of industries (percentage of employees in (a) lowest and (b) highest education categories),* c.*1989 (ranked by former only)*

France, 1990

	(a)	(b)
Petroleum, gas	16.74	19.60
Ships, planes, arms	18.79	10.96
Electrical machinery, etc.	25.92	12.27
Basic chemicals and fibres	29.36	10.12
Printing, publishing	29.48	8.79
Pharmaceuticals	30.26	11.97
Engineering	30.64	3.06
Minerals (non-ferrous)	36.10	5.72
Minerals (ferrous)	37.87	3.99
Foundry products	39.04	2.04
Coal, etc.	41.48	2.69
Other food industries	42.52	2.40
Vehicles	43.25	3.54
Rubber, plastic	43.91	3.17
Glass	44.99	3.36
Wood products, furniture	45.27	1.91
Household equipment	45.67	4.65
Meat and dairy products	46.01	2.46
Paper, etc.	47.72	3.03
Construction materials	49.76	3.06
Textiles, clothing	54.50	1.88
Leather and shoes	56.94	1.40
Agriculture	61.62	0.97

(a) % low education;
(b) % higher education.

Germany, 1987

	(a)	(b)
Ships and planes	13.03	29.43
Mineral oil	13.16	28.56
Office machinery	14.29	40.80
Petroleum	16.11	35.18
Engineering	20.49	22.95
Precision machines	24.25	21.87
Printing	25.23	16.05
Ores	25.65	25.65
Chemicals	26.35	25.01
Metal structures	27.48	14.56
Food	28.98	14.46

Electrical	29.68	26.46
Coal	31.10	14.12
Drink	35.03	15.91
Miscellaneous goods	35.37	15.26
Clothing	36.33	13.02
Minerals	36.83	15.06
Primary metal	39.50	13.64
Other mining	39.54	17.25
Road vehicles	41.22	17.19
Tobacco	41.48	15.43
Steel tubes	43.26	12.72
Footwear	43.52	11.83
Furniture	45.91	8.53
Textiles	47.55	12.83
Paper, etc.	47.65	13.72
Glass	47.74	13.34
Rubber, plastic goods	48.88	14.51
Leather goods	48.96	11.35

(a) % non-Fach;
(b) % advanced education.

Japan, 1989

	(a)	(b)
Petroleum products	16.22	21.62
Publishing, printing	18.34	25.79
Other manufacturing	18.49	14.38
Chemicals	18.89	25.42
Ceramic, etc.	20.48	13.25
Electrical	23.41	15.73
Precision	26.03	17.35
Machinery	31.89	17.22
Transport equipment	32.30	13.24
Food, tobacco	33.57	11.10
Pulp, paper	33.81	10.48
Iron and steel	34.80	10.66
Other metal	36.63	11.39
Rubber	40.83	10.00
Metal products	41.25	9.70
Clothing	43.48	4.08
Leather	47.06	8.82
Textiles	47.68	6.19
Furniture	50.00	7.81
Wood products	54.11	4.79
Mining	54.72	5.66

(a) % low education;
(b) % higher education.

Sweden, 1990

	(a)	(b)
Instruments	28.10	10.00
Electrical products	31.00	8.70
Engineering	35.40	5.80
Chemicals and petrol	36.00	10.20
Vehicles	36.40	5.20
Metal tools	46.40	1.80
Metal structures	47.10	2.80
Pulp and paper	47.20	3.70
Minerals and building products	47.40	2.60
Plastics	47.90	2.10
Food, etc.	50.50	2.70
Rubber	51.30	2.20
Wood	51.30	3.10
Non-metal mineral products	51.80	2.60
Other	53.30	3.10
Agriculture	57.60	2.10
Textiles, clothing, leather	60.40	1.80
Fish	61.50	1.90

(a) % low education;
(b) % higher education.

UK, 1989

	(a)	(b)
Office machinery	11.21	66.81
Petroleum, etc.	14.58	61.11
Ships and planes	18.44	64.42
Paper and printing	25.17	46.52
Electrical	26.15	49.59
Chemicals	26.16	49.45
Engineering	27.11	51.29
Precision goods	28.32	48.77
Wood, furniture	28.63	46.37
Metals	31.14	45.65
Coal	32.95	45.83
Rubber, plastic	33.40	38.30
Road vehicles	34.27	41.73
Mineral processes	36.18	35.25
Miscellaneous goods	36.89	31.11
Raw materials	38.36	30.14
Food etc.	39.76	32.19
Leather	50.85	28.81

Clothing, shoes	51.64	19.12
Textiles	53.27	21.44

(a) % no education qualifications;
(b) % higher education.

USA, 1989

	(a)	(b)
Computers	5.01	46.28
Medicines	5.55	46.43
Photographic goods	6.51	30.94
Inorganic chemicals	6.88	30.33
Petroleum products	7.02	30.89
TV, radio, electrical	8.09	31.65
Optical instruments	9.19	27.35
Newspapers	9.39	26.38
Precision goods	10.84	22.36
Engines and turbines	12.22	15.71
Planemaking	12.24	23.47
Construction machinery	12.25	13.99
Other machinery	13.1	21.85
Grain milling	13.81	20.65
Steam engines	14.89	13.38
Fertilizers	14.97	20.07
Diesel engines	15.03	12.84
Other engineering	15.61	13.72
Tobacco	15.77	17.98
Paper, printing	16.7	12.12
Road vehicles	17.08	13.47
Shipbuilding	17.59	11.46
General printing	17.87	16.13
Fishing	17.88	23.84
Other non-ferrous metals	18	12.55
Aluminium	18.47	12.55
Paper mill machinery	19.62	12.66
Plastics	21.78	12.27
Metal products	22	10.54
Mining, etc.	22.62	9.25
Animals	23	15.96
Crops, feed, oils	23.55	14.26
Metal and scrap	24.96	6.85
Wood	26.55	9.01
Canned vegetables	30.51	10.81
Meat	35.88	6.3
Textiles	37.83	7.33

(a) % high-school drop-outs;
(b) college graduates.
Sources: National census data.

We shall begin our consideration of the period of change with the late 1970s. The start of that period saw the end of the relatively easy post-war economy, in which the advanced countries had dominated the world with little threat from competition outside a few traditional sectors (for example, agriculture, textiles) within which they were, in any case, at least partly shielded from the impact of trade by protectionist policies. Although employment in manufacturing industry had peaked in most countries, the rich economies were still primarily unrivalled exporters of industrial goods; virtually full employment had been taken for granted. The dating of change is always difficult, as antecedents can always be traced further back: examples are militancy in the labour market in the late 1960s; some steep commodity price rises in the early 1970s before the spectacular case of rises in the price of crude oil, and so on. The oil shock itself came in two stages, 1973 and 1978. There is, however, a pragmatic solution to the problem of when to date the start of this analysis: in 1976 the system of classifying goods for international trade was changed. This therefore becomes the earliest available base year for the study.

The period which began then was one of economic restructuring for the advanced economies. During the subsequent years they had to adjust to high commodity prices. Meanwhile, the growth of microprocessor technology from the late 1970s led to major potential improvements in productivity and flexiblity of methods, enabling the entry of new producers in traditional fields, the development of new industries around high-technology products themselves, and the development of labour-saving production processes in the advanced countries. At the same time that many sectors in the advanced economies suffered from intensified competition in an increasingly integrated global market, there has also been growth in the demand for the products of the advanced countries from businesses and consumers in NICs as their wealth grows.

In many respects this set of changes is continuing, but in others a particular period can be considered to have ended. The political changes in eastern Europe at the end of the 1980s again altered the structure of global competition, while also creating major changes in the geography, society, and political economy of Germany, one of the most important advanced economies. Soon afterwards the world entered a new, prolonged recession, while a major round of international tariff reduction was achieved. It is therefore useful to regard the period 1976–89 as one of restructuring within the post-war international political economy; since then we have been living in a new, 'post-cold-war' environment. It is quite possible that the changes now taking place in national competitive advantages will be quite different from those of the earlier period; perhaps the answer to the Swedish anxiety referred to above is that the shift to a 'knowledge society' is only now occurring. It remains relevant to consider exactly what was taking place during that earlier period: did it mark the beginning of continuing processes, or was it the end of a line?

We then take a further look at change during the years since 1989; in effect this means until 1994, the latest date for which international trade statistics were available at the time of writing. This period is short and there is a danger that differences in the rhythms of national trade cycles distort the picture; these recent data must therefore be treated with reserve.

Changes in trade and skill patterns, 1976, 1989, and 1994

First of all, Table 3.7 demonstrates the different levels of involvement in international trade of our various countries. In general, of course, smaller countries have to be engaged in such trade more than large ones—the difference between Sweden on the one hand and Japan and the USA on the other is striking. It is, however, notable that Germany breaks this rule, being considerably more heavily engaged in the export of goods than any of the slightly smaller similar European economies (France, Italy, and the UK). These points are relevant to our central question. Much of the rhetoric about the learning society or the high-skilled economy assumes that there is a great premium on employment in the export sector. In fact, in all our countries the proportion of the workforce employed in producing goods and services for export is fairly small, but its size will clearly vary considerably given these different levels of involvement in external trade. For a small economy like Sweden, or one like Germany that has placed a particular emphasis on export activity, the need for concerted national skill policies is considerably greater than in Japan or the USA. It will be important to bear this in mind when, in later chapters, we note that Japan and the USA leave much skill formation to initiatives of individual firms. Since these countries require only a small proportion of the economy to be engaged in external trade, the strategy of leaving things to the individual firm may well have very different implications than for countries with a bigger exposed sector.

We now turn to a more detailed analysis of trade patterns. Appendix Table A.1 sets out, for each of our countries, the share of total world trade in all products represented by each of its exports. A country can be said to conform to the upskilling hypothesis if its exports move over time towards industries using more highly educated workforces; it defies the hypothesis if it moves in the opposite direction. Further alternatives would be for it to move in either of two curvilinear ways: to move in a straight U-shaped manner would mean a movement towards extremes, with both high- and low-education industries growing at the expense of middle-ranking ones; to move in an inverted U or a humped way would mean a movement towards goods requiring intermediate levels of education. Table 3.8 displays the relationships that we have been able to observe. Perhaps not surprisingly, given the crudity of the indicators we are having to use, patterns can be discerned in only a few cases, and very few are significant at the 5% level or better. These statistical observations are used to check the following brief narrative descriptions of what took place in the various countries.

France During the earlier period (1976–89) the French economy moved out of its previous specialization in food and textiles, and acquired a presence in such

TABLE 3.7. *Per capita exports, 1976–1995, seven countries*

	Exports ($) per capita of total population					
	1976	1989	1995	% change 1976–1989	% change 1989–1995	% change 1976–1995
France						
Goods	1,085.90	3,015.49	4,650.04	177.69	54.21	328.22
Services	386.79	1,113.87	1,681.34	187.98	50.95	334.69
Total	1,472.69	4,129.36	6,331.38	180.39	53.33	329.92
% services	26.26	26.97	26.56	2.70	−1.55	1.11
Germany*						
Goods	1,623.23	5,142.88	6,408.26	216.83		
Services	296.62	807.78	1,053.65	172.33		
Total	1,919.85	5,950.65	7,461.91	209.95		
% services	15.45	13.57	14.12	−12.14		
Germany, former western Federal Republic only						
Goods			7,547.06		46.75	364.94
Italy						
Goods	680.46	2,443.72	4,037.98	259.13	65.24	493.42
Services	155.77	590.59	1,135.33	279.13	92.24	628.84
Total	836.24	3,034.31	5,173.31	262.85	70.49	518.64
% services	18.63	19.46	21.95	4.49	12.75	17.81
Japan						
Goods	629.91	2,180.63	3,424.28	246.18	57.03	443.61
Services	104.43	321.17	521.33	207.55	62.32	399.22
Total	734.34	2,501.80	3,945.61	240.69	57.71	437.30
% services	14.22	12.84	13.21	−9.73	2.92	−7.09
Sweden						
Goods	2,264.11	5,939.20	8,967.50	162.32	50.99	296.07
Services	441.38	1,317.98	1,749.15	198.60	32.71	296.29
Total	2,705.49	7,257.18	10,716.65	168.24	47.67	296.11
% services	16.31	18.16	16.32	11.32	−10.13	0.05
UK						
Goods	811.19	2,644.08	4,145.73	225.95	56.79	411.07
Services	310.51	838.22	1,247.51	169.95	48.83	301.76
Total	1,121.70	3,482.29	5,393.24	210.45	54.88	380.81
% services	27.68	24.07	23.13	−13.05	−3.90	−16.44
USA						
Goods	564.68	1,433.36	2,195.62	153.84	53.18	288.83
Services	114.22	413.52	792.45	262.05	91.64	593.82
Total	678.89	1,846.88	2,988.07	172.04	61.79	340.14
% services	16.82	22.39	26.52	33.09	18.45	57.64

* Figures for 1976 and 1989 are for former western Republic only; that for 1995 is for unified Germany.
Sources: *ILO Yearbooks*, OECD Economic Indicators and UN World Trade Statistics; *IMF International Financial Statistics Yearbook*.

		Exports ($) per capita of total labour force			
1976	1989	1995	% change 1976–1989	% change 1989–1995	% change 1976–1995
2,612.26	6,737.92	10,364.36	157.93	53.82	296.76
930.47	2,488.88	3,747.50	167.49	50.57	302.75
3,542.73	9,226.80	14,111.86	160.44	52.94	298.33
3,699.74	10,360.01	13,052.17	180.02		
676.06	1,627.22	2,146.05	140.69		
4,375.80	11,987.22	15,198.21	173.94		
		17,034.57		64.43	360.43
1,859.95	5,820.06	10,200.00	212.92	75.26	448.40
425.78	1,406.56	2,867.86	230.35	103.89	573.55
2,285.73	7,226.63	13,067.86	216.16	80.83	471.71
1,236.48	4,234.38	6,451.77	242.45	52.37	421.78
204.99	623.65	982.24	204.24	57.50	379.17
1,441.47	4,858.03	7,434.01	237.02	53.03	415.73
5,358.56	11,355.24	18,333.64	111.91	61.46	242.14
1,044.64	2,519.87	3,576.06	141.22	41.91	242.33
6,403.20	13,875.12	21,909.70	116.69	57.91	242.17
1,751.22	5,253.83	8,543.38	200.01	62.61	387.85
670.34	1,665.56	2,574.47	148.46	54.57	284.05
2,421.57	6,919.39	11,117.86	185.74	60.68	359.12
1,384.24	2,849.13	4,367.37	105.83	53.29	215.51
279.98	821.96	1,576.29	193.57	91.77	462.99
1,664.23	3,671.09	5,943.66	120.59	61.90	257.14

TABLE 3.8. *Correlations between changes in export performance and educational background of workforces, seven countries, 1976–1989 and 1989–1994*

Country	Time period	Measure of educational level*	Character of change**	Significance (F-test)
France				
	1976–89	Low	None	None
		High	Inverted U	None
	1989–94	Low	U	None
		High	None	None
Germany				
	1976–89	Low	Positive	None
		High	Positive	None
	1989–94	Low	Negative	2%
		High	Positive	None
Japan				
	1976–89	Low	Negative	None
		High	Positive	None
	1989–94	Low	None	None
		High	Positive	None
Sweden				
	1976–89	Low	U	None
		High	U	not quite 5%
	1989–94	Low	U	5%
		High	Positive	not quite 5%
UK				
	1976–89	Low	Negative	None
		High	None	None
	1989–94	Low	Negative	1%
		High	Positive	1%
USA				
	1976–89	Low	U	5%
		High	U	0.5%
	1989–94	Low	None	None
		High	None	None

* Low = proportions of workforce with lowest educational backgrounds, *c.*1989.
High = proportions of workforce with highest educational backgrounds, *c.*1989.
(For details see Appendix Table A.1.)
** Negative = declining share of exports from industries with high proportions of workers at this educational level.
Positive = rising share of exports from industries with high proportions of workers at this educational level.
U-shaped = share of exports rose from industries with both high and low proportions of workers at this educational level.
Inverted U-shaped = share of exports declined from industries with both high and low proportions of workers at this educational level.
  (For details see Appendix Table A.1.)

advanced sectors as aircraft, office machinery, and some chemicals. Car production (a moderately skilled industry) declined slightly, in contrast with some other
countries. However, there were sharp declines in the higher-skilled engineering
sectors where France had previously had an important place. Overall the movements were therefore rather contradictory. They were also slight. No discernible
pattern reaches statistical significance.

In the more recent period (1989–94) there were slightly more pronounced rises
in exports from high-skill industries and declines in some lower-skilled ones—
in line with expectations of an advanced economy—but it is notable that some
of those with the very lowest skills have stabilized their relative importance
to the French economy after an initial decline during the 1980s. There is therefore some evidence of a U-shaped pattern, but no correlation reached statistical
significance.

Germany In the earlier period advances in German exports were almost entirely
concentrated in industries with medium skills—in particular in the car industry,
even though the country's overall share in the global market for cars was declining slightly. This masked slight declines in other sectors. There was no overall
education-related pattern in the country's changes between different product
markets, and the evidence from the low- and high-education measures is contradictory, though in neither case statistically significant.

Since 1989 there has been a clearer shift towards industries with higher educational backgrounds, according to both low- and high-education measures, the
former showing a statistically significant decline (at the 2% level) in the role of
low-skilled industries. This mainly takes the form of a relative decline in the
moderately skilled car industry (on which the country arguably became over-
dependent in the 1980s) and a resurgence of strength in its traditional past points
of emphasis: machine production and precision goods. These are moderately
highly skilled industries, rather than either highly skilled (as are pharmaceuticals or computers) or moderately skilled (as in motor vehicles). This is the model
of modernized traditional production that features prominently in discussions
of the German economy, but which had in fact declined somewhat during the
1980s. However in machine tools as such (the core of this kind of activity) there
has been declining performance.

In comparative terms Germany's export performance has been extraordinarily
strong, being second only to Sweden in relativized share of world trade and almost
rivalling that country in 1989. Even after dilution of its constant-population position after the addition of East Germany it continues in this position. Nevertheless,
the overall decline echoed in many sectors reflects the impact of that unification.
A vast labour force growth has taken the form of millions of people experienced
in the low-productivity economy of the former German Democratic Republic.
The point is obvious, but it serves as a useful reminder of the shock waves that
have hit the German economy.

Italy Of all the cases being considered here, Italy in the 1970s most closely corresponded to a low-skill model. It was thereafter, with Japan, the only country which saw a consistent and strong rise in overall share in world trade in both periods (1976–89 and 1989–94). While we have no direct data on the educational background of workers in various Italian industries, we can draw some provisional but untested conclusions on the basis of what we know generally about the skill levels of certain sectors. In the earlier period, Italian export success was achieved with a decline in exports from the highest-skilled industries and with increases concentrated at the lower skill levels; the country therefore defied the learning society thesis, increasing its market shares by moving to ostensibly lower-skilled industries. In the 1990s this seems to have changed, and there was probably a moderate upskill shift. Much more surprisingly, Italy has resembled Germany in having strong growth in machine tools, the heartland of the German formal apprenticeship system but one for which there are no outstanding formal Italian training institutions. This again raises the question of a diversity of routes to the high-skill economy (see Regini 1996*a* for an extended discussion of this issue, with particular reference to a comparison of Germany and Italy). Despite the many differences in their skill production systems, these two economies have both developed strong records in machine production and other capital goods.

Japan Like Italy, Japan has seen constantly increasing shares in world trade throughout the whole period, 1976–94. During the earlier period there was a decline in the role of industries with large numbers of workers with low educational backgrounds and a rise in those with large numbers of highly educated workers, though neither measure reaches a statistically significant level. In the later period the second measure shows a continued pattern of upskilling, though again there is no statistical significance. One very distinctive characteristic of Japanese success has been great strength in the moderately skilled motor vehicles sectors, alongside exceptional growth in a small number of highly skilled sectors (primarily computers).

Sweden Sweden is the only country being considered which did not see a rise in its world trade share during the 1990s, the 1980s decline having also been very severe. In the earlier period the changes taking place have no clear skill implications: both measures suggest a relative rise in the role of industries at opposite ends of the skill spectrum; neither is statistically significant, though that on the high-education score only slightly misses the 5% level. It is therefore not clear whether the findings are compatible with the findings of Landell and Victorsson (1991).

During the 1990s, however, there seems to have been a change in pattern consistent with the upskilling hypotheses. Both measures (of low and highly educated workers) are consistent in suggesting this, though on the former score a U-curved hypothesis emerges more strongly from the test. It reaches significance at the 5% level, the straight positive hypothesis on the high-education measure being slightly short of this. However, this evidence of some upskilling (plus some decline in the medium-skilled industries), exists in a context of declining overall performance.

United Kingdom Although the poor economic performance of the UK is frequently attributed to skills bottlenecks and poor training achievements, any deficiencies of this kind have not prevented the economy from changing more consistently with the upskilling thesis—at least at this aggregate industry level—than any other country in our sample. In the earlier period there was a slight (not statistically significant) decline in the export role of industries with large proportions of low-educated workers. By the later period the upskilling trend has acquired significance at the 1% level on both low- and high-education versions of the measure. This remains true even when the windfall from North Sea oil is discounted by removing the performance in the crude oil and natural gas sectors from the calculations.

The UK continues to have a relatively small export sector for a country of its size. Our findings are therefore not necessarily in conflict with those of the NIESR studies; the product markets of the highest-skilled sectors are relatively small, and it is possible for a strong performance here to be accompanied by weak ones elsewhere. Nevertheless, stronger versions of the low-skilled equilibrium thesis in the British case need to come to terms with this evidence of some major points of strength.

United States Finally, the USA showed a very marked trend towards a U-shaped development in the earlier period, suggesting a 'hollowing out' of performance in the medium-range skill industries in favour of both high- and low-skilled sectors. This is significant at the 5% level on the low-education measure, and at the 0.5% level for the higher measure. This is also consistent with the general image of US employment which emerged from Chapter 2. The more recent period shows no strong signs of any particular change. While the rise in the highest-skilled exports was exceptionally strong during the earlier period, it slackened off slightly during the 1990s. On the other hand there was some important recovery in certain moderately high-education industries (for example, engines), which had declined severely during the 1980s.

An analysis of specific industries

Much of the above account of total national performances depends on the problematic assumption that specific sub-industries possess educational profiles typical of the larger industries of which they are part. We can make more confident statements if we concentrate on a small number of industries where we can be fairly confident that skills are of a certain level. There is little doubt that the following make use of particularly high concentrations of well-educated employees and low numbers of poorly educated ones (the numbers in parentheses are those of the international classification of trade statistics): petrol and gas refining (334, 335, 34); organic chemicals (51); inorganic chemicals (52); dyes, paints, etc. (53); pharmaceuticals (541); office machinery (including computers) (75).[4]

There is similarly little doubt about the low educational levels of most work-forces in the following: animals, meat, and skins (00, 01, 21); rubber (23) and rubber goods (62); leather (61); and textiles (65).

Important 'upper-medium' goods are the industries of engine production and machine construction which are the capital goods at the heart of the industrial economy (engines (71), machine tools (72), metal machine tools (73), non-electric machinery (74)).

There is also particular interest in the 'lower-medium' motor car sector (78), which has been such a large export industry for most countries.

Table 3.9 shows data for these groups of products for our seven countries and for the world in general in 1976, 1989, and 1994, and shows overall change between the two end points. Globally, trade in the selected list of high-education products grew as a share of total world trade, the 1994 total being 117.86% of that in 1976. This is consistent with the thesis of a rising skill content of internationally traded goods. The country with the largest relative growth in share of world trade in high-skill goods was Japan, with the USA, Sweden, and the UK also increasing their relative share of this bundle of products. France was only just below the average, but Germany and Italy fell back. Clearly, many factors besides vocational education lie behind these developments; the figure for Japan in particular is part of that country's general entry into international trade from the 1970s onwards. The figures for the UK and the USA should not surprise us, as we have already described these countries as performing well in those industries which require very highly educated workers. For Sweden, too, we have noted the major and rapid improvements in the educational level of a country that had earlier had poor standards. The weak performance of Germany, however, is remarkable.

Goods requiring only low educational levels have declined as a proportion of world trade, again consistently with the education thesis. We should expect our countries, as the main advanced industrial economies, to show greater than average losses in trade shares here, and this is the case for France, Germany, Japan, Sweden, and the UK; the US figure also declined but not much more than the world average. It is difficult to interpret the Italian increase. Taken in conjunction with Italy's steep decline in share of goods requiring advanced education for their production, this might be evidence of the country moving down-market. However, since Italian prices were rising relative to world prices throughout the period, an alternative interpretation could be in line with the evidence that Italian skills improved informally and piecemeal in small firms.

---

[4] One might also include aircraft production, though there is some ambiguity about levels here and in any case much international trade in this commodity is the result of political and military arrangements rather than trade on the open market.

TABLE 3.9. *Changes in export shares of certain skill groups of industries, seven countries, 1976–1994*

Country and year	High skill sectors							All high skills	1994 as % 1976
	Petrol	Gas	Organic chem.	Inorganic chem.	Dyes, paints	Pharmaceuticals	Office equip.		
France									
1976	0.156	0.011	0.11	0.092	0.039	0.072	0.098	0.578	
1989	0.052	0.007	0.157	0.074	0.036	0.079	0.169	0.574	
1994	0.063	0.006	0.175	0.063	0.041	0.135	0.169	0.652	112.80
Germany									
1976	0.133	0.004	0.356	0.12	0.166	0.137	0.188	1.104	
1989	0.067	0.008	0.28	0.105	0.153	0.139	0.165	0.917	
1994	0.088	0.01	0.283	0.082	0.141	0.218	0.245	1.067	96.65
Italy									
1976	0.225	0.006	0.082	0.022	0.012	0.048	0.065	0.46	
1989	0.062	0.001	0.071	0.018	0.017	0.037	0.125	0.331	
1994	0.073	0.001	0.066	0.01	0.022	0.069	0.109	0.35	76.09
Japan									
1976	0.009	0	0.157	0.044	0.025	0.017	0.155	0.407	
1989	0.02	0	0.113	0.026	0.032	0.029	0.931	1.151	
1994	0.055	0	0.201	0.035	0.045	0.039	0.878	1.253	307.86
Sweden									
1976	0.0262	0.0003	0.0147	0.0112	0.0049	0.0152	0.0354	0.1079	
1989	0.0421	0.0006	0.0131	0.0103	0.0051	0.0219	0.0459	0.139	
1994	0.0345	0.0007	0.0155	0.007	0.0071	0.0616	0.0208	0.1472	136.42
UK									
1976	0.205	0.004	0.145	0.071	0.058	0.093	0.106	0.682	
1989	0.084	0.009	0.157	0.048	0.052	0.108	0.255	0.713	
1994	0.095	0.012	0.176	0.042	0.055	0.15	0.356	0.886	129.91
USA									
1976	0.12	0.028	0.255	0.148	0.036	0.116	0.341	1.044	
1989	0.156	0.018	0.312	0.137	0.047	0.119	0.959	1.748	
1994	0.14	0.014	0.326	0.104	0.058	0.154	0.883	1.679	160.82
World									
1976	4.14	4.14	1.7	0.75	0.53	0.81	1.2	13.27	
1989	2.54	2.54	2.46	0.89	0.64	1.13	4.28	14.48	
1994	1.99	1.99	2.22	2.74	0.64	1.47	4.59	15.64	117.86

TABLE 3.9. (Cont'd)

Country and year	Low skill sectors					All low skills	1994 as % 1976
	Meat, etc.	Rubber	Leather	Rubber goods	Textiles		
France							
1976	0.175	0.028	0.026	0.106	0.239	0.574	
1989	0.172	0.023	0.019	0.095	0.153	0.462	
1994	0.158	0.016	0.012	0.085	0.163	0.434	75.61
Germany							
1976	0.091	0.02	0.045	0.106	0.446	0.708	
1989	0.115	0.017	0.032	0.106	0.319	0.589	
1994	0.071	0.014	0.027	0.093	0.319	0.524	74.01
Italy							
1976	0.012	0.008	0.035	0.055	0.234	0.344	
1989	0.025	0.007	0.06	0.052	0.229	0.373	
1994	0.024	0.002	0.086	0.05	0.271	0.433	125.87
Japan							
1976	0.001	0.023	0.02	0.087	0.38	0.511	
1989	0.001	0.012	0.01	0.113	0.163	0.299	
1994	0.003	0.017	0.006	0.111	0.169	0.306	59.88
Sweden							
1976	0.0126	0.0013	0.0065	0.0143	0.0299	0.0646	
1989	0.0093	0.0007	0.0039	0.0106	0.0179	0.0424	
1994	0.0038	0.0012	0.0017	0.0065	0.0156	0.0288	44.58
UK							
1976	0.083	0.013	0.031	0.062	0.199	0.388	
1989	0.076	0.01	0.033	0.048	0.103	0.27	
1994	0.061	0.01	0.013	0.044	0.11	0.238	61.34
USA							
1976	0.192	0.042	0.026	0.057	0.229	0.546	
1989	0.193	0.032	0.021	0.063	0.131	0.44	
1994	0.183	0.027	0.026	0.078	0.165	0.479	87.73
World							
1976	1.76	0.52	0.35	0.68	3.32	6.63	
1989	1.58	0.35	0.45	0.79	3.2	6.37	
1994	1.37	0.26	0.47	0.77	3.25	6.12	92.31

TABLE 3.9. (Cont'd)

Country and year	Intermediate skill sectors				Intermediate skills	1994 as % 1976	Cars	1994 as % 1976
	Engines	Machine tools	Metal machine tools	Non-electric machines				
France								
1976	0.212	0.252	0.06	0.345	0.869		0.448	
1989	0.193	0.142	0.022	0.205	0.562		0.415	
1994	0.218	0.15	0.024	0.234	0.626	72.04	0.344	76.79
Germany								
1976	0.244	0.822	0.325	0.881	2.272		0.846	
1989	0.3	0.653	0.154	0.736	1.843		1.38	
1994	0.306	0.602	0.137	1.563	2.608	114.79	1.052	124.35
Italy								
1976	0.083	0.258	0.063	0.255	0.659		0.207	
1989	0.065	0.27	0.058	0.314	0.707		0.187	
1994	0.09	0.333	0.061	0.376	0.86	130.50	0.147	71.01
Japan								
1976	0.168	0.265	0.149	0.315	0.897		0.695	
1989	0.295	0.43	0.193	0.457	1.375		1.512	
1994	0.433	0.491	0.153	0.621	1.698	189.30	1.121	161.29
Sweden								
1976	0.0577	0.1077	0.0253	0.149	0.3397		0.0778	
1989	0.0456	0.0674	0.0128	0.102	0.2278		0.1114	
1994	0.0509	0.0749	0.0145	0.1125	0.2528	74.42	0.085	109.25
UK								
1976	0.283	0.327	0.067	0.27	0.947		0.135	
1989	0.181	0.175	0.033	0.204	0.593		0.167	
1994	0.231	0.167	0.029	0.219	0.646	68.22	0.192	142.22
USA								
1976	0.357	0.865	0.159	0.778	2.159		0.377	
1989	0.538	0.424	0.068	0.403	1.433		0.393	
1994	0.521	0.492	0.098	0.588	1.699	78.69	0.416	110.34
World								
1976	2.24	3.71	0.96	3.68	10.59		3.63	
1989	2.64	2.55	0.97	4.16	10.32		5.59	
1994	2.53	3.17	0.7	4.08	10.48	98.96	5.13	141.32

Shares of the bundle of intermediate-skill goods stayed relatively stable. Japan, Italy, and Germany all increased theirs, while the other countries all saw reductions. This is consistent with the thesis that Germany specializes in such goods. Japan appears to do both this and to rival the USA in high-skill products, which explains that country's extraordinary export success until the mid-1990s. Both Germany and Japan provide broad-ranging, company-based training for particularly high proportions of their workforces, albeit through very different means. Italian performance is more surprising, unless we again allow for the role of the advanced small-firm sector in providing skills through informal means.

Finally, the evidence from the key automotive industry shows a sector in very strong growth overall. However, of our countries, only Japan saw its relative share increase, though the UK managed to hold its own (coming from a weak base and thanks to substantial Japanese investment in assembly plants in the UK). German industry held on to most of its previous high share, but other countries saw larger declines, especially France and Italy. This is an industry where the literature tells us considerable achievements were made in the 1980s and 1990s by countries improving work organization and in-house training of workers with poor education levels (Kochan *et al.* 1997; Streeck 1985; Womack *et al.* 1990).

SUMMARY AND CONCLUSIONS

We can summarize these changes in the following way. Between 1976 and 1989 'successful' exporting countries (Germany and Japan) came increasingly to depend on motor vehicles, especially cars. This industry accounts for a high volume of exports and has been quite labour intensive. It is, however, only a moderately skilled industry, though considerable within-firm upskilling took place during the 1980s. At the same time, all countries under review except Japan and (to a more limited extent) Italy saw major declines in their world share of exports in machine tools and other engineering sectors. Several of these industries have generally been important employers of somewhat higher-skilled people than the motor industry. With the exception of Italy and Japan, therefore, the decline of engineering tended to offset the growth of certain highly skilled industries (most commonly office machinery and pharmaceuticals). Especially where (as in Germany and Sweden) the growing importance to the national economy of motor vehicles accompanied a decline in more skilled forms of engineering, the depressing effect on skill levels was enough to wipe out any discernible effect of the general global move towards higher skills within metal manufacturing. During the 1990s a relative decline of the motor industry and a recovery in skilled engineering sectors have been the main factors increasing the education profile of most countries' exports.

In Italy there has been a strange combination of progress in higher-skilled sectors of engineering, but also with some important growth in niches in the fashion sector and furniture, the skill implications of which it is unfortunately difficult to establish. France is in general the median country of the group, with few outstanding strengths or weaknesses.

Paradoxically, the UK and to some extent the USA (overall weak exporters with persistent negative trade balances) have seemed better able to conform to the upskilling thesis, partly because they lacked the earlier important boost to exports from the motor industry. Given the small size of the workforce in the high-tech industries, there was no reason why countries which are seen in general as 'poor trainers' for the bulk of the workforce should not develop very high skills in some areas. This is particularly true for the USA, which does not need to participate in international trade or worry about its trade deficit as much as smaller economies do. In any case, the USA produces very large numbers of generally educated people, providing a large reserve of potential skill within which firms needing such workers can recruit.

A joint British study by the former Manpower Services Commission, the former National Economic Development Council, and the Institute of Manpower Studies (1984) compared VET responses to the dislocations of the 1970s and early 1980s in the UK, Germany, the USA, and Japan. Its findings followed those of this and other studies. Compared with the other three countries, the UK was seen as deficient in its development of engineering education. While German institutions had been slow to respond to signs of skill shortage, eventually Germany's response had been extensive and impressive. In the USA individual companies responded rapidly by building up their own training capabilities or partnering with outside education providers. In Japan the emphasis on flexibility meant that there was less constraint from having too few engineers, as people could move in and out of jobs, building on what they already knew to redress the skills shortage at intermediate levels. The other three countries were also seen as having better arrangements for co-operation and information exchange: maintaining basic data on training levels, but also looking at the location of training courses, the qualifications being awarded, their quality, their projections for supply and demand. The concentration of activities on individual companies in Japan and, to a lesser extent, the USA, has not meant that these countries did not have important government-funded and/or joint industrial centres for such tasks.

Of the countries under discussion in this book, three (Germany, the UK, and the USA) have been in the past general industrial powers, operating across a wide range of core, standard engineering, electrical, and chemical industries. These depended for competitive advantage, not on any particular natural-resource niches, but on the price and quality of goods that could in principle have been produced in a wide range of countries. The USA was partly exempted from the pressure of global competition by its continental stature, as had the UK in its earlier imperial period. By the 1970s both Italy and Japan had found competitive niches in relatively down-market and probably low-skilled manufacturing sectors. France and Sweden were similar to the general industrial powers, but had certain natural-resource endowments affording particular competitive advantages: in France an unusually strong food and agriculture sector; in Sweden industries moving downstream from wood and, to a lesser extent, iron ore into paper and metal manufacture.

By 1989 Japan and (to a lesser extent) Italy had moved out of their down-market niches to challenge the general industrial powers in the heartland of their competitive advantage. They made major inroads in machine tools and similar mechanical engineering industries; in Japan's case also making significant progress in the new high-tech sectors, while Italy built on its strong history in developing a new distinctiveness in fashion-related goods. France (and the USA) lost some of their niches in food, but Sweden became even more dependent on pulp and paper. Motor vehicles became the principal new weapon of competitive advantage for most countries, with office machinery and pharmaceuticals being small but fast growing.

The relatively modest nature of skills in motor-vehicle manufacturing suggests that this sector could not long remain a key industry for high-cost producers; most countries were losing many of the important niches that they held in engineering; the new high-skill industries tended not to employ many people. Of course, this analysis has had to exclude services sectors, which were a major source of employment growth during the period, though not so much of export activity. More research is needed to analyse their skill levels. Overall, however, the analysis, crude though it is, lends general support to the conclusion of the Swedish research: the restructuring of the 1980s left us a long way from the knowledge society.

By the 1990s the idea of the learning society had acquired more practical relevance in most of our countries. However, the very highly skilled sectors continue to represent small shares of total trade, and they employ relatively few people. It remains important, as we indicated in the previous chapter, to separate the mass of developments in employment from potentialities for export growth.

4

The State and Skill Creation: Inevitable Failure?

Despite the general crisis of confidence that currently surrounds state economic action, in most countries government continues to play significant roles in VET. Among these are: direct provision of initial or further VET in state-run and/or funded institutions (as a continuation of its normal role as the central provider of compulsory mass education and one of the main, if not sole, providers of higher education); regulation of the activity of other providers, including setting and monitoring skill standards and whether they are being achieved by all kinds of provider; establishment of incentive mechanisms to encourage private sector skill investment, including use of tax policy to create incentives for skill by such mechanisms as tax breaks for employer-provided tuition, reimbursement of cost of tuition provided by employers, or imposition of training levies on firms to discourage free riders and increase the supply of transferable skills. This last mechanism may or may not be combined with a corporatist delegation to associations sharing responsibility for administering public policy, distributing training funds, and monitoring delivery.

Even if the state is not active as a direct provider, its role will nearly always be central. It has the capacity, through its legislative and fiscal powers, to alter the institutional structure and hence the definition of the others' roles in a way that will not normally be matched by other actors in the VET system, with the possible exception of dominant corporations within small countries or some major and powerful employer organizations. It can also be expected to maintain a commitment to national economic success, as both the electoral chances of the government of the day and its attempt to pursue its policy goals are usually dependent on such success; even a government totally committed to a neoliberal strategy and believing in the complete autonomy of capitalist firms has to face the fact that it is itself rooted within a particular territory with responsibilities to a particular population. It is hardly viable for it to adopt the view that the economic fate of that population must depend entirely on market forces and the decisions of firms, or to propose to its people that they move in large numbers to another country in order to find good work prospects. It cannot avoid having some strategy for making its people attractive as employees, even if that simply means making them as cheap and exploitable as possible. The state will be particularly central to what we have identified as a core contemporary policy challenge: pursuing the goal of creating as highly skilled a working population as possible.

Government (national or local) normally provides general, usually compulsory, education for the majority of a nation's children. There is considerable diversity, however, where this responsibility begins to merge with the more specific tasks of equipping individuals with work skills, a responsibility that might be and is performed by various combinations of agencies. When does education become voluntary? When does it turn from being a general preparation for personal competence and culture and become more specifically oriented towards subsequent employment?

In some cases, state-provided or funded VET is restricted to mostly general education, leaving most subsequent action on skill creation to other agencies. Within the group of countries being considered here, this is largely the case in both Japan and the USA. Although in many respects VET arrangements in these two countries are very different from one another, they both exhibit a mixture of extensive but very general school preparation with specific training concentrated within firms, though in both cases there are local schools and colleges specializing in vocational skills for certain kinds of employment. Also, the Japanese state provides an elaborate national skill-testing system for standards of competence (Okuda 1996; Sako 1995). This system, which is usually seen as fundamental to Japanese skill creation, is quite external to the firms and is autonomous of professional and occupational associations as well as training providers, imparting a general public-interest component into what might otherwise seem to be a thoroughly private skill-creation system. At the other extreme, in France, Italy, and Sweden VET for a large number of occupations is provided in public schools and colleges. Germany is an intermediate case, with the state playing a more detailed role than in Japan and the USA, but in partnership with other agencies: regional governments co-operate with representative bodies of business to deliver the apprenticeship system. As in Japan, standards of competence for German skilled occupations are established in law (Backes-Gellner 1996: 111). Britain is rather complex. During the 1980s and 1990s there has been simultaneously a withdrawal of government from detailed provision but a strengthening of central government's role as opposed to those of local government and interest organizations (Finegold 1992; King 1993).

In all cases, considerable attention needs to be paid to the state's relationship to the other skill-creation actors. Where government provision stops at a general level, does government have any role or interest in subsequent VET (as in the Japanese skill-testing system), or does it simply leave matters to the market? If government is a direct provider of VET, what relationship does it, or rather the teachers working for it, have with these other actors, including firms? Government is also in a strong position to influence the allocation of skill-creation costs.

We shall here explore the practical rather than theoretical potentialities for government action in skill creation in the context of contemporary pressures, by examining recent experience in the two countries which would historically be regarded as the most effective exemplars of detailed direct state-led systems: France and Sweden. Some consideration will also be given to Italy as a less successful version of the French approach that leads to some interesting implications, and to the UK where the role of the state has been subject to remarkably frequent change.

FRANCE: THE STRONG PROVIDER STATE

Following a strategy that dates back ultimately to Napoleon's use of the state educational system to modernize France and generate national unity, French VET has long been a matter for central government. The state provides a varied educational system catering for the full range of what are perceived to be the economy's needs. At the élite level, schools for the production of practical engineers and scientists have long been accorded high status, alongside that for administrators and more classical forms of academic training. In some cases these institutions date back to even before the Revolution of 1789. Lower down the occupational hierarchy, training for all important vocational skills has also been provided in state schools. This has normally been undertaken outside the firm and with virtually no involvement from employers; there has been very little use of apprenticeships.

Outside the traditional luxury trades and the agricultural sector, post-war French industrialism was rooted in Fordist industry (Boyer 1988). Skills needs were not high and for many years did not vary much (Rault 1994: 17). It is not coincidental that France was the country that gave birth to the *régulationiste* school of socio-economic analysis which saw the active state alongside mass production industry as the core elements of the Fordist system (Aglietta 1979; Boyer 1988). A standardized mass education system could provide the basic mass stock skills needed by workers in the core production industries, and also by employees in the centralized and standardized public administration. During the first decades of post-war growth there was a ready supply of school-leavers to fill these sectors as, late in the day for such a leading economy, France shed its vast peasant population. Traditional agricultural work often required considerable knowledge and skill, but not of a kind registered in formal educational attainment. The educational level of the French rural population had been low, and the growth of general, highly standardized secondary schooling therefore made a major contribution to raising the educational position of the working population within the framework of a modernizing, integrating nation.

As these basic tasks were accomplished, the nature of demands changed. At one level, as an advanced economy with an unusually large agricultural sector, France encountered major problems of employment adjustment; the decline of industrial employment common to all advanced industrial economies set in while agriculture was still declining too. It became increasingly difficult to sustain full employment, as we saw in Chapter 2. Second, once the problems of providing general mass education had been solved, more sophisticated educational demands grew, both from employers wanting more advanced skills from their workforces and from young people seeking better employment opportunities. From the mid-1960s onwards the state system responded with many new courses and forms of qualification; and from 1970 it moved away from its classic aloofness in dealing with employer and labour representatives in key areas of public policy.

Developments in initial skill creation

The term *formation professionnelle*, which most readily translates as 'vocational education', is used in France to refer only to what we call here further VET. The concept of 'initial VET' is simply seen as that part of the state education system which orients students towards their subsequent working lives and in many cases equips them with vocational qualifications. These activities of the state school and higher education system do not involve employers, and hence are considered as separate from *formation professionnelle*. Our discussion of the system must therefore make a sharp distinction between the two stages.

From the mid-1960s onwards, but with increasing frequency since the 1980s, the state system has provided many new technical and other vocationally oriented courses within schools (Rault 1994). As in many other national systems, these vocational routes have to compete with widely recognized élite educational paths leading to higher education. In France this latter has taken the form of the prestigious *baccalauréat*, the classical gateway to advanced academic studies. The flexible structure of the *baccalauréat* enables and requires young people to study a wide range of subjects, while developing some specialization in a chosen area of expertise, tapping a diversity of types of ability. This has been flexible enough to serve as the basis for reform of the system. The government launched more vocationally oriented professional and technical *baccalauréat* tracks to accommodate a wider range of ability and student interest, bringing it closer to technical subjects, but has done so while sustaining the idea that access to higher education is the best available path. As a result, when *baccalauréats technologiques* were introduced in the 1960s to provide the labour market with well-educated technicians, they quickly became instead alternative routes to higher education (CEDEFOP 1994: 39). To the extent that this raised the educational expectations of technologically oriented young people, its impact on French technical education levels was probably favourable. However, it left unfilled the gap perceived lower down the educational ladder.

These gaps were partly filled by various institutes offering shorter courses than universities, directed towards technological employment (*sections de techniciens supérieurs* and *instituts universitaires de technologie*), and it is currently government policy to try to steer more young people towards these than to the traditional universities. At the same time other technical qualifications as well as new types of vocationally oriented higher education institutions have been developed.

Those who were assessed after two years of secondary education as unlikely to succeed in the academic routes were directed towards vocational education tracks leading to two-year courses for the *certificat d'aptitude professionnelle*[1] (CAP) or the *brevet d'études professionnelles*, or, if considered more able, to the technological *baccalauréats* stream and possibly thereafter back into higher education. Concern at this very early specialization led, however, to further reforms (Büchtemann and Verdier 1998). Four years of comprehensive secondary education now precede decisions about whether young people should take the CAP or a *brevet d'études professionnelles*, or move into the *brevet de techniciens supérieurs* or *diplôme universitaire de techniciens*, qualifying for technician levels of occupations. However, many of these courses continue to be seen as indicators of failure, and most young people seem to prefer to continue in general or technical educational routes (CEDEFOP 1994: 37; Büchtemann and Verdier 1998; Rault 1994: 12, 18–20). Being on a vocational course is usually the result of progressive elimination from the general system (Goux and Maurin 1998).

This variety of initiatives has led to a major increase in the proportion of school-leavers having some kind of formal qualification. However, youth unemployment has remained very high. Since the late 1970s French governments, like their counterparts elsewhere, have therefore developed a wide number of initiatives for encouraging the young unemployed to take courses and to link with employers in order to do so. These include temporary and other work contracts during which training will be given. Employers are given an incentive to participate in these schemes through such measures as remission of social security contributions for young workers engaged in part-time training and the possibility of paying reduced wages to the trainees for the work that they contribute to the enterprise. Sometimes the emphasis of policies has been on make-work schemes with little educational content rather than actual training for high skills; sometimes there is training but with few subsequent employment prospects, so that the main consequence is merely temporary removal from the unemployment register. It therefore becomes difficult with many of these policies to distinguish training from temporary job creation. These training arrangements are typically limited in duration—between six months and a year—and thus rarely impart extensive skills or inculcate corporate culture. At the same time, the public employment service is required to follow policies of training provision which are in reality merely counter-unemployment measures. The fact that they are known to be such by employers undermines their credibility as skill-creation devices (Garraud 1995), and leads to qualifications in such courses becoming stigmas rather than signals of skills attained (Clémençon and Coutrot 1995). The multiplication of courses has been accompanied by a multiplication of sources of vocational guidance, to the extent that during the 1990s the government has intervened to reduce the resulting complexity by instigating *carrefours* (crossroads) for vocational guidance where employers and young people in search of work might come together.

---

[1] Introduced in 1911, the CAP has resisted various attempts to replace it, and has survived alongside its intended successors, becoming since the 1970s a qualification mainly for young people with unsuccessful school careers (Rault 1994: 12, 22).

As Büchtemann and Verdier (1998) point out, France (like the USA) continues to run a primarily Fordist employment system, in which most young people apart from those with higher education start in secondary parts of the labour market with high labour turnover and little stability. Their hope is eventually to be recruited by a large firm with an internal labour market system, where they might receive specific skills training and advance up the hierarchy (Verdier 1996). The lower-level formal qualifications of the system are not particularly relevant to this employment path.

In this context, the massive expansion of general educational opportunities and participation in higher education in France in recent years has led mainly to further downgrading of the vocational education and apprenticeship routes. Meanwhile, there seems to have been little response by employers to the fact that potentially more able young people have become available (Culpepper 1998); higher qualifications are serving mainly as a signalling device, increasing competition among young people for a static supply of posts (Büchtemann and Verdier 1998; Erbés-Seguin, Gilain, and Kieffer 1994; Verdier 1996), with the result that ever higher qualifications are needed to secure jobs at a certain level (Goux and Maurin 1995). Since employers find that the state's vocational training (the CAPs) does not provide the broad skills and capacity for communication that they now want, they recruit young people with higher education qualifications instead (Abattu and Bel 1996). Holders of CAPs thus find they have no access to the kind of occupation for which they believed they were being trained, while graduates are recruited to occupations below the level they had anticipated when they undertook their education. This all marks a change for France. Previously, with a relatively small proportion of the population undergoing advanced education and with firms relying on internal training rather than the state system alone, formal qualifications did not play an important screening role (König and Müller 1986).

France thus remains in a low-skill equilibrium. Despite the fact that it has a relatively high number of unqualified young people and low levels of skills among the existing workforce, there is talk of an over-production, even a waste or squandering (*gaspillage*), of skilled human capital (Béduwé and Espinasse 1995: 545). While individuals' chances of improved employment increase with educational level, the employment prospects of young people with a given educational grade have worsened (Bourdon 1995). Despite the fact that successive cohorts of young people leaving the education system have higher and more diverse educational backgrounds than their predecessors, they experience increasing difficulties in finding employment—a smaller proportion of them able to find positions on completion of their studies than of their less well-educated predecessors two decades ago (Verdier 1996: 49). Recent evidence also suggests that firms prefer to use long-lasting combinations of internal promotion and external recruitment, resulting in consistent age profiles, and are not interested in shifting the balance of their recruitment structure in order to recognize changes taking place in the educational background of young people (Béduwé and Espinasse 1995).

Social partnership in further VET

The other major change in French skill creation in recent decades has been the move to incorporate social-partner organizations in formulating and to some extent administering provision of further VET. The abrupt shift in the long tradition of the French state largely excluding organized interests from public policy formulation was part of the major attempt of French labour policy to adopt a less confrontational approach to industrial relations following the dramatic shocks of May 1968. From 1970 onwards one can perceive a distinct attempt by the French authorities to model new initiatives on a German neo-corporatist or social-partnership model, though using distinctly French means of doing so.

The new approach can be seen in a number of policies. First, the peak organizations of business and labour were encouraged to negotiate agreements on training provision, which were formalized in law in 1984. Second, in 1988 government tried to stimulate *contrats d'études prospectives*, whereby branch-level associations would carry out surveys of future qualification and training needs; and in 1993 it introduced shared training plans between local branch associations and local government. Third, at firm level unions were given the right to negotiate over further skill-creation provision in the enterprise.

Finally, there has been considerable encouragement of the apprenticeship and *alternance* models of training. The former has been developing within industry since the early 1970s, reviving the familiar old form of vocational preparation long abandoned in France. The latter is a recent (1980s) innovation by government which seems to be becoming a rival to apprenticeship (Rault 1994: 23–4; 38). Under apprenticeship young people and their training are primarily under the control of the employing firm, though there is an input from the school system; under *alternance* they remain pupils of the state education system which also finances the arrangements.

At the core of these developments lie two major elements of French state VET policy: all employees have a right to take a certain proportion of paid leave from work to follow vocational training, and all firms over a certain size are required to spend a certain sum annually on training. Firms can satisfy this requirement by providing training themselves, by contracting training to an external agency, or by contributing to general training funds. The combination of a pressure for collective negotiation by social partners, the individual training right and the levy create considerable pressure on French firms to carry out further VET.

These policies have led to an impressive increase in the level of training activity. Since the levy was first imposed in 1971, French firms have increased their involvement in further VET until they have overtaken many of their German counterparts (Aventur and Brochier 1996; Backes-Gellner 1996; Finegold and Keltner 1997; Keltner, Finegold, and Pager 1996; Regini 1996*a*). It is in fact the only major example in the countries we have studied of government action securing a systematic response in further VET from the majority of firms, although similar arrangements have succeeded in boosting the level of training investment in Singapore and Australia. This is of fundamental importance. At a time of rapid technological and organizational change, the capacity of firms frequently to upgrade the skills of their workforce becomes a central component of any national skills strategy. This is a clear collective interest, but the provision of within-firm training to an existing workforce is a subject where employers are highly resistant to collective action. As in several other countries, however, the training provided by French employers is spent disproportionately on courses for managers and other already well-educated groups (Aventur and Brochier 1996: 95–6; Clémençon and Coutrot 1995). Not only are these courses that firms might well have provided even without the levy, but they hardly amount to measures to assist those with weak positions in the labour market needing additional skills creation to secure their places in the future. On the other hand, they have probably helped to notch up the performance of some firms whose activities can benefit from advancing skill levels.

The interface between initial and further VET

In all these initiatives there are problems that can be related to the distance between the government education system and employers. Employers rarely feel they share ownership of the courses or the qualifications which emerge from them (Abattu and Bel 1996). Government initiatives are launched without any prolonged preparation of the response that might be secured from the business community. This was perhaps unimportant in the initial post-war decades, where the standardized state education system could produce both the general educational level and the standardized skills required by the Fordist economy. During this more stable period of skill development there seemed little evidence that firms were dissatisfied with the activities of the system. Not only does this change with post-Fordist developments, but the attempts of the state education and training system to innovate in the new climate have usually been regarded by business as remedial action for the unemployed and hard-to-employ. Such state skill-creation initiatives are not seen as part of a new modernization but as the rescue of the casualties of modernization.

This existing tendency of French practice was not changed by the move to involve social partners in further VET; if anything those reforms made things more difficult, since they brought the area of further VET within the framework of labour law, and hence erected new barriers between it and groups external to the labour contract—such as the state school system and its teachers (CEDEFOP 1994).

Given these segregations of concern, it is not surprising that the attempts to encourage apprenticeship have not been very successful, since apprenticeship requires the mutual engagement of education institutions and organizations of employers (and probably also representatives of employees). Whereas in Germany apprenticeship long ago succeeded in being extended from the craft sector to large-scale industry and services, the French revival has been limited almost solely to the craft sector (especially in food), and certain personal services. Large firms in the core industrial sectors are almost entirely absent (ibid.; Culpepper 1998).

In terms of the two principal dilemmas for skill creation established in Chapter 1—reconciling the provision of leading-edge training with reducing mass unemployment, and reconciling private and public priorities—the French experience offers only mildly encouraging prospects for state policy. It has contributed very little indeed to resolution of the first dilemma. Frequent educational innovations for school-leavers have had little impact on either unemployment or the capacity of young people at the lower end of the education system to acquire qualifications in high-tech fields. On the latter dilemma, that concerning public and private priorities, the situation is more promising. Advances have been made in integrating the role of government and that of individual firms at the further VET level, principally through the levies. Little has however been achieved at the level of initial VET, where the gap between the state education system and the world of employers seems as wide as ever. This is not surprising in terms of the history of French education, but it leads to the paradoxical outcome that for France it has been easier to assert the role of collective action in further VET (the particular province of employers) than in initial VET.

SWEDEN: THE STRONG SOCIAL DEMOCRATIC STATE

Until the recent decline in competitiveness and rise in unemployment, Sweden had enjoyed many years of remarkable success as a capitalist economy with an unusually advanced capacity for generating public goods, not only by the state, but also through collective organizations. Within the labour market in general the most prominent features have been powerful, centrally co-ordinated associations of capital and labour, and statutory tripartite institutions within which these co-operate with government in both formulating and administering policy. In much research Sweden has been presented as almost the ideal type of a neo-corporatist economy, including the operation of active labour-market policy. These aspects of Swedish policy will be discussed in Chapter 5. However, it is important at this stage to note that the corporatist active labour market policy was, for most of its history, not concerned at all with training and skill formation.

Most formal VET has been administered directly by the state, while a very important but largely unacknowledged role has been played by the large corporations which dominate the Swedish economy. The combination of these (tripartite labour market policy, state basic VET, and large company further training) produced what might be called a distinctive 'up-market mass' labour market in manufacturing industry, a kind of sophisticated Fordism—as the analysis in Chapters 2 and 3 showed, not a distinctly high-skill sector. The well-educated portions of the Swedish workforce have primarily been employed in non-traded sectors of the economy. On the other hand, Swedish mass-producers were usually using skills in advance of those associated with pure Fordism. For example, the country's important wood and paper industries have moved over the years to higher-quality niches as new producing countries have emerged at the bulk end of the market. Similarly, although the original Taylorist industry, the motor industry, has been dominant in Sweden, its two important motor firms (Volvo and Saab) have been clearly focused on the high-quality end of the market, not bulk production for mass markets, and therefore required relatively better skilled workers. Further, Sweden's historically tight labour markets encouraged motor industry employers to take special steps to attract workers to an industry with a reputation for boring production-line jobs. This precipitated radical experiments with self-managed work teams with polyvalent skills and job rotation at Volvo's Kalmar and, especially, Udevalla plants. These were later judged to have been unsuccessful (Lawler *et al.* 1992); while this new work organization achieved the desired impact on employee motivation and satisfaction, it proved unable to compete successfully with the less empowering, but more efficient, lean production model pioneered by Toyota. There has however been some suspicion that Udevalle was closed because management did not like its highly participative approach (Sandberg 1994).

A clear awareness of the skill challenges facing the Swedish labour market was demonstrated in the early 1960s by the appointment of the Yrkesutbildnings-utredning (Vocational Education Commission) that reported in 1966 (Sweden 1966), and on which (as usual in Sweden) the labour market partners were strongly represented. Although the Commission issued its report more than three decades ago, it shares the rhetoric of skill-creation policy documents being produced in most advanced countries in the 1990s. It spoke of the dependence of the future Swedish economy on skilled manpower and of the need in an automated age for workers with general vocationally relevant competence rather than specific work skills (ibid.: ch. 8). Because knowledge was changing so fast, schools needed to provide a strong general base, and companies would be expected to follow this up with frequent in-house training and retraining (ibid.: 116, 117, 122–7). It went on to propose major changes in the structure of Swedish education, which were largely adopted.

Until 1970 academically oriented children had moved at the age of 14 to *gymnasie*, those more interested in technical subjects went to a small number of technical schools, those seeking to follow a skilled manual craft went to appren-ticeship-based *yrkesskolor*, and the rest went straight into employment. The *yrkesskolor* had developed from earlier, more apprenticeship-like institutions in a joint policy initiative by the SAF and LO in 1944 (Sweden 1966: chs. 2 and 4). These two organizations had maintained a joint committee (Yrkesutbilding-skomitet, later Arbetsmarknadsråd) to oversee the system and to regulate those aspects of it that retained its apprenticeship features through collective agree-ments. Apprenticeships, however, were increasingly evaluated negatively by the policy-makers, although they had once been the main form of preparation of skilled manual workers, and still are in neighbouring Denmark. From early in the post-war period (1955) it had been social-democratic strategy to bring vocational education out of the workplace and into the schools. This was not an attack on vocationalism as such, only on the role of firms as its lead providers; within the schools the Social Democratic Labour Party (SAP) and the unions wanted vocational education to be increased, but with scope for mobility into other forms of education so that young people did not have to commit themselves to careers in manual work at an early age with little scope for subsequent career mobility (Axelsson 1989: 46). In this way the provision of skill creation in this most corporatist of labour markets ceased to take corporatist form and became a more statist model, like the French.

The Commission proposed bringing together the previously separate academic, technical, and vocational schools into single institutions (*gymnasieskolor*), with frequent opportunities for transfer and therefore maintenance of a good deal of common curricula. Pupils would, however, have to choose a specific branch of the school, and within the vocational branch they could specialize in a specific 'line' (*linje*), relating to the skills and techniques needed within a particular branch of industry. It was assumed by the reformers that labour demand from firms would broadly determine the number of places available in the various vocational lines, with freedom of choice for individual pupils within those constraints (ibid.: 104, ch. 10). Pupils would receive a mix of theoretical and work-related education, the latter making use of realistic workshops within schools, but not entry into the real shop-floor as in apprenticeship. Social democrats and trade unionists were adamant that young people at school should be pupils under school jurisdiction and not cheap employees.

The primary aim of the major school reform introduced following the report in 1970 was to improve general educational opportunities. But this central social democratic ideal dovetailed neatly with the views of both sides of industry on the educational needs of future employment. The vocationalist contribution to school reform was strong. It is, however, important to note how the introduction of *gymnasieskolor* led to the state effectively further marginalizing the interest organizations in the administration of foundation VET (Nilsson 1981: ch. 5). The Yrkesmarknadssråd remained in existence; employers' organizations and trade unions remained represented both nationally and locally in school administration; and employers' organizations continued to help formulate curricula for school vocational lines. But individual companies as well as the organizations were considerably less involved in day-to-day administration, quality assurance, and change than their counterparts in Germany, Denmark, or Austria working within an apprenticeship model.

This was still not considered a problem by business interests, as firms were confident that the school sector could deliver the general vocational skills that were needed; each school had allocated to it a bipartite advisory committee for each vocational line. Although practical training would be in school workshops rather than in company ones, these were meant to be as 'realistic' as possible, and the positive features of the old apprenticeship system were commended in the 1966 report (Sweden 1966: 222). The move to two-year school courses rested on an assumption that firms would themselves provide an initial year's training for new entrants.

Problems of under-achievement and work–school links

Once the system had been established policy concern shifted to early leavers and drop-outs (Standing 1988: 99; Sweden 1976; 1979; 1980; 1989*b*: 278), to the bottom 15% of the achievement range, and to other social (class, regional, gender, etc.) goals (Nilsson 1981: 223–8). Politicians and social policy experts dominated policy making rather than the labour market interest organizations (ibid.: 236–42). There was continued dissatisfaction with the rate of success in keeping young people in education, leading to a new government inquiry and a new programme (Sweden 1986*a*, *b*) that outlined measures (easy transitions between grades, slow lanes, part-time study, counselling services) aimed at persuading all potential early leavers to stay at school. Because the school system itself was widely seen as too rigid, the task of administering these programmes was given to a group within the tripartite body supervising the national labour market policy, Arbetsmarknadstyrelsen (AMS, the Labour Market Board), working on the problems of following up early leavers, though using the schools as the locations for study (Sweden 1989*c*: 127–32). Certain other state initiatives outside the school system and related to skill-creation needs were also introduced, but still as a by-product of social democratic concerns about welfare and full employment.

Unlike France, Sweden was not at that stage faced with widespread youth unemployment; problems were rather perceived as those of motivation and vocational orientation. By 1989, 50% of young people in *gymnasieskolor* were taking vocational courses, 35% academic courses, and 15% technical courses (Sweden 1989*a*: 18–31). The proportion of young people staying on at school beyond the compulsory school-leaving age of 16 had risen from about 70% in the mid-1970s, to 85% of 16–17-year-olds by 1987, and the great majority were remaining there until 18 or 19 (Sweden 1989*c*: 74). There were, however, continuing problems in encouraging students to take examinations and qualifications. Further, although 95% of the school-leavers of the mid-1980s sought a place at a *gymnasieskola*, 10% dropped out after one year, and another 7% a year later (though some later returned) (Sweden 1989*c*: 114–16, 121). Only 56% of those seeking a vocational skills line secured their first choice. Some lines (such as engineering) had been kept large because in the long run labour demand was expected to be high within them, though in practice this demand fluctuates over time. Young people were reluctant to enter these lines because of an apparent scarcity of jobs, though they were forced into doing so by the relatively greater availability of educational places in them. The young people's apprehensions often proved justified, as many engineering graduates from the programme found that they could not get work (Axelsson 1989: 133–4; Sweden 1989*c*: 117–20).

Employers, especially those in engineering, had been critical of the level of mathematics teaching and its lack of integration with the training, including hands-on practical aspects of training, in technical subjects (ibid.: 144). There was also anxiety that the education system was adapting only slowly to changes in the workplace (Standing 1988: 99). The school system concentrated its training for the engineering industry on machine tooling, which catered for about 30% of the workforce. The other 70% of frontline employees in the sector were recruited from various different educational backgrounds and lacked specific skills. In contrast, some people who had taken four-year technical courses in engineering found themselves in manual jobs in the industry. This solved some problems of skill, but at a cost in terms of workers' morale. Given that all but the largest firms tended not to provide an initial year's training, there was growing disillusion with the initial skill-creation system among both employers and young people.

An analysis of competence levels in the Swedish economy (Landell and Victorsson 1991) was sceptical of the contribution being made by skill development to Swedish economic performance, finding the educational level of employees, especially manual workers, to be directly related to company profitability in only some sectors (ibid.: 52–8). Those which had grown most in size and profits in recent years had often not been those with the most skilled workforces, though there had often been a positive association with a high proportion of white-collar and technological staff in the workforce (ibid.: ch. 3). In some knowledge-intensive and other key export sectors (for example, drugs, machine tools, transport equipment, and motor vehicles) there had been a polarization between a low-skilled manual workforce and highly qualified non-manual employees (see also the official statistics in Sweden 1992*a*: 111–34).

Widespread agreement was developing that the country would need to relocate itself within high-skilled labour markets to regain international competitiveness. The government therefore appointed the Kompetensutredning or Competence Commission, with the usual representatives of major organized interests and political parties. In a number of publications, including its final report (Sweden 1992*b*), the Commission presented the detailed case for a high-skilled Sweden to compete in high value-added niches within a highly competitive, post-Fordist international economy. There was agreement on all these central arguments. The report argued a need for Swedish firms to move to the model of *den lärende organisationen* (the learning (or teaching) organization)—a concept that had been earlier used by the SAF. In an interim report the Commission had signalled an important change in Swedish thinking by stressing the centrality of the workplace as the main locus of change, and therefore the need for policy to address that and not just the societal level (Sweden 1991*a*: 25–33); though use of the word 'workplace' rather than 'company' glossed over major differences of understanding between employers and unions.

The otherwise broad agreement within the Commission could not progress beyond this point. Representatives of the SAF and the Moderate Party wished to make training the responsibility of employers alone. They therefore opposed

the concept of a tax subsidy for collectively agreed training programmes, advocating instead just a general reduction in business taxes so that employers might
provide some training with the retained resources if they so chose (Sweden 1992*b*:
85–6, 90, 91). This was a radical departure for Swedish business policy making
on training; it went beyond the principle of rejecting union participation in training and denied the entire public goods concept within training provision. The
SAF's representatives had the changing political situation in mind. By the time
the report was published the government had changed, and one committed to a
'British' neo-liberal economic policy had been elected. Although the Commission's reports continued to be published they now embodied no agreed strategy
for the future.

Although the bourgeois government that took office in 1991 wished to change
the high-wage, high social cost trajectory of the social democratic period, it accepted
that Sweden would not be able to find its competitive edge in low-cost production, but rather in high value-added products (Sweden 1992*a*: 125). No one argued
that the existing skill-creation system was able to provide this. No important voices
sought protection from a growing internationalization of the economy as an escape
from the need to adapt. Employers and unions were also united in believing that
the 'world of work' or *arbetsliv* must move closer to young people during their
period of initial VET than the 1970 model provided. There was consensus over
the need to move beyond the 'up-market mass worker' to the skilled post-Fordist
employee, and some limited acceptance on the union side that this meant some
gestures towards greater involvement by individual companies.

The new government interpreted this consensus in ways that favoured the
new policy preferences of the employers' organizations, which were far from universally accepted. The context within which skill-creation policy was being made
now comprised a more rapid deterioration of the country's economic position
and a collapse of the familiar tripartite system.

The government's main opportunities for a policy initiative lay in foundation
VET within the schools, where it instituted some distinctive changes to a policy
that had already been developing under the previous social democratic administration (Sweden 1991*b*). First, there would be an increase in the post-secondary
(post-16) stage of school education from two to three years (Sweden 1992*c*: 55).
Under the bourgeois government's amended proposals, anxieties about motivat-
ing young Swedes for vocational study, especially for industrial skills, continued
to dominate thinking (ibid.: 80–90). There would be a considerable articulation
and decentralization of policy, with national curricula being capable of local
adjustment (ibid.: 52–3, 74 ff.).

Second, the curriculum was restructured on more strongly vocational lines
(Ball and Larsson 1989: 13–14), with students spending periods of time within
firms. As in France there were also moves for a return to apprenticeship. A parallel apprenticeship model was provided for, to exist alongside the school model
for each school programme, should industries and local education authorities
want to take advantage of it. Within this model, at least 15% of students' total

time is spent at a workplace, but the local school authority remains responsible for the quality of training provided by the firm. There are joint advisory bodies between schools and trade and industry organizations at local levels to supervise the programmes. Meanwhile, within the school part of their education, students on these programmes continue to study general subjects to ensure that the knowledge base they acquire is not too narrow.

More radically, some large firms sought a return to a nineteenth-century Swedish pattern of 'company schools', in which children might, if their parents so chose, take their secondary education at a school controlled by a firm rather than by the local authority. The Education Act of 1992 provided that if a company wished to establish a school, public funds that would otherwise have gone to the local *kommun* schools would be diverted to it. By 1994 some large firms had established such schools.

Summary

As the above discussion shows, there has been little anxiety in Sweden that the large companies that dominate the economy would not participate in skill creation. As long as they regarded Sweden as their major base, such firms were likely to be sensitive to arguments about collective goods. This collective orientation of large Swedish firms has to be set alongside the country's more frequently acknowledged history of social democracy when assessing the particular ease with which Sweden has, until recently, pursued collectively oriented public policy. However, in recent years there has been a loosening of the bond of Swedish firms to Sweden. Liberalization of Swedish capital markets increased the opportunities for Swedish multinationals to develop manufacturing capacity abroad. At the same time the solidaristic collective bargaining system also began to break down. Elements of the Swedish model which enabled the various partners to take a certain level of co-operation for granted were collapsing. This affected the set of institutions governing the labour market.

Although the Swedish state had acquired a strong reputation for the efficiency of its active labour market policy and the universalism of its welfare state, it is important to note that this had not extended to the creation of a particularly highly skilled manufacturing workforce. The corporatist structures that had made possible an effective job placement service, as will be described in the next chapter, did not play much of a role in VET provision. They were therefore not available to provide a nuanced mediation between educational service and employing organizations. Initial VET provided the skills for a Fordist workforce at skill levels only slightly superior to the French system. It is too early to see how recent reforms have affected this situation, though it would seem that the country's capacity to generate high levels of vocational skill will depend increasingly on the preferences of the large corporations, which, as we have seen, are less and less dependent on the Swedish economy and workforce for their success.

ITALY: THE WEAK PROVIDER STATE

France and Sweden demonstrate how even states with strong historical records of skill provision encounter severe difficulties under current competitive conditions of rapid occupational change, the pivotal role of individual firms, and attempts at combining national strategies for equipping the 'learning society' with measures to help the unemployed and those hard to employ, usually because of some educational deficiency. These problems of state failure are seen even more clearly if we examine two states with weak past records of state-led skill creation activity, Italy and the UK.

The Italian Republic inherited an education system that partly imitated the French model of strong, autonomous central state action and partly followed lines established during the Fascist period, being based on strict segregation of educational routes, devoted to the production of a classically educated élite and a rudimentarily educated mass, schools for the latter including some basic vocational education (Cobalti and Schizzerotto 1998). The radical centralization of previously fragmented systems that it involved played an important part in the establishment of a common language spoken and understood by most Italians. Reforms did not begin until the 1960s; the system of the pre-war period was therefore that under which much of today's Italian workforce has been educated.

The reform process was primarily geared towards changing the radical inequalities of opportunity and early segregation of the Fascist period. A system of 'comprehensive' schools (*scuole medie uniche*) was established in 1962 to take children through the first stage of secondary schooling without segregation into different tracks, thereby postponing the point at which they would be required to choose between academic and vocational education. Further reforms in the late 1960s made possible transfer to university by students from the two main higher grades of vocational school, *istituti tecnici* and *istituti professionali*.

There was little concern in these reforms for vocational skills, the main political aim being to provide possibilities of access to university education to pupils from disadvantaged backgrounds. Even within these terms, little was done substantively to improve opportunities, the main consequences being an extension of formal rights and theoretical possibilities. They have led to no diminution in inequalities in the chances of children from underprivileged backgrounds achieving social mobility (Cobalti and Schizzerotto 1998; Shavit and Westerbeek 1995). Although the principle of pupil (or pupil and parent) choice of direction after the first stage of secondary schooling seemed to be enshrined, young people and their families were heavily constrained in their choices by teachers' advice and by their own perceptions and knowledge of possibilities, risks, and opportunities. The level of inter-generational occupational mobility has, not surprisingly, remained one of the most limited in western Europe (ibid.). In addition, large numbers of young people leave school with no qualifications at all (Gambetta 1987).

For many years after the Second World War the country's primary economic project had been to move from low-skilled agriculture to the low-skilled Fordist industries of the north. This did not require a national goal of maximizing all individuals' competences. The education system managed to produce an educated élite to man a relatively small advanced sector in oil refining, machine tools, and some branches of chemicals. Whilst the decline of agriculture produced a labour surplus, the growing industries of the north had large appetites for relatively unskilled labour. And there was considerable migration from the depressed south of the country to the north. Beyond that, the country still made use of considerable labour emigration.

Change came during the 1980s. The production of a highly skilled labour force became an issue of national political importance and not just a private matter for firms and VET institutions (Bresciani 1987: 55). There was now a more or less formal public commitment by virtually all political forces and the social partners to turn Italy into a country with an advanced, high-skilled labour force (D'Avanzo 1992). Also, as in many other countries, work skills were coming to be seen more in terms of flexible, general competences and developed intelligence rather than specific 'skills' in the sense of the former industrial economy— whether Fordist or craft based (Meghnagi 1989; 1991). Experts began to talk of needs for advanced general capacities, for the ability to learn how to learn, for the fusion of humanistic and technical skills (Cevoli, Palmieri, and Tagliaferro 1992; Zuccon 1992).

Given the deadlocked and untrusted character of the Italian state itself—a considerable contrast with France—the most important thing that central government has achieved so far has been to facilitate potential action by regional authorities (Infelise 1996: 175). In 1976 a new tier of government was established at the level of the region, in addition to the *comune* and provincial levels that already existed. In many fields of policy there was subsequently a struggle between the political centre and the regions over respective competences. Within the field of skill creation the new elected regional authorities were in 1978 (*legge* (law) 845) granted comprehensive responsibilities for lower-level VET, provided they acted in consonance with the state schools (Napoli 1984). They used their new powers, including a limited power to legislate, to establish courses primarily for relatively low-level manual and technical skills, but by the early 1990s several had moved on also to organize some continuing education for existing workers (Isfol 1992: 25–8), and second-level (post-secondary) courses (mainly for the tertiary and information technology sectors (ibid.: 34–42)). Courses have increasingly been oriented to the world of work through relations with interest organizations, including the development of apprenticeships (ibid.: 40–1). These activities have been an important supplement to the pattern of provision, though they have contributed further to the overall lack of integration of the system. There has continued to be overlap between the vocational components of the state schools' mission and the role of the regions, while the latter have sometimes sought to provide more general education than strict VET. The boundary between the roles of the two levels of authority was never clearly defined in law and remained more of an aspiration than a clear rule (Napoli 1984: ii: 4).

Public policy instruments have at least started to leave the rigid bureaucratic models of the past; more effort is being devoted to relations with industry; and the growing prominence of the regions brings labour market policy a little closer to the main loci of action in the Italian small-business economy (discussed further in Chapter 6). However, in general one cannot yet conclude that the flexibility of local levels of Italian government have really begun to compensate for the cumbersome nature of the national state; nor has that state reformed itself so that it presents an example of successful government involvement in vocational training, and certainly not one engaged in equipping its national workforce with the highest possible skills. As in several other countries, public agencies tend to concentrate on remedial activity for the unemployed, while private training providers provide short courses for specific company needs (Infelise 1996: 182). The version of Fordism for which the main education system prepared young Italians was a particularly low-skilled form, and moving from that to the skills required in a contemporary advanced economy has not proved easy.

Meanwhile the phenomenon of apparent over-qualification that we noted in connection with France also affects Italy. Unemployment rates are notoriously far higher in the depressed south of the country than in the northern and central regions. However, education levels are higher in the south, particular in comparison with the prosperous centre (Shavit and Westerbeek 1995; Iannelli 1999). This is particularly true for young women, where unemployment is concentrated among those with high educational qualifications. The reasons for this are not fully known, but it is likely that formal education is not particularly important for occupational success in the north-east and central regions of the country, where the economy is dominated by small family firms. Meanwhile, as Esping-Andersen (1996) has pointed out, southern Italy (and Spain) are notable for their poor development of professional public service employment (especially education, health, and welfare), which as we saw in Chapter 2 is a major employer of qualified female labour in virtually all advanced countries.

THE STATE AND THE FIRM: THE CASE OF THE UK

Historically the UK has had apprenticeships in many sectors, working, as these normally must, through organizations of employers. This was closer to a 'German' corporatist approach than the direct state-school provision systems predominating in the other countries discussed in this chapter. However, corporatist arrangements in the UK have usually been weak, and concern has long been expressed about their adequacy, leading to various bouts of government intervention. These have mainly taken the form of reinforcements to corporatism, but by the late 1980s this was entirely abandoned, at least as an object of government policy. Indeed, the intention of subsequent policy initiatives was to dismantle the last vestiges of corporatism. This has not led the UK to move to a direct state-provision model, but to state encouragement of voluntary, non-corporatist participation by firms in initial VET arrangements. From this emerge certain novelties that make the country worth considering under the heading of state policy.

In both general and vocational education there were two important moments of policy initiative in Britain in the years between the post-war establishment of the welfare state and the start of its dismemberment in 1979. In the mid-1960s major institutional innovations were made and related to important needs of national competitiveness, but not pursued with any sense of urgency. In the mid-1970s both the general crises around the oil-price shocks and more specific anxieties about the state of the British economy produced further policy responses. As in other countries, most concern during the 1960s focused on the general education system and the issue of educational opportunities. The main development was the introduction of comprehensive schools, aimed at breaking down barriers erected by the school system to children acquiring educational qualifications. The policy was impelled partly by a concern to satisfy anxious parents at a time of a growing school-age population, and also to increase the number of people who might secure qualifications. Under the previous system, only the top third of the ability range who passed the entrance exam at the age of 11 to attend grammar schools stood much chance of obtaining recognized academic qualifications and remaining in school past the age of 15. A minority, mostly male, of the remaining two-thirds secured apprenticeships, and the rest of young people entered the workforce unqualified. Reforms to the vocational part of the system largely took a corporatist form, encouraged by a state levy, and will be discussed in that context in the following chapter.

When schools policy returned to the agenda in the mid-1970s there was a less optimistic mood. Standards of school achievement were generally perceived to be low, but the causes were seen variously as being about inadequate resources, modern educational methods, or mismatch between education and vocational needs—depending on the political position of those making the criticism (Finegold 1992: 197–200). Concern about the vocational relevance of education was included in this agenda, but mainly in terms of the possible vocational implications of deficiencies in general skills, such as mathematics—an issue raised in particular by the then Prime Minister, James Callaghan (Callaghan 1976). Specific concern about skill creation concentrated as before on the adequacy of co-operation between state institutions and the business world, and the main response was a strengthening of corporatism through the establishment of the Manpower Services Commission (MSC). Its work will be considered in detail in the next chapter, but since for a period it was the main vehicle of government skill-creation policy, it is important here to note its main initiatives.

The main neo-liberal thrust of policy began in 1979 with the prolonged period of Conservative rule. The Thatcher government did not want the MSC to interfere with the private choices of firms to move to new levels of achievement in the general skill-creation area. Its tripartite structure was not therefore used to take major initiatives on apprenticeship (as in Germany), active labour-market policy (as in Sweden and its own early years), or within-firm further VET. Its focus was partly remedial, which meant, as in other countries, providing training opportunities for the unemployed. Perhaps even more than elsewhere, the belief that government should concern itself only with residual welfare tasks and not interfere at levels of initiative and enterprise, led to these skill-creation policies being concentrated at the low end of the skills spectrum. Also, the emphasis of neo-liberal policy was on employability through reducing the price of labour rather than on skill creation by government involvement in economic decisions. The Youth Training Scheme (YTS), with its relatively low weekly allowance, was used to make young people more attractive to employers by reducing individuals' reservation wage and giving firms an opportunity to screen young people before making a job offer, so reducing job security (Boyle 1997); young people who did not accept a training place were cut off from all state benefits. The MSC was also able to concern itself with what was happening in schools, which, being public institutions, were not included in the government's preference for *laissez faire*.

A growing proportion of government educational spending was channelled through the MSC, which began to encroach on the territory of the still traditionalist Department of Education (Finegold 1992: 223–6), in particular launching experiments in teaching style and content in vocational education. It often worked in partnership with local education authorities (LEAs), towards whose autonomy the Education Department was becoming hostile. Its most interesting programme was the Technical and Vocational Education Initiative (TVEI) (ibid.). This concentrated on trying to create a separate, more work-oriented technical and vocational path within full-time education to rival the dominance of the academic track, not through the creation of new qualifications, but through innovations in teaching techniques and content. Given its temporary and experimental nature, it did not manage to produce great changes in the content of the curriculum, but it had considerable impact in challenging teaching methods and subject boundaries (Bennett and McCoshan 1993: 144), though its hopes that local businesses would become more heavily involved were largely disappointed, for various structural reasons (ibid.: 144–5).

The Department of Education began to fight back. In 1987, a year of crisis in the MSC (see Chapter 5), the department produced its own major reform of the entire education system embodied in the Education Reform Act 1988. This departed from the MSC's legacy in two major respects. First, it established a national curriculum of subject content and teaching and assessment methods, which marked a move back towards traditionalism and left little time in the school day for vocational subjects. Second, whereas the MSC had worked closely with LEAs and co-operative networks of schools and further education colleges established by them, the new Act considerably increased the autonomy and mutual competition of individual schools and reduced the authority and role of LEAs.

A subsequent Education Act in 1991 removed further education colleges, the main providers of skill-creation courses, from the LEA ambit altogether, and established them as autonomous institutions competing for central government funds with each other and with private providers. The Education Department's final revenge over encroachment from employment policy on to its turf came in 1995, when the Department of Employment itself was abolished and its residual functions absorbed into the renamed Department for Education and Employment. The main significance of this last move was the government's neo-liberal assertion that there was no such thing as a general policy on employment.

All these changes did not mean that the government had ceased to regard skill creation as a relevant area for policy making, though reversal of the MSC's experiments and the search for another new approach after only six years produced new discontinuities and reinforced the difficulties of developing long-term horizons in British VET policy. However, the principal emphasis remained unchanged: there was a focus on employability (through such measures as labour-market deregulation and removal of the right of young people to unemployment benefit) as much as on skills; and the skill-creation component of the strategy concentrated on very basic skills. There was, however, a renewed attempt to engage the interest of business people, especially at local levels. Two developments were particularly significant: the formation of Training and Enterprise Councils (TECs) (which will be discussed in Chapter 6 and which have been the principal instrument of business participation), and the introduction of National Vocational Qualifications (NVQs) and General NVQs (GNVQs). The two were related in that TECs have had an important role in the provision of training for NVQs.

NVQs have primarily been pursued by people in relatively low-skilled work, since they are designed to demonstrate competence within a particular job rather than to show how well individuals are prepared for a range of jobs. Among young people, this has meant that the main use of NVQs has been by those not considered adequately academically qualified to take the General Certificate of Education ('A' Level) examinations, the main route into higher education that represents the core academic channel for pupils until the age of 18. NVQs are not, however, limited only to young people but might be taken at any age.

NVQs comprise a system of competence-based qualifications intended primarily for people who have already secured a job. They constitute the first nationally integrated system of certifying non-academic vocational courses in Britain. They exist at a number of levels: NVQ 1 (basic); NVQ 2 (semi-skilled);[2] NVQ 3 (craft/technician); NVQ 4 (technician/supervisor); NVQ 5 (professional). It is hoped that the standards of NVQ 3 will rival those of the German *Facharbeiter*

---

[2] Officially NVQ 2 is described by the British government as 'basic craft', but given the narrowness of the competences assessed it is unlikely that it can really be considered equivalent to craft in the normally understood sense of skilled work. It is agreed by most impartial observers that it is only at level 3 that NVQ corresponds to European Union definitions of skilled work (Backes-Gellner 1996: 111; Prais 1989).

grade. NVQs 4 and 5 are said to be equivalent to higher education, but to date there have been too few cases of qualifications at these levels to determine the validity of this. Work towards NVQs levels 1–3 is often carried out all or in part on employers' premises. Young people not pursuing academic courses leading to examinations are equipped with vouchers for a certain amount of training leading to NVQs. They lodge these vouchers with the college or employer providing the in-service component of the training, and the employer can claim back funding from the government to the value of the voucher to compensate for having provided training.

The NVQ system is presided over by a National Council for Vocational Qualifications (NCVQ) which includes persons from the business world, though it is dominated by bureaucrats capable of administering NCVQ's complex competence-based approach to creating standards. Standards for specific qualifications are, however, developed by so-called 'Lead Bodies', which are dominated by employer representatives.

NVQs differ from the traditional certification systems often associated with apprenticeships in that they prescribe no amount or particular form of training, rather focusing solely on the demonstration of a capacity to perform closely specified tasks. While this in theory can foster greater innovation among VET providers, the absence of theoretical components means that there is much less preparation in polyvalency than in German apprenticeships; there is no necessary attempt to teach understanding of a work task rather than its mere execution (Backes-Gellner 1996: 121; Prais 1989: 53). The competences may be learned entirely on the job, or training may be given by a number of agencies, including established colleges of further education and also private training firms, the numbers of which have grown considerably in recent years. Institutions wishing to provide courses are required to enter a cost competition to do so. Local TECs have the responsibility for awarding contracts to provide particular courses for accreditation, the costs of courses being a prime consideration to which they must have regard. This tends to favour the new training companies over the established colleges (which had in any case often been regarded by employers as out of touch with their needs (Bennett and McCoshan 1993: ch. 7)), as the private training firms tend not to have the burden of full-time, trained, and often unionized staff.

Much day-to-day quality control is in the hands of assessors in individual firms and TECs, which have a financial incentive to claim large numbers of successful candidates. The system is monitored by only a small inspectorate of the NCVQ, which also has an incentive to proclaim the success of the scheme. In addition to potentially undermining confidence in the quality of the system, this leads to difficulties in securing reliable information on its progress and, more important, problems in ensuring reliability across sites (Wolf 1995). For example, Robinson and Steedman (1996) have shown that claims by NCVQ that three million people had completed or were working towards NVQs in 1995 were deceptive since they counted as separate persons for each course entry. In fact, most people entered for several courses, and the authors conclude that only about 600,000 separate individuals were enrolled.

It was in recognition of the fact that NVQs did not provide the broad occupational foundation young people require that NCVQ created the GNVQ, which is mainly intended for young people still in full-time education, to be taken as an alternative to academic qualifications. It exists at three levels, Foundation, Intermediate, and Advanced, the last being officially deemed equivalent to two 'A' Levels and therefore qualifying for entry into higher education. In this way the NVQ system is in principle related back and made equivalent to qualifications in the academic system. In addition, beginning in late 1993 the government attempted to revive and modernize apprenticeships, using GNVQ's competence-based framework, rather than the old time-served model.

NVQs and GNVQs have become the main form of training accreditation for a wide range of occupations, but mainly in the sheltered sectors of the economy. Traditional forms of qualification continue to outnumber it in exposed sectors and for crafts and other more advanced technical occupations (Robinson and Steedman 1996). However, although they often lack the base of support from employer associations and trade unions enjoyed by the old craft apprenticeships, while doubts persist about their educational and occupational value, and although they still embody a separation of academic from skill-creation education within schools, NVQs have at least established for the first time in England a chain of nationally recognized VET qualifications that have, via the GNVQ, some relationship to the academic streams (Backes-Gellner 1996: 129).

It is too early yet to determine whether NVQs will acquire a reputation as good qualifications for skills. The NVQ system is still in its relative infancy, and the numbers going through to higher levels remain very small. A major anxiety which will only be resolved in time is whether its standards really will be high enough, and how many employers will bother to take part (Bennett and McCoshan 1993: 193). In 1991 the government established the target that 50% of the workforce be working for an NVQ by 1996, but this had to be dropped when in 1995 only 2% of the workforce was in fact doing so (Robinson and Steedman 1996). By 1996 the only net growth in vocational qualifications awarded as a result of the introduction of NVQ was at the low levels of 1 and 2, while GNVQ has only replaced existing qualifications, not resulted in any overall growth (ibid.). Also, the existing structure of vocational qualifications which was to be replaced and rationalized by NVQ has continued to exist (ibid.).

NVQs constitute a rare example of an employer-based training system without corporatist monitoring. That does, however, raise questions about the ability of the policy-makers to resolve the collective action problem among employers. Given its avoidance of high public spending, government is unwilling to offer more than small financial inducements to replace the pressure that might come from employer organizations in a more corporatist system. Also, the system depends very heavily on firms' definitions of their skill needs and ambitions. Novel though it is, it is difficult to see the system overcoming the problems of inadequate scale and ambition that plagued British apprenticeships. Also, skill-creation systems need to remain in place for a considerable period if knowledge and trust of them is to develop among firms and young people alike. Here the British strategy of changing arrangements every few years may inhibit that from occurring.

Summary: making a virtue of short-termism

Among the implications of the shift to neo-liberalism at the end of the 1970s was an overall reduction in flows of public finance to support collective goods and social infrastructure activities, a decline in government involvement in business affairs (including training), and a rejection of the involvement of organized interests in the shaping of policy. This might be thought to require a weakening of any government commitment to a national skill-creation strategy; the proportion of GDP devoted to education spending in overall in the UK has declined from an already low level. However, within overall education policy there was an increase in state spending on VET. Also, neo-liberalism was not interpreted as requiring either a reduction of state direction or a decentralization to local levels of government (as it would in the USA). Instead, there has been a process of centralization, intensified government intervention, and rapid policy change. Some of the changes, which have included some major changes of direction, have resulted from tensions between modernizers and traditionalists. The latter, who held sway during the initial years after 1979 and in some respects again during the 1990s, are not defined by their aversion to neo-liberalism; rather, they interpreted this as meaning little state intervention in the system, which would then imply little attempt at interfering with the curriculum. Also sharing the neoliberal aversion to public spending, they wished to reduce local authorities' discretion, but only in terms of spending money, not to interfere with their autonomy *per se* (Finegold 1992: 211–13).

Rapid and frequent policy change has itself been a policy, consistent with the emerging British model of placing maximum emphasis on flexibility and short-term appraisal of institutions' performance. With this has come a concomitant downgrading of the role of experience and of stable institutions, which were likely to be seen as sources of rigidity and resistance to rapid change. This development of central policy, which was probably based explicitly on Olson's (1982) theory of the rigidifying effect of institutions, exemplifies the main concept for understanding recent British developments: to make a virtue of the country's weak institutional capacity for producing collective goods, and to encourage flexibility through short-termism in decision making. This is a consequence of viewing all institutions other than the market as interferences with and sources of rigidity within market processes, which are in turn viewed as the sole source of efficiency. In only slightly less extreme form than in the UK, this has become a dominant orthodoxy among many industrial societies during the 1990s.

This leaves for the state, as argued in Chapter 2, the residual and limiting-case form of intervention as being to intervene in order to deregulate and prevent intervention, though as the above discussion has shown this is not quite an adequate means of describing the highly interventionist role of the British state during its neo-liberal period. This puzzle may be resolved in two ways. First, and consistent with at least some interpretations of the neo-liberal paradigm, a first step in the weakening of the institutions that interfere with the 'free market' is their containment. This requires the paradox of first concentrating intervention in the one institution of the central state—away from corporatist institutions (as in both the UK and Sweden) and from local levels of government (an interpretation rather limited to the UK) (Hall 1986; Finegold 1992). This is, however, not enough to explain the battles between traditionalists and modernizers and the gradual victory of the former within new-right education policy. This is where the second part of the explanation is required: neo-liberalism's main hostility towards the state is concentrated on welfare interventions; outside that arena neo-liberals, in keeping with the traditions of British Conservative Party statecraft, may well be found intervening heavily (Boyle 1992).

CONCLUSIONS

Both general discussion and the more detailed analyses of some national cases suggest three main reasons for the crisis of state competence within the VET sector: the association of government action with residual care of the unemployed; difficulties of the gulf between government agencies and companies at a time both of rapid technological and organizational change and of growing demands by companies to be able to develop cultures of their own; and the particular hostilities to certain kinds of government action by neo-liberal orthodoxy. Not even the most impressive cases of direct state action, France and Sweden, provide examples of state-led skill creation enabling the successful pursuit of a universally highly skilled workforce.

This very specific area of skill-creation policy thus demonstrates some general points concerning the current predicament of public policy. First, in all cases that we have considered in detail—France, Italy, Sweden, and the UK—government is associated with ameliorating social failure and not with dynamism, the latter therefore being seen as resting solely with private corporations whose initiatives the state can only weaken by diluting with social concerns. Neo-liberal strategy is self-reinforcing here. First it residualizes the state's role to one of a welfare safety net, and then it limits it further because it is associated with residual tasks. In both the French and the Swedish state this contrasts strongly with earlier periods: those of Gaullist high-profile projects and those of the original Swedish active labour-market policy. Similar consequences of the state becoming identified with social repair and the unemployed are reported from Germany (Voelzkow 1990: 116–17) and the USA (Finegold *et al.* 1994*b*).

Second, the difficulties of responding flexibly to companies' needs and their desire to shape their own workforce strategies appear as major constraints on the state if it wants to go beyond providing the basic requirements of a Fordist workforce and to play a part at the forefront of the development of new skills designed to assist the great majority of its young people. There are some possible responses to this. In France we have seen some gains from the policy of subsidizing and encouraging firms' own efforts at continued VET, which directly addresses the contemporary need for constant reskilling and upskilling; but clearly many problems remain if an adequate rapport between government services and individual firms is to be secured.

In the Italian and British cases there are signs of a different response: the development of small, flexible agency units. However, and as we shall see further in Chapter 6, there is considerable difference between a government agency working with the grain of the needs of a firm already engaged in skill maximization and one seeking to ratchet up the skill needs of companies lacking such an approach. The more responsive and sensitive to firms an agency is, the more difficulty it has in being proactive and strategic, unless it is deeply embedded in the day-to-day practice of individual industries and in particular their leading-edge opportunities. If this enviable but difficult position cannot be reached, a merely reactive agency will be of little use to a national goal of maximizing both the supply and the demand for skills. Responsive, 'customer-sensitive' agencies might help maximize skill utilization by firms, but at unambitious levels.

As recent responses of Swedish employers have made clear, even when business leaders share the objectives of improving skills, they do not want this to proceed at a pace any faster, or under a direction other, than those of individual companies. On the other hand, governments cannot pursue skill-maximization strategies unless they are in close touch with business interpretations of what this means in practice. Once their officials and professionals retreat to a position of just finding means of providing space for company autonomy, or to the residual role of caring for social casualties, they cease to be plausible participants in the development of a high-skill economy and lose the possibility of acquiring and maintaining the expertise necessary to function as well-informed participants in the provision of advanced skills. They also thereby lose the capacity to pursue policies designed to improve the skill positions of their populations beyond the levels that companies operating within the borders of their states find to be in their own immediate interests.

One solution to this problem has often been seen as resting with corporatist intermediary organizations that move between individual firms and the public policy arena, providing a collective goods component while remaining within the business community. It is to these that we now turn.

5

Corporatist Organizations and the Problem of Rigidity

Collective organizations of businesses are potentially important actors in the provision of workforce skills. They combine an important characteristic that the state possesses but the individual employer lacks (capacity for strategy at a collective level) with one that the state lacks (closeness to business needs). On the other hand, such organizations present problems. First, how are they able to secure co-operation among firms to satisfy common skill needs given that these same firms are likely to be competitors for labour, even if not in product markets? Second, if businesses develop powerful collective organizations, will they use these for protectionist, cartel purposes, conspiring against the public interest and preventing important change? Third, can collective organizations, which depend on elaborate consultative and discursive methods to reach agreements, respond sufficiently quickly to changing needs in fast-moving markets? In order to appraise these questions we need to examine some evidence; but we must first consider relevant theories of collective action.

Pure public goods are both non-excludable and non-rival; that is, it is not possible to exclude people from having access to them; and access by one does not prejudice access by another. Skilled labour is in this sense not a pure public good; it is rarely possible to exclude a firm from offering improved conditions to a worker whose skills it wants; but it is rival, since if the employee changes firms he or she is lost to the original employer. Impure public goods with characteristics opposite to those of vocational skill, that is, those that are excludable but non-rival, can be provided via 'clubs' in economists' sense of that term (Sandler 1992: ch. 3). A club is a voluntary organization of actors (in this case, firms) who develop means of restricting access to a good. Only those who pay a membership contribution and abide by a set of rules are permitted access. If congestion in use of the good threatens its non-rival character, access is controlled and limited. Within the club access to its facilities can be provided on a non-market basis.

Although in the case of skills and training the opposite conditions of non-excludability and rivalry are present, it is possible to construct a similar argument, as suggested by Olson's (1965) original solution to the problem of collective action. This involved an organization overcoming the disincentive that individuals have to contribute adequately to collective action by generating secondary benefits that were consumable individually and on a basis of excludability. Individuals would be induced to join the organization to secure the secondary benefits even if they lacked the incentive to secure the primary collective benefits which they could obtain without becoming members.

A problem with Olson's account is that the distinction between primary and secondary benefits is often unclear. In practice a membership organization may have a variety of functions, some collective, some individual, which are not necessarily ranked. The important point at the heart of Olson's thesis is the lateral step by which an organization might use control over excludable benefits in order to elicit contributions to collective goods over which it has no control. Let us assume that it is concerned with two goods: X, a normal club good that it provides to its members on the usual club basis; and Z, a non-excludable good. The organization may be able to induce contributions to, or regulate the use of, Z by making access to X conditional on making such contributions. The control thereby indirectly achieved over Z can be used to reduce congestion in its use (either by restraining use or, more relevantly to the case of vocational education, by guaranteeing adequate increases in supply) and therefore to ensure conditions of non-rivalry.

For an organization to be able to do this it must have a virtual monopoly over supplies of X; and individuals wanting access to Z must want X sufficiently strongly: to be willing to become members, paying club fees adequate to give access to X; to pay for the administration of the club; and to make a contribution to Z. The character of the monopoly over X requires some investigation. If it is solely a *de facto* monopoly one should expect new producers of X to appear on the market who would be able to offer X more cheaply because they were not also trying to finance the overall administration of the club and simultaneously to control behaviour and extract contributions with respect to Z.

An organization will stand a better chance of meeting these difficult conditions if it can do certain things. It might offer a range of excludable goods, X to N, such that even if monopoly conditions are not possible on each one, the particular package offered for the membership fee is distinctive and particularly attractive. Alternatively, or additionally, an organization may secure a monopoly position that is not easily challenged. For example, it may have secured legal monopolies to the provision of certain facilities, or may have a distinctive set of ties to a particular community, perhaps defined by religion, ethnicity, or political party.

All such organizations are no longer clubs in the strict sense of the economic theory. Clubs are necessarily voluntary, while we are here describing a monopolistic, possibly compulsory organization that has a capacity to impose disciplinary rules over members, and shall use the term 'association' to distinguish it from a club. Such an association will work dynamically to expand the range of interactions it has with members, and perhaps with others in its field, in order to generate further its capacity to induce co-operation, thus approaching closely Marin's (1990) concept of generalized exchange.

Once they have a multiplicity of functions, a dense web of exchanges, and longevity, associations may develop their capacity further. By operating cumulatively the structure builds up both knowledge and trust among members and between them and the officials administering the association. Trust and knowledge are both commodities in which it is difficult to be a new entrant into a monopolistic market. The latter may be particularly important where co-operative behaviour among competitors is concerned. By repeatedly participating over a lengthy period of time, the actors either become able literally to trust each other on the basis of repeated co-operative behaviour (as in an iterative game), or acquire a large number of potential 'holds' over each other. The actors become locked in a co-operative situation that maximizes the resources able to be deployed. The price for this might be a slowness of response because of interdependence and the need for extensive agreement, though if real trust develops it becomes possible for short cuts to be made, obviating this problem.

Work skills may become associational goods of this kind in various ways. In the most obvious case, a business association acquires control over access to a set of functions such that virtually all firms employing workers within a given set of labour markets find it advantageous to join. These functions might include such items as technical and marketing advice, but perhaps also a share in the administration of some publicly provided resource, such that non-members will be at a disadvantage. These latter examples might more effectively fulfil the monopoly criterion than the provision of individual membership services. The association can use the sanctions at its disposal in these areas to require member firms to contribute to training, whether through carrying out training themselves or by financing others to provide it.

Objections may be made to the role of associations, as defined here, following the important thesis produced by Olson (1982). This starts from the premise that, over time, organized interests will resolve the problem of collective action that Olson had posed for them in his earlier (1965) work, and acquire the capacity to influence policy. They will do this in order to maximize the interests of their group. In other words they will act as a cartel, using their organizational power to extract artificial rents at the expense of the general public, in particular by protecting the security of the status quo against innovation and change. They thus become an obstacle to growth and change. They may do so through cartel behaviour within markets, but also by using their organizational resources to influence governments to act in ways favourable to them.

Olson sought empirical confirmation for his argument by contrasting economic growth in the UK and the USA with that in Germany and Japan. The former two countries (the principal victors of the Second World War) had experienced far slower rates of growth since the war than the latter pair (the war's losers). This evidence was consistent with Olson's thesis; victory in war, he argued, had enabled the structure of organized interests in the Anglophone countries to survive and grow without interruption; in contrast, German and Japanese institutions had been destroyed by war, and had to reconstruct themselves. Given that Olson regarded organizational strength as a function of the time over which organizations have an opportunity to develop, German and Japanese organizations were expected to be weaker than those in the UK and the USA and therefore less able to impose cartel restraints on growth.

Critics have pointed out that very soon after the war both Germany and Japan had quickly reconstructed organizations very much in line with their institutional traditions (Abramovitz 1982). From immediate post-war reconstruction onwards these two economies developed distinctively institutional forms of capitalism (though different from each other). Olson misunderstood the implications of the German and Japanese cases for his thesis. Elsewhere in his work he developed the special case of encompassing organizations, which are organizations that represent such high proportions of the overall population of a given unit that they are unable to maximize their own position at the expense of the rest of that unit because their own constituency forms a significant part of it. That argument can be extended to cover organizations which, while not encompassing, might for other reasons be prevented from acting narrowly. In the German case the country's commitment to an open trading regime, replacing the former protectionism, combined with the disinflationary stance of the Bundesbank and the generally pro-competition stance of the social market regime, gave firms little choice but to use their representative associations for constructive, productivity-enhancing strategies rather than rent-seeking ones—though the country's strong adherence to the ideas of high standards of production quality has sometimes been used to restrict imports.

Seen in this way, post-war Germany presents a case, not of weak associations, but of strong associations forced to act in non-protectionist ways. The collective services they developed for their members were therefore of a kind that enhanced rather than impeded efficiency, becoming thereby a resource conferring competitive advantage of a kind not available to pure market economies which lacked a capacity to generate collective goods. Such an interpretation is highly relevant to the practical implications of Olson's argument. To date the main conclusion which has been drawn from his work—particularly in the UK —is that governments can best serve the needs of a competitive strategy by weakening or destroying collective organizations, or at least (as we saw in the previous chapter) by frequently changing policy and its associated institutional arrangements so that organized interests rarely have a chance to establish themselves, or again by freeing policy implementation as much as possible from involvement with interest organizations. While this might prevent the development of narrow rent-seeking behaviour, it can never generate the constructive pursuit of distinctive competitive advantage through the provision of collective goods. To do this would require, not weakening interest associations, but changing the terms on which they operate by giving them positive incentives to behave in an efficiency-enhancing way. Presumably, if a government has sufficient autonomy from, or power over, interest organizations to weaken them or bypass them, it should also have the capacity instead to restructure their mode of operation. This is the true lesson of post-war German and Japanese experience.

There are thus alternative approaches that can be taken to the role of institutions. They both have costs. The Olsonian preference for breaking down the role of organizations both embodies (in its bias towards frequent change) an inability to take advantage of the learning curve, and prevents the pursuit of collective goods as a form of competitive advantage. In particular it sacrifices the gains that can come from co-opting the co-operation of organized interests, including the gains of shared knowledge and the ability to co-opt the organizational resources of the interest groups to those required to run the policy. Overall, this approach has the strengths and weaknesses of 'travelling light': an ability to move flexibly and quickly, but at the cost of limits on what can be achieved. The alternative associational or corporatist model embodies an opposite series of preferences. The theoretical starting point is the advantages that come from a deep integration of organized interests in policy making and policy administration in order to secure impure public goods.

There is an interesting paradox in this analysis: the more state-interventionist model is Olsonian, the one associated with neo-liberal theory and practice. As we saw in the previous chapter with reference to recent British and Swedish experience, although it might leave much to market forces, the neo-liberal state adopts a powerful role in rejecting interaction with organized interests and in being free to break up institutions without much consultation. This is quite consistent with the concept of 'the free economy and the strong state' (Gamble 1994) that has accompanied the neo-liberal revival since the late 1970s. Given that economic liberalism is not anarchism, it has a role for the state; and in the interests of free competition the state had to be disentangled from the economy. By the same token, when the state's involvement in the economy does become necessary, it also follows that the state must be autonomous.

As already noted, the German system presents the fullest example of the role of corporatist associations in the provision of vocational skills, and its strengths and emerging weaknesses will be discussed below. Very similar approaches are found in the two other German-speaking nations, Austria and Switzerland, and in Denmark. There will also be some further discussion of the Swedish and British systems. Sweden was noted in the previous chapter as being far less corporatist in the training area than in most of its other labour market institutions; the relationship of Swedish labour-market corporatism to skills provision therefore requires some exploration. Finally, the British case will be considered as one of failed corporatism.

THE CORPORATISM OF THE GERMAN APPRENTICESHIP SYSTEM

The main outlines of the German vocational educational and training (VET) system are well known (especially as summarized in Streeck *et al.* 1987). At the core of the formal system is the dualist structure whereby most young people leaving education (other than those going on to university or those failing to continue their education beyond the statutory level) enter an apprenticeship where they divide their educational time between school and a firm. In the 1950s about half German school-leavers entered the system; it has now grown to about 70% (Müller 1994), largely through the growing entry of girls (Blossfeld *et al.* 1993).

Over the years the system has successfully moved upwards with the improving level of completed formal education. Originally most people entered apprenticeships at the age of 15 from *Realschulen*, the most basic form of compulsory education. Now however, apprenticeship is more likely to draw on those who have attended a middle-level school (*Mittlere Reife*), or, especially in the financial services sector, even the academic, university-oriented *Gymnasium* (Müller 1994). An increasing proportion of young people (12% in 1995) enter university after completing an apprenticeship. In recent years the classical entry route from schooling into manufacturing industry via apprenticeship has declined in popularity, as young people have wanted to pursue wider educational horizons than those permitted by the traditional apprenticeship (Büchtemann and Vogler-Ludwig 1995). However, this has coincided with the general decline in employment opportunities in manufacturing, as German firms have focused new investment in lower-wage locations (Finegold and Wagner 1997). This is partly compensated by the spread of the system to post-*Abitur* entry in certain services sectors or advanced parts of manufacturing. For employers a university degree combined with a practical apprenticeship is often seen as an ideal preparation for a management career. Technical universities (*technische Hochschulen*) are growing in importance, further helping to bridge the gap between different models of education in line with changes in the occupational structure itself.

The origins of the system are strongly rooted in *Handwerk* and the tradition of the master handing on his skills. However, the system has shown capacity for adaptation, first to the needs of big industry (Streeck 1992), and (as noted above) in more recent years to the requirements of the service sectors, including finance, the social services, and the civil service (Müller 1994). It is also related to the system of training for the professions (including the civil service) established in the nineteenth century, which similarly embodied strong concepts of occupational identity and a partnership between government and industry (the users of many professional skills) (ibid.). Like the French state, the Prussian took a lead in forming the skills of the new industrial society; however, unlike the French case, it did this always in partnership with representative bodies of industry. This reflects the different origins of the two states—the French seeing itself in a *tutelle* relationship to its society in the task of modernization, the German one accepting and making use of industry and industrial associations that had developed at national level in advance of the state itself.

This fundamentally important characteristic of the system is principally embodied in the way that it is controlled and monitored by the distinctive German institution of the *Kammern* (chambers of commerce and industry). These are compulsory but self-governing membership organizations of firms, organized by industrial branch and by locality and endowed with statutory power to make and administer public policy in certain areas—pure expressions of corporatism. Skill provision is an important part of the mission of the *Kammern*. It is provided in law that they set the syllabi and provide the inspectorate and certification. One-third of the membership of the governing bodies of *Kammern* are required by law to be employee representatives (Backes-Gellner 1996: 155–6). They also engage in frequent consultations with their member firms as well as with trade unions and the formal school system over changes and amendments to those syllabuses.

A statutory national body, the *Bundesinstitut für Berufsbildung* (BIBB), is responsible for reporting regularly on the state of training developments and improving the courses. The BIBB is a bipartite organization, with equal representatives of both sides of industry; the representatives are not political figures or negotiators, but technical experts (ibid.: 157–9). External certification, supported by inspections to check on the quality of training provision, is important to employers and employees alike. For the employer, a certificate issued by a source with which it can identify and in which it can have confidence is the guarantee that an employee it hires will have the necessary skills. For the employee the certificate is the passport to mobility. It is interesting that, despite (though really because of) its corporatist character, the German external labour market is active; employees expect to change firms from time to time to advance in their occupation (Marsden and Ryan 1991). The inclusive character of the dual training system and the validity of its certificates enable this to happen without undermining employers' willingness to train. And, as Backes-Gellner (1995) notes, the costs of information exchange are low among these closely linked institutions, which enables efficient communication among different actors, extending to training in the newest technologies.

The system thereby embodies both public regulation and objectives—including a maximization of training goals—and sensitivity to business needs. It is a sensitivity to the long-term needs of sectors competing in high-skill niches in a global economy, not just to the more immediate needs of individual firms. The logic of the 'association' characteristics of certain kinds of membership organizations as spelled out at the outset of this chapter operates here: firms will from time to time need resources and assistance from their *Kammern* or other form of association. If they have a reputation as training laggards the association and its other members will be reluctant to help. It is important to note how the real day-to-day power of the associational networks is not limited to their formal and legal authority. In a model of this kind, the formal system is supplemented by an informal web of pressures that becomes established around the former. Especially in the *Handwerk* (artisanal craft) context, but also more generally in the large number of small and medium-sized firms in Germany, there are distinctive communities of business people. These will put pressure on colleagues not participating adequately in the training system (Streeck 1992). 'Trust transactions' are generated (Soskice 1991*b*). Given the close relations that many German firms develop with their suppliers, this can then move down the value chain (Streeck 1989: 101). This helps give an initial answer to the problem of rigidity which might be assumed to be implied by a formal and legal structure.

The way in which informal networks will grow up around formal bureaucracies, provided there are elements of community in the life of the business world, is a major but very neglected aspect of corporatism. Minor adjustments can be made without calling into question the overall formal structure, reform of which requires extensive consultation and can take a very long time.

In the past the significance of all this has been seen in the system's capacity to restrain what would otherwise be the temptation of the individual firm to cut back heavily on training apprentices during recessions. While such behaviour would be entirely logical from the point of view of the individual firm, it is not rational for the system overall. Given the time lags involved in workforce training, a reduction in training during a recession will result in shortages, labour supply bottlenecks, and consequent inflationary pressure during the subsequent recovery. It is rational to smooth out the impact on the labour market of product market demand fluctuations, but there is a familiar collective action problem in the inability of firms to achieve this without a co-ordination function. The *Kammern* have provided this. Streeck (1989: 95–6) gives the example of how this was achieved by the motor industry during the post-oil-shock recessions of the 1970s. In particular, during this period the industry equipped both its new apprentices and existing staff with skills that could be used during the subsequent period of remarkable restructuring and changed work methods of the 1980s. This in turn enabled German industry to protect its market share, as was shown in Chapter 3. We can also see how the system as a whole is able to adjust to cyclical fluctuations (Soskice 1991*b*). Large firms, which provide the most sought after and costly apprentice places, do more than their share of training during boom times, and are reasonably content to do this provided they know that their main competitors, who are other large firms, are doing the same. When there is an economic downturn, large firms scale back on apprenticeships and the *Handwerk* sector is willing to take up the slack, since firms incur little if any net cost per trainee (Wagner 1998).

Furthermore, an apprenticeship system enables costs to be shared between employers providing training and their trainees, without the latter being required to pay fees. Apprentice wages are low; this is accepted by trade unions (who have a stake in the operation of the system) and also by trainees themselves. They know that within the German system, where such arrangements are so extensive, virtually the only routes to successful subsequent careers are through following an apprenticeship (Soskice 1991*b*; 1994). The small number of young people who enter the labour force with only the social minimum of compulsory education find it difficult ever to obtain good employment (Mayer and Blossfeld 1990; Shavit and Müller 1998). Young people are thus concerned to compete for the better apprenticeships—those in the largest firms or the most advanced industries (ibid.). The other side of this coin is that there is little choice of educational route (Bynner and Roberts 1991).[1] It becomes very difficult in later life to change the occupational track on which one was set by an apprenticeship (König and Müller 1986).

---

[1] Bynner and Roberts (1991) compare Germany explicitly with the UK. In the former case there is clarity in the transition from education to employment with concomitant lack of choice; in the latter, the opposite combination.

The prolonged weak product markets and intensified international competition of the 1990s, alongside the constraints imposed on the German economy of preparing for the introduction of the Single European Currency and of absorbing the former East Germany, have begun to strain these qualities of the system (Finegold and Wagner 1997; Finegold and Levine 1997). If firms are determined to shift production from Germany to lower-wage nations, and hence are trying to reduce employment, they will resist taking on new trainees, however strong the moral pressures; there is no point preparing the young for skilled jobs if those jobs are not going to be available. There have therefore been many recent cases of firms refusing to do their share of apprentice training, leading eventually to informal intervention by the *Bundeskanzler* (Federal Chancellor) himself to put pressure on employers' associations to put pressure in turn on member firms to raise the level of apprentice training. As early as the 1970s government had threatened to introduce a training levy system, but had never proceeded with it. More recently government has established its own training places and employment subsidies, especially in the new eastern *Länder*, to support weak points in the corporatist arrangements (Culpepper 1998).

Since apprentices make a contribution to actual output while they are doing their practical work in a firm and the training allowance has been low relative to the adult skilled worker's wage, it has been estimated that there is little or no net cost to firms which provide the training in the *Handwerk* sectors and that the benefits outweighed the costs for most employers (Wagner 1998). However, changes in the last decade may have altered this equation. The move away from apprenticeship to higher education is leading to a decline in the quality of those left as apprentices, threatening a decline in their productivity and desirability as future employees, and a consequent reluctance by firms to use the apprenticeship system (Büchtemann and Vogler-Ludwig 1995). In addition, the reforms of the apprenticeship system in the 1980s to increase its educational content and length (to 3.5 years in metalworking, for example) and increases in the apprentice wage have both raised the net costs of an apprenticeship and thus further reduced incentives for employer participation in the system.

The strong occupational identity encouraged by the system is often viewed stereotypically as a German corporatist rigidity (Geißler 1991; Grabher (ed.) 1993) and a potential barrier to the introduction of multifunctional skills (Herrigel 1996; 1998). There are, however, important elements of built-in flexibility, which have enabled it to be a constantly changing system, integrating theoretical and practical education and stressing general, flexible skills (Blossfeld 1990: 7; Finegold and Wagner 1997). To an important extent this follows from the day-to-day involvement of firms, not only through the *Kammern* but, probably more significantly, through the in-firm component of the training. Staff employed as trainers (*Meister*) spend some of their time in normal work, so that they are constantly kept up to date with changing practices in a way that cannot be achieved by someone working full-time within a specialist training organization or school.

There have also been major formal reforms to the system, though these have usually taken a long time to arrange as so many groups have to give their consent (Keltner *et al*. 1996). As Backes-Gellner (1996: 165) points out, however, once a lengthy process of syllabus reform has been completed, firms have a record of rapid implementation of it. In the 1950s a total of 900 occupations had formal VET preparations. By 1970 this had been reduced to 500 (Müller 1994). By 1992 it was down to 377, including the addition of new occupations in services and high-tech sectors (Sadowski and Decker 1993: 29). The most recent reforms in particular have moved from tight job definitions to a flexible preparation in order to produce what are called polyvalent skills. Trainees are equipped initially with core, key skills (*Schlüsselqualifikationen*), on to which more specific skills can be added, or which can be changed (Streeck 1989: 97; Blossfeld 1990: 7). When it was recognized that traditional apprenticeship concepts were inappropriate to industries dominated by teams of workers using programmable machines, a major reform process was initiated in the metalworking industry, which led to a reduction from 37 to seven qualification categories after a decade of discussion and research (Casey 1990; Feldhoff and Jacke 1990; Finegold *et al*. 1994*a*). Reforms can make it difficult for some small and medium-sized enterprises to offer a full range of training. While this might lead these firms to oppose and delay change, they have also shown a capacity to cope by forming partnerships to share costs and capabilities.

Trade unions have only a limited formal role in the training system, except in the construction industry where the casual nature of even skilled employment makes co-operation from organized labour particularly necessary. Elsewhere they are limited to participation in the albeit important task of the definition of training standards. They have, however, also contributed indirectly to the system's effective operation as part of the informal set of pressures that gather in an associational framework. In this they have been considerably assisted by the *Betriebsräte* (works councils), which have an important statutory role in German business and which can therefore maintain their own watch on the quality of training being provided by a firm. In addition to raising issues of this kind directly with management, the councils can also pass information on to the unions.

Unions and works councils can therefore often be part of the channel whereby sanctions are exercised against recalcitrant employers who are not fulfilling their training obligations. Since unions have a strong interest in the provision of training, they will be less co-operative with firms which are not pulling their weight within the apprenticeship scheme. Certain aspects of the collective bargaining system also help sustain the apprenticeship model. Combining qualifications with seniority in a sectoral formula for setting wages, as occurs with manual workers in the main manufacturing industries in Germany, gives young people an incentive to enter an apprenticeship and makes it harder for firms to 'poach' (that is, to offer wage premiums to lure away skilled workers) (Soskice 1994). This can be related to a general argument about collective labour markets. Certain systems of wage determination may reduce poaching by making it more difficult for an employer to tailor rewards to an individual's characteristics, or to solve skill shortages by bidding up wages—instead, encouraging the more societally beneficial strategy of training and retraining (Soskice 1991*b*). One way in which this can be achieved is by linking pay in a given sector or across industries closely to the qualifications which an individual possesses. Such a system continues to reward employers who invest time and effort—sometimes money—in higher levels of skill provision, but restricts the ability of free-riding firms to offer a premium to other companies' skilled workers. Mechanisms of this kind have the effect of internalizing the reward structure across a number of companies.

The exclusion of further VET

The German apprenticeship model does not extend to further training, and Germany is not a particularly strong provider of such training (Sauter 1996). The relatively weak provision of information technology in German firms may be related to this (Keltner *et al.* 1996). It might be considered that the strength of the apprenticeship system makes this kind of skill provision less necessary since in some countries much further training is 'remedial', compensating for the deficiencies of initial training. However, in recent years, in-service training has been becoming increasingly important for firms in all countries which wish constantly to upgrade their workers (Regini (ed.) 1996). This is experienced by many German firms as an increasing problem with the current training system (Bahnmüller 1996). There are, however, some indirect inducements to firms to operate a high level of further training.

First, since German firms are pressed to compete on the basis of labour-force quality by the wider institutional system, they will be forced by market pressures to ensure that they maintain the skill levels of their existing workforces. For example, when the German motor industry reconstructed its Fordist production methods on a basis of job enlargement and polyvalent skills in the 1980s, it did so very successfully by providing in-house further VET (Kern and Schumann 1987; Streeck 1985).

Second, the *Betriebsrat* found in most German firms must be consulted if management wishes to introduce job reductions, and it has veto rights over the 'social plan' that the management must produce in such circumstances. The *Betriebsräte* place a major emphasis on measures for retraining and re-equipping the existing workforce, though they have no role in the provision of in-firm training. This is, of course, an 'insider market' response of the kind associated in neo-liberal economic theory with high unemployment among 'excluded' young workers. However, as we saw in Chapter 2, the apprenticeship system has provided an alternative solution to this, and Germany (along with other dual system countries) has been unique in having lower youth than adult rates of unemployment.

However, during the current period of strain, the absence of specific collective policy at the level of further VET in a context of highly elaborate initial VET is beginning to have a perverse effect. Many companies are solving the problems they are now facing by putting considerable emphasis on retraining small parts of their workforce, using company-level schemes of further training—the kind of training that will be particularly important in the future for innovative firms and high-skill sectors (Backes-Gellner 1995; Finegold and Wagner 1997). It is significant that these signs are strongly evident in Baden-Württemberg, the country's strongest high-tech region (Bahnmüller 1996). With all the institutional elements of the dual system almost completely absent at this level of further training, the great bulk of it takes place entirely under management auspices in individual companies (CEDEFOP 1992; Bahnmüller 1996; Sadowski and Decker 1993: 36 ff.; Voelzkow 1990). Firms want arrangements to remain like this, though they do accept some limited role for the *Kammern*. As a result, most of this further VET has a very different character from initial VET.

Continuing vocational education is also distinguished by the fact that it is an extremely obscure market, for example, with regard to what courses are available and how good the training providers are. Furthermore, the conflicting interests of the social partners leave their mark on continuing vocational training as a whole. The consensus that is typical among the parties involved in developing initial VET is an exception rather than the rule in continuing VET (Sauter 1996: 115).

In a similar fashion to the cases to be considered in Chapter 7, this training tends to be firm specific and—with some important long-established exceptions, such as training for *Meister* or *Facharbeiter* certificates—does not lead to the award of portable certificated qualifications of use in the external labour market. As Sauter notes (ibid.: 126): 'Since every provider of continuing training can award certificates, consumers are now confronted with an utterly confusing certification market.' Similarly, and again with important exceptions, the training tends to be concentrated on those who already have a high level of skill and education (Sadowski and Decker 1993; Voelzkow 1990). Very little further training comes the way of the country's small number of semi-skilled workers who missed out on the initial opportunities of the dual system (Bechtle and Dull 1992). However, it is notable that the co-operative pattern spills over; research also reports considerable voluntary co-operation between firms on this training (Sadowski and Decker 1993: 45).

As in Italy, Sweden, and the USA, there have been attempts by trade unions to negotiate over further training, for example, to create an entitlement for employees to receive training leading to certificated achievements, whether bargained for at the level of an individual firm or a whole industry (Voelzkow 1990). It is the policy of unions that skill acquisition should be seen in this way. There have been some successful outcomes (Sadowski and Decker 1993), but such training accounts for only a small proportion of total further training effort.

Summary and future prospects

Accounts of German skills provision both here and elsewhere in the literature differ from those discussing most other countries' systems in that there is less emphasis on government policy and less narrative of policy change. This is partly because policy making and administration through the *Kammer* system assign a smaller role to government policy and, in consequence, a smaller role generally to discrete policy innovations. The unique linkage between public policy and the world of business that *Kammern* provide makes possible a more dialogistic pattern of repeated interactions to produce minor change. The idea of occasional interventions by an external central government, that is so important in some other systems, is lacking.

Another reason for the lack of policy movement is that, within a system of this kind, major changes tend to be hard and slow to negotiate, and therefore occur more rarely than in less consultative cases. This is consistent with the expectations of Olsonian theory that change will be slow and cumbersome within large-scale associational structures, and is often taken as evidence of a major weakness of the German and any other corporatist cases. Indeed, Rose and Page (1990) have attempted a quantitative analysis of policy innovation in British and German training that regards the smaller number of government policy actions in Germany as substantive evidence of the superiority of the British approach. Several objections can be made to this.

First, it ignores the process of incremental adjustment which is easier for the embedded *Kammern* to make than for an external government agency. Second, and similarly, in looking at *government* policy Rose and Page were not necessarily considering the most appropriate institution for a study of German VET policy. But third, it is more than possible that frequency of policy change reflects mistakes and failure of previous attempts; it may well be that the dialogistic approach to policy making, while definitely slower, also reduces the number of errors. In a curious way the capacity for speed of action in British policy making may provide the need for itself and therefore its own justification through the number of mistakes which it produces, and which must be speedily addressed, as the more flexible bureaucracy responds to politicians' short-term priorities. Finally, the German policy process combines both design and implementation; since all relevant parties are involved in the policy change there can be a strong presumption that they will all ensure its implementation after it has been introduced (Finegold and Keltner 1996). The British (or French) government may have considerably more autonomy in decreeing what changes it will introduce, but may then depend for implementation on reluctant or even opposed groups which had not been involved in the design of the change and might feel no commitment to it. It is notable that, as we saw in Chapter 3, all research comparing intermediate skill levels in Germany, France, and the UK has concluded that the first-mentioned country is usually ahead (Backes-Gellner 1996; Finegold and

Soskice 1988; Marsden and Ryan 1991; Prais 1981; Prais and Wagner 1985; Steedman, Mason, and Wagner 1991).

However, as already noted in connection with the declining willingness of firms to provide apprenticeships, there is clear evidence that the German dual system has come under considerable strain in very recent years. It is true that government intervention to encourage firms to produce more apprenticeships and to create state-run schemes which ensure that all young people who want them can have training places testifies to a public commitment to sustain the system through a period of crisis. However, the fact that such action was necessary demonstrates that the system's own in-built stabilization measures are failing to function. There appear to be at least six reasons for this.

First, the highly consultative model of development and change, while crucial to the trust capacity of the system, imposes delays in making major adjustments which, at a time of rapid occupational, technical, and economic change such as the present, constitute an important problem.

Second, the slow speed of adjustments is not just a product of the search for consensus; it also results from the sense that one's occupation, one's *Beruf* or *Fach*, has been fundamental to much of the past success of the German approach, but might now be causing problems (Blossfeld 1990). A sense of identity, indeed pride, in one's calling has encouraged a sense of responsibility for work quality, extending widely among manual workers, including many who in other industrial systems are likely to be seen as poorly motivated hands requiring constant supervision. The Anglo-German comparisons conducted by the NIESR in the 1980s and discussed in Chapter 3 noted frequently the extent to which responsibilities requiring a separate supervisory or managerial tier in the UK would be carried out by skilled manual workers in Germany. However, today this increasingly means that the training which equips workers with this kind of occupational identity is providing a static concept of the occupation that can run counter to the flexibility required of new forms (Finegold and Wagner 1997; Geißler 1991; Herrigel 1996). This is not just a matter of amending courses, but of adopting a more fluid concept of one's occupational role. It also means accepting that initial training for a particular kind of work function needs frequent updating and retraining, in many cases to the extent that the specific occupation for which people considered they have been trained even ceases to exist.

Third is the degree of rigidity imposed on young people by the dual system. Decisions taken early in life about which school path to follow determine rather fundamentally the subsequent career an individual will follow. School selection is rigid, and although there is a strong external labour market within occupations, there is relatively little occupational mobility, change of occupation, in German society (Blossfeld 1990; Hinz 1998). There are also dangers that, if one has not been able to secure a place with an apprenticeship (as is increasingly likely with *Realschule* graduates at a time of high unemployment), one will find it difficult to acquire any recognized occupational position at all and will become marginalized (Müller 1994). In particular, women and foreigners are found in these positions (Mayer and Blossfeld 1990; Krüger 1998).

Fourth, there is some evidence of the atrophy and cartel behaviour predicted by the Olsonian theory of organizational behaviour. As was noted in Chapter 3, the German economy has not been successful at entering new fields: German firms have definitely lost ground within such branches as office equipment and advanced electronics, areas where the premium has been on innovation rather than amending past practice. Corporatist models, as would be anticipated by Olson's arguments, are better at improving and rejigging practices in industries covered by existing interest organizations than at innovating totally new ones (Herrigel 1998).

Fifth, as initiatives in the modern economy have slipped increasingly to the individual firm, there is impatience with intermediary organizations like *Kammern*. Firms complain at the constraints imposed on them (Regini 1996*b*). It is important to remember that they may be exaggerating and ignoring their capacity to adjust the details of training through their individual contributions to the dual system; firms find it convenient to criticize the dual system in order to reduce their training costs. However, although, as we have seen, major reforms of the corporatist system are possible, have taken place and will have to take place again, there is impatience among firms at the slow speed and at the difficulty of radical innovation. This could be particularly problematic if the continuing pace of change makes radical reform a more frequent requirement than can easily be achieved by the dialogistic and consensual approach. *Kammern* are responding to the situation in an Anglo-American market model, turning themselves into organizations offering customer services to firms on a contract basis, as though they were business service firms rather than membership associations with authority. While this might preserve their activities, it may do so at the expense of their capacity to act strategically and authoritatively.

Finally, the key attributes of the initial training system are all almost completely absent at the level of further VET. Here the German system resembles the British or the American—though without the history of college support for firms' own activities that is important in the US case. Most of this further training does not lead to the award of portable certificated qualifications of use in the external labour market, and tends to be concentrated on those who already have a high level of skill and education (Sadowski and Decker 1993; Voelzkow 1990).

As more German corporations develop global reach, they may find it quicker and cheaper to shift production than to reform the German system—though as has been shown by some recent decisions by German firms with plants in the UK to switch investment back to Germany because of British skill shortages, the German skilled labour force continues to possess major advantages in skill competition. Also, it is easy to forget that much of Germany's current problems are exaggerated by reunification and the effort to transfer the existing training system to east Germany, which lacks a critical mass of internationally competitive firms (Culpepper 1998).

There is a real danger that the crisis in the German system will continue. Some aspects of the crisis are 'unnecessary', in the sense that the two basic problems are amenable to solution within the terms of the system: there is no reason in principle why a dual system could not be extended to deal with both further skills provision and the disappearance of settled long-term occupational identities.[2] *Kammern* could operate a levy system *à la française*, but without the problems of remoteness from the firm of state action. The capacity of the system to secure a sharing of costs among employers, the state, and individual employees is also a valuable attribute that could easily be squandered by a shift to a different model. Perceptions of it as 'rigid' are in danger of leading German businesses themselves to overlook its opportunities for adaptation. One recalls that the German system is almost alone in having a youth unemployment rate lower than the adult one. A relatively high rate of youth unemployment is a good indicator of the extent to which labour markets have been closed by rent-seeking insiders, who use various regulative devices to protect their own position at the expense of outsiders and general efficiency. According to *a priori* neo-liberal thinking a regulated, *Kammern*-dominated labour market of the German kind should be the epitome of an insider market and should therefore be expected to have a high relative level of youth unemployment. The fact that it does not shows how, provided they are structured in certain ways, organized systems can produce their own compensatory checks and balances.

Further, the system's role in producing a strong sector of entrepreneurial small firms must be set against its alleged rigidity. Because of the strength of the qualification system, most self-employed persons and small business owners in Germany have acquired a *Meister* certificate, in contrast with France and many other industrialized countries where the majority of self-employed have a low educational level (König and Müller 1986).[3]

The problems are not practical but political. An increasing number of German firms want the autonomy from collective provision, and indeed from commitment to the German national scene with its high labour and other costs, that a

---

[2] Lutz (1992) argues similarly that there is something unnecessary and probably damaging about the flight from apprenticeship to higher education. According to Lutz, this flight is not produced by the emerging needs of the production system but, as in France, by parents believing that improved qualifications will assist their children in the job market. Employers then respond to the changed supply of recruits by developing more hierarchical and meritocratic structures. This then leads to the vocational system becoming a second-class system and it becomes neglected by young people and the business world alike. Reform of vocational systems would, however, probably produce more relevant as well as less hierarchical occupational structures and be more useful to less academic children. Buttler and Tessaring (1995) point out that, while firms share the cost of the dual system, the state pays the full cost of university education. This gives firms an incentive to move to graduate recruitment, which further undermines both the shared-cost approach which has been an important part of the success of the German model and the career opportunities previously available to those educated through the apprenticeship system.

[3] The study cited is specifically concerned with a Franco-German comparison, but a similar contrast could be made between Germany and either Italy or the UK.

move to a company-only approach to training brings. Other difficulties, which extend far beyond the adaptability of the training, are currently causing the main problems for the German economy. For example, can it bear the cost of modernizing the former East Germany? Does German business know how to enter new high-tech industries? Are firms able and willing to create jobs for young people? However, firms are encouraged to see the dual system as one aspect of the general problem of high labour costs. The collective action pressures of the German system, like those of all national systems, are based on ensuring that individual firms within the jurisdiction of the system do not free-ride. There can, however, be no protection against competition from firms in countries which do not have a national project of upskilling the labour force and where therefore the costs of the training system, even if nationally imposed, will not have the same cost implications. If German firms were responsible for training only those employees whom they had an immediate need to upskill, they would, even if providing this training at a high level, save on training expenditures.

It does not follow from the above difficulties that the apprenticeship system is likely to be dismantled; this would be too big a break from the German social consensus model, would cause conflict with the trade unions and public opinion, and also would destroy the country's unrivalled reputation for producing a stream of high-quality young employees. What is far more likely to happen is that the dual system will become frozen in time, performing its current range of tasks, but gradually covering a smaller share of employment, with a risk that it might fail to advance and to spearhead the new challenges of preparing the really advanced workforce, which will depend on continuing and further VET. In the advanced companies, the consequence would be severe damage to the German model of industrial citizenship.

CORPORATISM IN SWEDISH ACTIVE LABOUR MARKET POLICY

We have already seen in Chapter 4 that Sweden abolished its apprenticeship model. Nilsson has shown (1981: 273–7) how Swedish policy-makers began to depart from a German kind of apprenticeship during the 1930s—not a decade in which social democrats were likely to be enthusiastic about German approaches. Significantly, they believed that their weak small-firm sector could never bear its full share of the burden; therefore large companies would have to take the lead in training; and training would have to be based around mass-production industry rather than craft-type skills. It should be noted that, despite the strength of the Swedish associational system, it was not seen as able to guarantee small-company participation in skills provision. There were no equivalents in Sweden to the German *Kammern*. After the Second World War thinking became strongly influenced by the US Training Within Industry model (ibid.: 279–97), a piece of pure Fordism which aimed at providing low-level and highly segmented work-role skills for mass-production workers. This did not mean that Sweden was seeking to move down-market; instead the declining need for specific skills perceived in modern large-scale industry was seen to make possible an increase in general but vocationally useful education.

There had been considerable co-operation between schools and industry in the provision of courses during this initial post-war system, and Skolöverstyrelsen (Sö, the national school board) and Arbetsmarknadsstyrelsen (AMS, the Labour Market Board) co-operated in predicting local labour force needs via the labour mobility policy (Sweden 1966: ch. 4). AMS is a tripartite, multilevel, and administrative (as well as policy-making) institution on the typical Swedish model. It has comprised not only a national tripartite central board, but a similarly tripartite regional and local structure. At these lower levels representatives of the various partners have been in an interdependent relationship with the centre: they depended on its policies and resource allocation, but their co-operation and success were also necessary to the centre's delivery of its aims. Neither government nor the representative associations of employers and workers could give simple orders to the lay representatives who controlled these lower levels.

It was AMS that became the central instrument of Swedish active labour market policy (ALMP), widely perceived as a particularly successful example of such policy (King and Rothstein 1993)—though without a significant training mandate other than for the provision of basic skills. The organization's initial mission was to provide a labour exchange system to help overcome the mass unemployment of the 1930s. Early twentieth-century labour exchange administrations in Sweden, as elsewhere, had acquired a reputation among workers as mechanisms for forcing people to take inappropriate work so that the state would not have to pay them unemployment benefit. The Social Democratic government of the late 1930s set out to replace this with an administration that workers could trust, and the staff of the new body were largely trade unionists and other social democrats (Rothstein 1985). The employers' organizations co-operated, but it was undoubtedly partisan rather than consensus administration. Nevertheless, as with many components of Swedish policy from those years (like the solidaristic wage policy), the internal needs of the labour movement were capable of adaptation to national needs.

By the late 1960s the ALMP was specializing in assisting labour mobility and upgrading basic skill levels, often through help with adult education. The new industries in southern Sweden were expanding, and employment in the mining and forest industries of the north was declining. Against a background of unambiguous government commitment to full employment, trade unions were willing to co-operate in a policy of labour mobility. Because the AMS system was well connected to local labour markets, it was able to provide each district with information concerning job vacancies and skill needs throughout the country (Johansson 1991: 36–7). All workers seeking employment benefit would come to the exchanges and, more controversially, private employment exchanges were made illegal.

The maintenance of full employment became more difficult in the 1970s and early 1980s and labour-market policy began to concentrate on short-term measures, such as the provision of temporary jobs, subsidizing the stockpiling of goods, and make-work schemes. Such defensive measures were common in the industrial world at that time, but were of a kind that Swedish policy had typically tried to avoid. The distinctive social democratic Keynesianism that Gösta Rehn and other economists had developed for post-war Sweden had typically stressed supply-side improvements rather than simple demand management. The policies of AMS to encourage geographical mobility had been important examples.

The lapse by AMS into temporary remedies had been based on the assumption that the post-oil-shock recession was a temporary interruption to the normal course of post-war growth. By the mid-1980s, Sweden's main economic actors realized that the new instability of world markets was something more serious and that a major restructuring was required. The emphasis of labour market policy therefore shifted to more constructive tasks of improving the quality of labour supply and the competitive base of the economy (Thalén 1988: 16–19). From this time dates a shift in the role of AMS towards training for the competitive needs of the new flexible economy, including work for specific companies (Johansson 1991: 153–65; Standing 1988; Dahlberg and Tuijnman 1991: 153–9; Sweden 1984*a*).

The AMS information network, which had become a very sophisticated computerized operation, was used to make available detailed information concerning the supply of and demand for various skills. This became an essential aid to skills policy, for example in planning the size of various vocational lines in schools in different parts of the country. Further, the network enabled young people to make well-informed and therefore not speculative choices about the careers for which they would prepare themselves. However, the AMS system did not reach into the content or organization of school-based initial skill generation.

Meanwhile the new appreciation of the importance of the individual institutional company, and its implications for further VET, began to grow in Sweden as elsewhere. There was a considerable growth in in-house training activities; by the end of the 1980s about 25% of the workforce had some educational activity in the workplace in any one year, about the same level as was being catered for in the state adult education system, with a further 10% in the voluntary sector (Sweden 1992*b*: 16). Concepts of 'lifelong learning' and the 'learning enterprise' began to be used extensively in Swedish policy making. Flexibility and rapid adaptability as shaped by quickly changing product markets became central concerns across the political spectrum (see, for example, Sweden 1991*a*: 51, 52). Further, as elsewhere, Swedish employers wished to encourage company identity among their employees, and increasingly saw an understanding of the company's specific style and ethos as an element of 'skill', or at least as a necessary element of young workers' vocational preparation. Skills might be more general, but their application may be specific to a company and prone to rapid change. Companies wanted to be directly involved in training young people for speedy adaptation; at the same time there was awareness that the country's low proportion of small and medium-sized businesses might be a disadvantage when there was a need for rapid adaptation and the pursuit of high value-added market niches —though the record of small firms in training is not particularly good.

An important change took place following a report of the KAFU Commission (Sweden 1983). Until then AMS had provided all its courses directly, but in 1984 a separate Labour Market Training Board (Arbetsmarknadsutbildningen, AMU) was established. This is a tripartite body with a small headquarters staff and extensive regional and local networks whose task it is to commission training from a range of providers (mainly but not solely in the public sector). It therefore operates in a quasi-market and needs to attract the interest of companies. This was a move towards more market determination and company sensitivity in AMS's operation. The novelty of this should not be exaggerated; for example, as early as the 1960s AMS would work with individual firms to ensure a labour force in a new region (Sweden 1986*b*: 72). The new developments were, however, part of a larger change in the mid-1980s, as the governing Social Democratic party began to develop public agencies that would service private firms. Within labour market policy this means less concern with the job needs of individual workers than with improving the general level of workplace skills (Hjer 1980; Tuijnman 1989: 49, 50).

While most of its commissions come from AMS, AMU also works directly with employers. It can support employers' training costs (through either in-house or specialist courses) for the following purposes: easing bottlenecks in labour supply, avoiding redundancies, facilitating structural adjustment, removing gender inequalities. So far the first of these is the most important. Particular use has been made of these possibilities by AMU, on behalf of AMS, in order to place less skilled workers who would otherwise be unemployed into vacancies released by existing workers who are being retrained for higher posts for which there are currently shortages of candidates.

All sectors of the economy have made use of the new link with AMU, but especially manufacturing. Companies approach local AMS staff with a training plan, and the latter has to decide whether it is appropriate. Details are then established between the employer and the union. There are sometimes conflicts here. AMS, spending public money on behalf of taxpayers and the general public, needs to have concern for trainees' longer-term interests; companies sometimes want to deal with their own narrower, specific needs. There is therefore a delicate balance between the pursuit of collective goods and of companies' private goods. A complete privatization of AMS, as was being discussed among groups close to the bourgeois government before it fell in 1994, would raise important issues concerning whether a national labour-market body served only client company needs or wider concepts of skills policy.

The rationale behind the company-oriented strategy when it started under the social democratic administration was the collective goal that firms' private costs needed social support if the national strategy of pursuing high skill was to be achieved (Thalén 1988: 27), though this led to some concern that longer-term future needs of the labour market, and those of hard-to-place workers, might be neglected (Sweden 1989a: 187). Similarly, adult education has expanded considerably (Tuijnman 1989: 55), but mainly because it has been pressed further into commissioned work for companies. As with similar policy ideas in the USA, this has caused concern to some observers, who feel that public policy is being subordinated to firms' needs (Abrahamsson, Hultinger, and Svenningsson 1990: 74, 75; Tuijnman 1989: 50).

AMS itself has also become more decentralized. Policy is increasingly set at *lan* (regional) and even *kommun* (local government) levels, where local AMS staff can work closely with firms and educational authorities on local labour market issues. This is a major development in policy, marking a new stage in the growth of the ALMP: from its original days as a simple labour-exchange system, through its now famous years as probably the world's most sophisticated proactive device for labour market information capable of acting as a signal of training needs and provider of training courses, representing the national commitment to a skill economy, and now to a response to the acknowledged rigidities in the system, acquiring a new capacity to respond to individual firms' needs.

Overall, the AMS system had been well equipped to support the long-term collective goods needs of an economy dominated by manual workers in Fordist manufacturing industry. A striking characteristic of the original labour-mobility policy was its encouragement of considerable adaptability on the part of Swedish workers—not a characteristic normally associated with systems partly administered by strong trade unions. Outside the Fordist sector its initial role was less well oriented to long-term needs or adaptability, and most of the changes during the 1970s and 1980s described above were attempts to respond to these deficiencies. In so responding there may have been some shift away from the pursuit of collective goods, and the AMS system may not have solved the problem of pursuing long-term needs, since individual firms cannot themselves anticipate these. These are dilemmas intrinsic to the attempt to transcend short-term market calculation in a post-Fordist economy.

A further problem has been a changing significance of ALMP in a period of prolonged structural unemployment. The aim of ALMP is to use public funds for the unemployed, not just passively to give them income support, but to provide them with skills training, temporary work experience, and career advice. This assumes that the unemployed will relatively quickly and successfully re-enter employment. However, if unemployment is high and persistent, it may not be easy for them to do this, and attendance on a training course or participation in a special scheme becomes almost as passive as receipt of unemployment benefit. Eventually the point is reached where courses and schemes are initiated, not because it is really believed that they will lead to a chance of rapid re-employment, but because they keep people out of the unemployment register. So-called active labour market measures then become virtually indistinguishable from passive ones. This may be happening now to Sweden's ALMP—it is a change which is not limited to Sweden but which is most evident there, given the country's leadership in such policies.

The employers' revolt

The AMS system might indicate a path that can be taken by corporatist structures adapting to local and corporate training needs, though conflict over its corporatist status has complicated the position. Swedish employers, as represented in SAF, have become increasingly dissatisfied with the outcomes of the country's corporatism. From the 1980s onwards the collective bargaining system failed to deliver the stability and inflation aversion which had been the trade-off for powerful union influence which employers had accepted for many years; and it was leaving Sweden anomalous at a time when some other countries—primarily the UK and the USA—were embarking on neo-liberal economic policies that excluded union involvement in economic matters. Employers also believed that recent developments in social democratic policies were moving beyond the compromises that underpinned the Swedish consensus. As part of their diagnosis of the country's declining international competitiveness, employers therefore concluded that the role of unions needed to be weakened. Further, Swedish business had become increasingly international. There had been considerable outward investment and many Swedish companies no longer depended on the national workforce for their profits. Their dependence on co-operation with the practices of Swedish labour was therefore much reduced (Pestoff 1991: 31–3).

These changes had two direct implications for training. First, employers now wished to exclude unions from participation in training policy. In defending this stance they argued that in the past unions' main concern in collective bargaining over training had been restricted to financial terms of time off for study rather than the content and purpose of training. Second, SAF had decided some years previously that it would maximize employers' political interests better within a US-style 'lobbying' system than through Swedish neo-corporatism, in which organized interests share in the administration of state policy (Myrdal 1991; Pestoff 1991). Under the latter there is a requirement for workers' interests to be represented alongside those of employers; under a lobbying system unions would be at a disadvantage. SAF therefore demanded a break-up of all neo-corporatist structures. In the early 1990s it began to withdraw its representatives from all bi- and tripartite *styrelsar* (boards). It had excepted AMS from this new ideological stance, on the grounds that its work was very constructive and that labour-market policy was an area in which it was right and proper for business and labour interests to be represented. However, following the election of the bourgeois government, SAF also withdrew from participation in AMS.

After a period in which the agency continued to function without employer representatives, the government restructured it on what might appear internationally more conventional, less historically Swedish lines. Union and employer representation (private and public) has continued on a series of advisory panels and a general consultative committee (*rådgivande nämnd*), but administration of the system has been placed squarely in the hands of the civil service and a government department. Members of the *styrelse* (board) itself are politicians, state officials, and experts only. Whether this will threaten the capacity of the organizations, and particularly labour, to participate actively in the development and implementation of new skill strategies remains to be seen, given SAF's aim of excluding unions from matters such as training.

In the late 1980s it had been assumed that the labour market organizations would be involved in curriculum development and in other relations with schools in developing the new vocational lines (Abrahamsson, Hultinger, and Svenningsson 1990: 74). So far branch-level employer organizations still seem to accept direct participation of this kind. If the SAF alone assumes a new 'US style' lobbying role, then much of the substance of Swedish policy administration may stay in familiar paths, with a useful decentralizing of authority to a level closer to individual companies. If, on the other hand, the industry associations eventually follow SAF's course, then much of the work being achieved by bringing business and education closer together might be undercut by a weakening of business's capacity to participate. A simultaneous growth of company training (especially if it is to include an element of apprenticeship) and of the small and medium-sized firms that Sweden lacks is likely to be achieved only if business associations retain the power of sanction that mere lobbying organizations usually lack.

Swedish skills provision remains in a state of considerable flux. It is not yet possible to describe the outlines of a coherent and accepted new model. Will the state-led system of the past become a company model after the US fashion? Or will it become more corporatist—in line with Swedish active labour market policy rather than with German *Kammern*—and if so will it prove more successful than the German one at extending to further VET? How significant will be the attempts at an adaptation of manpower policy, now including training, which responds to local and company needs without sacrificing capacity for a national strategy of producing a 'learning society'?

FAILED CORPORATISM IN THE UK

Finally, it is worth considering the fate of corporatist policy attempts in the UK as an example of a system under similar but more intense neo-liberal pressures than the German and Swedish cases, and without a past lengthy record of success for neo-corporatist structures in either collective bargaining or the labour market. The comparison is particularly useful in that for a period (from the mid-1970s until some point in the 1980s) British manpower policy institutions were modelled on Swedish ones, while for a period in the early 1990s

British government sometimes claimed that it was seeking to imitate the German involvement of business interests in national policy (Wood 1998).

An apprenticeship system had long been part of the British training legacy, but it remained poorly developed. Unlike in Germany, there was no strong corporatist structure of firms, certainly nothing remotely resembling the *Kammern*, which could impose a regime of high performance and expanding quality and volume of training as occurred in the German model. Trade unions had a more entrenched role in the administration of the system than their German counterparts, but used this in a restrictive way. Definitions of skilled work were slow to change and provided craft workers with protected job niches and made possible the elaboration of restrictive practices.

There was an important attempt at reforming the system under the Industrial Training Act 1964, which established a system of levies and subsidies in order to ensure that firms either provided training or at least contributed to a fund from which those who were providing training could draw (Senker 1990). The system was administered for each identified industry by corporatist boards (Industrial Training Boards, ITBs) drawn from employers and trade unionists from the industries concerned. It reached primarily existing skilled trades in the production sector (manufacturing, construction, public utilities) and distribution. There was, however, little evidence that government regarded this as a particularly high-priority activity. The Central Training Council established to supervise the operation had very limited advisory powers and no authority to insist on enlarged ambitions from the boards (King 1993). Its successor body, the Manpower Services Commission (MSC), claimed that the Council had not produced 'any sustained growth in the number of people trained beyond the needs of individual firms' (MSC 1975, quoted in King 1993)—a complaint that was to be made about every subsequent initiative, including those of the MSC itself.

By 1973 the rise in unemployment and the general increase in the country's economic vulnerability led to renewed concern over vocational skills. The new Manpower Services Commission was created by government to preside over manpower policy. This was a fully corporatist institution, modelled explicitly on the Swedish AMS, managed jointly by representatives of government, the Confederation of British Industry (CBI) and the Trades Union Congress (TUC), with the social partner representatives having equal status to government ones in policy making and administration, not merely a consultative role. Health and safety, and conciliation and arbitration services were restructured in a similar way. The ITBs were incorporated in the new system, but since the political emphasis was concentrated on action against unemployment they were initially left very much to their own unambitious devices (King 1993).

In comparison with German and Swedish equivalents, British employers' associations and trade unions were relatively weak in these extended roles. They usually had little capacity to determine policy in an authoritative way that could be binding on their industrial branch. Neither side devoted much attention to skills provision issues, being primarily concerned with collective bargaining.

Further, as the more dramatic conflicts over industrial relations and incomes were revealing at this time, both unions and employers' associations lacked authority among their own memberships. The underlying structure of industrial relations and wage bargaining failed to support the role of social partner organizations in advancing dynamic training activity (Finegold 1992: 140–1). Both weaknesses inhibited any attempts that might have been made to develop either a strategy or a system of detailed enforcement. The main instrument was the training levy which, though it should not be underestimated, was also limited as it never rose above modest levels. It was fixed initially at between 0.5% and 1.5% of payroll and was reduced after 1976 when government assumed most of the administrative costs of the system.[4]

It cannot be said that the ITB system under the aegis of the MSC proved to be a failure, as it did not have long enough to demonstrate its capacity and the Commission did not have time to develop a strategic role. Emerging as it did at a time of severe strain in social partnership, it nevertheless managed to be a forum of tripartite co-operation and did oversee a large programme of apprenticeship. Whether the social partners would have been able to develop further and innovate new arrangements for rapid technological change, and whether unions could have adapted from their identity-protecting role, it is difficult now to say, as major changes were to arrive before the end of 1979, less than six years after the MSC system had begun operation.

As noted in the previous chapter the MSC, as a piece of surviving neo-corporatism, including the participation of trade unions, and being an agency likely to spend money on interfering with the free market and managerial autonomy, was in many respects out of kilter with the neo-liberal orthodoxy that has dominated British policy in all areas since 1979 (ibid.: 208–10, 213–14). However, after a period of initial neglect in the first few years of the Thatcher government, it acquired a new prominence during the deep recession of 1981. Not only did unemployment begin to reach very high levels, but apprenticeship schemes collapsed in nearly all industries. This was partly a result of the recession, but partly also consequent on the government's abolition of the training levy system and the subsidies it provided for apprentices, and the winding-up of most of the ITBs on the grounds that they were an unnecessary burden on and an interference with industry and firms' own assessments of their training needs. Now, suddenly, training became urgent.

Endowed with new responsibilities and having a growing proportion of government educational spending channelled through it, the MSC set the pace of change and began increasingly to encroach on the territory of the still traditionalist Department of Education (ibid.: 223–6). Because the main impetus for its new prominence stemmed from the unemployment crisis, much of the MSC's funding and programmes were for remedial action. For example, the central

---

[4] The payroll levy was comparable to that introduced at around the same time and still existing in France. However, while the French system is aimed at financing further within-firm training within a state-led initial training system, the British levy was intended to assist initial training too.

initiative was the government's Youth Training Scheme (YTS), launched in 1983 as a means of equipping early school-leavers with some basic skills and administered through the MSC. As such, it was unlikely to contribute to providing new, higher skills (Steedman and Wagner 1989). It was also based heavily on perceptions of employers' existing needs rather than any future-oriented perspective to increase their ambitions (Lee *et al*. 1990). Even so, many apprenticeship schemes were relaunched within the framework of YTS and, associated though it was with remedial action, it became the country's main vehicle for training in manual skills, as was discussed in more detail in the previous chapter.

If the weaknesses of British training can be attributed to the weakness of institutions within the business world and the poor set of incentives offered, the MSC's response can be seen as tackling the former by an enormous head of energy of its own through which it sustained the support of the main central social partner organizations. It did not do much at a more decentralized level to spread responsibility and active participation among social partner or even business associations (King and Schnack 1990). Neither could it tackle the fundamental problems of short-termism in British managerial decision making. However, it was not these defects that caused its demise. This can instead be attributed to a number of factors.

First, the government wished to use the MSC as a channel through which the payment of unemployment benefit would increasingly be linked to the willingness of the unemployed to participate in training schemes. The TUC representatives on the MSC were not prepared to accept this element of 'compulsion' in treatment of unemployed people, and in 1987 refused to co-operate with it. Within months the government expelled union representatives from the Commission (a reduction in their role had already been planned), then abolished the Commission itself and took its powers back into the government apparatus.

Second, even during its brief heyday, the potential effectiveness of the MSC's operations was being undermined by the more general weakening of corporatism —not just through the marginalization of unions, but also through the undermining of employers' organizations that followed the collapse of industry-wide collective bargaining in many sectors. The role of unions in national training strategy was further weakened in 1989, when the government ended their right to be consulted over proposals for YTS training at unionized workplaces (King 1993).

Third, as discussed in Chapter 4, the Department of Education had begun to fight back against the MSC's encroachments and was probably instrumental in its final demise.

Since 1987 there has been no important role at all for organized interests, even of employers, in running VET, except in the construction industry, in which a combination of casual labour markets and high skill needs raises the problems of training as a collective good particularly acutely.[5] As a result,

---

[5] The involvement of business people as individuals through Training and Enterprise Councils continues to be very important, but that is a separate matter. The TECs will be discussed in some detail in the following chapter.

apprenticeship schemes have gradually declined into being small quantities of non-transferable on-the-job training (Marsden 1995). As Marsden argues, a considerable amount of this training takes place, and employers are spending large sums on it. However, it tends to be concentrated (as in other countries) on already well-educated employees, to come in non-certifiable forms of short in-service courses that cannot be easily related to other bodies of knowledge, and (as Robinson and Steedman (1996) also argue in relation to NVQs) to be found more in the sheltered than in the export-competitive sectors, in fact predominantly in public services.

Summary of the British case

The potential for interest associations, whether bipartite or of employers only, playing a continuing part during the 1980s was weakened by two forces. First, Conservative governments were thoroughly opposed to their role, especially on the labour side. Second, the institutions of industry-wide collective bargaining, which provided the main diet of activity for such organizations, went into a period of decline. Any significant level of industrial relations activity above the level of the company having become minimal, employers' associations have lost much of their *raison d'être*—certainly nearly all their authority in the business community—and in some cases they have disappeared altogether. It may therefore be the case that the option of working through representative bodies of business would not have been practical, even if it had been less ideologically unattractive to government. Therefore, while the MSC persisted curiously with a tripartite approach to an increasingly neo-liberal agenda (Finegold 1992: 215–22, 239), it is doubtful whether many of the associations involved in it could have made use of their wider legitimacy within their community to any effect.

Because in Britain, and in contrast with Germany, the role of associations in training has long been dependent on any stimulus given by government policy, much of the story of the final years of neo-corporatist experiments has been discussed above in connection with the role of the state through the MSC. In retrospect the Commission's half decade of hyperactivity in the mid-1980s appears as an anomaly, a mechanism left over from an earlier period but temporarily reinvigorated as the government needed it as an instrument, both of remedial action within the unemployment crisis and for its radically centralizing drive against local government and the educational establishment. By the time the MSC had finished, it had dramatically changed the landscape of policy and qualifications, but because it was operating within a context of frequent policy change and continuing struggle over modernizing and traditional educational forces, little of its legacy survived, and nothing of its corporatism at all. In its place, the Training and Enterprise Councils embody no structured role for interest associations at all, rather the reverse. They are, however, central to the idea of informal business networks as we shall see in the following chapter.

CONCLUSIONS

Neo-corporatist structures bring together strategic public-policy responsibilities and sensitivity to business needs. They should consequently be well placed to resolve some of the dilemmas in creating high-skilled societies; the German case demonstrates past capacity to achieve this. However, the capability of existing structures to perform in this way is weakened by a number of factors which emerge from the above discussion of examples.

First, even when they have been designed to facilitate considerable inter-action with individual firms, corporatist organizations experience difficulties in developing adequate sensitivity to company needs. This is partly because the pace of change is now so fast; partly because firms (especially in the services sectors) increasingly want that problematic entity 'social skills' rather than competence at easily definable tasks; and partly because these skills are frequently defined to mean aptitude at operating within the firm's distinctive culture. Meeting these challenges requires considerable adjustment from neo-corporatist institutions— of the kind that we have seen AMS trying to make in Sweden.

Second, the changeability and flexibility of new skill concepts shifts emphasis from initial towards ongoing training. As discussion of the German case showed, it is easier to organize neo-corporatist involvement in initial skills provision, because this concerns a necessary interface between, on the one hand, the public and social sphere of the school system and the general education of young people, and on the other, the private sphere of work and the acquisition of occupational iden-tity. Further VET takes place within this private sphere, after young people have been turned into company employees; employers are less likely to accept inter-action with public institutions, even those drawn from their own entrepreneurial community, at this point. Again, this will especially be the case when the fur-ther training takes the form of further induction into a specific corporate culture.

Third, while it is in principle possible to redesign corporatist structures in order to adapt them to new tasks, the balance of power in the business world at pre-sent inhibits this. In all three countries that we have examined in this chapter, there is a growing hostility of individual enterprises to engagement with public agencies. In the Swedish and British cases this is tied particularly to the power struggle between capital and organized labour. In German VET organization (though not of course in industrial relations), labour is not a very significant actor; but opposition to extra-firm constraints, while not as strong as in the other cases, can still be seen. The *Kammern*, although part of the business community, are seen as embodying collective concerns, sometimes also government concerns, which are increasingly perceived as implying additions to the cost burden which weakens international competitiveness in a world where there are many coun-tries, the firms of which face no such obligations.

Finally, there is some evidence in both Germany and Sweden for the Olsonian prediction that, as systems of organized interests become entrenched around a particular set of activities, they have a sclerotic effect on performance. As we

noted earlier, Olson's misunderstanding of the state of German and Japanese interest organizations in the wake of the Second World War has contributed to the
policy conclusion that therefore the best thing to do with such systems is to destroy
them. This has been the general strategy of the British government since the start
of the 1980s; it is the policy goal of SAF in Sweden, and an increasing number
of German firms is starting to take the same approach. An alternative, rooted in
a different interpretation of post-war Germany and Japan, would argue for a radical redefinition of the competences and areas of coverage of these organizations,
not a dismantling of their structures and capacities. In principle, if a government has the power to destroy organizations in the manner achieved in recent
years by the British state, it has the power to encourage their redesign instead.
However, two practical considerations inhibit this course of action.

First, institutional redesign and reconstruction require more skill and time
than demolition; and second, as we have already noted, the power constellation
in the business community currently favours the destruction rather than the recon-
stitution of institutions embodying public policy constraints on firms desperately
seeking freedom from all restraint in an increasingly competitive world. At the
same time employers want their new employees to be equipped with certain
relevant foundational skills by the public school system (see, for example, USA
NCEE and NAB 1994); and they want business interests to have a chance to
influence the changing content of these competences. Unless this task is to be
given to certain individual business people who thereby gain a special insider
position in relations with government and an exceptional chance to have government heed their particular views, it is difficult to envisage a means for achieving business involvement in the creation and development of these essential
competences other than some kind of redesigned corporatist structure.

6

Local Agencies for Skill Creation

Discussion of corporatist networks demonstrates the trade-off between encompassingness and strategic capacity, on the one hand, and flexible and local responsiveness, on the other. Within the realm of membership organizations, but at the opposite end of the continuum, are local, informal networks. Whereas associations operate through principles of hierarchical order, these latter work through norms of reciprocity and community exchange (Mingione 1991: ch. 1). By association we mean an explicitly and formally constructed organization which members join in a formal way, and which is bound by more or less clearly established rules of governance. Networks are informal. They may be explicitly recognized, but possibly in only a vague way; for example, a network might not have a name, any more than groups of friends have names. Rules of appropriate behaviour within the network, such as who holds a senior position in it, how one joins it, and who actually constitute the members, often remain uncodified and unwritten; they exist largely in the shared subjective understandings of those who are commonly regarded as being the core members. Normally therefore there has to be considerable interaction among members to sustain and develop these understandings, and this means that networks usually have a geographically precise and small location, though some exceptions to this might be found (for example, in specialized professional networks) if sufficient steps are taken to sustain frequent electronic and other forms of communication.

If analysis of formal associations requires an understanding of law, organizational theory, and probably political science, the study of networks belongs with sociology (in particular the sociology of community), cultural anthropology, and social geography. At its most general, the study of networks is the study of friendship and informal co-operation. Here, however, we are concerned with the more specific topic of networks among firms, or between firms and other organizations (such as local government, local trade unions, churches, and political parties) which might be relevant to their business activities. To see firms in this way is to regard them as embedded in a social structure (Grabher (ed.) 1993) which enables them to engage in co-operative relations and develop trust in each other and other institutions within the network and wider community (Granovetter 1985). A fundamental aspect of network relations is that they do not take the form of market transactions; exchanges are diffuse, long term, possibly even uncalculated. This is possible because the trust that exists makes it unnecessary to make precise exchanges, and the embeddedness makes it unlikely that firms will leave the community context before they have made reciprocal (but not strictly measured) contributions to the common stock of co-operative acts. The economic relevance of this kind of behaviour is that the accumulated results of co-operative acts become a form of shared assets for member firms, providing what Trigilia (1991) has called 'collective competition goods': firms are able to draw on the bank of assets to help them compete in wider markets.

For example, small firms in the same or related industries in an area might assist each other to complete an order from a distant customer firm when the firm with the order is overloaded and the firms lending assistance have spare capacity. The work itself will here be compensated through normal market means, and it is in the interests of all firms to participate in the deal. In strong networks of this type, firms may even co-ordinate purchases of different pieces of specialized equipment, knowing that they can all benefit from distributing these investment costs, rather than each firm buying all of the same equipment. The collective and non-quantified resource provided by the network is the understood and recognized a priori commitment to co-operate in such a circumstance without extensive negotiation and haggling over price. A firm within such a network is able confidently to take on contracts, knowing that if the deadline becomes difficult it will be able to draw on the willingness of its neighbours to co-operate. A firm which lacks such contacts might be able to subcontract in such circumstances, but through purely traded and calculated arrangements that might be difficult and expensive to organize. An even more diffuse and implicit example was uncovered by Bagnasco and Trigilia (1984; Bagnasco 1988) in Bassano in the Veneto region of Italy. They documented the coexistence of two such different industries as machine tools and garments within the same district as a part of the mutually supportive community character of these economies. The two sectors were not at all similar. They were not even related economically; it was not the case that the machine tool industry made machinery for the clothing industry. Instead, it was the very fact of their difference that made them complementary: product demand cycles for the machine-tool firms with primarily male workforces were quite different from those of the predominantly female garment industry, enabling the community to withstand fluctuating demand in either of the industries. Thus the community base facilitated labour flexibility.

As we saw during the course of the discussion in the previous chapter, ostensibly formal corporatist structures of the German kind can also embody elements of this informality; the distinction is not extreme. A group of small firms in a community might be able to act like an association by, say, threatening various sanctions of social exclusion towards firms which will not contribute to shared training activities. The issues selected for sanctions in this way can be diffuse, informal, and constantly developing. Streeck (1992) has described such processes among German employers. Other important examples of mixed cases may be drawn from Japanese supplier networks (Nishiguchi 1994; Smitka 1991; Sako 1992; 1996; Sako and Helper 1998; Friedman 1988). Here a large customer firm organizes in a fairly formal way an association of its suppliers, but as Sako (1996) shows, considerable effort is then devoted to developing patterns of social interaction and personal friendships to cement the relationships and encourage the supplier firms to trust and co-operate with each other. Firms in such connections develop close relations or partnerships with each other to avoid the high transaction costs of renegotiating complex deals at every new exchange (Aoki 1988; Asanuma 1989; Sako 1988; 1996; Sako and Helper 1998; Williamson 1985). Where suppliers' contracts are stable for a number of years, not only will small firms be able to risk some decisions of this kind, but the large corporation is also more likely to take an interest in their development. If it is concerned that suppliers are not keeping up with the latest skills and technology, it will need to discuss with them what they are planning; in the short-term, arm's-length context it would simply shop around to find firms that have managed to do so.

The geographical character of most networks led the scholars who 'discovered' them (for example, Bagnasco 1977; Becattini 1989; Becattini (ed.) 1987; Trigilia 1986)[1] to turn back to the concept of the 'industrial district' developed at the beginning of this century by the British economist Alfred Marshall (1912). Marshall asked why, in such cities such as Birmingham and Sheffield, manufacturers of similar items tended to congregate in the same neighbourhoods. He found the answer in the capacity for easy sharing of facilities that this afforded —including a shared skill base and process of learning. Allied to the modern concept of transaction-cost reduction and collective-competition goods, this theme has emerged again as a potential explanation of why some geographical regions seem able to advance economically far more rapidly than others. Researchers have looked to the existence of inter-firm networks as possible explanations of at least some of these cases of strong growth regions.

As noted, much of the literature about this phenomenon has focused on Italy, in particular the industrial districts of small firms in sectors such as engineering, advanced ceramics, and textiles in the north-east and central regions (see Bagnasco 1977; Best 1990; Hirst and Zeitlin 1989; Leborgne and Lipietz 1988; Trigilia 1986). While firms continue to compete, their co-operative relationship has facilitated product specialization, with enterprises concentrating on those markets where they have a competitive edge. Local networks have also been described as important in Denmark (Banke 1991; Hjalagar 1990) as well as in Germany (especially Baden-Württemberg (Herrigel 1996; Sabel *et al.* 1989), but also in parts of Nordrhein-Westfalen (Grabher (ed.) 1993; Voelzkow 1990)); only rarely in France or Sweden (Sweden 1991*a*: ch. 5; 1992*b*: ch. 4), though there is considerable debate about their desirability in both countries.

There are also extensive accounts from certain parts of the USA (for example, the metalworking sector in Wisconsin and Connecticut (Rogers and Streeck 1991; Mason and Finegold 1995); or the computer-oriented high-technology clusters in Silicon Valley (Saxenian 1994), Route 128 in Massachusetts (ibid.;

---

[1] The fact that these were Italians reflects the prominence of the phenomenon in some regions of that country, mainly the belt stretching from the Veneto in the north-east to Emilia-Romagna, Tuscany, Umbria, and the Marche in the centre. This is the area now generally known as the Third Italy, the First and Second Italies being the backward south (the Mezzogiorno) and the Fordist industrial north-west (Bagnasco 1977).

Finegold 1998*a*; Sabel *et al*. 1989), Austin (Texas) and Oregon (Best 1990; Porter 1990)). The preconditions for this are often present in the US context: strong local community identities, autonomous local governments with some economic competence, important local networks of businesses, excellent links between business and local colleges and universities. In some cases (for example, Fairchild Semiconductor and Hewlett Packard in Silicon Valley, California) this has led firms to provide substantial general training and development which helps fuel regional growth. Some US industrial districts comprise small and medium-sized firms in particularly highly skilled and innovative branches, especially in the high-tech sectors. Local university research centres, such as the world-class facilities at Stanford and Berkeley in Silicon Valley, are often intimately involved in the high-technology networks, providing ideas for start-up businesses, ongoing training and technology transfer, and infusions of new talent (Saxenian 1994). Similar roles for universities have been developed in Germany (Esser 1991; Voelzkow 1990).

In principle, in the absence of governing institutions within the sectors, one might expect firms of this kind to be very wary about developing expertise in their staff, and in any case they often lack the time and infrastructure to do so. The retention problem can be real, and may include anxieties about industrial espionage. It is partly offset by offering generous stock-options—which only vest after three or four years—to retain valued staff, but in these particular sectors there may also be a positive spin-off from the general optimism about the gains from future technological development in the sector. If the market is constantly expanding, if there are general gains from considerable cross-fertilization of ideas, and if local producers are only a sub-set of total producers in a global market, the frequent movement of expert staff may be experienced as positive, rather than zero-sum. For example, von Hippel (1987) has argued on the basis of research on small US steel mills that much positive-sum know-how trading occurred among engineers working for competitor firms. Saxenian (1994) found a similar dynamic among software and electronic engineers in Silicon Valley. There is often a strong onus on the individual employee continuously to develop his or her own skill base by frequent job moves or even by starting up one's own firm. These actions are made relatively easier by the geographical concentration of large numbers of firms in similar lines of business, giving employees the confidence to contemplate job moves without disrupting family life and children's schooling. This new pattern is often regarded as marking a shift from firm-based job security to individually based employment security; but behind the individual lies the industrial district, implicitly and informally providing firms with the collective-competition good of security which they cannot provide individually themselves but which their employees want.

As we saw in previous chapters on the state and on corporatist organizations, and as we shall see in the next chapter on the market, mechanisms for achieving goals do not always function positively. The same is true of networks. As Granovetter (1985) has discussed in theory and as Grabher ((ed.) 1993) has shown in his study of the Ruhr towns, 'too strong ties' to community and co-operative networks can inhibit change.[2] While a strength of networks (and associations and institutional companies) is that, by making it difficult for firms to use exit to solve problems, they encourage them to work at improvement, this can become a weakness if it locks firms and others into situations where incremental improvement is no longer a viable option (Herrigel 1998). This might happen, for example, in the case of industries that have declined beyond the hope of recovery. Also, Trigilia (1991: 317) has pointed to some of the disadvantages of trust, where the strength of that commodity in purely interpersonal terms can inhibit the development of arrangements for institutionalized trust (see also Fukuyama 1995). Institutionalized trust exists where A is willing to trust B, not because he has personal, community knowledge of B (who might be a complete stranger), but because B is a representative of an institution (for example, a bank or a government agency) which A has learned to regard as trustworthy. Communities which rely very heavily on personal trust may find it difficult to make the transition to institutionalized trust. One consequence of this will be that they find it hard to have extensive dealings outside their immediate circle, which limits the size and scope of their activities.

Training enters the frame as one of the collective goods that might be produced within co-operative networks. Potentially networks share some of the collectivist and non-state qualities of corporatist associations, while possessing more flexibility and proximity to firms' needs. This greater flexibility could be valuable in resolving some of the issues of skill creation through larger institutions that we have encountered in previous chapters. At the same time, smallness of scale and difficulties in transcending interpersonal trust might limit networks' training ambitions as well as other co-operative projects.

Since it has been Italy, more than any other European country, which has led observers in recent years to reconsider the role of informal networks in the analysis of modern economies, Italian experience will be discussed in some detail here, and this will be followed by some consideration of the Japanese supplier networks and of the British Training and Enterprise Council (TEC) experiment; the TECs are more appropriately regarded as an attempt at local network creation than as either corporatism or direct state action.

LOCAL BUSINESS NETWORKS IN ITALY

The Italian industrial districts are good examples of informal group formation in a context where intensified international competition may facilitate ventures with other companies in the same industrial sector. The firms involved are defined

---

[2] On the other hand, in precisely the Ruhr area where Grabher saw an incapacity to innovate, other authors have described an eventual capacity to respond and pursue new economic solutions (Hennings and Kunzmann 1990; Voelzkow 1990).

geographically, and compete in global markets against competitors from other geographical areas. While they continue to compete with each other for home markets, they have an incentive to co-operate in those parts of their operations— perhaps including advanced skill training—which no single firm may be able to finance, but which would benefit them all in the competition for foreign customers. The fact that they are still facing competition within the international market prevents them from using their combination to restrict competition. They must, however, possess the institutional resources necessary to construct the network; such arrangements are far from universal among producers in such situations.

The community base of Italian industrial districts, with their family and friendship relationships, church and political party links, made it possible for very small firms to develop relations of trust, enabling them to co-operate while still competing (see, for example, Becattini 1989; Trigilia 1989). Assisting with informal continued training of workers who had come through the inadequate formal system of skill creation was among the kinds of collaborative tasks taken on by these networks, though it did not figure as largely as some others, such as marketing assistance. A major obstacle to flexibility occurs when employees feel threatened with insecurity by change. A community provides an alternative or supplementary basis for trust and security. If people lose their jobs they will be supported by the family network, efforts will be made to employ them elsewhere, and they will have trust that this will be done (Franchi and Rieser 1991: 457–8).

Such an informal small-firm pattern might easily be associated with economic backwardness, and it was in that light that the artisanal economy had hitherto been seen. In addition, the search for a basis for trust at such local, face-to-face levels was taken as evidence of the chronic problems of low trust, inefficiency, and downright corruption of large-scale and official structures in Italian life. Informal networks might be remarkable in what they could achieve, but in some respects they were *faute de mieux*. What had become notable by the 1970s was that these districts were no longer backward, but included some of the most prosperous and internationally successful parts of Italy and indeed Europe. Further, in acquiring these attributes, they had reinforced rather than lost their small-firm, community characteristics. From the early 1970s onwards Emilia-Romagna, Tuscany, and the Veneto in particular had the interesting characteristics of being the regions of Italy that had some of the highest concentrations both of workers in manufacturing industry and of small firms (Trigilia 1986: 162).

There was also a surprising mix in the kind of products being produced (ibid.: 161). Many of them were in food, clothing, shoes, and other fashion goods. All these are close to agriculture: food, obviously; the garment industry of Emilia-Romagna is heavily wool based; the shoe and fashion product industries are leather based. These might be seen to continue the image of simple, 'post-peasant' structures. However, the industries of these regions have also notably included ceramics (to some extent a traditional industry dating back to Roman times, but also one capable of producing advanced modern industrial products), sophisticated machine-tools sectors, specialized motor vehicles, various precision metal products, and a clothing industry based on industrially reprocessing used fabrics rather than on primary materials.

More recently the north-western region of Lombardy has been found to have similar networks to those usually seen as particularly characteristic of the centre and north-east (Colombo and Regalia 1996). The system in all these regions needs to be distinguished from the black economies or illegal sectors of southern Italy, where small firms are able to survive on the basis of lower-quality goods produced by low-skilled labour because of the price advantages of untaxed illegal production (Bagnasco 1988: 34–7). While such firms are not absent from the lower ends of the fashion goods industries of the central regions, the most significant parts of those economies do not depend on illegality. In some cases entrepreneurial associations assist local government in ensuring fiscal regularity, and competitive edge has depended more on the quality reputation of well-known brand names. The small firms of the southern regions rarely developed resourceful, self-reliant industrial districts in the same way, partly because of the dependence of those regions on political favours from the central state and its political figures—though by the late 1990s these were signs of the emergence of some true industrial districts in parts of the Mezzogiorno, especially in the furniture industry.

The search for alternatives to the state to provide collective goods—again, making use of traditional community links (kinship, religion, neighbourhood) rather than specifically 'modern' constructions to do so—has been an important characteristic of the industrial districts. It is notable that small firms in central Italy neither became dependent on state clientelism nor turned their backs on the possibility of collective action to devote themselves to pure market competition, but made use of facilities for such action (Best 1990). Gradually during the 1970s, local (that is, *comune*) government often became accepted as potentially part of the networks in many areas (Trigilia 1986: 170). Rather than rely on national government resources that would probably not be delivered, or would be delivered inefficiently, firms grouped together with various other local actors to provide public goods for themselves. Within both Communist and Catholic subcultures it was possible for local regulation of labour markets to develop in which employers, unions, and other local networks assisted in the collective sharing of the costs of economic reorganization (ibid.: 162 ff.).

Unusually for small-firm sectors, trade unions played an important role in at least some of these districts. It was a different kind of unionism from the alienated, conflictual kind found in the large factories of northern Italy in the early post-war decades; the workforce was not proletarian and the level of conflict was much lower (Locke 1995). Firms themselves were also more likely than is usual with small enterprises to belong to their representative associations (ibid.: 169). In principle therefore the industrial networks and their communities were well oriented to the production of collective goods for businesses, and might be expected to play a part in skill creation.

Industrial districts and the challenge of skill formation

Training is often listed among the collective-competition goods delivered by the Italian small-firm system, but it is not prominently discussed. It has been typically informal; the owners of the small firms are usually skilled craftsmen (*artigiani*) who practise their trade themselves; they pass on the skills, in an implicit form of on-the-job training, to their own sons and daughters and also give assistance with particular specialist tasks to neighbours in the same trade. It has also been a deficit model of training. Young workers emerge from the state schools and training institutes with some basic knowledge which will be refined and made more practical through informal local networks.

It is possible that this almost invisible, certainly uncertified, pattern explains one of Italy's educational paradoxes: the highest incidences of failures to complete education to the point of qualification occur in the north-east and central regions of the country, where numbers dropping out of school are higher than in either the industrial north-west or the depressed south (CENSIS 1994; Jobert 1995). It is argued that in the north-west the large factories have required formal qualifications as a screening device for hiring, even though the skill demands of their Fordist production had traditionally been relatively modest; in the south young people desperately acquire educational qualifications in the hope that they will help their employment chances. Meanwhile, in the small-firm zones of the north-east and centre people are able to find work, often with their own family, and acquire the necessary skills from the locality. Recent research (Iannelli 1998) shows that young Italians who pursue some higher education secure better jobs than those who have none, even if they do not complete their courses and acquire certificates. This is consistent with the model of recruitment within a local community, when the formal certification needed in anonymous settings will be less important than the fact that one is known to have received a certain type of education. This certainly fits the classic pattern of the role of small-firm communities and networks in the Italian context, and it has clearly enjoyed some success; it is in this part of Italy that one finds the specialized machine-tool firms which, as we saw in Chapter 3, held their own against the Germans and Japanese when British and American firms failed to do so in the 1980s; it is also the key area for the production of up-market fashion goods. Is this system able to confront the latest challenges of a 'learning society'?

As elsewhere in western Europe, by the 1980s the production of a highly skilled labour force had become an issue of national political importance in Italy and not just a private matter for firms and VET institutions (Bresciani 1987: 55). There is now a more or less formal public commitment by government, Confindustria (the main manufacturing employers' association), and the main unions to turn Italy into a country with an advanced, high-skilled labour force (D'Avanzo 1992). As in many other countries, skills were also coming to be seen more in terms of flexible, general competencies and developed intelligence rather than specific 'skills' in the sense of the former industrial economy—whether Fordist or craft based (Meghnagi 1991; Colombo and Regalia 1996). As we saw in Chapter 4, Italy's existing public training institutions were evaluated during this process and found to be deficient. Further, training options have not related very clearly to the needs and preferences of employers, whose organizations, in general, have been neither involved nor interested in the content and organization of courses. In general, Italian industry was developing its market strategies and accompanying work organizations either at low levels of skill demand or with demands that could be met by informally imparted skills. The country was not embarked on a course for high-competence competition, but was excelling in precisely the areas in which poor countries could eventually become rivals.

The critical reappraisal of labour-market policy also affected the industrial districts. The kinds of skill that could be imparted through informal networks seemed to be limited; perhaps the districts were reaching the limits of their achievements. Also, as Bianchi (1992) has pointed out, within Europe generally by the early 1990s large companies had made a powerful response to the gains that had been made in market share by small firms in a number of sectors; industrial concentration within the European Union, the emergence of new competitors from outside the EU (such as the new market economies of eastern Europe), and private market regulation increased the competitive challenge on the small firms. In many industries this required a change of strategy by them. This proved to be a severe challenge. Local production systems needed a capacity to improve their competitiveness by a number of actions, including retraining their labour forces. This required action going beyond the local networks themselves.

Regional governments have attempted to fill the gap between central state initiatives that are remote from the localities and the growing inadequacies of informal provision, though often these initiatives added to the confusion and excessive complexity of Italian formal education by duplicating national provision (Infelise 1996: 181). By the early 1990s the regional governments (which had been established during the 1970s) were organizing, not just basic vocational courses for young workers, but also a considerable amount of continuing education for existing workers (Isfol 1992: 25–8). They have now also begun to organize second-level (post-secondary) courses at intermediate and advanced levels; these second-level courses have come increasingly to be concentrated on the tertiary sector and information technology (ibid.: 34–42). And courses have increasingly been oriented to the real needs of the workplace through relations with interest organizations, apprenticeship, etc. (ibid.: 40–1). Partly in an attempt to operate in a manner more similar to that of the business world, rather similarly to the British TECs (see below), the regional governments rely heavily on placing contracts with private-sector firms or non-profit entities under local authority supervision to provide their courses (ibid.: 160). About 70% of these training providers are in the private sector and about 30% are public. In each case their activities are validated by a bilateral body—representing employers and unions —which sets standards of content and certification. There are then national accords for the mutual recognition of certificates, based on numbers of hours of study.

Additional new institutions working at this interface have been regional agencies for employment (*agenzie regionali per l'impiego*). These developed gradually as a response to a felt need to have an active labour market policy in general, including the area of training (Carinci 1990). Lombardy was the first region to do this in 1983, but others followed fast and they were soon established as entities of the central state (which finances them) but with regional administrations consulted on their membership. They have a duty to work closely with regions, local authorities, and social partners on training and career advice issues. The regions have to approve their programmes. Their legal status is innovative, as peripheral agencies of the central state working in co-operation with the regions. Again, during their brief history agencies have moved from a bureaucratic to a managerial mode of operation (ibid.). Although in theory their role is advisory, they have sometimes become involved in organizing training, as it is possible for regional governments to delegate competences to them. This has mainly been done in the autonomous provinces of Val d'Aosta and Trentino, where authorities hope that the agencies might serve as links spanning the gulf between government and business (Pitton 1991).

Brusco, Reyneri, and Seravalli (1990) see local agencies as a useful breakthrough, or synthesis, in creative institution building after a period of rigid state regulation had been succeeded by its antithesis: deregulation, neo-liberalism, and the dismantling of institutions. The structure of agencies also made possible recognition of the different needs of different parts of the country. In the south their role has to be very basic, in trying to link the large numbers of unemployed young people to the labour market. In the north and centre, there is scope for more sophisticated careers advice to individual job-seekers and also assistance to new firms in securing a good labour force. The latter includes helping firms to train workers they have engaged as a result of the agencies' work, at least by subsidizing the training and possibly by helping to provide it. They have had to struggle against firms' usual suspicions of anything to do with state activity, and union suspicions that they were just handing out a new swathe of subsidies to businesses. The most alert agencies have therefore involved the social partners at every stage—particularly for assistance in the task of distinguishing between those firms which are just subsidizing their wages bill and those which are providing real training.[3]

The numbers of people being trained by the regional authorities is still small, smaller than the numbers in apprenticeship or in the national state training

---

[3] On-the-job training schemes were, like those in many countries, developed in the 1980s (*legge* 863 of 1984) to deal with the growing youth unemployment problem. They provide subsidies to enable people between the ages of 15 and 29 to be hired by employers for two years only, stipulating that the individual receive training supervised and approved by the regional authorities. A later scheme (*legge* 113 of 1986) was directed at the long-term unemployed aged 18–29, especially in the south. Because many in Italy are aware that the country has much ground to make up, there is interest in continuing education for the high proportion of untrained people. In some regions such as Emilia-Romagna, employers can be subsidized for taking on redundant employees, provided they appoint a tutor to help them acquire new skills.

system (Isfol 1992: 162). Some concern has also been expressed about whether the agency model of much recent policy development is leading to yet further fragmentation of provision and the monitoring of standards. There is also some suspicion that agencies tend to organize courses that are prestigious but not very useful to young people or the needs of the local labour market (ibid.: 112–13; Infelise 1996: 181). Considerable work also remains to be done in developing validation and certification.

A further initiative by regional governments to enable local networks to extend their scope has been the establishment of 'service centres'.[4] Bianchi (1992: 310–11) lists 33 examples of such centres, in regions running from Friuli to Sicily, 14 of which included training among the services offered. Bianchi and Bellini (1991) have argued that, once a network has reached the limits of achievement, policy action has to try to assist the whole network of firms and its surrounding community to enlarge the basis of its tasks. In their view this requires policy intervention by public authority; left to itself the network will be unable to upgrade its activities; assistance based on individual firms will destroy the basis of the network. This is seen as necessary because the firms and the networks themselves lack access to the kind of competence needed.

The policy response has taken the form of centres for 'real services' (*servizi reali*). These are organized either by local or regional public authorities themselves or by consultancy groups operating under their auspices. Like the other agencies discussed above, they have embodied a model of non-bureaucratic operation, both entrepreneurial and co-operative, and an attempt to get closer to local networks than was usually possible for public agencies: sufficiently external to the local system and therefore not trapped by the limitations of its increasingly inadequate horizons, but close enough to it to work within rather than against the network concept.

The coverage of these centres closely corresponds to the coverage of industrial districts, being at their most dense in Emilia-Romagna and Tuscany. Regions in the south have very few, even though the resources for them are available; they have not spent all the national and European funds for which they are eligible to finance co-operative training schemes, and have shown little interest in this area of policy (Isfol 1992: 261).

The government of Emilia-Romagna first produced a regional law on vocational training in 1979 (*legge regionale* 19/79). This delegated to the provinces of the region powers to organize training and guidance services. As a result, a considerable variety of institutes and organizations has developed throughout the region, specializing in providing services for different kinds of firms and for different training needs. The kinds of activity have included training for various technical skills, and also—very important in a region of very small enterprises—in management and entrepreneurship. In small firms a particular skills issue

---

[4] See Bianchi 1985 and 1990 for a theoretical analysis of the role of such services and the significance of a local and network base for their organization.

concerns entrepreneurs themselves: Do they know how to formulate a business plan? To take advantage of computer systems? To market in remote countries? How will they solve problems of labour management? Very few indeed of the large number of entrepreneurs in the Third Italy have had any formal training in these areas, and it would be difficult to provide the resources from within the local communities themselves unless, as is now happening, they draw on the resources of neighbouring universities and other local sources of expertise.

In the mid-1980s the regional government, in co-operation with all relevant labour and employer organizations within its territory, produced a plan for improving training in the region, devoting increasing resources to supporting a series of training courses subsidized by integrating European Social Fund grants into the arrangements (Benedetti 1991). Plans for apprenticeship schemes in partnership with local firms were incorporated (ibid.: 44). The region recognized the need for its courses to become more entrepreneurial and in tune with the needs and aspirations of companies (ibid.: 62), though by 1989 budget cuts had forced reductions in the programmes, placing its future in some jeopardy.

Similar developments have taken place in Tuscany. A report for the regional government (Freschi 1992) expressed concern that the small-scale networks of the industrial district model were not adequately addressing the challenges of both global competition and the response of large corporations. Towards the end of the 1980s the region had established a number of *servizi reali*—in particular, centres for vocational training (*centri di formazione professionale*)—to assist small business communities to adjust to face these challenges. In all, 17 of the 27 initiatives launched were concerned with training. In addition to services explicitly labelled as training, many of the other activities of the centres (for example, technology transfer, creation of new enterprises, personnel relations, diffusion of innovative ideas) also include a training element.

The record of activity has been considerable, but it has also met the obstacle that might have been expected. Regions, provinces, and their service centres, local though they may be in focus, still represent external forces in the eyes of some business networks; they are sufficiently remote from actual communities to have to be the objects of institutional rather than personal trust. They therefore encounter trust problems similar to those of central state institutions, if not quite so strong.

The Tuscan centres were established in partnership with representative organizations, though in practice trade union involvement has been very low (Freschi 1992: 31). Associations of small businesses participated more seriously, but were both jealous of the centres as possible rivals to themselves and concerned at what might be state intervention in the market. The centres experienced a major trust problem (ibid.: 76). Firms themselves were also reluctant to take on tasks going beyond their immediate perception of market needs, so it was difficult to use the centres to raise horizons; centres trying most clearly to carry out the task of doing this were less likely to be successful than those offering services corresponding to existing perceived demands (ibid.: 59–60), including in particular services within the area of training (ibid.: 65). This provides a good illustration of the difficulty of moving firms which have been operating within a low-skill equilibrium to accept the challenge of trying to move to a high-skill one. Similarly, the most successful centres are those that have depended on particular respected local individuals and not on formal representation (ibid.: 33, 77–8). Likewise, because of the lack of a basis for mutual trust, centres have also found it very difficult to co-operate with each other and share experiences.

To the extent that they succeed in orienting themselves more successfully to the perceived needs of companies and local networks, centres, agencies, and other co-operative mechanisms run into different problems: while relating themselves to the endogenous needs of companies, bodies responsible for raising skill levels also need to ensure the achievement of standards capable of external monitoring—this being a particular issue in small and medium-sized enterprises (Isfol 1992: 149, 168–9). Also, because entrepreneurs' own associational resources are informal and local, they tend not to have strategic capacity or to perceive the broad picture. The local production system was after all, as has been noted above, partly a response to the felt need to protect threatened local community institutions from invasion by the state and by market forces (Trigilia 1986: 165). The networks are likely therefore to be mistrustful of initiatives that try to reach beyond what firms are currently doing. To the extent that centres, etc. then adapt themselves to local perspectives, they have to drop the strategic ambitions that they were designed to promote in the first place. In the Italian context the general challenge of moving from low- to high-skill equilibria has to embrace this additional specific problem.

Summary

The strengths of the local networks have therefore continued to be simultaneously their limitations, though there have been changes and improvements. We have seen examples of Trigilia's (1991: 317) argument that the very strength of the local ties and personal trust that produced effective community action prevents the possibility of collaboration through institutional trust at higher levels such as the region, where co-ordination may be necessary for more ambitious tasks. He also points to the paradox whereby, at the very moment that the regions were beginning to get off the ground, national-level industrial relations were also finally starting to operate effectively, and much of the activity that helped stabilize that level undermined the growth of the regions (ibid.: 318). Such regions as Lombardy, with a larger scale of industry, were better equipped to operate through associations active at the regional government level than in the classic industrial district regions of the centre (ibid.: 319). As has been pointed out elsewhere, the co-operation within industrial districts is based to some extent on custom (*consuetudine*) (Franchi and Rieser 1991); this can impart a distinct conservatism to the kind of co-operation that it makes possible. It may also well be that when firms which take for granted customary neighbourhood co-operation are asked to think more explicitly about their activities, they begin to think more 'rationally' in the sense of putting the interests of their individual firm first, and start to destroy the basis of co-operation and sharing.

Bianchi and Gualtieri (1990) have also described a process of company take-overs within Emilia-Romagna which is threatening to undermine the essential characteristics of this small-firm economy, the distinctiveness of which may be being 'crushed' between the growing role of large firms and competition from newly industrialized countries (NICs) (ibid.: 100). Part of the problem lies in the difficulties of adaptation by networks, since they rely on considerable inter-action and communication to change their production model.

So far the response of the Italian economy to the challenges of new com-petition has been partly to revive and update the large corporations of the north, with (as before) a mixture of Fordist hierarchical companies providing their own relatively modest skill needs, and more up-market institutional companies, also again avoiding the problems of collective action in their production of skill. Partly, however, there have been attempts to upskill the small- and medium-sized firm sector of central Italy and elsewhere that has proved to possess exactly the dynam-ism and flexibility required by the late twentieth-century economy. At present that seems to be happening more in the Veneto region of the north-east, in par-ticular under the leadership of the Benetton clothing empire acting as a large cus-tomer corporation for which very small enterprises carry out contracts. Although Benetton is not part of the separatist movement currently seeking independence from Italy for this and other northern regions, the strong sense of regional iden-tity is important to economic co-operation there. As we have seen above, the small-firm economy embodies a problem: dependent for its very vitality and suc-cess on using informality and localism because of the difficulties involved in dealing with formal, especially state, institutions, it encounters a certain block if resources from outside the capacity of the local area are needed in order to move into new areas of competence and enterprise.

To argue in this way is to assume that Italy should now start to find its dis-tinctive niches by adopting strategies which seem to be the common aim of all advanced countries: the production of goods and services specific to high-value-added, educated workforces adept at generalized, flexible competences attuned to local company culture but with publicly validated levels of achievement. But why should very similar means be used for the pursuit of diverse niches? A by no means illogical alternative would be to retain distinctive approaches. Central Italy's generation of relatively informal, non-bureaucratic, partly entrepreneurial, partly tripartite agencies and entities of various kinds does at least provide a distinctive approach to the crucial issue of the gulf between public authority and local entrepreneurial community which is not being very satisfactorily resolved in any of the other countries we are considering. The bewildering array of *enti* and *agienze* might be simply reproducing the disorder and overlapping or parallel routes for training and other managerial services that have dogged the country for so long; but they might, like the small firms the extraordinary variety of which they seem to mirror, also embody significant points of initiative and success.

SMALL BUSINESS NETWORKS IN JAPAN

Industrial districts of small firms called *sanchi*, on roughly the Italian pattern, have been a part of the structure of Japanese industry, as they are today in south China. It has been government policy to encourage their growth. Of the 500 or so officially registered *sanchi*, around 70% date back to before the Second World War, and over 30% to the Edo period (1603–1867) (SMEA 1995: 276). However, the system is not part of the dynamic heart of Japanese industry. The products range from traditional crafts (such as lacquerware and pottery) to consumer goods from the cheap, low-quality phase of Japanese industrialization and, as such, face severe competition from cheaper producers elsewhere in Asia. Also, depending, like the Italian firms, on family networks, they face severe problems now that young people no longer wish to carry on such businesses.

Supplier networks led by large firms

If one seeks small-business networks making an important economic contribution in contemporary Japan it is more relevant to look to the supplier networks created and maintained by the great corporations. As noted above, this phenomenon is not absent in Italy; the Benetton clothing chain and some other large firms in the Veneto region have established something similar. In the post-war Japanese economy however, these networks play a more central role. At the heart of a network is an exchange between a large customer firm and a number of first-tier suppliers, in which the customer offers long-term partnerships (including security of contract) in exchange for high-quality, just-in-time supply closely suited to its needs and capable of rapid adaptation. By committing to long-term orders from a given supplier, rather than relying on a pure market system of frequent renegotiation and precisely calibrated exchange, the customer takes a risk.[5] The risk is partly offset by the close interest the large firm takes in the business of the suppliers; it requires detailed knowledge of their business and it gives advice on changes required to maintain adaptation to its needs. It is in this way that the long-term supplier relationship can offer assistance with training and other expensive and collective forms of provision that would probably be beyond the reach of small firms left to their own devices and in competition with each other.

---

[5] While the relationships between customers and suppliers are longer in Japan than in more market-oriented economies such as the USA and the UK, the actual formal contracts, if they exist at all, are typically only one year in length; the partnership, or implicit contract to continue doing business together, thus needs to be differentiated from the formal agreements, which are renegotiated to take into account changes in material costs, technology, etc. (Helper and Sako 1995).

In adapting itself so closely to the large firm's needs, however, a supplier is also taking a risk that the large firm will not honour the long-term nature of the arrangement. If the implicit contract were repudiated, much of the customer-specific investment in both physical and human capital would have to be written off. These relationships therefore require mutual trust, since they lack the constant recourse to enforcement of written contract terms that characterizes purer market forms of doing business. Such mutual trust, say between Toyota and its suppliers, has been cultivated by Toyota devoting much of its own resources to technical assistance, by sending in its own engineers to the suppliers' shop-floor to provide hands-on training in how to implement just-in-time production or quality-control procedures (Sako and Helper 1997). Toyota's show of commitment to a particular supplier in this way encourages the supplier to make investments and to accumulate know-how which are specific to that relationship (Asanuma 1989). This incentive to invest in 'relationship-specific skills' is considered a major source of competitive advantage of Japanese firms.

An even more interesting aspect of these relationships and their capacity to transcend pure contract is that there is not merely a number of bilateral relations between customer and supplier, but a set of multilateral ties binding the suppliers to each other as well as to the large firm. This is what is meant by a supplier network, and is enforced by the formation of supplier associations (*kyoryokukai*) (Sako 1996). Since these suppliers are in principle in competition with each other for trade from the customer, these networks have been carefully structured by and are maintained by the customer firms. Their incentive to do this results from the gains they achieve from a rapid diffusion among their suppliers of improvements and innovations taking place in any one or more firms. If the suppliers were in fierce competition with each other, they would jealously protect any innovations and would keep them secret from the customer, threatening the whole basis of the close relationship. Therefore the customer not only offers long-term commitment to limit competition, but also encourages close relations, exchanges of information, and the development of a community of interest among the suppliers themselves. In this way they are able to develop co-operation on issues like quality improvements and cost reduction. Training and broader learning in this context take the form of off-the-job courses, study groups, and mutual factory visits which are arranged as part of the activities of supplier associations. Instruction may typically be given by someone from the large customer company, but the quality of the learning is enhanced by the suppliers' willingness to offer advice to each other. Trust is therefore also needed and developed among the supplier firms.

Since this trust involves a variety of salaried managers from the large firm and groups of suppliers who have been brought together by the large firm rather than forming part of a pre-existing community, it is a rather different form of trust from the Italian variety. As we saw, the Italian model depends heavily on family, neighbourhood, and other forms of face-to-face contact. The Japanese relationships have institutionalized trust more successfully (Fukuyama 1995); one does not trust the manager from company X because his aunt is married to one's second cousin, but because he is working as part of a firm that has shown itself to be worthy of trust in the past, and because the network of which both are part is an example of an institution which has been shown to work successfully in many circumstances in one's country in the past. This form of trust is more like that generated by German business associations than Italian communities— though, as with German associations, an interpersonal network is often super- imposed on the more formal one, helping to expedite its business and add a component of personal trust. It differs from an association, of course, in that the supplier firms are not participating members of the customer firm but are pro- ducing goods which are purchased by it; this gives them their primary incentive to join the group of suppliers and to respect what the customer firm asks them to do. There is no problem of collective action. Nor are the supplier firms con- cerned with orientation to public policy goals; any questions of this kind will be dealt with between the government and the management of the customer firm. The Japanese customer firms regularly organize dinners and other social gatherings—typically golf and baseball—at which their managers and the leaders of the supplier firms meet, creating what Germans would call *Gemütlichkeit*.

Metropolitan small-firm networks without a single large focal firm

A trust-based supplier relationship has its advantages; but there are limits to the number of direct suppliers with which any one large firm can develop such a relationship. This is why, while the US 'Big Three' vehicle producers at one time retained thousands of direct suppliers, Japanese car manufacturers typically kept only a few hundred. In order to narrow the number of direct suppliers, Japan- ese large companies developed multiple tiers in their supplier networks, with smaller firm size as one goes down the tiers. Many of the same institutions for the provision of collective goods (such as training for a group of suppliers) have been duplicated for the lower tiers; for instance supplier associations of second- tier companies have been organized by first-tier suppliers, in order to diffuse what they learned from their large customer firms. This process of imitation and trick- ling down enables each tier of small firms to benefit from the collective-goods provision capability of the tier higher than their own.

   The lower tiers of these supplier networks led by a large firm consist of gen- uinely small firms, and for some of them which are owner-managed, the distinc- tion between interpersonal trust and institutional trust becomes blurred. Added to this is the strong sense of geographical identification and community among them. Admittedly, the origin of some of the locally based supplier networks, such as those in and around Toyota City or Hitachi City, can be clearly traced back to the establishment of a large firm, which has come to entertain a sense of social obligation in the company town. But other networks, such as Hamamatsu in Shizuoka Prefecture, existed before the establishment of relatively large firms in the area such as Suzuki Motors and Yamaha.

Geographically concentrated small-firm networks which do not rely on a single large focal firm tend to exist in metropolitan areas in Japan, in particular in Otaku in south Tokyo and East Osaka (SMEA 1995: 265; Ueda *et al.* 1996; Watanabe 1995; Whittaker 1997). The main point of similarity with the successful Italian industrial districts lies in the nature of flexible specialization. Not only is Otaku or East Osaka a regional cluster of a large number of small firms (each containing around 7,000 to 9,000 manufacturing firms, with 80% of them employing fewer than ten workers (SMEA 1995)); much functional flexibility exists within the cluster, so that each firm is able to fulfil a broad range of small-lot orders with very short lead times by calling upon other firms to act as subcontractors. This interdependence among the small firms is maintained by the following two mechanisms.

First, 'ties of blood, friendship and neighbourliness underlie many of these relations' in Otaku (Whittaker 1997: 111), and these ties are reinforced by the fact that it is an area with little segregation between residential and manufacturing space; just over half of Otaku factories and workshops have owner-managers' housing on the same premises (ibid.: 131).

Second, while there is no lifetime employment at these firms (and there remains something of the legacy of wandering journeymen, changing their place of work before settling down as master craftsmen), poaching appears to be rare. This is not only because of the community orientation, but also because some new firms have been established by former employees of existing firms with the blessing and support of their ex-employers (SMEA 1994: 262).[6] In these start-ups, a manual employee becomes an independent owner-manager with the financial help of the former employer, who may provide second-hand equipment, factory premises, and some subcontract orders. Thus, not all exits are bad from the point of view of skill formation, and the mode of start-ups within the same area ensures co-operation among firms over such matters as the fulfilment of orders, or the joint purchase of materials.

Japanese government policy towards small firms has been underpinned by the idea that they would be able to exploit economies of scale and emulate large firms by forming associations. In fact as many as 45,566 SME organizations were identified by the Small and Medium-sized Enterprise Agency (SMEA) in 1990, and 85% of them were co-operative business associations. They were mostly small associations with perhaps two dozen member firms, all in a single industrial sector, most commonly in such areas as woodworking, textiles, pottery, retail, wholesale, transportation, and construction. Around a third of all co-operatives claimed to provide some education and training, considering this 'service' as the fourth most important activity (after the collection and provision

---

[6] This has also been a characteristic of much new company formation in Germany, contributing to the maintenance of business communities there (Streeck 1992).

of information, joint purchase of materials, and the provision of welfare services for member firms and their employees) (Whittaker 1997: 114–16). As co-operatives, they can also obtain government loans and subsidies on favourable terms.

There are, however, limits to the capacity of such associational networks to provide VET, particularly when it concerns not a mere regeneration of existing skills but upgrading for new technology and new products. The social esteem of the small-firm sector is under attack, as the '3K' image (*kitsui* (hard), *kitanai* (dirty), *kiken* (dangerous)) is leading to serious recruitment difficulties, particularly for technicians and blue-collar workers. Temporary labour shortages, particularly in the bubble economy of the late 1980s, were satisfied by recruiting foreign workers. The government also devised a number of schemes for the training of foreign workers as part of its overseas development assistance policy, whereby it provides subsidies to small firms which train and employ foreign workers (mainly from China) for a limited period of time (Imano 1997). But on a more secular trend, small firms in Japan have a poor prospect of securing good-quality labour in a society in which the overall attainment of general education is not considered problematic. The main 'human resource' problem for small firms in Japan is not the poor educational attainments of young people in excess supply, but how to make small firms an attractive workplace for well-educated young people increasingly in shortage in a rapidly ageing society. The more recent incentives for inter-firm co-operation, and public policy supporting it, have arisen from the need to solve this common problem.

One policy initiative in this area is the so-called fusion programme, which is an attempt by the SMEA to bring small firms from different industrial sectors to innovate and develop new products. For this purpose, 'technology exchange plazas' have been constructed to encourage exchange of ideas among the firms (Whittaker 1997: 122). This encourages the setting up of groups of around 30 firms which meet regularly to discuss technical and managerial issues, visit model factories, and hear speeches from invited speakers. It is hoped that some of these groups will go beyond information exchange to develop new products and 'fusion', a new joint venture. The government support is not just in terms of finance (funds, tax relief, etc.), but also in kind (access to government testing facilities and advisers known as 'catalysers'). Ultimately, small firms may consider starting a new venture as another way of attracting good-quality new recruits.

Summary

In recent years the Japanese supplier network system led by large firms has come under some pressure. This is partly a response to the growing uncertainty of world markets and the fears of large companies that they can no longer risk such extensive long-term agreements for certain levels of supply. Helper and Sako (1995) report declining customer commitment at the margin and growing uncertainty about future orders among automotive suppliers. (Ironically they also report a growth of long-contract relations and supplier networks in the USA, as American firms react positively to the spread of Japanese business practice, the two learning processes leading to a certain amount of convergence.) However, the character of the Japanese response continues along the high-trust trajectory. Customer firms have suggested to their suppliers that, while remaining members of the supplier network, they should also become contractors to other (in theory, rival) large firms, and join their networks. This means, of course, an increased flow of information between the networks of large firms, a development that is possible only in a business context where high-trust relations reduce the intensity of competitive practices.

Every one in four employees in manufacturing in Japan works at an establishment with fewer than 20 workers, and this figure excludes owner-managers and family workers. While large institutional firms can provide training in-house (a subject to which we shall return in the next chapter), smaller firms do not have the resources and therefore rely on outside agents. But these outside agents are typically firms with which small firms have a business link, such as customer firms and suppliers of equipment and machinery (Koike 1994: 20). Even within small firms, some education and training are undertaken with a view to providing an incubation period before employees become independent and set up their own businesses. In these ways, training activities which cross the firm's boundary are carried out as part of business links, providing a customer focus for the need to make improvements.

LOCAL SKILL-CREATION INITIATIVES IN THE UK

Historically the British VET system suffered from the weaknesses of institutions (for linking firms with each other and with educational institutions) which thereby hindered the provision of collective goods, combined with short-termism in decision making by both firms and individual members of the labour force. By the early 1990s policy had come to concentrate on making a virtue of some of these weaknesses. The weakness of institutions became an opportunity for flexibility. Short-termism became an opportunity to make more use of immediate market incentives. The weakness of collective-goods provision became a reason for leaving more autonomy to individual companies, which could pursue entrepreneurial opportunities without much interference from the state, business associations, or other external institutions. All three characteristics became a means of ensuring frequent and rapid change. However, by the end of the Conservative government's long rule in 1997, some ambivalence about the virtues of weak institutions could be detected.

In 1991 the government adopted a new strategy which openly and formally rejected the corporatist or associational path, but which acknowledged a role for local, informal business networks. The key institutions in the new policy were the 82 Training and Enterprise Councils (TECs) (in Scotland there are another 23 somewhat more broadly empowered Local Enterprise Companies (LECs)). These replaced all existing structures for organizing and supervising government policy for skill creation and were charged with the task of getting the training activities of British firms to a point where they could compete with the best that Germany, Japan, or the great American corporations had to offer. At the same time they were given the task of administering all programmes for assisting the young and adult unemployed, groups which tended in general to be at the low end of the skills range and unlikely to be manning the spearhead of a national high-skills challenge.

TECs were developed in deliberate imitation of US Private Industry Councils (PICs), with some changes designed to remedy problems PICs had encountered (Bailey 1993).[7] Their members are drawn primarily from the business community, but they rarely hold representative positions in business organizations. TECs are local, but with no necessary relationship to local government and with boundaries which do not always follow those of local government. They are creatures of central government but operating in an entrepreneurial rather than a bureaucratic mode. Their mission includes working closely with the local business community. In many cases local chambers of commerce, education–industry partnerships, or previous MSC regional or area offices, became the focal point for creating the TEC, but they have no necessary links with pre-existing local business organizations.

The changes which took place in collective bargaining in the UK during the 1980s, virtually destroying any significant level of industrial relations activity above the level of the company, considerably weakened, and in some cases led to the demise of, employers' associations. It may therefore be the case that the option of working through representative bodies of business would not have been practical, even if it had been ideologically acceptable to government. Similarly, the weakness of contacts with local government, though sometimes a problem, became less significant in the early 1990s when local education authorities (LEAs) were stripped of many of their responsibilities for non-academic education after the compulsory school-leaving age. The local colleges of further education (CFEs), the leading public providers of VET, were removed from their ambit and established as competitive rivals with LEAs in the provision of some types of course. This considerably reduced the strategic capacity of the LEAs to have any general responsibility for post-school provision in their areas. Government policy encouraged the formation of private training firms as additional rivals to the colleges. The relationship between TECs, LEAs, and colleges was then placed on a purchaser/provider, rather than colleague, basis. There is therefore a local training market rather than a local training policy arena, the only local bodies having a capacity for policy in this area being the TECs, though they too

---

[7] The US government established PICs in the early 1980s to bring together groups of local business men who might co-operate in helping to tackle youth unemployment. Training was not, in fact, a prominent component of their agenda.

do this by placing contracts for courses on an economic basis rather than by devising strategies.

The TECs, the local education authorities, and the CFEs have to build new links and relationships if they want to start co-operating with each other, and in most areas they seem to have done this. In general, the field of British economic institutional networks is considerably fragmented, and it is a matter of some debate whether the appearance of the TECs has helped resolve or merely contributed to that fragmentation (Bennett and McCoshan 1993: chs. 4 and 5). Partly in response to the US PIC examples, there had been a number of small local experiments in relations between central government agencies and firms as local government and formal business associations declined in power and importance during the 1980s. In partnership with networks of firms, individual ministries began developing enterprise agencies for encouraging business activity in individual localities. These rarely had much to do with training, but concerned themselves with numerous other business questions that embodied some element of collective action (ibid.: 114–19). At the same time, chambers of commerce, which had tended to have a very low profile, began to expand their role (ibid.: 119–25). Unlike German *Kammern*, British chambers have had no historical involvement in labour questions. Often concerned mainly with relations between local businesses and local government planning controls, they also have none of the authority and statutory power of their nominal counterparts in several continental European countries, and they have rarely been involved in questions of business strategy. This was clearly changing, though skill creation was rarely on their agenda.

VET was of far more direct concern to some further government initiatives in the mid-1980s for seeking the involvement of business in links with schools and LEAs, launched by the Department of Education as part of its initial riposte to the MSC usurpation described in Chapter 4 (ibid.: 147–55). This included a scheme called Compact which worked through local business associations and encouraged firms in inner-city areas to take an interest in their local schools and offer job guarantees to certain pupils staying on to take various courses (Richardson 1993). Developing from local rather than central government around the same time were education and business partnerships, again centred on LEAs (Bennett and McCoshan 1993: 156–63). As Bennett and McCoshan point out, all these initiatives were separate from TVEI and were eventually in tension with the Education Reform Act's devaluation of the role of LEAs as centres for co-ordination of local schools' activities.

Also operating at the level of business networks had been local enterprise agencies, a movement pioneered since the early 1980s by a private initiative with government support, Business in the Community. These agencies usually took the form of partnerships between local business and local authorities. They helped small and medium-sized firms with a variety of different problems where some collective-goods activity might be useful, though their concerns with training were, rather as in central Italy, largely limited to training for the small business entrepreneurs themselves (ibid.: 114).

TECs and business communities

The establishment of TECs was a logical development of this multiple discovery of the importance of local networks, and one that reduced the growing incoherence of a maze of overlapping agencies and initiatives by being used also to replace much of the MSC's activity. It was also (at least initially) consistent with central government's aversion to local government involvement. The members of TECs are required by law to be chief executives. Representative business organizations quite explicitly have no role: individual business people are appointed to the TECs because, as individuals, they might set an example to others, not because through associations they might have access to wider networks, complex exchanges, sanctions, and encouragement of both the formal and the informal kind as happens in the German case—or more informally in the Italian industrial districts. It is a 'charismatic hero' model of policy imitation; that is why they have to be chief executives, leaders, even if in practice personnel and training matters in their companies are delegated to specialists.

Individuals from LEAs or elsewhere in local government, and from trade unions, can be members of TECs if co-opted by the existing members, subject to the requirement that two-thirds of the members must be from private-sector businesses, and only if the individuals nominated conform to the chief executive model. In the case of education personnel this usually means chief officers of local authorities or their education departments, or head teachers of individual schools. In theory, therefore, they are there because they are organization leaders, not because it might be relevant to a body concerned with training in a locality to have strong links with the central providers of young people's education in part of that area. That would be a form of corporatism, or would recognize the role of educational or local government, rather than entrepreneurial, expertise. The appropriate relationship envisaged in current British legislation between a TEC and the local education service is the pure market transaction between purchaser and provider.

In practice and over time the hard ideological corners have been worn down, mainly by the TECs and their local business communities themselves, but also by government. Most TECs have included persons from the local education service in their board membership. (It is interesting to note that, when the Employment Department carried out a national survey of TEC members in 1993 (Vaughan 1993) it specifically ignored the existence of all public-sector members. It is therefore not easy to give precise estimates of their numbers or background.) They have also developed wider networks with local public-sector education providers in subgroups and subcommittees (Richardson 1993). Anecdotal evidence suggests that bonding between local government, firms, and other local institutions has been strongest in areas facing economic crisis and decline, as people have come together to defend their area, like mediaeval people running to support a city under siege. This has emerged from studies of Marshall's original

(1912) example of industrial districts in Sheffield (Lawless 1994), and also Coventry (Healey and Dunham 1994).[8]

In some cases trade union leaders have also been significant figures within TECs. In particular, in cities in the declining industrial areas of northern England unions, local government, and local employers have grouped together in projects for economic revival, and TECs have played an important part as the meeting point for much of this activity. In more prosperous areas and those in which service-sector employment dominates, this has been far less evident. In general the form chosen for the structure of the TECs has reduced the role formerly played in skill-creation activities by trade unions. It could be argued that this has been a useful development, since in the past unions had often used qualifications and training merely as a means of maintaining labour shortages in artificially defined occupations. Ironically, however, in recent years they had started to play a very different role. Nearly all the old restrictive practices have gone; some British unions, at least at their senior levels, have acquired an appreciation of the role of work skills in modern economies—and perhaps in attracting members to their organizations. The former Electrical, Electronic, Telecommunications, and Plumbing Union even established its own training school in technical skills, providing a service which was valuable both to its members and the firms that employed them. British unions in general do, however, tend to be poorly informed about new possibilities and the implications of technical change—a weakness that they might have started to overcome had they been centrally involved in continual detailed discussions of skill creation (Coffield 1992: 28).

More generally, both the Employment Department's own enquiry (Vaughan 1993) and academic research (Bennett and McCoshan 1993: 187–8) report that TECs have found it difficult to recruit persons from small and medium-sized firms, and the latter also found considerable under-representation on TECs from the services sectors—this latter being consistent with the general finding that TEC activity has been stronger in older manufacturing areas than in those dominated by the new tertiary economy.

For its part, government had second thoughts concerning the desirability of cutting TECs off from organized business.[9] Increasingly it looked to local

---

[8] This is a striking contrast with Italy, where networks flourish in areas of prosperity and are generally absent in depressed areas. This may reflect an important difference in the political geography of the two countries. In Italy the depressed southern regions were, throughout the half-century of Christian Democratic dominance (1944–94), close to the political centre and came to depend on political favours from the central state for help. In the UK economic problems have been concentrated in the old industrial heartlands of the north, the Midlands, Scotland, and Wales, which have been remote from the political centre of gravity of the Conservative Party, which has been the dominant political force in the country, particularly during the 1980s, the main decade of decline. This may have imparted a stronger sense of self-reliance to the British depressed areas. Also, some of the main areas of Italian small-firm communities developed in formerly communist areas (especially in and around the city of Bologna) which in the post-war decades saw themselves as virtually in a state of siege against a hostile national state.

[9] The changes described here took place before the change of government in May 1997. At the time of writing this change has had no implications for the role of TECs.

chambers of commerce to become partners of the TECs, providing a 'one-stop shop' for business services. Chambers were therefore encouraged to merge with TECs, and in some towns they have done so. Elsewhere this proposal has been seen as a threat to chambers' autonomy and there has been considerable friction (Vickerstaff and Parker 1995). Chambers vary considerably; some are impressive organizations which collate a considerable amount of data on economic conditions in their area and speak authoritatively of its needs to government; others are little more than social gatherings—though as our discussion of Japan has suggested, the importance of social gatherings to business trust and collective action should not be underestimated.

At times it seemed that government was seeking gently to nudge British employers in a German direction, by linking chambers (which would remain fully voluntary) to the statutorily supported TECs, thereby bringing the former more fully into the public policy arena and collective-goods provision, and also giving government an opportunity to encourage all of them to become serious organizations. However, this kind of corporatist imitation of Germany became unpopular as British politicians, Conservative and Labour alike, came to identify themselves as part of an Anglo-American approach that had solved problems of the labour market through deregulation and to contrast themselves with 'high-unemployment' Europe. Government is therefore more likely to use a market rhetoric for its policy—hence the use of the American-sounding term 'one-stop shop' which is very different indeed from the idea of a membership organization persuading its members to participate in the provision of collective goods.

Unlike the Italian business networks, neither TECs nor the small firms they are primarily meant to serve are necessarily rooted in communities. Small firms in Britain are often isolated from each other and reluctant to join groups. This makes it difficult for TECs to identify them and make contact; TECs have made much more progress in their relations with large, geographically concentrated corporations than with small companies (ibid.).[10] TECs are after all externally imposed organs, established by central government and initially financed by it. Subsequent appointment is by the existing members and the TECs are encouraged to look to private sources for additional funds.[11] However, beyond that they have little support from government; they are not like an agency of the state, as in France, powerfully extending the arm of central policy in the provinces. The model on which their own activity is based, like all innovations in contemporary British public agencies, is that of the small firm, required to find its way in the market by offering services that local businesses will pay for. They can indeed go bankrupt, and this has already happened to a large TEC in south London.

[10] The local basis of TECs has also caused problems for some of the UK's largest firms, such as the retail chains, which are among the country's largest employers, but have a relatively small presence in each TEC area. They thus have to deal with 82 separate training agreements, rather than the single national training contract they used to sign with the MSC.
[11] It was a telling indication of where the balance of priorities lay, between the TECs' role in leading-edge skill promotion and that of remedial action for the unemployed, that their budgets were initially related to local unemployment rates; as that rate declines, so a TEC's resources are reduced.

There is however a paradox here: if they have been set up as an element of public policy, they must be concerned with the provision of collective goods (and skill creation is at least in part an example of such a good). But if they must model their operations on those of companies, then they must act within a market and, therefore, not in a collective-goods framework. This tension affects a number of TEC operations.

The fact that they are more like firms than like either administrative institutions or membership associations improves their acceptability among the companies with which they must work, but it also gives them certain problems. For example, one of the major tasks of the TECs has to be to develop a high profile among the local business community: to make their own existence known, to become associated with certain activities, to achieve recognition. Because they have no systematic links with local institutions, this is a challenge that they have had to meet in the manner of new companies, by advertising and profile-raising publicity events. Most have succeeded in this in the sense that large numbers of businesses recognize their names and have some idea what they do (Crowley-Bainton 1993).

On the other hand, there is some evidence that TECs have been most successful where they have developed strong community roots. For example, small firms have responded most readily to either small TECs or TECs with branch offices in localities (ibid.: 21–2; Parker and Vickerstaff 1996: 254–5); and TECs have had most success in encouraging an interest in training where TEC board members have been able to use local network contacts—in particular in manufacturing—and where TEC board members used to be part of old ITB networks and retain their contacts from these (ibid.).

The Scottish equivalents of the TECs, LECs, have a wider economic development brief. This explicitly goes considerably beyond training (though many TECs have done that in practice too). This has given them a wider range of points of interaction with local authorities and other bodies concerned with local development. They generally behave more like an Italian local agency; it is notable that Scotland and its various cities have some of the attributes of autonomous regional and municipal identities that characterize the Italian regions. In general they seem to have been more successful at integrating themselves within their districts.

When the government uses TECs as an instrument of policy, it continues to do so as though they were competitive firms rather than administrative channels. Thus, the TECs are equipped by the government with resources that they must spend in the market with various training providers in such a way as to show a maximum number of trainee places for a given expenditure, primarily aimed at the unemployed. Their central incentive in the area of skill creation is therefore to provide training cheaply, by choosing the cheapest providers, concentrating on those skills that can be most quickly and cheaply provided, and making provision that most obviously meets the existing expressed needs of firms:

the outcome measures . . . which are used to judge TEC performance create incentives for them to perpetuate the low-skill equilibrium; they can best satisfy their targets by providing narrow, employer-specific training, concentrating on low-cost, low-capital intensive courses (e.g. hairdressing over engineering), and focusing on those low-skilled occupations, such as retailing, where high turnover rates make it easier to place people in jobs . . . Those TECs that seek to develop a strategy for investing in higher-level skills must also overcome the short-termism built into their contracts with the government which are assessed and renegotiated each year with no guarantee of future resources. (Finegold 1992: 242.)

This emerges as the TECs' central dilemma: there is no point in being a local-level initiative if they are not responsive to local business needs; but local business needs are, especially among small businesses, needs as currently perceived. Pursuing these existing needs is not well suited to a strategy of trying to raise corporate ambitions to meet new long-term challenges (see Parker and Vickerstaff 1996 for a similar argument). The new system of national vocational qualifications (NVQs) described in Chapter 4, which serves as the main outcome measure used to determine TECs' funding, suffers from the same problem: the content of the skills being learned is determined very much by the existing day-to-day practice of the firms in which the training takes place. Meanwhile the TECs are not equipped with the resources which might enable them to speak authoritatively to firms about what they ought to be recognizing as their needs. Their staff are not necessarily professionally skilled in this field; there is little in the way of a national resource base on which they can draw.

As noted, some TECs have found it wise to underemphasize the 'training' part of their mission, since this is an issue which firms are often not very interested in discussing—an experience similar to that of the *servizi reali* in Italy. This is especially true for the very basic kind of training for which they are still receiving most of the state funding. Instead, they stress the second part of their mission: general help with enterprise services, where firms can often more readily see some value. In moving in this direction TECs are clearly moving to fulfil some important needs that may well improve firms' competitiveness in otherwise unrealizable ways; they may also, by winning firms' confidence through this initial contact, be able to move on to training questions later. There is also a meeting point between the two tasks in the Investors in People project (IIP) discussed below. However, in general such developments cast some doubt on the whole training project, or at least on the suitability of the TECs for fulfilling it.

A further major problem has been that, although TECs are seen as the main instrument with which the UK will rival German and Japanese skills provision for the advanced economy of the future, their principal state-funded activities are for short-term programmes for the young and adult unemployed, in particular for those needing rudimentary VET. Further, they have gradually been shifted increasingly to this kind of work (Bennett and McCoshan 1993: 190), and have complained to government about it. Not only does this activity take time and energy, but the TECs acquire a reputation among both local businesses and young people as being the remedial agencies for those at the bottom of the skills heap. This destroys much of what they have been trying to achieve in the self-publicizing activities that already absorb a large part of their resources. It is not at all what employers were promised when the TECs were initiated, and it is also not work that contributes to the building of local business networks. It further means that the proportion of their resources over which they have any discretion is very small (ibid.: 188).

We have noted a similar phenomenon in virtually all the countries discussed in this study. The British case brings out the core of the general problem very sharply: while most aspects of TEC work have been placed on a market basis, responding to firms' needs rather than trying to develop collective policy, this activity remains clearly part of the public-policy arena. When as much as is possible of an area is privatized, that which remains within the irreducible public arena is likely to be a residuum unattractive to the market. The point applies, whether the residuum is a product or a group of potential recipients of VET programmes.

In contrast, one of the TECs' most effective instruments has been their role in implementing the government's IIP strategy, which involves the TECs in awarding an IIP certificate to firms the labour practices of which have been inspected and found to reach certain standards of excellence on a number of dimensions, mainly related to skills development, including (at least in theory) measuring the returns to training. These awards are not merely symbolic, because access to certain government grants for training is limited to firms possessing the IIP award. Very large numbers of firms, including major ones, have therefore been eager to qualify for this certification. The only weaknesses of this strategy are that: (a) the government funding that provides the central incentive has been subject to repeated reductions in value, reducing the incentive to obtain IIP centification; (b) the criteria of IIP, which stress long-term investment in employees, run counter to the strong opposite trend among British businesses, with government encouragement, for the casualization of staff and a move to temporary, short-term contracts; and (c) since TECs are often the main determiners of who is awarded IIP certificates, the fact that the government then includes the number of certificates they issue among the quantitative progress indicators by which it assesses them has led to some scepticism about the meaning of the IIP standard.

Summary

So far the TECs have had three main achievements. First, they have pioneered the development of a new, flexible form of public intervention that is regarded sympathetically by local businesses. Within this, they have provided valuable enterprise services within their areas.

Second, they have been part of a successful general national effort for encouraging more and more young people to extend their education, both generally and in ways related to vocational skills. By rewarding TECs on the basis of the number of young people obtaining qualifications, rather than just the number participating in certain training schemes, the government has removed some of the old conflict between the MSC's youth training programmes and the full-time education courses of schools and colleges. The short-term consequences of encouraging more young people to participate in further and higher education might be only to intensify competition and to bring disillusion and resentment when young people find they are overqualified for the work they eventually achieve, but it is at least consistent with the goal of establishing a base for a generally more highly skilled workforce.

Finally, in some areas they have helped build and rebuild strong and genuine links and networks among firms and among them, trade unions, and local government. Despite the competitive, market basis on which relations among TECs, LEAs, and colleges have been placed by recent law and policy, often all parties involved have fought to sustain co-operative relationships going beyond their market transactions, developing something of a model of co-operative competition.

It cannot, however, be claimed that TECs have yet demonstrated a capacity to put the UK on an upskilling path; their funding bias towards low-level training and their tendency to move towards other aspects of enterprise services to meet firms' preferences may well mean that they can never do this. They have been unable to develop as a prominent national lobby in favour of skills, though they have now established their own national body—something which was encouraged by government.[12] In some respects their failures can be seen as intrinsic consequences of the British attempt to make virtues of institutional weakness and short-termism, and therefore count as successes in the terms of that strategy. Because of the insistence on the value of flexibility and insecurity in providing work incentives to people working in agencies like TECs, there has been frequent institutional change, and no establishment of bodies with clear durability and rootedness within the community. Public funding has been low, which puts policy-making instruments on the same footing as insecure firms—an explicit rejection of any argument that public policy and market behaviour have distinctive *modi operandi* is an important feature of contemporary British approaches to public service.

CONCLUSIONS

In all three countries the 'proposers' of co-operation (*agenzie*, customer firms, TECs) have to win trust for their projects of generating co-operative networks. The resources at their disposal for doing this vary widely. Most strongly placed are the Japanese customer firms, which are powerful actors in the market on whom

---

[12] It is notable that this is a lobbying body; it has no administrative function within some national system of provision.

the supplier firms are strongly dependent, and where trust has become institutional and therefore more flexible and transferable than in most Italian situations. Italian trust is strong, but has great difficulty transcending face-to-face communities; British TECs, as newcomers to this activity with neither market power nor local roots, have to work hard to develop trust. They are aided in this where real local business communities already exist; in contrast to Italy, where these seem most important in prosperous, innovative small-firm regions, in the UK business communities seem to be mainly defensive devices in situations of decline, particularly in Scotland and northern England.

The contrasts among the network institutions developed in the three countries discussed here are strong: most Italian institutions have developed locally; Japanese networks (and a small number of Italian cases) sprang from individual large corporations; British TECs came from central government. Both the Italian and the Japanese examples originated from the business community itself and have from the outset involved social as well as purely business networks. Local trade unions and local government have played a major role in Italy, and to some extent local government has been active in Japan and the UK. Over time the Italians have moved towards both the Japanese and the British TEC model in the adoption of a managerial, business mode of operation. One can see some convergence between Italy and the UK: towards an entrepreneurial model on the Italian side; and towards an appreciation of local community networks among at least some British TECs. There are also major similarities among the countries: the Italian Benetton cases resemble the Japanese supplier networks; Japanese metropolitan small-firm networks without a focal firm have several features in common with Italian industrial districts; and the British government has been encouraging its Japanese inward investors to stimulate some supplier networks among their British contractors.[13]

Neither Italy nor the UK has found policy mechanisms that might speed a move to what was defined in Chapter 1 as a long-term rather than a short-term skill-creation model. To some extent the reasons are different. In Italy a deep mistrust of anything beyond very local institutions has proved a major stumbling block, an attitude that can be of considerable importance when the most dynamic sectors of the economy have been very local and small scale but where measures to take advantage of new skills and technologies are beyond the capacity of these relatively small local institutions. In the UK the problem has been an almost deliberate destruction of capacity for public policy by making public agencies behave as though they were private, market actors, except in the residual task of caring for the hard-to-employ. Agencies in both countries, and the others considered in this volume, have experienced difficulties in combining assistance for the unemployed and poorly skilled with attempts at persuading already sceptical businesses that these agencies can help to push forward the frontiers of high-level skill creation.

---

[13] A similar strategy has been pursued towards Japanese firms in the USA.

Perhaps most important, however, is the fact that in none of the three countries has training been at the forefront of services sought by firms. In Italy training has been just one among a number of *servizi reali* being offered, with the agencies giving no particular priority to workforce training—though to an important extent the provision of any service to very small enterprises of the Tuscan kind amounts to training: that of the entrepreneur. Formal training has featured among the services demanded, but it has a minor profile. The British TECs were similarly intended to deliver a range of services (not specifically to small firms), but training was clearly picked out as at least *primus inter pares*—'training and enterprise', as their name puts it. Further, the great bulk of state finance that they receive is for training. However, in practice TECs have found that it is by emphasizing their non-training, 'enterprise' services that they can best win the attention of local businesses. Training is more important in the Japanese networks, though it is not a primary focus.

This factor raises yet again the dilemma between a market-oriented, 'service-selling' approach that tries to get as close as possible to the defined needs of firms as customers, and a national policy goal that seeks to shift firms from currently perceived needs to something more ambitious. Given that even corporatist agencies like German *Kammern* and the Swedish AMS are increasingly defining their relationship to their constituencies in customer-service terms, this is no minor point. Of course, as the world of the 'real' market routinely demonstrates, being oriented to customers' preferences in no way necessitates a passive approach to those preferences. The most successful businesses try to stimulate wants among potential customers which correspond to what they plan to provide. Businesses are not bound to remain with a 'mission' to sell a particular product, and marketing strategies are a complex negotiation between existing customer preferences and the firm's capacities. Also, the shaping of preferences is easier when the customers are a mass market of individual consumers rather than other firms, which can be expected to be more hard headed. However, the idea of using marketing techniques to persuade firms that they want to upskill their workforce needs would have to be part of the mission of any close-to-the-market public-policy agencies in this field. There would then be considerable difficulties for policy-makers if such agencies were given a brief that was too close to a naive version of the market analogy, following closely the concept of customer sovereignty and failing to appreciate the demand-shaping role of truly entrepreneurial firms. They might also be required to maximize sales of services in general, which might well lead to the neglect of the public-policy goal of improved workforce skills and an abandonment of the concept of public policy as meaning anything other than customer service to enterprises. This is to some extent already the case in the UK.

None of these cases offers a fully successful solution to one of the fundamental concerns of this book: how to combine the general national social-policy goal of an educated workforce with the growing dependence of skill-formation and enhancement projects on individual firms which have no public responsibilities.

The Japanese networks are oriented in a different way to these problems. By definition they do not have to win acceptance within the business world, since they are of it. As international market leaders the customer firms do not have difficulty persuading their suppliers, if it is necessary, to move to more ambitious levels of skill. Although they are primarily concerned with the product and labour markets within their industries and have no wider responsibilities to Japanese society, they do frequently acknowledge a community concern to the regions within which they are located.[14] Large Japanese firms have a privileged position within the polity and society which causes difficulties for both free-market and citizenship ideologies in many western countries; but in exchange for that privilege there is often a greater acceptance of community constraint on the corporation.

Given this importance of the individual firm, we must finally consider in the following chapter whether mere reliance on its capabilities, with some encouragement from government, might be the best available approach to the construction of a 'knowledge society'.

[14] Every Japanese car manufacturer has a local community concern for its smaller subcontractors, many of which are still owner managed (for example, Suzuki in the Hamamatsu area, Toyota in Toyota City, Mazda in Hiroshima, Mitsubishi in Mizushima).

7

Markets and Corporate Hierarchies

The simplest market model of initial VET avoids the need for the different kinds of institutions discussed in preceding chapters: individuals equip themselves with skills in order to find jobs, and potential employers provide them with an incentive to do this by paying a premium for the skills they possess. A number of labour markets work in precisely this way, notable examples being those for lawyers and secretaries. However, for this to happen, the individual needs to be fairly confident that the training investment will lead to employment; and firms must have some certainty that appropriate skills have been acquired. These criteria will tend to be limited to skills with certain characteristics: the vocational possibilities of acquiring them must be easily understood by applicants for training; demand for them must be high and stable; and their content must be relatively standard and either slow to change or changing in predictable and widely recognized ways. There are many occupations where these conditions do not hold, in particular those with advanced, rapidly changing, but not easily transferred skills which need to be closely related to the direct production activities of the organization (whether of goods or of services). Software programmers are a good example.

Further, this simplest case argument tacitly assumes that firms are merely aggregations of a mass of individual labour contracts, in which individual employers passively respond to the skills produced by the market signals made by themselves and others. However, as managerial economics and transaction-cost economics have shown us (Williamson 1975; 1985), firms, other than the very smallest, are organizations with hierarchies of managerial authority, senses of strategy and mission, sometimes with a distinct internal culture. They therefore develop strategies that include taking an active, creative approach to the formation of skills. This may involve them in becoming skill providers rather than skill purchasers. Within a firm that has become a true 'learning organization' it is almost impossible to separate the development of skills from execution of the work task, since the latter involves constantly finding new and better ways of performing operations and using one's abilities. As discussed in Chapter 1, to the extent that these skills are company specific, no particular public policy questions are raised; to the extent that they are transferable, there is potentially a poaching risk. However, this will not necessarily be a fundamental deterrent to skill provision. A number of conditions may induce firms to be active trainers irrespective of any incentives provided by public policy or institutional structure.

The argument that trained labour is an example of what were called in Chapter 1 impure public goods rests on the assumption that labour markets are fully open. There are however very many situations in which this is not true. When access to employment is limited to a small number of clearly defined qualification points, and exit from it is to retirement or some other form of employment termination, firms both have an incentive to provide their own training and are free from the fear of poaching should they do so. This may occur in the case of labour-market monopsonists, institutional companies, and firms with particular kinds of product market (three categories which are by no means mutually exclusive).

Labour-market monopsonists   A typical example of labour market monopsony would be a large company dominating specialized labour markets within a particular journey-to-work region. Such a firm will be less prone to fears of labour 'poaching' for the bulk of its staff, though not for the very highly qualified who might be expected to set their job search within far wider geographical horizons. Other large firms in the same region using very different labour skills are not competing in the same labour market, while small firms in the same sector may make such small inroads into labour supply that it still pays the large firm to provide training. The long-term supplier relationships characteristic of Japan and discussed in the previous chapter provide, as we saw, contexts within which large customer firms have an interest in developing the capacities of, and sharing knowledge with, the small supplying companies.

Even if the skills that monopsonists provide are quite general within their sector, they are in a similar position to a firm with firm-specific skills. They therefore have no disincentive to train. Such firms may well be found within countries, regions, or sectors that in general display a low-skill equilibrium; the firm develops its own high-skill product-market niches, and its very distinctiveness becomes one of its attractions for potential workers. On the other hand, where the customers of such firms are producing for similarly geographically constrained consumer markets or where the firms are in general monopolistic producers (as will sometimes be the case with labour-market monopsonists), they face little incentive to upgrade skill content and product quality, since customers cannot easily look elsewhere for alternative goods and services (Rose 1991). It should be noted that as global markets spread this is becoming true of fewer and fewer firms. In capital-intensive industries, where direct labour is a relatively low proportion of overall production costs, there may be additional incentives to train.

Institutional companies   Firms of the kind identified in Chapter 1 as 'institutional companies', developing strong corporate cultures around their hierarchies, protect themselves from the open labour market. For example, they may develop strong internal labour markets, encouraging workers to develop careers within the organization. The labour-market monopsonists will be in a good position to do this, but it is also a policy that can be pursued by firms in more competitive labour markets, either if they develop reputations as attractive employers, or if most leading firms in their region or nation share an emphasis on recruitment at limited points, long-term relations between firms and employees, and a virtual bar on cross-recruitment. Seniority-based pay systems may be part of such a strategy, by creating a disincentive for individuals to leave a firm, since they would be forced to start at the foot of the pay scale in a new enterprise, or at least to lose service-related pension and other benefits. Such systems also make it harder for firms to bring in highly paid outsiders without upsetting their internal reward systems. On the other hand, strict seniority-based reward structures may fail to provide financial incentives for individuals to invest in their own skill acquisition, by emphasizing age and tenure with a firm rather than the skills of the individual.

There are good reasons why particularly innovative firms are likely to develop institutional strategies of this kind. To make the investment in training and other components of a high-skill strategy pay off, a company must be able to organize the work process in a way that encourages continuous innovation. It makes no sense, for example, to raise the competence and expectations of a production worker if he or she is then given a job that consists of a series of repetitive tasks. Moving from a Fordist to a more flexible model of work organization, however, can pose a threat to individuals—not only to workers, who may be reluctant to embrace new work practices that could lead to redundancies, but also to line managers, who may be forced to relinquish or share some of their powers with work teams. Companies may be able to use the threat of increased international competition and plant closures to force employees to go along with changes in the organization of work, but they cannot compel individuals to innovate. Innovation requires active co-operation, not acquiescence (Williamson 1985: 262–3; Walton 1985). Thus, for a high-skill strategy to succeed, a firm must develop co-operative internal relationships. These are easier to establish within a strong, corporate culture which encourages long-term identity—something which in turn requires expectations of long-term employment among employees. Such firms therefore sacrifice some of the advantages of numerical flexibility available to those which offer only insecure and short-term contracts. They compensate for this by trying to instil more functional flexibility into their skilled workforce. However, it should be noted that this does not necessarily apply to the whole of a firm's workforce; there can be a strong segmentation between a core of highly skilled employees encouraged to develop a company career, and a margin of the less skilled, who may be treated as far more disposable (Atkinson and Coleman 1989; OECD 1996*a*).

Product strategy   Some firms will be located in highly advanced product markets where it is absolutely necessary to have advanced skills to compete or lose market position. In these markets there are two strategies open to firms: to develop some of the competencies themselves or to attempt to hire them on the open market. The latter strategy, however, presupposes the former: there must be some firms investing heavily in skills and other aspects of a learning infrastructure or there will be no one on the external labour market to hire with the relevant skills. Some firms may choose the skill-development option, although knowing that they will lose the investment in some key talent in competitive labour markets, because they view it as the best means to compete in market segments that require high-quality customer service and rapid innovation. The internal skill-development strategy offers a number of advantages that may offset the additional costs: it enables firms to tailor the skills developed, even if they are of use to other companies in the sector, to their particular technical needs and corporate culture; it allows firms to screen trainees, typically at a lower salary than if they hired an already skilled person, to determine who has the greatest potential; and it can foster a positive attitude to the firm even among those who leave.[1] In high-tech sectors, skill development and new product and process innovation are often synonymous with the process of developing new competence, at the same time improving corporate performance (for example, a team may be formed to reduce product defects which, in the process, learns new quality techniques). By building skill development into the work process itself, a firm can both reduce the costs of building capabilities and make it more difficult for competitors to replicate this strategy. It is always possible that pirate firms will develop in these sectors that try to poach without developing their own skills, but these are unlikely to be at the cutting edge. If these sectors are to exist at all, they will have to consist of high-quality firms investing heavily in skills and other aspects of infrastructure. If their activities create barriers to entry, these will raise profitability within those firms that manage to become established, making them attractive to venture capital and other forms of high-risk investment. In these sectors, therefore, financial systems which in general punish long-termism in managerial strategies may include financial institutions specializing in niche markets of this kind, offsetting the general tendencies of the system.

As long as there are some firms pursuing these high-skill strategies, it is possible for others to compete alongside them, without offering their own training programmes. Indeed, at the top of the skills range—for example scientists and engineers in research-oriented firms in pharmaceuticals or computers—few technical skills are developed through formal firm-based training. Firms hire the most talented people with aptitudes in the general field, and attempt to create a learning environment where they can work with their peers to solve problems. Expertise is developed continuously, on the job as they go, not primarily through formal training, although external networking and conferences with peers on the cutting edge of knowledge creation are likely to be an important prior preparation. Such occupations are not, however, paradigms for an entire economy.

Where further training of existing staff at more routine levels is concerned, a large number of firms find themselves in situations where to stay in front in a market technology which is changing requires constant upgrading of the capacity of all levels of staff. This can often be done in ways that are of use to, and specific to, the individual firms, reducing the portability of the skills being acquired

---

[1] For example, McKinsey, one of the world's leading management consulting firms, expects nine out of every ten young people it hires and trains extensively to leave the firm, knowing that its best source of future business is former McKinsey employees who have advanced to senior management positions in large firms.

—and therefore being covered by what Becker (1962) calls 'non-transferable skills'. Recent research on four so-called dynamo regions of western Europe—located in France, Germany, Italy, and Spain—shows that a large amount of training of this kind takes place (Regini (ed.) 1996). Admittedly these were firms noted for their market success and therefore probably not 'average' firms, so the authors found no evidence of fear of poaching. However, the authors also note that (in accordance with the Becker thesis) training tended to be limited to non-portable skills, with virtually no certification and little concern for updating basic skills; they also found that it was concentrated on small numbers of key staff—typically those who were already the most skilled. Similarly, recent research in the UK, a country with a poor reputation for initial training (Finegold 1992), reveals a considerable amount of company-level action at the further training level. In many cases this is training that compensates for deficiencies in initial VET that firms need to remedy in order to move towards a higher skill strategy (Mason and Finegold 1995).

THE SCOPE FOR COMPANY-ONLY SKILL CREATION

The preceding discussion makes it clear that, *a priori*, a strong public policy on skill creation is not a necessary requirement for the production of advanced skills. Under a number of conditions, firms will invest in skills themselves, and the problem posed in Chapter 1 of how to reconcile a need for public policy with a need for company autonomy does not arise. This helps explain the evidence we encountered in Chapter 3, where the UK economy, long noted for the weakness of its VET provision, was nevertheless able to show several examples of excellent performance in activities requiring highly skilled personnel. But relying on the excellence of a small group of companies cannot go beyond points of quality and enable a country to fulfil the public policy goal posited at the outset of this book: the enskilling of the average firm and of the great majority of a nation's working population.

There are two reasons for this. First, it is only advanced firms which are likely to provide these levels of training; second, even they are likely to restrict training to certain categories of staff. The only exception to this would be a country in which the great majority of firms happened to fall into one of the advanced sectors of likely high-level trainers, and in circumstances where the system of production required this training to be given to a very high proportion of the workforce. In the more likely situation, countries relying primarily on firm-level action will have a relatively small proportion of their workforce trained to high levels, and these will predominantly be in large, institutional organizations that provide large amounts of training. There will then be considerable inequality between persons in skilled positions in those firms and the rest of the population, who will be either in marginal jobs in the same firms or in firms within a low-skill equilibrium.

Two countries among the group being studied in this volume exhibit considerable prominence of company autonomy in training provision and little direct involvement by public or other external collective actors, but in very different ways: Japan and the USA. These will be studied below in some detail. Examples of company-level provision can of course be found in all countries, but we concentrate on these two because these countries rely particularly, in their different ways, on this form of VET provision. Some attention will also be devoted to the UK, which has imitated some US approaches.

VOCATIONAL TRAINING IN JAPAN

Japanese large corporations present the ideal-typical cases of institutional companies. They recruit employees from the external labour market at only very few points, typically at school-leaving and university-leaving ages. From then on labour markets are strongly internal, with well-established promotion and seniority criteria. Core employees of these firms are offered guarantees of lifetime employment (provided their performance remains high) and in turn are rarely able to change firms in mid-career, leading, as we saw in Chapter 2, to Japan having the longest employee tenures of any country where measurements have been made. The fact that the turnover rate for new employees is also low shows that long-term tenure is part of an initial expectation for new recruits too. Within this framework Japanese corporations are well known for their tendency to promote very strong corporate identities—what we have called here company cultures. In fact, firms constitute communities, employees finding within them networks of personal relationships and also welfare services of a kind that in western societies will often be found (if at all) in the locality rather than the employing organization.

Our theoretical argument above would suggest that such firms would provide good environments for both initial and further VET, and, more generally, for informal, ongoing learning within the organization. There is considerable evidence that this is the case (Dore and Sako 1998). The emphasis on internal labour markets and lifetime employment reduces anxieties about poaching, while the concept of firms as communities with distinctive cultures clearly requires strong induction processes to function effectively. Little training is provided outside the firms, most Japanese school and university education being very general, with vocational schools being seen as second best.[2] Firms are concerned to recruit new

---

[2] The main exceptions to this are correspondence courses for skill certificates. There are also Public Human Resource Development Centres which provide vocational training for school-leavers, turning them into skilled workers in various fields. Polytechnic colleges also provide practical training for potential technicians before they go to work in a company (Okuda 1996: 306). However, according to data collected in 1992, only 3.6% of off-the-job training is accounted for by these centres, and a further 0.7% at universities and special training schools; 18.5% of such training was performed by industry associations, and 3% by miscellaneous sources, leaving 72.9% performed by the company itself or other commercial organizations (ibid.: 311).

entrants with high general educational achievements, but then expect to train them in the general techniques of the work and in the specific needs of that corporation. Even the more vocational courses in schools and universities have a high general, theoretical content.

Institutions of corporate governance support these arrangements. Each large group of manufacturers also contains a bank which advances long-term loans for investment. In addition, cross-shareholding within the group reduces the threat of hostile takeover, further enabling managers to adopt a long-term view of training and other aspects of infrastructure. As we have seen in Chapter 4, the company-centred character of training is complemented by nationally accepted skills tests administered by the Ministry of Labour (Sako 1995). Company-level training and little inter-firm mobility does not mean that skills and qualifications lose general validity and transparency. However, the testing system suits the needs of corporations rather than creating separate individual skill identities and occupations by treating skills as 'discrete and miscellaneous, rather than as components of a particular occupation or trade' (ibid.: 6).

The fact that virtually all training is in-house means that there is no sharp discontinuity between initial and further VET, which in turn suits the Japanese corporate model of constant innovation and change in product technology. A further important characteristic is that, given their high general educational level and their presumed commitment to the firm, employees in the great corporations are expected to be motivated to teach each other and to keep trying to upgrade their own skills. Willingness to work in a team and to teach others are often explicit criteria in employee appraisals which are linked clearly to promotion, although not so much to pay. Therefore, much within-firm further training is informal and does not show up in measurable data of numbers of specialized training staff or size of further VET budgets. One exception to this rule has recently been the resurrection of the role of formal company schools—some of which date back to the nineteenth century—for training in theoretical knowledge for new technology.

Further, the fact that employees expect to spend most of their working lives with one corporation, which becomes a community for them, means that, in contrast with skilled German workers, they identify as members of the firm rather than as the practitioners of particular occupations or professions. This has proved very useful in a period of rapid change, since employees can be trained to adapt to new kinds of skill and to set their hands and minds to very different work tasks without feeling a need to resist in order to defend their occupational identity. It was, for example, first in Japan that firms developed multifunctional teams and the idea of continuous improvement (*kaizen*).

Most important, this eventually made possible the important breakthrough of diversified mass production in the automotive and other engineering industries, now commonplace but pioneered in Japan in the 1970s and 1980s. Previously, changing the specification of a mass production-line good involved specialized toolsetting staff coming to change parts of the equipment and setting so that a differently shaped product, or one with different attachments, could be produced. Such changes required considerable notice and organization and were therefore limited in number and type. Once production workers were trained to change the tooling of their machines themselves, adaptations could be made quickly and in more complex ways, leading to variations in products that had previously been possible in only craft, not mass, production. A very strong form of that key attribute of late twentieth-century industry, flexibility, was therefore made possible, given the Japanese company context of corporate rather than occupational identity and constant, even informal, upskilling. However, as Dore (1986) has pointed out, this is really an example of the 'flexible rigidities' which are fundamental to the Japanese model. The flexibility is rooted in and made possible by the rigid form of the large companies, their limited points of recruitment, and the lifetime employment system.

This system raises certain questions. First, if these corporate giants are able to dominate the economy in this way, do they not produce a set of uncompetitive, slothful cartels and oligopolies? At the heart of this book is a dilemma between a public interest in the maximization of skill levels and the fact that the key to these skills lies within firms which, if they are to be sufficiently dynamic to produce constantly advancing skills, are most likely to be found in the most market-driven (and therefore least publicly responsive) parts of the economy. If Japanese firms manage to maximize skills provision, is this not because their form defies the rules of the pure competitive market? Must this not be because they are not facing competitive challenges?

One answer to that question is to point out that, for a number of reasons, Japanese business and political élites have committed themselves to the task of ensuring that their national economy is internationally highly competitive. There is a sufficient basis for securing an effective social and cultural consensus in Japan for state policy devices, associational practices, and the self-perception of firms themselves to rule out the option of becoming 'sleeping giants' even though, from a point of view shaped by the peculiarities of a British or American cultural concept of the logic of action, that is what Japanese corporations might seem to have every incentive to do.

However, that is not the only answer. The community of the great firms is in no way coextensive with the whole economy. Therefore a second question arises: Is a system of this kind able to produce collective action at the wider societal level? Specifically, is it able to produce skills that are recognized as such outside the individual firm? What implications does it have for the majority of the Japanese workforce who work either in small firms or as temporary workers in the large ones? Does it extend beyond the export sector of manufacturing industry?

The answers to these questions are complex and multidirectional. First, it is important to recognize that the characteristics of the Japanese economy that make it a particularly strong example of an 'institutional' economy do not consist solely of the great institutional companies; formal organizations and the state

both make important contributions too. As is recognized in much of the literature on the Japanese economy, ministries of the central government have always
been important in guiding firms to maximize national performance, often through
informal pressures and understandings rather than formal legislation. In the case
of training, the Ministry of Labour and some other ministries play a more formal role, maintaining a wide range of skill tests for the performance of operations considered to be of national importance. Workers in jobs where health and
safety or quality standards are important need not only to satisfy the criteria of
these tests when they initially qualify, but also to be retested at regular intervals.
The tests themselves change in response to changing technologies and needs
because the Ministry works on them in close association with the business
associations for the various sectors. They constitute a constant encouragement,
on a national rather than solely corporate basis, to improve skills. The Ministry
also subsidizes training by firms during recessions (Finegold *et al.* 1994*a*), enabling
firms to retain the employment bargain with core employees who might otherwise be laid off, and encourages internal labour markets in general.

Associational networks also play a part in diffusing training and ideas for developing skills from the large firms to smaller ones. We saw in Chapter 6 how this
worked through supplier associations, but more important is the role of the dense
network of contacts linking firms of different sizes within sectors. For example,
the Japan Industrial Training Association and the Japanese Union of Scientists
and Engineers were important in diffusing Training-within-Industry from the
USA immediately after the Second World War, and Quality Control Circles in
the 1960s (Cole 1989). More recently a survey by the Ministry of Labour (Japan
1994) showed considerable diffusion of small-group activities (including quality circles), particularly in manufacturing, from large firms to smaller ones.[3]

We can therefore conclude that Japan exhibits a combination of most of the
different types of collective-goods institutions discussed in this book. Therefore, while it is true that the community of the great firms is very different from
the notion of a collective public interest, there are strong components of such a
notion. Japanese economy and society can in no way be reduced to a company
economy and society.

However, to turn the account back some way in the opposite direction, there
are clear limits to the extent of the collective public interest that is pursued. Several
parts of the economy remain outside the scope of the model. As we saw in Chapter
2, if Japan and the USA have higher levels of employment than many other industrial societies, it is because of their high numbers in the distributive sector, which
is not noted for its high skills. The public policy concerns of the Japanese state
and business associations are heavily oriented to an export-performance model.
The social and community services sector, which provides high-skill employment
for many people in the USA and several European countries, is particularly

---

[3] The Labour Management Communication Surveys were carried out in 1972, 1977, 1984, 1989,
and 1994. Small-group activities spread from 40% of all firms with 100 or more employees in 1972
to 59% in 1989. Much diffusion took place in the 1960s.

poorly developed. Also, even within the great export-oriented manufacturing firms, most female employees and the many temporary workers (heavily overlapping categories in fact) are often excluded from the self-motivated skill-improvement system.

As Japanese firms face the unpredictable markets of the post-Keynesian economy, the size of the workforce guaranteed lifetime employment is shrinking. While, as we have seen, the model has means of diffusing itself to small firms, there must be some doubt whether it can diffuse its characteristics to a workforce that is not offered or may not want the exchange of commitment for security that has been its most salient characteristic until now.

Further, although Japanese society is relatively egalitarian,[4] there is no national commitment to extending and spreading opportunities. Access to the best universities (and hence eventually to the best employers) is heavily dependent on school performance, which in turn is strongly affected by the ability of parents to supplement their children's education, by sending them either to private schools and/or to after-school cram courses. Since the lifetime employment system means that there is not much chance of later correction of poor early occupational placement, parental income is a heavy determinant of subsequent chances to share in Japan's learning society (Higuchi 1987).

VOCATIONAL TRAINING IN THE USA: ADVANTAGES AND LIMITATIONS OF A WEAK COLLECTIVE SECTOR

The most obvious characteristic of skill creation in the USA is the absence of any generalizable system. The reasons for this are also obvious: the sheer size and diversity of the country's economy; its complex and highly decentralized political system; in comparison with countries in western Europe or the Far East, the more powerful role of individual companies alongside the weakness of both public institutions and collective associations of business interests. Indeed, the very concept of the improvement of workforce skills as a national project is difficult to envisage in the USA, where it is not clear that there can be national projects for what are essentially seen as matters for individual persons and individual companies, with possibly some contribution from local or state governments.

Apart from professional associations for such occupations as medical practitioners and lawyers, which have played an important part in skills development, the role of economic interest associations has been weak. As discussed in the previous chapter, business networks or industrial districts can also be found in certain parts of the USA, notably in high-tech regions like Silicon Valley and the Los Angeles multimedia industry. However, in general it is reasonable to regard the market and the individual company as constituting the crucial training

---

[4] Japan's income distribution is more like that of northern Europe than the USA or southern Europe.

institutions when considering the US case, with one important exception: the role of the largely public education system.

American public education, like the Japanese system, does not value certified vocational or occupational skills. It is, however, geared towards providing educational opportunities on a mass basis; despite the country's internal heterogeneity there is a relatively uniform system of basic education—necessary for a large country with high geographical mobility. The university system is particularly extensive, if highly diverse in quality; and the state system is supplemented by many private initiatives, a large number of which are highly vocational. An extensive, national system of public education, alongside many further opportunities in the private sector, and a historical willingness of individuals to invest in education as the best route to mobility has, in a sense, both been a 'skill strategy' and rendered a more specific one unnecessary. The USA does not therefore provide a pure case of a market or market-and-hierarchy model of skill provision: the important public-policy component of a high level of basic educational provision, and a general cultural disposition of much of the population to regard education as a family investment, are also parts of the model.

A factor that in the past reduced the role of workforce skill in the US economy was the phenomenal success of the country's use of mass-production methods. Starting with relatively unskilled labour in the early part of this century, Taylorist or Fordist production strategies placed an emphasis on the achievement of very high levels of productivity based on the application of capital equipment, work organization, and skilful managerial control, rather than front-line worker skills. These Fordist firms, as well as important primary-product and low-skilled services sectors, still exist today (Mason and Finegold 1995), but it is increasingly important to recognize that a growing proportion of large US firms have adopted post-Fordist models, such as the 'high performance workplace' that depend on a high level of skills throughout the organizations (Lawler *et al*. 1995). At the same time, the USA has been extremely successful at fostering the development of small, entrepreneurial firms in the high-technology and services sectors, often started by individuals who have invested heavily in their own human capital. Both large and small firms have been able to draw on the high level of college-educated Americans.

The Fordist firm and the high-performance firm

Three recent national surveys of US employers enable us to gain some impression of the extent to which the average firm has pursued a high-skill strategy. One looked at a nationally representative sample of 694 manufacturing plants with 50 or more employees to see the extent to which they had adopted four key aspects of high-performance workplaces: (a) self-directed work teams, (b) job rotation, (c) quality circles/problem-solving groups, and (d) total quality management (Osterman 1994). This study found that approximately 35% of plants had implemented at least two of these practices for the majority of their 'core' workers. Firms which adopted these workplace practices were more likely to be in internationally competitive product markets, to compete on the basis of quality and customer service rather than cost, to use technologies that required high skills, to invest in high levels of training, and to adopt innovative pay systems.

The Census Bureau's more comprehensive survey, which included smaller firms (that is those employing fewer than 20 persons rather than the usual fewer than 50) and private service sector enterprises, found somewhat more modest levels of high-performance work practices. The important exception to this was the use of formal training; more than 80% of firms provided formal training in the last year, either in-house or through an external provider (EQW 1995).

A third survey focused on the largest 1,000 manufacturing and service sector corporations in the USA, the firms that would be expected to be leaders in the adoption of new work practices (Lawler *et al.* 1995). The survey, administered in 1987, 1990, and 1993, found that a growing number of large firms has attempted to increase employee involvement, and that this was related to an increase in skill development at the lower levels of the organization. The survey also revealed a significant increase in training of all types between 1990 and 1993, along with a greater use of knowledge- or skill-related pay, although the latter was still generally confined to a small subset of employees.

Even if the transformation of workplaces is still incomplete, the results of these restructuring efforts have been paying off for US firms. The USA has enjoyed strong and sustained growth in productivity—in manufacturing since the the late 1980s and early 1990s, and more recently in the services sector, where growth was stagnant in the previous decade (Roach 1994). Our analysis of changes in the growing sectors of US foreign trade performance in Chapter 3 told a similar story.

There is some evidence that size of firm is a key determinant of skill investment, with smaller companies far less likely to devote resources to training. This finding is compatible with both the monopsony and institutional company hypotheses (though it is also explained more simply by the difficulty of small firms establishing training departments and offering formal courses). A recent survey of a nationally representative sample of nearly 12,000 US employers (USA 1994) showed that 71% of all establishments offered some type of formal training to their employees in 1993. Small firms (here fewer than 50 employees) were significantly less likely to do this (69%) than medium or large establishments, virtually all of which had formal training programmes.

Meanwhile, as noted in Chapter 1, some major corporations are coming to reconcile their own needs for skill-conscious staff with the increasing unpredictability of their own ability to offer continued employment to these staff, by subsidizing courses chosen privately by employees rather than organizing in-house training designed for company needs (Finegold 1998).

An important new trend that demonstrates a more specific skill-creation role for collective action has been the growth of customized training (Creticos and Sheets

1990; Lynch *et al.* 1991). Custom training uses the specific business problems faced by the company as course material and incorporates the firm's business requirements and strategy, rather than focusing on the general development of the individual. This trend toward customization has been demand driven. Corporate directors are questioning the economic returns to the company from costly executive education or other general-audience short courses, and turning toward programmes that explicitly link human-resource development and corporate strategic objectives (see Finegold *et al.* 1994*a*; Morgenson 1992).

In custom courses, the education provider—which may be the executive-education departments of business schools, community college professional-development centres, or private consultants—tailors coursework to the business needs of individual companies, and teaches selected employees from that company, often on site. The courses may be only a few days, or part of an ongoing partnership between the provider and the firm. Custom courses represent the most rapidly growing form of workforce development for business schools and private providers (Finegold *et al.* 1994*a*). In many cases, this growth has been fuelled by state funding; all but three of the 50 states provide some support for customized training, although in most cases the funds are quite limited (only eight states provide more than $10 million/year (McDonnell and Zellman 1993)). Some economists (for example, Grubb and Stern 1989) have questioned the rationale for providing public subsidies for custom training, but these programmes have proved popular with both employers and employees because they are more closely related to actual skill needs than most government-funded training. A study of a Michigan programme that subsidizes training in small firms found that it led firms to triple the amount of training they provided to employees in the year before the grant and that this was related to a reduction in scrap rates (Holzer *et al.* 1993).

Another approach by institutional companies is to establish firm-focused company schools or universities (Finegold *et al.* 1994*a*). Firms such as Motorola, General Electric, and Xerox have developed autonomous business units whose primary function is to meet the ambitious continuous education requirements of all the firm's employees and its suppliers' and customers' workforces. Because of the level of resources required to sustain these activities, such units are limited to very large companies.

There are, however, still grounds for believing that the structure of the US business environment leads to a relative neglect of investment in human capital. A recent study (MacDuffie and Kochan 1993) sampled 70 automobile assembly plants in western Europe, Japan, and the USA. It concluded that US firms invested significantly less in training than their competitors, and that the difference could be related to the production strategies pursued by the firms and some characteristics of the national environments, even when they were investing overseas. For example, Japanese auto plants provided 310 hours of training to newly hired assembly workers in the mid-1980s, compared to 280 hours in Japanese-owned plants firms in the USA, and just 48 hours in traditional American-owned US plants (Krafcik 1990). Blanchflower and Lynch (1992) have shown that most skills acquired on the job are incapable of being transferred to other firms. There are two features of the US institutional environment that create disincentives for even large firms to engage in training, which relate to two issues indicated in our theoretical discussion: labour turnover and the role of financial markets.

Labour turnover First, a peculiarly high rate of labour turnover discourages the retention necessary to give firms the incentive to regard employees as long-term investments, and therefore to invest in the creation of transferable skills.[5] The USA has relatively few constraints on employers' ability to dismiss workers and, as we saw in Chapter 2, has the highest rates of labour mobility among the large industrial countries. Several of the country's largest machine-tool firms abandoned their well-respected apprenticeships in the 1970s because nearby aerospace firms were 'poaching' their young machinists as soon as they completed the training (Finegold *et al.* 1994*a*). As we saw in Chapter 3, US performance in most parts of the machine-tool sector collapsed during the 1980s.

Likewise, in a recent comparison of service strategies, work organization, and human-resource policies in the US and German banking sectors, Keltner (1995) found a strong relationship between the much lower labour turnover rates in German banks and their willingness to make significantly larger training investments in each new employee. US banks, faced with demands to tailor products more closely to customer needs and turnover rates of up to 30% per year for key categories of workers, have coped by adopting a modular training strategy—providing short training courses to new employees and then offering opportunities for greater job responsibilities and additional training to individuals who stay with the firm and show a desire for advancement. In other, lower-skilled areas of the services sector, such as fast food and hotels, turnover rates can exceed 100% annually, with a strong negative impact on service quality and the skills of the workforce (Schlesinger and Heskett 1991).

It is not clear from the aggregate data on turnover rates to what extent high turnover represents a conscious choice by employers to treat labour as a variable cost that can be cut when demand slackens, and to what extent it is an external constraint on managers, imposed by the behaviour of other firms and Americans' preference for greater mobility. A variety of evidence suggests that US managers could reduce turnover if they desired, but prefer to minimize the size of their core, long-term workforce. There has, for example, been a dramatic growth in the size of the temporary workforce in the USA, with Manpower Inc.— an agency providing temporary employees—now the largest single US employer (Seavey and Kazis 1994). In his study of the banking sector, Keltner (1995) found

---

[5] To some extent the process is circular. Because there is a weak relationship between the education system and the skills needed for jobs, and because firms are reluctant to train, much emphasis is placed on a 'trial and error' approach to recruitment, the screening of young recruits by employing them for short periods while their suitability is assessed (Büchtemann and Verdier 1998; Tan and Peterson 1992).

that one US bank was able to attain dramatically lower turnover rates (averaging 8% per year) by offering employees, including part-timers, greater employment security, pay tied to the firm's performance, more input into corporate decision making, and opportunities for ongoing learning. Most banks elected not to pursue this strategy, however, because it was perceived to limit their employment flexibility.

There are other examples of firms that have been able to reduce turnover, and make substantial investments in transferable skills, by constructing strong internal labour markets and other attributes of the institutional company pattern (see, for example, Schlesinger and Heskett 1991; Appelbaum and Batt 1994). Some companies have done this by following the model of the labour monopsonist and locating in areas where there are no direct competitors for their set of skills; Daimler-Benz surprised many commentators by choosing to build its first US automobile plant in rural Alabama, one of the poorest, and least educated parts of the country. In addition to the generous investment incentives, relatively low wages, and non-union environment, one of the key factors in the firm's decision was the strong sense of community in this rural area and the absence of comparable firms for several hundred miles (Andressen 1994). Small high-tech firms, which are often clustered together in regions such as California's Silicon Valley, the Research Triangle in North Carolina, and Massachusetts's Route 128, seek to retain their highly skilled employees by offering stock options that can soar in value as the firms grow.

Financial markets   Second, although the USA has arguably the world's most efficient capital markets, these are prime examples of what were called in Chapter 1 'capital-based markets', and appear to deter many companies from making long-term investments in the skills of their workforce (Dertouzos *et al.* 1989; Porter 1992; Soskice 1991*a*). The problem arises because the costs of investing in training appear immediately on the balance sheet, while the benefits take time to accrue, are difficult to quantify, and often require other concurrent changes in organization in order to be fully successful (Finegold 1991; OECD 1996*b*). Survey evidence suggests that the heads of US corporations have a significantly shorter investment time-frame than their counterparts in Japan and Germany (Poterba and Summers 1991; Abegglen and Stalk 1985). There are several features of US capital markets and corporations that appear to encourage this short-term investment time-frame and discourage sustained workforce development: (a) corporate governance regulations which require US chief executives to focus solely on the interest of shareholders, while Japanese and German firms take into account the interests of all stakeholders, including the firm's employees; (b) the impact of hostile takeovers and leveraged buyouts that compel managers to maximize short-term returns in order to sustain cash flow; (c) the relationship between companies and stockholders that tends to limit the flow of information to easily quantifiable indicators, such as quarterly profits, and discounts factors such as human capital investment (Soskice 1991*a*); (d) and the educational background of those leading many US firms, who have taken MBAs which emphasize financial management over human-resources issues (Finegold *et al*. 1994*a*).

Reviewing these and other factors, a major recent study of the system of corporate finance in the US concluded:

American firms invest too little in those assets and capabilities most required for competitiveness (*such as employee training*), while wasting capital on investments with limited financial or social rewards (such as unrelated acquisitions). (Porter 1992; italics in original.)

The effects of the US financial system on company managers' decisions regarding training, however, vary significantly by sector and firm type. US venture-capital firms provide far more long-term finance for high-tech start-ups than is available in other nations, while many family-owned businesses rely primarily on retained earnings for funding investments, and can take a longer-term view toward training if they desire. Even in firms where there is clear pressure to demonstrate the short-term returns to any investment, there can be a beneficial effect on workforce development as the human-resource department seeks new ways to demonstrate the effectiveness of education and training programmes and tie them more closely to the organization's needs (Leyda *et al*. 1995).

Summary

Perhaps more than in any other country in our study, recent changes in the USA seem set to reinforce the country's existing pattern in the development and use of human skills: strong performance in a number of particularly high-skilled sectors; a far less impressive average performance; and an extremely wide distribution, with a substantial group of the population (of both persons and firms) with low skill levels. The system creates disincentives for the average firm to pursue a high-skill strategy, alongside many instances of very advanced training in high-performance companies—primarily because they are labour monopsonists, institutional companies, or firms in very advanced sectors. In sum, this makes for a patchy provision of training to select groups of employees. It also makes it difficult to develop a national strategy that might aim at achieving overall high skill levels (as opposed to residual remedial aid for those left behind), with policy-makers continuing to rely on a pattern of company and individual incentives that combine to produce excellence in leading sectors but under-performance elsewhere—including within firms. These are the outcomes which the theoretical account at the outset of this chapter led us to expect from a market- and company-led training system. The USA does, however, also possess a truly vast quantity of both public and private educational activities; this is not necessarily implied by a market- and company-based system, so it is therefore useful to look below at the UK as an example of such a system with a much smaller educational base.

The USA has less need to be concerned over the failure of a system of its kind to produce a skill-maximizing strategy for the whole nation than smaller countries: as we saw in Chapter 3, the proportion of the country's output that is internationally traded is considerably lower than that of smaller nations; its prestige as the sole world superpower gives it competitive advantages of a unique kind, quite apart from competition based on skills; its dominant position in the world means that it can carry virtual permanent trade deficits without crisis—in fact, were the USA to start running long-term surpluses, there would be a problem for the world economy, which relies on the US market acting as an engine for growth; and its highly individualistic culture does not seem to require the kind of egalitarian social cohesion of many European societies and, in some respects, Japan. However, as noted earlier, the growth in inequality—which is linked to educational problems—is regarded by many as the most pressing problem facing the US economy (USA 1995*b*).

For the trade that it does require, it has both a number of existing world-class companies and a base of raw materials and primary products that give it further market advantages. Manufacturing production occupies a smaller proportion of US output than that of most other advanced countries, greater importance being held by both agriculture and the increasingly dominant services sector, many areas of which are still far less exposed to international competition. Evidence of its changing occupational structure in Chapter 3 (growth at both high and low levels, with almost an 'excluded middle'), as well as recent evidence of growing inequalities of income (OECD 1996*a*), also indicate the lack of progress in a project of achieving 'high average' performance. Other evidence (US Department of Labor 1997) suggests that, despite the strong growth in higher-skilled managerial, technical, and professional occupations, the largest absolute growth in employment is occurring in relatively low-skilled ones (for example, retail sales, janitor, waiter/waitress). However, there are clear signs that employers' skill demands are increasing—in a new survey of a nationally representative sample of firms with more than 20 employees, the Census Bureau found that 57% had increased skill requirements in the last three years, while only 5% had experienced a decrease, and 39% reported no change (EQW 1995).

In recent years many in the USA have shared the general concern of advanced industrial countries that ground was being lost in the production and sale of many standard manufacturing products to new producers, while the country's capacity to succeed in an adequate range of high-tech areas has also been in doubt.[6] As elsewhere, there have been those in the USA who have argued that there should therefore be more concerted public-policy attempts to move production of goods and services up-market, including upgrading the skills capacity of the labour force (Reich 1992). The labour markets themselves are responding to this situation without public policy. The growing inequality of incomes has intensified incentives for individuals to invest in skills. Opportunities to respond to this incentive are plentiful, as they have been increased by growth in the amount

---

[6] It remains to be seen if this will change following the crisis of the Japanese and other Asian economies.

and variety of provision as well as the flexible way in which the US education and further training system enables individuals to add modules of various skills.

On the other hand, Federal and state budget cuts have worsened the chances of people from relatively low-earning backgrounds being able to take advantage of these opportunities. Also, these incentives may be being undermined by the growing insecurity of employment, the temporary nature of many job contracts, and the shorter lifespan of companies. All of these factors increase the risk of the investment in education that individuals are being called upon to make, with the effect that, if they are rational actors, they might be less willing to do so. Signs of concern at these possibilities and at growing income inequalities can be seen in some policy responses, such as the School to Work Opportunities Act 1994, designed to encourage more widespread uptake of training opportunities.

There will not be problems of this kind in those sectors of the labour market where potential rewards are very high (justifying the risks), or where individuals can be confident that their skills will be in high demand whatever the insecurity of individual job placements. This will apply in particular to rapidly developing, very highly skilled sectors, particularly in geographical areas where employment opportunities in such sectors are concentrated.

This raises an interesting question for the relationship between the performance of the average company (or worker) and that of the best. Is it possible that within a system (or non-system) of the US kind that imposes few pressures towards achieving a high average, it might be easier for some firms to concentrate on achieving the very highest standards for a minority of staff? This puts at its most extreme the dilemma between the social goal of maximizing high skill and the role of corporate autonomy, and is an issue to which we shall return in the final chapter.

BRITISH IMITATIONS OF THE US MODEL

Discussion of British vocational skill creation has mainly presented a picture of generally unsatisfactory performance—or, more accurately, a rather bipolar system with exceptionally strong performances in some high-skilled industries, with a long tail of low-skilled industries and people, and in general a missing level of middle-range skills. This was a major finding of the research carried out by the NIESR in the 1980s and summarized in Chapter 3. Comparative studies of British and German industries suggested differences in skill levels of persons employed, leading to differences in the quality of output, in a number of industries and occupations in the two countries: mechanical fitters, electricians, construction workers, office workers, and shop assistants (Prais and Wagner 1985); the metalworking industry (Daly, Hitchens, and Wagner 1985); foremen (Prais and Wagner 1988); fitted kitchens (Steedman and Wagner 1987); women's outerwear (Steedman and Wagner 1989); and mechanical engineering and food processing (Mason and Finegold 1995).

More recently, a comparison of training of bank employees in France, Germany, and the UK (Quack, O'Reilly, and Hilderbrandt 1995) shows British banks struggling with both poorly developed corporatist structures for assisting the industry as a whole, and a low level of general educational provision. They tended to solve the problem by concentrating training on a small élite of staff, programming skill into the machines for the rest who would remain inadequately trained. Similar results are found from research in engineering design (Campbell and Warner 1991; Lam and Marsden 1992; Thurley and Lam 1989), where narrow specialization is often used to overcome skill deficiency, which in turn seems to create disillusion and a sense of working below their capacities among young engineers. Some authors have seen British firms' 'solution' to their chronic skill problems as having been to produce simpler and less sophisticated goods than German and other rival firms (Steedman and Wagner 1987; 1989). However, as we saw in Chapter 3, this is only part of the story; the UK also has had, and increasingly has, a small but strong performance in some highly skilled sectors. It is better to see UK performance, like that of the USA, as bifurcated between high- and low-skill activities.

There is the same issue here as in the USA of the relationship between the performance of the average company (or worker) and that of the best. Again, as with the USA, a system (or non-system) that is not geared towards a high average may actually be better equipped to provide a minority of the best—though in the UK there may be an additional problem that in several sectors the latter is increasingly dependent on inward investment.

However, as Lam and Marsden (1992) record, there is evidence that following the deindustrialization of the early 1980s that removed many low-performing firms, the remaining British firms have considerably improved their training efforts. In a study of microelectronics in the engineering industries of the UK and Germany, Campbell and Warner (1991) reported some signs of change in both countries. Results from their sample of 27 firms in each country suggested that companies were developing better links than in the past with public education, expanding training for front-line employees, and developing training for employees in supervisory positions. These had, however, been initiatives taken by individual firms within the voluntarist UK system and in no way represented a systemic change. There has also been important evidence of an increase in firms' own expenditure on training after years of very low levels (Blundell *et al.* 1995; Davis 1996). As in most other countries we have examined, employers tended to concentrate this training on employees with higher education (Blundell *et al.* 1995), which corresponded to the characteristically British extended skills gap between managerial and professional staffs on the one hand, and routine non-manual and all manual workers on the other. Employer-provided training is also concentrated in industries in the midst of major technological advance (ibid.).

In Chapter 3 we were able to confirm important elements of this account. The role of firms as seen in this record follows that which would be expected in a market-led system, with fear of poaching and few incentives for firms to invest in skills unless they are in one of the very high-skilled sectors which cannot survive without them and able to draw upon the strong record of British élite higher education. Attention in both academic writing and much policy discussion has therefore concentrated on improving the basic human resource being provided to firms by the general education system, and on links between that system and the business world. The general context of dissatisfaction with the country's performance has led, as we have seen in preceding chapters, to various attempts at imitating practice in other countries. While much of this originally concentrated on Germany, the clear differences between some aspects of German institutional structure and the British, together with a strong political preference for resembling a neo-liberal rather than a neo-corporatist system, has led in more recent years to imitations of US institutions. Some evidence of this has already been noted in the modelling of TECs on American PICs.

For example, Daly (1986) undertook a systematic comparison between Britain and the USA, based on the assumption that, both countries having a more market-based system than Germany, the American model might provide a more accessible guide to changes needed in the British pattern than the more institutionalized German one. Dominant US features included: flexibility in manning arrangements, with less demarcation between skilled and unskilled activities and few restrictions on entry into craft work; large numbers of management and business graduates, and in general more vocational graduates. She also found relevant a school system in which a much higher percentage of the population received a basic education with a vocational component; and a much higher number of school-leavers going on to higher education. Within the school system there was an emphasis on high and intermediate skills. The main difference here from Britain was the sheer number of people undergoing education, especially to university level. As Daly pointed out, Britain had neither the large proportion of graduates that the USA enjoyed nor the high number of workers with intermediate qualifications found in Germany. However, a recent study from the US Economic Policy Institute (Rasell and Mishel, no date) draws attention to an unusual feature of US education. While both enrolments in and expenditure on higher education are the highest in the world, its per capita expenditure on pre-primary, primary, and secondary levels is among the lowest in the OECD area.

Recent changes in British VET have been aimed at engineering a shift towards elements of this US pattern: a high level of general educational provision alongside strong incentives for individuals to secure opportunities and a general dismantling of institutional as opposed to market structures (King 1993). There has been considerable growth in young people staying on at school, entering colleges of further education, and taking up other educational opportunities (Finegold 1992: 236–8). Consistent with this preference for US models, it has become customary for governments to play down their own role in skills-creation policy, while not playing down the role of skills *per se*:

It is the view of the UK Government that economic success, and the social benefits that can be provided only by a successful economy, require vocational education and training arrangements that are responsive to the needs of firms and the aspirations of individual workers. However, the Government does not believe that such arrangements can be brought about by national legislation or regulations at a time when flexibility and constant adaptation in training are required in order to respond to the challenges facing firms and workers. (Davis 1996: 265.)

Skills policy has therefore been concentrated on the supply side, increasing the number of educated young people coming on to the labour market.[7] However, this approach is not entirely straightforward. In the first place, the size of the educational base of the population remains smaller than that in the USA and may have hit a ceiling of growth without a cultural change accepting the need to treat advanced education as an investment. Second, the outcome of such a strategy—points of excellence within a less highly skilled general context—is less well suited to the UK's need to engage strongly in international trade than it is to an economy the size of the USA. It is also not at all clear that the emerging pattern of provision is consistent with a goal of maximizing the proportion of the working population able to compete internationally in terms of the quality and skill of their labour. Improvements in productivity in UK export industries have often been achieved by reducing the overall size and output of those industries, leading to the country relying on an even smaller export sector than in the past. Meanwhile, small firms have a particularly poor record of providing training (Blundell *et al.* 1995; Davis 1996: 271).

It is therefore doubtful whether the market model can operate in the UK in quite the same way as in the USA, and it is certainly notable that, even during the strongly neo-liberal Thatcher period, and despite the formal stance of government and employers in Britain that the country has a primarily market-led approach to training, there has been far more national public policy in the UK than in the USA (Finegold, McFarland, and Richardson 1993). Felstead and Green (1994) challenge the stereotype of British firms fitting into a pure market model, where firms reduce training in recessions. They argue that industry-specific standards, the corporatist role of professional bodies, national and European Union regulations have all served to stabilize training efforts. The UK therefore only partly fits the concept of having a 'market-led' approach to skill creation. Indeed, as previous chapters have shown, it has been a country in which a greater diversity of approaches has been taken to training than in any of the other cases surveyed.

Governments have also tried to import a strong form of the idea of the institutional company through their success in attracting inward investment by Japanese multinationals. In particular, and as noted in the previous chapter, it is hoped

---

[7] The change of government in May 1997 did not result in any major shift in the emphasis either on increasing supply or in generally abstaining from action on the demand for skilled labour or on creating intermediary institutions between the business and educational sectors other than the existing TECs.

that the Japanese firms will develop supplier networks in Britain of the kind they built in Japan, whereby a large customer company stimulates best practice among the suppliers. It is then hoped that some large UK firms will begin to copy Japanese practices, both in investing in the skills of their workers and forming partnerships with suppliers. For example, the Department of Trade and Industry and the Society of Motor Manufacturers and Traders not only advocate but devote some resources to encouraging 'partnership' sourcing and the development of supplier networks in the car industry. The kind of co-operative relationships, both between suppliers and customers and among suppliers, which this involves, makes a strong contrast with the preferred adversarial and pure contract-exchange approach of normal British commercial relations.

Sako (1994) compared the experience of Japanese multinational companies setting up plants in Britain and Germany. In Germany the Japanese firms' main problem lay in getting around the rigid qualification system in order to provide more flexible learning and promotion opportunities for semi-skilled workers. In Britain the major problem lay in the unavailability of people comparable to German *Meister* who could take on both supervisory and technical roles. The Japanese firms in Britain had to choose, on the one hand, between training supervisors in technical skills and making supervisors out of reluctant technicians, and on the other being content with the British norm of a more centralized technical department supporting the shop-floor. She found only a few making the long-term commitment involved in transposing a Japanese system.

Japanese imitations have had an important symbolic and demonstration effect within Britain, but whether their impact can be big enough to have a national effect must be open to some doubt. Not only are Japanese transplants very small in relation to the total size of the UK labour force, but Japanese corporate institutions are very different from British ones.

CONCLUSIONS

Firms, left to themselves, will engage in a large amount of vocational training, especially the reskilling or further skilling of appropriate existing workers, provided that they are located in product markets where such an upskilling is necessary for market survival. Company-led skill creation is likely to be exceptionally adaptable and seems to be associated, at least in the strongest if different cases of Japan and the USA, with strong performance in particularly highly skilled and innovative areas. Strict collective choice approaches of the kind associated with Becker (1962) would seem to underestimate the extent to which firms will accept some wastage of workers they have trained, even if these go to rival firms, if provision of the necessary training is vital to sustaining a presence in market niches to which they have become heavily committed through various sunk costs.

However, it remains extremely doubtful whether, by itself, an approach of reliance on firms and individuals in the market can achieve the goal of upskilling most of a working population—even where, as in the USA, reliance on firms is linked to a public policy and general cultural bias in favour of extensive general education. It cannot be claimed that in any country relying primarily on autonomous company initiative the majority of firms is operating at this standard; the USA and Japan in particular enter international trade for a relatively low proportion of their economic activity and sustain large low-productivity service sectors that do not provide their workforces with strong prospects. Where firms make a major contribution to training and retraining their employees, the evidence suggests that many do so for only a minority of their staff, and limit further training to Beckerian firm-specific skills which do not contribute to labour-market flexibility. As we saw in Chapter 5, similar problems are reported of firm-level further training in Germany (Voelzkow 1990: 114–19), which lacks the collective co-operation and regulation of the *Kammern* that are essential if the initial training system is not carried over into further training—an area where the writ of the *Kammern* does not run.

There are, therefore, no inherent tendencies in firms' market-driven search for improved skills to supply a strategy for skill maximization for a society as a whole. Overall, there is no evidence from existing cases that the pursuit of the learning society as a general collective goal can be achieved by reliance on individual firms.

8

Conclusions and Policy Implications

On the basis of our analysis of VET systems in these seven leading industrialized countries, we can now draw some more general conclusions about what kinds of institutional arrangements for skills creation seem to promise most prospects of attaining the goal of the learning society. In some respects the worst placed are those systems that provide specific vocational courses remote from the enterprise: among the countries studied here, that means primarily the central state-regulated regimes for initial VET of France, Italy, and also, to some extent, Sweden. As we have seen in Chapter 4, where the public education system is the main direct provider of vocational education there is almost inevitably a gulf between education providers and firms. While this might not have been important at a time of relatively slowly changing skills and technologies, it is today becoming a major handicap. It is extremely difficult for systems of this kind to respond quickly to market opportunities for making new and better uses of work skills, as has been widely recognized in the Swedish debate and in French and Italian attempts to revive apprenticeship.

Separately, we have seen how in most systems the role of direct state provision of training has been adversely affected by two self-reinforcing factors: the association of government action with residual provision for the unemployed; and the hostility of current neo-liberal orthodoxy to most kinds of government action. Here we saw that this specific area of skills-creation policy demonstrates the current general predicament of public policy. Government becomes associated with care for social failure and not with dynamism, and the latter therefore comes to be seen as resting solely with private corporations whose initiatives the state can only weaken by diluting them with social concerns. Neo-liberal strategies are self-reinforcing in that they first residualize the state's role to one of a safety net for the welfare casualties of the economy, and then residualize it further because it has become associated with such tasks and is therefore seen as inimical to innovation.

On the other hand, at the increasingly important level of further VET there is evidence that the French state-led strategy of creating incentives for subsidizing firms to train through a levy system can have beneficial effects. The rationale of the policy is that, because of cash-flow problems or difficult investment risks, firms might not be taking advantage of opportunities to improve their market prospects by upgrading the quality of their existing labour force. A combination of levy and subsidy might enable them to do this. However, as the French debate shows, there are considerable anxieties about whether firms are making proper use of the system as intended. Monitoring such expenditure is extremely difficult;

in many cases firms have probably secured a subsidy for doing something which they would in any case have done for themselves. By itself a subsidy may well not be enough to enable an unadventurous firm to discover new ways of using work skills to conquer new markets. Effort is concentrated on managerial and other already highly educated employees rather than on upskilling those in danger of falling out of the march to the learning society—though this is also an issue in the USA, Germany, Sweden, the UK, and other countries where state subsidies are not at stake.

In general, the state, even the French state, is losing its claim to be able to guide firms that have not found dynamic new paths for themselves into appropriate courses of action. Are any institutions today in a position to carry out such a task? As recent actions of Swedish employers have made clear, even when business leaders share the objectives of improving skills, they want to leave the initiative with individual companies. On the other hand, governments cannot pursue skill-maximization strategies unless they are in close touch with business interpretations of what this means in practice. Once their officials and professionals retreat to a role of deregulating in order to leave space for company autonomy, and to the residual role of caring for social casualties, they cease to be plausible participants in the development of a high-skill economy and lose the possibility of acquiring and maintaining the expertise necessary to function as well-informed participants in the provision of advanced skills. They also thereby lose the capacity to improve the skill positions of their populations beyond the extent to which the companies operating within the borders of their states are willing to support. They end, as Dresser and Rogers (1997: 8) describe on the basis of US experience:[1]

with local governments or educational institutions stumbling along after what they take to be the latest industry 'trend' without the resources to drive it, and almost always finding that by the time new programming arrives, the underlying economic conditions have changed.

In the Italian, British, and, to some extent, Swedish cases we saw signs of a response to this problem in the development of small, flexible government agencies close to local business communities. However, there is considerable difference between a government agency working with the grain of the needs of firms already engaged in skill maximization and one seeking to ratchet up the skill needs of companies lacking such an approach. Where firms are not themselves enterprising, the more responsive and firm sensitive an agency is, the less capable it is of being proactive and strategic. This is of little use to a goal of maximizing national skill creation and utilization.

---

[1] Dresser and Rogers regard this as being the way government 'is and always has been' (ibid.). This is not, however, a generalization that one would apply to all past experiences of governments in countries where government roles have not been marginalized as extensively as in the USA (for example, the Swedish active labour market programme (King and Rothstein 1993); the Japanese skill certification system (Sako 1995); or some forms of the French professional training system).

Our survey of Italian and British experience in Chapter 6 demonstrated this and some other weaknesses of local strategies. Neither country has found policy mechanisms favourable to a long-term rather than a short-term skill-creation model. In addition to suffering from the general problem of government policy trying to combine assistance for the unemployed and poorly skilled with attempts at pushing forward the frontiers of high-level skill creation, in neither country had training been at the forefront of services sought by firms. Therefore, of course, it declines in importance among the services offered, illustrating the dilemma between a market-oriented, 'service-selling' approach that tries to get as close as possible to the defined needs of firms as customers, and a national policy goal that seeks to shift firms from currently perceived needs to something more ambitious.

The danger of being trapped between uninformed interference by public agencies and an incapacity of many firms to take advantage of new possibilities has in many ways been resolved through systems of the German kind. These not only combine, through the dual system, formal education with real work experience, but also mediate collective concerns through authoritative representative business organizations (the *Kammern*) rather than through government departments. As we have seen in Chapter 5, such arrangements can solve many problems, but they can be slow to adapt to change because they depend on carrying the commitment of a large number of interests that have to be consulted before a major adjustment is undertaken. The German system is currently having difficulty adapting to the needs for social skills and to a more service- rather than manufacturing-oriented economy. At the same time it has encountered severe problems of declining competitiveness in manufacturing, caused partly by the over-valuation of its currency, partly by its high labour costs, and partly by the cost of renovating the former East Germany.

We also noted that, although the changeability and flexibility of new skill concepts are shifting emphasis towards further rather than initial VET, it is difficult to organize neo-corporatist involvement in the former. Initial training concerns a necessary interface between, on the one hand, the public and social sphere of the school system and, on the other, the private sphere of work and the acquisition of occupational identity. Further training takes place within this private sphere, after young people have been turned into company employees; employers are therefore less likely here to accept interaction with external institutions, even those drawn from their own entrepreneurial community. This will especially be the case when the further training takes the form of further induction into a specific corporate culture. French public policy would seem to be performing better than German in the area of further VET because of the greater role permitted to state action in the French context.

Adaptations could be made to the German apprenticeship system. It has changed much in the past; and in principle the dual system could be extended to further VET. If these changes do not happen, it will be because firms do not want external intervention in their affairs, not because apprenticeship and interest associations are inherently incapable of adaptation.

PROBLEMS OF COMPANY AUTONOMY

In the present international neo-liberal political climate we must give particular consideration to the argument that public policy should more or less vacate
the field other than to provide or encourage the provision of continually higher
levels of general educational provision so that those firms which are able to see
ways of making use of better-qualified staff will have good material with which
to work. While many companies will not participate in this process, there might
be little that can be done by an external agency to help them. Japanese firms have
shown that a very high level of commitment to skill improvement can be pursued within a corporate-dominated model. The Japanese economy is not, however, a true example of neo-liberalism, but one to which the institutions of supplier
associations, business associations in general, and strong internal labour markets
are essential.

   There are some difficulties in establishing firms' preferences here. On the one
hand they increasingly want good general standards of education rather than highly
specific skills. This is a reflection of three major changes taking place in the
character of work: the demand for individuals capable of operating in multifunctional teams with a broad understanding of the business (Mohrman, Cohen, and
Mohrman 1995); the frequency of change itself (change in the skills required to
perform a job and the need for flexibility and adaptability); and the growing
importance, even in the manufacturing sector, of service skills, skills of personal
communication (Regini 1996a). These changes lead employers to seek in new
recruits both a continuing ability to learn and what they usually call 'social skills',
which might mean anything from ability to co-ordinate and secure co-operation,
through ability to communicate effectively, to simple willingness to obey orders.
With the exception of the last mentioned, these are the kinds of abilities that
general education is best at providing. On the other hand, firms are often very
critical of general education systems, saying that they want an education more
closely geared to the world of employment.

   Their position is not necessarily contradictory. There are three possibilities:
this may be a matter of different employers, or employers of different types of
labour, having different requirements; firms may be seeking a general education
but of a different kind from that being provided by educational institutions; or
firms may want people with the adaptability that a general education can give,
but articulated according to a specific corporate culture. We shall discuss these
issues in this order.

   First, there is the question of a diversity of requirements. For some tasks, those
likely to lead to managerial or professional positions, or where the employee has
to represent the firm in its relations with customers, suppliers, and others, the
versatility of general education is wanted. In other cases, perhaps for those lower
down the firm's hierarchy, more specific skills are sought (or, if 'social skills'
are desired it is largely those of obedience—a commodity which modern education systems find it difficult to combine with their job of developing enquiring,

critical minds, both important components of the ability to learn). In this context, whether a young person should pursue a general or a highly specific course will depend on the part of the occupational hierarchy for which he or she seems destined. *Ceteris paribus*, for the individual there must be a bias in favour of conserving the possibility of aiming high, and therefore of taking more general courses. However, for the majority who will not be among the more successful, this may turn out to be poor advice, as in a world of generally increasing uptake of educational opportunities a relatively unsuccessful general education is likely to deliver worse prospects than a more specific, though potentially less ambitious, course. Büchtemann and Verdier (1998) go so far as to speak of the '*déstabilisation*' of specialized vocational education as a result of this process, and cite studies by Büchtemann and Vogler-Ludwig (1995), Ryan (1995), and Verdier (1995) for evidence of the process in Germany, the UK, and France respectively. Lutz (1992) puts the point even more strongly, arguing that Germany is in danger of avoiding reforming its dual system by shifting to increased emphasis on general education, which will leave vocational training as an appendage to the main educational system—as happened in France with negative consequences.

Second, if firms are seeking what they regard as a general education but this differs from that being provided by educational institutions, then effective means of communication do not exist between employers and the educational world. This may be a problem of educational process, as many schools and colleges continue to deliver general content in a traditional lecture format, when what employers (and many educational researchers) prefer is an action-learning approach, where individuals are taught to take control over their own learning and master general concepts in the context of real-world problems. It may also be a problem of mismatched content. Young people may then suffer by wasting their time in inappropriate learning, discovering eventually that firms were solving the problem by providing in-firm training for people recruited through a quite separate route.

Finally, firms may want a general, educated adaptability, but defined and articulated according to a specific corporate culture, leading the new employee to identify with the firm and its goals. If firms take this position, they are usually prepared to provide such an acculturation themselves, but the position is not without its paradoxes. While employers increasingly stress the specificity of their cultures and their desire to inculcate their employees in them, they also increasingly stress the need for greater ease of hiring and firing and tell employees that they must expect to change jobs more frequently than was common in the past (Rousseau 1995). The short, and declining, length of time spent with a particular employer by the average US employee is today seen as a mark of the superiority of that country's employment system, in contrast with, in particular, Japan.[2] A decline in average employment tenure is meanwhile being recorded in Japan,

[2] There is, however, evidence that some of the very brief periods that young people spend with employers are not so much examples of flexibility of employment as inefficient job matching caused by failures of communication between general education and vocational needs.

Germany, and other nations which in the past had lengthy average employment periods.

Even more challenging to the company culture idea is the trend towards ending the concept of employment altogether and replacing it by a series of contracts between a customer firm and a mass of small labour-contracting firms, temporary agencies, or, in extreme cases, individual providers of labour services. These can be accompanied by the growth of supplier communities as in Japan, in which case they can be made fully compatible with a company culture model, at least for the hub of the firm network and its largest suppliers. If, as is often the case, supplier networks are advocated as cost-cutting and commitment-reducing strategies, this is unlikely to occur. This will be particularly the case if, as in the UK, subcontracting and franchising are not really examples of small-firm formation but of self-employment without infrastructural support.

It is likely that often these paradoxes are being resolved by segmentation, with firms retaining a long-serving group of key staff who are inculcated into a culture and with whom they have relational contracts, and a larger number of more marginalized individuals who are employed on a shorter-term transactional basis (ibid.).[3] However, it is also possible that, in the present context of intensified competition, some firms are seeking to discover how far they can proceed with a policy of 'having one's cake and eating it too': seeking strong but unreciprocated commitment and loyalty from staff. Anxieties about the constant pressure to demonstrate to shareholders adequate returns, and the fact that it is often easier to achieve these returns through downsizing and delayering than through 'growing' the business, lead managers to do this, despite the face that these managers themselves are thereby made vulnerable to redundancy. Certain basic requirements of the contemporary corporate environment are difficult to reconcile with the requirements of the learning society.

Nevertheless, there will be those who respond positively to this situation: people confident in the scarcity of their skills and of their chances of gaining new employment once the current contract ends. This will be common among people with particularly rare skills, able to charge very high fees for their services which provide them with security during any temporary periods of unemployment. This has long been the case of leading figures in the artistic and cultural world, especially performing artists; in the eighteenth century Ricardo formulated his concept of 'rent' specifically to explain their high incomes. Many modern technological occupations embody elements of this. Such people are most likely to be found at the sharp edges of new technology or science-based innovation, where the high morale produced by being involved in exciting innovation can provide that combination of total dedication to the task in hand with willingness to accept a high level of insecurity which is, for contemporary employers, the philosopher's stone of the ideal worker. It is a quality rarely found

---

[3] Regini (1996*a*) suggests that numerical flexibility (that is, easy disposability) is mainly wanted from occupational groups in decline.

among German or French employee cultures, but quite common in certain parts of the USA. It is unlikely anywhere to be the predominant form of worker, rather something to be found in highly specific circumstances.

However, even these qualities may have collective and institutional components. It will be easier for a highly skilled worker to accept insecure employment in one firm if that enterprise is part of a network of similar firms the managers and staff of which know each other well, since there will be a reasonable chance that the end of a contract at one firm will be quickly replaced by one at another with which the worker may already be in contact. It will be very different for employees of isolated companies not so mutually connected. These are among the advantages of industrial districts, whether they feature co-operation through intermediate institutions, as is common in Italy and Germany, or simply a dense concentration of employers with similar needs that have multiple partnerships among independent firms, as is common in US high-technology clusters.

Firms can resolve the dilemma of the relationship of their specific needs to employees' general educational background in three contexts. The first is an apprenticeship system of the German type, provided this can respond sufficiently rapidly to needs for change. The second, which corresponds to the position in the USA, is for the general education system to provide a vast, unstructured diversity of opportunities, some of which will be wasted and misguided, but others of which will hit the target of providing employers with their needs. Third, the Japanese large-firm model represents a particular combination of the other two: general educational provision of a US kind, but within a more 'German' context of a clear indication of the likely successful routes.

The second form may well be preferred by many employers, in Germany and Japan as much as in the USA, as it meets some of their current preoccupations with reducing commitments beyond the firm. On the one hand, little is required from firms in terms of interaction with governments, agencies, schools, even business associations or *Kammern*, interactions which might add to firms' costs and slow responses at a time when labour costs and speed of response are a priority. The model also assumes a large supply of potential labour from which some can be selected and many rejected—a characteristic which did not commend itself to employers at a time of consistently high employment as in the 1950s and 1960s, but is quite acceptable in a prolonged period of slack labour markets. Such a system corresponds to a pure market in labour, within which employers act as pure customers, indicating their needs through the market signals of their hiring policies, rather than a Hirschmanian or Williamsonian market in which participants must communicate and interact more directly. However, even the USA, which has tight labour markets in the 1990s, cannot assume a large available labour supply in the future.

If we view the situation through the eyes of young persons on the other side of the labour market, such a system may look less attractive. Virtually by definition they are poorly informed and unable to assess the variety of courses knowledgeably. They must, however, make decisions that will not be easily reversed but which must predict accurately the state of labour market opportunities in a future time period—the period after they have completed their educational preparation. They must also make extensive investments of time, energy, and possibly money. They cannot afford to make mistakes, since when all one is taking to market is one's own labour, one is offering only one item for sale, and one which has taken a lengthy period of preparation.

We may summarize the position that has been reached in the encounter between firms' need for autonomy and the social priority on generally increasing skills as follows. In many circumstances there are no reasons why firms, left to themselves, will not engage in a large amount of vocational training, especially the increasingly important reskilling of existing workers—though the new emphasis on dissolving the employment contract into labour subcontracting and a shortening of the length of time that workers spend with a particular firm creates severe problems here. Where it does take place, company-led VET is likely to be exceptionally adaptable and seems to be associated, at least in the strong if different cases of Japan and the USA, with high performance in particularly highly skilled and innovative areas. However, it remains doubtful whether, by itself, a strategy that relies on an approach of reliance on firms can in any way produce the frequently stipulated requirement of an upskilling of most of a working population—even where, as in the USA, that reliance is linked to a public policy and general cultural bias in favour of extensive general education. It cannot be claimed that in any country relying primarily on autonomous company initiative the majority of firms is operating at this standard. Even where firms do make a major contribution to training and retraining their employees, the evidence suggests that only a few, true leading-edge firms have a strategy of decentralizing authority to front-line employees and providing all workers with the skills needed to handle these new responsibilities (Lawler, Mohrman, and Ledford 1995). Most firms are pursuing upskilling for only a minority of their employees, and limit further training to Beckerian firm-specific skills which do not contribute to labour-market flexibility. Regini (1996*b*) concluded from his study of leading firms in Baden-Württemberg, Catalonia, Lombardy, and Rhône-Alpes that even in periods of expansion their approach to upskilling was selective and *ad hoc* and was not geared towards creating reservoirs of human resources which would favour innovation. Similar problems are reported of firm-level further VET in Germany, where the collective co-operation of the apprenticeship system is not carried over into further training.

The current period is one of uncertain product markets and intensified global competition in which firms need to reduce their costs wherever possible, but in which a combination of rising educational standards and high unemployment is making skilled labour a plentiful commodity. In this context firms have strong incentives to move from a voice to an exit approach in their labour-market behaviour, stressing the need for complete ease and freedom in hiring and firing policy while reducing their engagement in all institutions that require interaction and communication. In this environment the pursuit of the learning society as a general collective goal or object of public policy cannot be fully delegated entirely to firms. The growing paradox of the simultaneous demand by firms for both higher general education and vocational training to provide greater adaptation to the milieu of the individual firm requires change from every system: greater adaptability on the part of the dual system; far more effective advice to young people facing the deceptively helpful diversity of so-called free market systems, a task with which employers and their associations must expect to give considerable help rather than leave to the educational and careers advice services; and some fundamental reconsideration of state-led systems that provide rather narrow, public training schemes with little contact with industry itself.

THE LIMITATIONS OF A HIGH-SKILL STRATEGY

The implicit, often explicit, assumptions behind much public discussion of the need for improved vocational education are that, in a context of growing international competition, sustainable competitive advantage can only be secured in export markets (or in import substitution) by high-cost producers in the advanced countries in product-market niches requiring high skill. There are two problems with this strategy. First, only a minority of the working population is involved in producing internationally traded goods and services; second, competitive niches are gained at least in part because of the increased productivity of the highly skilled labour that is produced by the training, which in turn reduces the amount of labour required for a given level of output. Therefore, while skills-creation strategies aimed at increasing national presences in high value-added markets are necessary for countries' economic success and for sustaining and improving employment opportunities for skilled people, it is highly unlikely that employment of this kind will ever be the major, or even a major, source of new jobs.

The evidence presented in Chapter 3 demonstrated aspects of this. A few obvious generally high-skill export sectors can be identified: information technology, pharmaceuticals, aircraft manufacture. No country has been able to base more than a small amount of its export activity in these sectors. Even if skills increase in the medium-high technology areas, such as machine-tool production, they are (especially as productivity advances) unlikely to employ large numbers of people. It must be remembered that some important service industries, which we were unable to consider in Chapter 3, employ highly skilled workers and are internationally traded: aspects of financial services or, indirectly, other business services which are used by manufacturing and other firms engaged in export. However, these remain small and, given the direct nature of much service delivery, need to have large numbers of their staff employed in (and usually from) the countries where the service is being delivered, even if ownership and top management are located in a home country.

Sectors which provide high-skill employment and those which provide advantages in the international economy are by no means synonymous. In most countries the biggest single employers of highly educated labour have been the
health, education, and welfare sectors, which are only marginally involved in international trade and usually are publicly provided or subsidized. One might expect
some expansion in the range of tradable services as trade barriers are reduced,
especially within groups of nations like the European Union. However, even in
those cases local labour forces will usually be used for most service delivery. If
anything, the proportion of a nation's workforce, as opposed to its capital, which
is engaged in internationally traded activity is declining—despite the growth of
world trade (Deutsches Institut für Wirtschaftsforschung 1996).

One implication of this argument is that the challenge posed to employment
in the advanced countries by new low-cost producers or by the switch of production to cheaper countries is less direct than is often believed (Krugman 1994).
To some extent what happens is that the savings that domestic consumers make
through buying cheaper imported goods are spent by them on domestically produced services, either directly or indirectly though their capacity to pay higher
levels of tax to finance public spending. For some parts of the labour force
—the growing number of highly skilled people working in education, health,
and luxury services—this logic has clearly been at work. However, some other
services and manufacturing industries are subject to a different logic. When
productivity is rising in some sectors, those where productivity remains low will
have to compete by being low cost, which primarily means having low labour
costs. By definition, a low-productivity sector will produce more jobs per unit
of turnover than a high-productivity one. Low-productivity sectors have therefore recently acquired a new prominence in job creation. Low-productivity jobs
have to be relatively low paid and are likely to require lower levels of educational background.[4] It was shown in Chapter 2 that in most countries, but especially in the USA where the labour market responds particularly quickly to change,
recent job creation has taken a bimodal form, with expansion at the top and bottom levels of the skill range. This reflects, on the one hand, the gradual growth
of educational levels and capacity of the economy to make use of them and, on
the other, the disproportionate employment gains that come from expansion in
low-productivity areas.

The likelihood that low-skill, low-wage jobs will be a major source of employment in economies where productivity is improving quickly in globally traded
sectors has a number of serious implications. Most prominent in general academic and political debate has been its consequences for income distribution

---

[4] There is, however, still an optimistic argument concerning the role of education in employment
of this type. It can be argued that, if the educational level of those performing low-skilled tasks rises,
the productivity of their work rises, making possible improvements in their income. For this reason
skill-enhancement policies for the low skilled are often an important counterpart to policies for introducing or improving minimum wages. The argument is optimistic because it has to assume that use
can and will be made of a worker's improved skill level, rather than its being 'wasted'.

and labour protection. The two countries in which this form of employment has expanded most, the UK and the USA, have experienced an extraordinary polarization in their income distributions in recent years, with the bottom 10% of the working population in the USA now being absolutely poorer than they were at the end of the 1970s despite a near doubling of the nation's wealth (OECD 1996*a*). Job creation of this kind is likely to be very sensitive to costs, and is likely to take place only if security, protective measures, and social insurance costs as well as wages are reduced. Since encouragement of such employment has now become an official policy of the OECD as one of the major means of resolving the problem of continuing high unemployment, a deliberate worsening of labour standards is being advocated by international agencies for possibly the first time in the history of modern employment systems.

To date, labour-market deregulation strategies among the advanced countries are free-riders on other countries' continued regulation. Were all countries to adopt current Anglo-American policies there would be a risk of an uncontrollable downward spiral of declining labour conditions and security, which would in turn undermine consumer confidence and hence production. Of course, the advocates of such policies do not accept such a categorization, but would argue that universal adoption of their proposals would yield universal benefits. However, this could only be expected to happen over the long term, which would leave neoclassical policy proposals with the same problems that Keynes analysed during the 1930s. They are at present protected from that experience and able to point to employment gains for countries which do follow the prescription by virtue of the fact that these countries are gaining at the expense of those which have not followed it. These are relative gains which are, by definition, not generalizable.

Another consequence of such a strategy is that the unemployment problem is 'solved' by making the conditions of employment increasingly resemble those of unemployment. People seek work, *inter alia*, in order to escape poverty, insecurity, and lack of self-respect. If the circumstances of employment for many require low wages, a high level of insecurity, and the performance of humble, low-level service tasks, the gains from moving from unemployment to employment may appear small, even though entire national systems of employment regulation will have been swept aside in order to provide it. However, governments view the problem of unemployment quite differently from those unemployed or fearing unemployment, for unemployed people are usually eligible for some kind of expensive benefit; an eligibility which they lose if employed in any way.

There are signs of unease at some of these implications even among the authorities which have urged the deregulatory approach. The OECD, having encouraged greater income inequality in general and a harsher approach towards the unemployed in order to make them accept low-paid work and poor conditions (OECD 1994*a* and *b*), has more recently shown anxiety at the social problems caused by extreme inequalities and has entertained the thought that poverty and the prospect of a succession of poorly paid, insecure jobs might have adverse effects on work motivation (OECD 1996*a*). The G7 group of nations has at least recognized the need to avoid the competitive downward spiral of employment regulation, though concrete agreement on consequent policy measures will be very difficult to achieve.

These wider issues are not our immediate concern here. The most likely implication of declining general labour standards in the field of skills creation will be intensified demand for education among young people, seeking to avoid being drawn into growing low-productivity forms of employment. Employers are likely to respond to this improved educational supply with a demand for relatively high levels of qualification among the people taking on the low-productivity jobs. This would be wasteful because the educational level is being used solely as a screening device and not substantively on the job. The clash of expectations that results from this leads many young people to prefer to stay out of the labour force until something suited to their educational achievements becomes available, rather than be perceived by potential employers as someone working in a low-skilled job. The response of policy to this is to force people to accept whatever work is offered to them if they wish to be eligible for pub-lic support during their period of unemployment, which changes considerably the entire face of welfare and job-search policy.

It is possible that in some circumstances, situations of this kind will eventu-ally lead some young people to cease bothering with education, because despite all its sacrifices it might lead to nothing better than could have been attained without it. There is some evidence of this among populations with particularly poor employment prospects, such as young women in the Italian south, where the poor development of the welfare state has prevented them from taking advant-age of the main source of employment opportunities for women in northern Europe (Esping-Andersen 1996), or young males in America's most deprived inner-city areas. However, the more likely response will be an even more des-perate search for qualifications, perceived as a means of gaining an advantage in the struggle.

POLICY IMPLICATIONS[5]

The approach to public VET policy in many countries has been a pattern of the following kind: considerable effort around general educational participation and basic skills provision; many programmes for helping the unemployed (or, more accurately, helping the unemployed compete with others and thereby perhaps increasing the rate of flow through unemployment); some specific bargaining for in-firm training between unions and employers or associations of employers;

---

[5] A portion of this section is drawn substantially from Finegold and Levine (1997) and due credit should be given to David Levine who was the originator of many of these ideas.

some sparks of innovative activity among first-class firms; and hesitant, uncertain efforts by various combinations of actors to take action oriented to the coveted long term.

Our analysis has suggested a number of worrying features of this pattern. Growing dependence on the individual enterprise rather than general public policy as the source of major initiatives in work skills raises the central paradox on which we have concentrated: the acquisition of skill has become a fundamental public policy issue, being almost a requirement for future guarantees of effective citizenship when the price of poor or inappropriate educational preparation for work is likely to be a low-paid job in a low-productivity sector with diminished security; but for its provision we are increasingly dependent on the private sphere of the individual firms which can have no responsibility for general needs. We must now move beyond demonstrating the existence of problems and indicate some possible ways forward.

Reasserting the role of public agencies for pursuing high skills

Public agencies (including business associations) must be able to play an effective part in trying to maximize the role of advanced skills in the economy if we are to transcend this dependence on individual firms. To do this they must be equipped with appropriate and rapidly changing knowledge. This does not lead to the fashionable solution of public agencies working with companies through a mode of 'market' provision of advice like any other consultancy, since this merely follows firms' existing perceptions. Public skills-creation bodies must certainly work far more closely with firms than in the classic mode of, say, French or Italian state provision, but they must do so from positions of authority, based partly on being channels of funds allocated authoritatively, and partly on the fact that their decisions are rooted in extensive knowledge, so that they will win the respect of firms. They must therefore be well resourced and well staffed, offering long-term contracts to professional experts who have years of relevant experience, including work in the private sector, and with long-term commitments to this field of work. The model of short-term employment contracts—with agencies fighting for their own survival and as worried about possible bankruptcy as about becoming major sources of expertise on skill requirements—that has been imposed on British TECs (following the rather unsuccessful model of British small firms in general) is not a helpful guide. A neo-liberal residualized concept of public service, in which all attractive activities have been hived off to private consultancies, leaving public policy in the hands of a rump agency with poor-quality staff, scant resources, and low prestige cannot provide the basis for an authoritative service.

In particular the role required will not be achieved by agencies which have as their principal responsibility catering for the unemployed, especially where responsibility for placing the unemployed in jobs is linked to that for disciplining them and requiring them to accept work offers. When these strategies are used, the public service cannot then become associated in employers' minds with advanced developments in VET. King (1995) has described how, during the 1970s, employment placement services in many countries adopted a path of moving up-market, delivering high-quality services from High Street premises, and extending their appeal to a wide range of potential employees. This was part of an upgrading of public labour-market policy in order to help people maximize their match to career opportunities. A central aspect of this task was the complete separation of this career guidance service from that of paying unemployment benefit and checking on the job searches of those registered as unemployed.

He then describes how this strategy has been completely reversed since the late 1980s, initially in the UK and the USA, but more recently in reforms introduced in other, less market-oriented economies, through a policy which has now been recommended to all its member states by the OECD. There are two reasons for this. First, job-placement services are being privatized as part of the general contemporary strategy of stripping back public activities. Clearly, private job-placement agencies want to take over the task of advising and placing those for whom it is easy to find employment. The remaining state service therefore becomes again a residual one, the staff of which will not gain experience in tracking high-quality labour needs. Second, in order more closely to monitor the behaviour of the unemployed, services of benefit payment, job search, and policing are all concentrated in the one residual employment department.

The story is an interesting case of how perceptions of the employment problem among government departments in a number of countries have changed, away from trying to ratchet up the skill needs and practices of firms and towards finding low-wage jobs towards which the unemployed can be channelled. Our discussion of the TECs in the UK showed a similar record affecting, not job-placement services, but agencies designed originally to be the spearhead of Britain's challenge to German and Japanese skill levels.

A central conclusion of our review of VET policies in various countries is therefore that public agencies in this field need to be able: (a) to relate closely to individual firms; but (b) to advise firms on the basis of an authority based on constantly updated knowledge, so that competences can be ratcheted up and so that educational institutions and relevant government departments can be kept in touch with what is required; (c) to influence firms' further VET efforts as well as their participation in initial training; and (d) to link skills creation with the other services (for example, technology transfer, access to capital, assistance in work process redesign, export marketing, etc.) that can help firms make the transition to internationally competitive, high-skill, high value-added strategies.

This has a number of implications for the design of policy and policy agencies. They must be well resourced and able to develop high-quality expertise so that they can become associated with success. They will probably be best equipped to operate authoritatively if they work closely with business networks and neo-corporatist associations. In countries where such employer associations have traditionally been weak, there may be an opportunity for state policy-makers to foster inter-firm networks. Historically, US and, to some extent, UK firms have been reluctant to co-operate through associations because of anti-trust concerns, cultural opposition to behaviour that is viewed as contrary to the free market, and a relatively weak and fragmented employer organization structure. Since the mid-1980s, however, there has been a major transformation in inter-firm relations in these more market-based economies, as many large corporations have sought to emulate the Japanese lean production strategy in building close partnerships—including co-operative training agreements—with suppliers. There are also a number of examples of employer networks of an 'Italian' kind that have emerged at the local level, both in thriving high-tech areas like Silicon Valley (Saxenian 1994), or more defensively as we saw in connection with some British TECs and LECs in Chapter 6. The British cases suggest that government can bolster these nascent networks by providing support for co-ordination activities and using them as a vehicle for the delivery of services.

To work effectively with employer organizations or networks, however, the state must be endowed with sufficient authority to counter cartelistic tendencies within these employer groups. Depending on what most suits local political cultures (and care needs to be taken with the precise design), such requirements could be embodied in a number of different institutional forms: departments of central government, provided they are capable of responding genuinely to local initiative; less formally structured agencies, provided they are not compelled to act in a passively responsive mode; chambers or similar representative bodies of business, provided they have sufficient coverage of the local employer base and are free to support innovation and new industries; community colleges linked with local economic development agencies. It is particularly important that however training is provided, a public agency has responsibility for standard setting (see below) and monitoring.

In creating such policy instruments, it is important to think carefully about which types of services should be universal and which should be targeted at particular groups. Some public services may benefit from being comprehensive. Perhaps the clearest example is a labour-market information system, where a comprehensive and up-to-date database that lists all available vacancies in a region and/ or sector and those available for employment can provide a valuable service to companies and individuals while providing policy-makers and training providers with a powerful tool for continually updating their programmes. Sweden has developed the most sophisticated version of such a system as a central component of its active labour-market policy. With new information technologies, such as the Internet, it is possible to link such databases across the country or internationally, as well as to tailor searches to an organization's particular requirements.

Reasserting publicly funded education

The current trend towards low taxation and concomitant reduced public services has unavoidable implications for skills and employment. All the countries we have studied devote a substantial portion of public spending to education, usually concentrated on the young. There are strong public-goods aspects of education, which make it impossible to treat it as just another consumption or even invest-ment good. A commitment to a learning society requires more and constantly improving education at all levels. There is a strong case, based on differences observed in educational attainment within and across countries, that more effect-ive use could be made of the substantial resources already devoted to education and training.

There are at least three main areas which call out for additional educational investment: early childhood development, mass post-compulsory education, and universal further training. The first of these is beyond the main focus of this vol-ume on work-related education and training, but is so vital for overall skill devel-opment that it must be included in any discussion of policy options and priorities for education investment. The need for placing a priority on this area of devel-opment is made clear by a growing body of research which suggests that much of people's learning capacity and subsequent life chances are determined by the learning that they do in the first two years of life, long before they reach the for-mal educational system. At the same time, however, the significant increase in the number of women in the paid workforce and of two-career families, along with the increase in single-parent families, has meant that an increasing propor-tion of children are not at home with a full-time parent during this crucial stage of development. Thus, there is a strong societal need to develop high-quality, affordable safe child care outside the home—such as the French *crêche* and *école maternelle*, Swedish care systems designed specifically to help working mothers, and current British experiments of a similar kind—along with flexible employment arrangements and other supports for families where one or both par-ents are sharing primary child-rearing responsibilities.

A second educational priority is to expand learning opportunities—whether part time or full time—for young people after compulsory schooling, so that the vast majority are able to develop an advanced skill set. With secondary educa-tion increasingly becoming the norm for many developing countries, and with some NICs (such as Singapore, South Korea, and Taiwan) already producing world-leading literacy rates and educational attainment, it is essential that the advanced industrial countries provide their young people with a strong educational founda-tion if they are to compete successfully in the world market-place. Although most of the countries included in this study have, in the last two decades, begun the shift from élite to mass higher education systems, it is only in the USA that more than half of each new cohort participates in some form of higher education, and even there the percentage obtaining a bachelor's degree has been relatively stable, at about 25%.[6] While traditional, more academic forms of higher edu-cation may not be appropriate for the majority of the population, it is clear that

---

[6] One contrast between US and most European education systems is the existence of a substan-tial sub-degree higher education sector in the former.

most individuals can benefit from some form of structured, more advanced learning after compulsory schooling. Countries like Denmark and Germany, for example, have expanded their higher education systems, while maintaining and modernizing their technical education and apprenticeship systems, to ensure that 85–90% of the population enter the workforce with a recognized occupational qualification and/or a degree.

A final area where greater skill investment is required is in ensuring that high-quality further training is available to the entire workforce. With the rapid pace of technological and organizational change, individuals at all points on the skill spectrum will need to update their skills, if not entirely change their careers, periodically over the course of their working lives. This need is particularly important for those who have lost their jobs or who have taken time off from their careers for family reasons, and do not have the support of a firm to retool their skill set.

The market alone is unlikely to provide sufficient levels of skill investment to meet these pressing needs. At younger age levels the expenditure is that of parents rather than of individuals themselves. Since children can rarely be expected to repay their parents' expenditures on them, such spending does not take the form of purely rational investment expenditure in anticipation of individual gains on the part of the investor. It is far more likely to be determined by parents' current income and wealth. A shift towards increased parental contributions to educational spending would therefore produce a strong shift in the take-up of educational opportunities towards young people from wealthy families. Such a development would ease the problems of governments based on parties drawing much of their support from such families, as their voters would feel less anxious than at present that their children will face competition from others for what promises to be a declining proportion of well-rewarded secure positions in the economy of the future. It would, however, be incompatible, not only with the promise of equality of opportunity which remains a universally accepted educational slogan among all shades of political opinion in most societies, but also with the concept of a learning society.

After compulsory schooling, the issue for policy-makers is how to finance an expansion of ongoing learning opportunities given public fiscal constraints, and yet at the same time not discourage individuals from poorer backgrounds from pursuing education because of a lack of personal resources or access to credit. There is a strong argument that individuals should be asked to bear some of the costs of further and higher education. While there are positive externalities to this investment, most of the returns accrue to the individual in terms of future income. Currently, in those countries where the majority of young people are asked to finance a portion of their own advanced education they have to do so by working part time during their studies. We saw in Chapter 2 that large numbers do this in the USA, the Netherlands, Denmark, the UK, and elsewhere. In many ways this can be a useful development, in keeping with the fact that an increasing percentage of those in higher education are more mature students who are already in the workforce. It also encourages individuals to view education as an investment in their own human capital which has real costs, rather than a natural right or consumption good that they have earned by passing an entrance examination, as is now the case in some European countries. Likewise, the part-time route can give students work experience and provide a supply of workers who do not seek security or full-time work while still bringing to the routine tasks they perform, mainly in the retail and catering sectors, a level of alertness and ability that would not otherwise be available to employers in these sectors.

There are, however, limits to the part-time approach and relying on individuals to finance their own post-compulsory education. First, the inequality effect of differential parental wealth still operates; children from wealthy families do not need to take paid employment during their studies, which might enable them to secure better grades. Beyond a certain point simultaneous study and paid work will affect academic performance and therefore lower the quality of the educational enterprise. In addition, the highly educated student workforce has the effect of crowding out employment opportunities for others with lower educational qualifications.

Alternatively, firms might be expected to make more of a contribution to subsidizing the development of transferable skills. Government policies may also have a direct effect on managers' willingness to invest in skills. This can take the form of a carrot that induces firms to spend more on training, such as tax breaks or subsidies for training certain categories of workers. In Japan, the Ministry of Labour operates an unemployment scheme that has a dual benefit for workforce development (Finegold *et al.* 1994*b*). In sectors that have been hard hit by the recession, the government pays part of the worker's salary. The programme not only requires training during the recession, but also encourages managers to develop their employees' skills when the economy recovers, since the firm knows that it will not have to lay off employees quickly if demand slackens.

An alternative is for the government to penalize firms that do not invest in human capital, through mechanisms such as a training levy introduced at different times in France, Australia, the UK, and Singapore. These programmes generally require all employers above a certain size to spend a certain percentage of their payroll on training, or pay an equivalent amount into a fund that supports worker training. While a training tax almost certainly will lead to a one-time increase in the quantity of training, the danger is that some of this human capital investment will be wasted if firms are doing it to comply with regulations, rather than as part of a co-ordinated high-skill strategy. For countries considering this option, there is a strong argument for first putting in place a well-functioning system of national skill standards, so that employers who are providing transferable, certified skills are rewarded.

But again the scope for such policies is limited. If the free-rider problem suggests that most firms will not voluntarily provide vocational education, leading virtually all countries to develop policies for encouraging them to do this, it will be commensurately more difficult to persuade more than a certain number of them to assume a growing share of the task of funding investment in general skills. But if one reason for trying to move to a low-tax economy is to reduce the cost burden on companies that must complete globally with countries that impose few costs on firms, there is little to be gained from replacing taxes by direct contributions from firms to fund the same services.

The challenge for policy-makers is to devise a means of financing an expansion in the supply of higher education and ongoing training that shares the costs equitably among the three main sources of skill investment: the state, individuals, and employers. One possibility is to provide every school-leaver with an entitlement to two to three years of further or higher education or the monetary equivalent, which could be used directly after finishing compulsory education or in the future, after they have entered the workforce. Those who require additional resources for completing a degree(s) (including living expenses) would be given a loan by the state that could be paid back through a graduate tax once individuals have entered the workforce and started to receive the returns on their educational investment (for additional details see Finegold *et al.* 1992); a similar system has already been put in place successfully by Australia to expand its higher education system (Chapman and Chia 1989).

In addition, people could be given lifelong learning accounts that could be used throughout their careers to finance education and training investments for themselves or their children. Individuals could make tax-free contributions similar to the payroll deductions now made for pension plans in the USA, while employers could be required or encouraged to make small contributions (similar to the tuition-reimbursement programmes that many firms now offer). When an individual became unemployed, the state could make an additional contribution to the account that would enable the individual to purchase retraining and other job-placement assistance from either public or private providers.

When considering how much the society generally, and the government in particular, can afford to spend on education and training it is vital to keep in mind that these are investments that can have important pay-offs. To see the potential for pay-offs to investments in human resources, consider the case of preventing drop-outs (Finegold and Levine 1997). In the USA, the average high school drop-out earns 49% less than high school graduates with no additional education, leading to lower average tax payments by drop-outs. In addition, the present value of total welfare, prison, and parole costs averages about $70,000 for high school drop-outs (almost entirely prison for men, and welfare for women). This figure is far above the $30,000 cost for each high school graduate who does not attend college, and the $15,000 cost for those who do attend college (USA 1995*a*: 188).[7] Thus a programme capable of influencing typical high school drop-outs to behave like typical high school graduates would reduce spending on welfare and the criminal justice system by about $40,000 in present value terms for each

---

[7] These figures are the net present value at age 18 of the costs incurred between the ages of 18 to 54, using 1992 data. Costs are discounted at a 4% annual rate (ibid.).

youth affected. Differences in taxes paid would increase this figure. Of course, it cannot be assumed that such gains would be realized in their entirety, as an increased supply of educated people would lead to some reductions in their incomes and security, and not all would win jobs associated with that level of education when the supply was smaller. However, neither should it be assumed that all gains would be lost in this way. This example shows that investments in human resources can take years to pay off, but potentially have large returns.

These figures are almost the reverse of US public spending on education and training: the typical college graduate is the beneficiary of over $25,000 in public spending between the ages of 16 and 24, while the typical high school graduate receives about $11,000 and the typical high school drop-out less than $6,000. Compared to the USA, most other industrialized nations have smaller wage gaps and rates of incarceration, but larger employment rate gaps and more generous spending on social welfare. Thus, the total benefit of preventing drop-outs may be similar to that in the USA. Moreover, programmes exist that appear effective in improving the life chances of at-risk youth, while saving governments money. For example, there are the various remedial schemes in Sweden which offer chances of completing education some years after normal school-leaving ages for those who had dropped out of school. Likewise, the Quantum Opportunities Program in the USA provides an array of after-school, tutoring, mentoring, and summer programmes in a number of cities, and has been shown cost effectively to reduce drop-outs and teenage pregnancies (see the review of evidence for this and other programmes in USA 1995b).

Thus, to achieve the twin aims of promoting an increase in the average standard of living while reducing or at least halting the growth in income inequality, it is difficult to see any major democratic alternative to a prolonged and intensified commitment by governments to publicly funded education at most levels as part of the learning society strategy.

Reasserting the role of public-service employment

Even with substantially increased educational investments, an important minority of the workforce will be unable to participate in the employment provided by the learning society; even specific skill-upgrading agencies will not be the route through which the majority of the unemployed will find work. Indeed in their work for further skills training these agencies will be helping predominantly those already in employment, not even labour-market entrants; and, as we have seen at a number of points, involvement with work for the mass of unemployed diminishes at least the image and probably the substance of agencies' attempts to operate at the top end of the skills range. This challenges the position of those who posit improvements in VET as an alternative to the growth of low-productivity jobs, and also that of those who claim that deregulating labour markets and leaving firms free within the market will both reduce unemployment and encourage improvements in vocational education quality.

For years to come many members of the workforce will be unable, as a result of both demand and supply factors, to gain high-quality places in the labour market. It should not be pretended that, if they only showed adequate initiative and responded to the education opportunities available, most people would be able to do so. Many will be forced to compete for the low-productivity opportunities that will not require high levels of education except as the filtering device through which, by definition, many will not pass. If people in this position are to avoid facing both low wages and high insecurity by competing for jobs in deregulated private services as their long-term prospect, there will have to be an expansion of public services, which can provide secure though still low-paid work for people capable of only low productivity.

Such choices are beyond the scope of this study, but consideration needs to be given to the future of public services as sources of employment. The public sector plays two vital roles in creating jobs at opposite ends of the skill spectrum. As we saw in Chapter 2, at the high end the primarily public social and community services sector of the economy is the principal employer of highly educated labour in all countries. That sector and the services it supplies, some of which make a central if indirect contribution to competitiveness, have therefore been a fundamental component of the high-skill economy. A concentration of public policy preoccupation on reducing the size of the public service would not, of course, lead to a complete loss of all occupations and services currently being performed there; some would thrive in the private sector under privatization and marketization. There would, however, be a large net loss: to take only the example closest to our current concerns, a complete privatization of education would lead to a decline in its uptake by poor and moderate-income families, with a consequent loss in both high-skill teaching jobs themselves and in the economic contribution that results from an educated workforce.

At the same time, public services have been important sources of employment for relatively low-skilled workers. One thinks immediately of the whole range of environmental cleansing services: refuse collection, street cleaning, maintenance of public spaces; also of child care, and some jobs within health care and public transportation. These services have often made a distinctive contribution to the structure of employment available in the advanced societies: work that required relatively modest skills, paid rather low wages, but offered security of employment and (because of the commitment of most public employers to concepts of 'the good employer') freedom from the brutalization often associated with low-skilled and low-paid work. Anxiety to reduce the size of public employment and of taxation has recently led most national and local governments to make working conditions for this kind of employment more closely resemble that to be found at the low end of the private sector, either by privatizing it or changing its regime through marketization within the public service.

If we must accept that a sizeable number of people are destined to remain in low-skilled employment, the former public-service model will require rehabilitation. A dilemma currently preoccupying the OECD is that while wages should fall at the lower end of the skill range in order to increase the supply of jobs, poor and insecure working conditions and frequent job changes have a demoralizing effect (OECD 1996*a*: xx). The public-service model of low pay combined with decent conditions, which it is difficult to achieve in the down-market private sector, can square that circle and did so for many years in most countries.

Creating new institutions and policies to support high-skill societies

However desirable increased public expenditure on education and training and employment may be, the political reality is that these investments are unlikely to occur so long as the power of global capital and corporations continues to increase relative to that of nation states. Rather, there is intensifying pressure on the continental European economies to cut back on their existing levels of public spending and deregulate, in the short term to meet the conditions for European Monetary Union (EMU), but more generally to try to emulate the success of the USA and the UK in creating jobs. The danger, as we have already suggested however, is that this will create a downward spiral, with countries competing with each other to attract firms and international investment by cutting the size and regulatory power of government, and weakening the safety net for the least powerful groups in society.

In the Uruguay round of global trade negotiations there was some recognition of the need for supranational regulation of corporations to accompany the increasing liberalization of flows of goods, services, capital, and labour. These restrictions, however, were only minimal—for example, sanctions against child or slave or prison labour—and even these have proved difficult to enforce. In the long run there is likely to be an increasingly compelling argument for the creation of a much stronger international regulatory regime that would set some basic standards—a living wage, access to health care, a clean environment—that would be a floor below which firms would not compete. Initially, this regime would probably need to be limited to the advanced industrial nations (for example, members of the OECD), which continue to account for the vast majority (over 85%) of all global trade and have more comparable living standards.

In the absence of such a large change in the international governance of corporate activities, those countries (such as the USA, Germany, and Japan) that have traditionally relied on an employer-based system for key elements of the welfare state (such as health care and pensions) may need to rethink their basic model of delivery. The need for restructuring is driven by several factors. First, as individuals move more frequently between organizations and an increasing portion of the workforce is accounted for by part-time, temporary, and self-employed workers, an employer-based system is increasingly impractical and a barrier to mobility. In addition, as the pressures of international competition continue to increase, there is a real danger that firms will reduce or eliminate these essential benefits altogether on the grounds of remaining cost competitive.

There appear to be two alternatives to an employer-based system. One, already in place in some European countries, is a universal state system. While this has many advantages, including the containment of health-care costs, it also suffers from the general pressures that neo-liberal policies and globalization have generated to reduce the size of the public sector. The alternative is to create a more individual-based system of portable benefits, so that people are given greater control and responsibility for their own health care and retirement, with the state providing a regulatory framework and safety net. Such a system could also include lifelong learning accounts, where individuals, employers, and the government share the costs of ongoing human capital investment.

Meanwhile there is a range of policy initiatives which governments can take, which will both improve VET standards and, whatever the form taken by the national system, will enable them (and corporatist organizations, if they are in a position to share roles with them) to regain authority and an expert role in skills provision.

Improving information　One of the more incremental ways in which governments in all types of institutional systems can encourage greater and more efficient investment in skills is by improving the quality of information about employment and training providers that decision-makers—whether individuals, firms, or VET providers—require to operate effectively. Ideally, improvements in information should be both qualitative and quantitative. Better quality information is needed for both providers of training and consumers on what types of training are available. In particular, there would be a benefit from better dissemination of information on new approaches to enhancing skills that are being tried and the success of these experiments (*vide infra* on international benchmarking for some of the potential sources of this information). Where possible, the government's role in this dissemination should be indirect, supplying data and other forms of support to intermediate employer and trade-union organizations that are in a better position to relay information to individual firms and their employees. Where such organizations do not exist, government may want to help start them. The Japanese Training within Industry (TWI) programme provides an excellent example of how a sustained information dissemination effort can raise both the level and the quality of skill provision.

The other form of information that is vital, particularly in market-based systems, is enhanced data on the quantity of investment in skill development. As we shall shortly demonstrate, at present there is massive mismeasurement of investment in human resources. This matters, because decision-makers in both the public and private sectors rely on mismeasured government deficits and on poorly measured human resources in making decisions.[8] Most obviously, voters rely on measured government deficits in evaluating the fiscal responsibility of governments. Because of these pressures, many countries (for example, the

---

[8] For discussion of the difficulty in measuring human resources, see Flamholtz 1985.

United States) have rules encouraging or requiring the government to eliminate or reduce the (mismeasured) deficit. In many nations, governments agree to reduce the deficit to win approval from multinational organizations. Membership in the EMU requires large reductions in most members' measured deficits. In other parts of the world, the International Monetary Fund (IMF) conditions often require such reductions before the Fund will provide financial assistance to developing nations. In either case, although achieving the deficit goal is voluntary, nations forgo something they value if they do not reduce their current measured deficit—even if this is at the expense of increasing the present value of future deficits.

Decision-makers in the private sector also rely on mismeasured deficits and human resources. International financial markets may punish nations which appear to run large government budget deficits, even if the measured deficit is due to the lack of capital budgeting. Direct foreign investment is also responsive to both measured deficits (if they are thought to predict future instability) and to measured human resources. Improving measures of human resources would encourage companies to invest in nations that are building up the capabilities of their workforce. Because these stakeholders currently rely on mismeasured deficits and investments, governments have incentives to avoid investments involving high pay-offs, even if the present value of future deficits would fall with higher spending. Thus, we need to develop new forms of information on skills that credit successful educational and active labour-market policies with some portion of the future costs saved. To begin filling the major gaps that exist in our understanding of human capital investment and how it is related to economic performance, we can build on collaborative work already under way in many countries to identify reliable and valid measures of workplace practices. This approach encourages the adoption of a number of techniques: human capital accounting procedures; comparative research; matched-firm comparisons; national surveys of firms and individuals; and policy demonstrations and evaluations across countries.

Current accounting practices for government systematically mismeasure long-term investments by failing adequately to account for human capital (Miller 1996; Levine 1995). When a corporation makes an investment in a new building that lasts thirty years, private-sector accounting rules charge only about one-thirtieth of the cost of the investment as an expense in the first year. This accounting procedure makes sense because of the long-term nature of the investment. Unfortunately, most governments do not follow this sensible procedure. Each expense is charged to the deficit in the year paid, even for a training programme that pays off over the next thirty years. A more accurate measure of the deficit would have a capital budget that identified those expenditures that provided benefits over many years. Unless governments measure the deficit correctly, they will face incentives to starve long-term investments for short-term gains. For example, under many nations' accounting systems, selling a school building and then leasing it back at high cost from the new owner shows up as saving money in the short run, while introducing a programme for at-risk youth that would avoid expensive future time in prison or on welfare shows up as costing money.[9]

Governments need to restructure their accounting rules to put investment in people and in quality on a more even footing with investment in plant, equipment, or research. These changes should occur in both the public and private sectors. In the United States, organizations as varied as the American Institute of Certified Public Accountants, the Association for Investment Management and Research (which charters financial analysts), and the Financial Executives Institute have issued reports emphasizing the need for better measures of non-financial aspects of investment (see, for example, AICPA 1995). International organizations, governments, industry, and the accounting profession must work together to create standard measures of workplace investments that are comparable across time, across nations, and across companies. Only then can investors understand which companies are investing for the long term. Moreover, only then can international investors understand which nations truly have budget deficits, and which are investing in the future.

The current lack of a common definition of training and the fact that most firms do not measure training expenditure makes it impossible to arrive at an accurate estimate of training investment within each country, much less to compare the levels of workforce development across countries.

To illustrate the immense methodological problems in this area,[10] consider two concurrent workforce surveys in a single country, the USA (Zemsky and Shapiro 1994). The surveys—the Current Population Survey (CPS) and Survey of Income Program Participation (SIPP)—asked virtually identical questions regarding whether individuals had received training to qualify for their most recent job and whether they had undergone training to improve their skills once on the job. The responses, however, were diametrically opposed: the CPS found that approximately two-thirds of individuals had received some form of training, while SIPP found that 75% of workers had no training. And while the CPS, like most other training surveys in the USA and abroad, found that individuals with the highest prior educational levels and income were most likely to receive training, the SIPP revealed that more schooling did not lead to increased training; indeed, it found that individuals with a college degree were less likely to receive training.

Zemsky and Shapiro (ibid.) attribute this discrepancy to the context in which the questions were asked on the two surveys that reflects a wider division between private and public training in the USA. While the CPS focuses on an employee's occupation and work history, the SIPP concentrates on federal programmes for the disadvantaged, with training questions following after a series of questions about food stamps, social security, and federal income-maintenance programmes. Thus, while the training questions themselves were virtually identical, the SIPP results reflected 'the negative image most Americans attach to

---

[9] Eisner (1994) makes these points in general; we here emphasize their relevance to investments in human resources.

[10] See OECD (1993: ch. 5) for a far more detailed discussion of methodological problems.

welfare programmes, even though the respondents were being asked about job-related training that had little to do with welfare' (ibid.: 4). This example also serves as a more general caution for researchers of the difficulty of interpreting even the most basic information on training in isolation from its surrounding cultural and institutional context.

Future measures should build, wherever available, on existing work, both to lower research costs and to encourage comparability of findings. There has been a recent growth in the number of national, individual, and employer training surveys (see, for example, Eliasson 1994 for a review of British survey data; for the USA: Zemsky and Shapiro 1994; Osterman 1994; Lawler *et al.* 1995). In a few cases, researchers have even attempted to co-ordinate similar training surveys across a number of countries (for example, OECD and Statistics Canada 1995; Tan and Batra 1995). Future research must ensure that measures of human resources policies are also linked to measures of organizational performance. The International Adult Literacy Survey (IALS) of the OECD and Statistics Canada (1995) offers a promising step in this direction, with detailed measures of adult workers' literacy, numeracy, and problem-solving abilities in seven countries. The OECD plans to link employer and individual data in subsequent waves of the survey and expand the number of countries participating.

Supporting skill standards   The training and workplace measures should identify training outcomes such as skills learned as well as training inputs such as hours in class or money spent. Such outcome measures typically involve skill standards. This can take the form of a competence-based model such as the NVQ system in the UK (which has been adopted in modified form in Australia and New Zealand), or a more traditional set of occupational standards linked to recognized courses, as found in the Germanic countries' apprenticeship systems, or the skill certification programmes run by the Japanese Ministry of Labour. Unfortunately, rapid organizational and technological changes can soon make industry- or occupation-specific skill standards obsolete if they are written too narrowly.

Fortunately, general problem-solving skills appear to remain useful for long periods of time. International organizations should work with member governments and the private sector to create a common set of building blocks that measure these general skills. Industries and nations could then voluntarily adopt these building blocks in future generations of skill standards. Having generic standards (and sample test instruments and training materials) would lower the cost of creating high-quality skill standards. Importantly, these skill standards would emphasize the skills of solving problems and working together in groups that researchers have identified as crucial for high-performance workplaces. Ideally, people moving between nations, industries, or occupations would only need to receive training in those skills not already covered by the generic building blocks included in their previous certifications.

Moreover, international comparisons of skill attainment could enrich the current measures of literacy and of standardized test scores with measures of work-related general skills. The OECD's IALS mentioned above is an excellent example of such an approach, constructing careful measures of workers' demonstrated numeracy, literacy, and problem-solving abilities that are comparable across countries and can be related to prior education, training, and workplace variables (OECD and Statistics Canada 1995).[11] In addition to expanding both the range of countries and skills included in IALS, standard labour-market surveys should include questions on whether employees are learning on the job. These questions should cover both work practices (enrolment in formal training programmes, extent of on-the-job training) and the work itself (agreement with statements such as: 'I solve problems on my job', 'I learn new skills on my job'). Both financial institutions judging which nations have sustainable growth-oriented policies and companies choosing where to site new facilities could use these measures to help assess labour market quality more precisely. If two economies have similar wage and output levels, the one with more on-the-job learning (not just training) at all levels will probably have better long-term growth and income equality.

Validating measures: training and performance   Measures of on-the-job learning will be taken more seriously if they have been shown to predict important outcomes. For example, one cross-national study (Krafcik 1990) compared automobile assembly plants. The researchers found that plants with innovative work systems (including extensive training, work teams, and decentralization of responsibilities for quality control to line workers) manufactured vehicles in an average of 22 hours with an average of 0.5 defects per vehicle. In contrast, more traditional plants took 30 hours with 0.8 defects per vehicle. We need additional studies, particularly those that compare similar plants (perhaps with a single owner) across national boundaries. Employee-oriented outcomes such as safety, wages, employment stability, and job satisfaction should be included in these studies, as well as employer-oriented outcomes.

Public-sector education and active labour-market policies should be validated in the same way. The evaluation results should be converted into expected future expenditure savings; these savings, in turn, should be built into the government's capital budget and the measured budget deficit. In addition, the evaluation should then feed back into continuous improvement of the programmes and into reallocation of resources into programmes with successful track records. In many cases, randomized experiments can perform the validation. These experiments can be built into the work of many employment and training service providers. In many cases, service providers with a waiting list can easily perform a randomized experiment by selecting from the waiting list, and comparing outcomes of those served with those who remained in the queue. In other cases, a service provider can randomly allocate clients to different subunits or programmes and compare results.

---

[11] The inclusion of 'adult literacy' in the title of this project has unfortunately caused many researchers to ignore this potential resource, which actually measures worker competences from very basic to quite a high level, and in numeracy as well as literacy and verbal comprehension.

In any region with more than a minimal number of people receiving services, local governments can monitor the performance of subcontractors by randomly assigning clients to them. The relative performance of each contractor's clients can be used to determine the value added of services. This knowledge can then be used both for improving services and for allocating performance-based pay. In the USA the Upjohn Institute is implementing such an experiment with three welfare-to-work service providers in Michigan (Bartel 1995). Where randomized experiments are not feasible, government labour-market information systems can track citizens' employment and earnings histories to determine which interventions add the most value. Because most of these data are already collected for administrative purposes, the key is to link them in ways that protect confidentiality yet permit automated evaluations of schools and other training providers.

Improving certifications of employers   International organizations, member governments, and large private-sector customers should work together to create certifications that measure which companies produce high quality and are organized to improve their quality. Suppliers of high-quality goods and services tend to rely on their workers for help in improving quality. Thus, these efforts to purchase from high-quality suppliers should not only save the government money but also increase the quality of jobs.

Many companies are adopting the International Standards Organization (ISO) 9000 series quality standards. These standards require that companies maintain and follow documented procedures for almost everything they do. Unfortunately, the ISO standard has no requirement that the procedures be continuously improved. Levine (1995) has suggested an addition to the ISO standard which would increase its usefulness for identifying excellent suppliers:[12]

Improving Quality Plans: The supplier shall establish and maintain documented procedures for continuously improving all documented procedures. The supplier shall ensure that this procedure is understood, implemented, and maintained at all levels of the organization.

Because high-quality suppliers tend to rely on their workforce, a move to improve product and service quality will also improve the quality and skill of jobs. The multi-industry Process Certification Standard is becoming widely accepted in the private sector. International standards-setting organizations must ensure that this standard and its successors identify employers where each employee has the incentive, ability, authority and responsibility constantly to improve the workplace. The important public characteristic of standard certification and the role of state institutions in maintaining inspection systems also becomes one of the means by which public authorities can continue an authoritative and expert role

---

[12] Guidance on procedures for continuous improvement is given in ISO 9004-4, Guidelines for Quality Improvement. A more complete proposal for improving ISO 9000 is found in Levine 1995: 140–1.

within training systems despite the shift to corporate economy and to customer–supplier rather than authority relationships in the connections between government and the private sector. The place of public–private co-operation achieved by the Japanese skill-testing and certification system (Sako 1995: 1, 21) is an outstanding example of this.

In addition to general quality-management standards, governments may also want to expand the use of exemplar employer quality or skill standards or kitemarks, such as the Deming Award in Japan, or the US emulation of it in the Malcolm Baldridge Award. While these awards are about quality only, the UK's Investors in People scheme is more closely related to training, recognizing organizations that have demonstrated excellence in their development of employees' capabilities. Unlike ISO 9000, which sets a common, minimum process standard that can be applied across all sectors, these awards should be designed to recognize outstanding examples of quality or skill-development systems. They can help an economy move towards a higher-skill equilibrium in several ways. They provide free publicity and positive recognition to the winners and act as an example that other organizations can emulate. Also, through the criteria for the award, they provide guidelines on how to improve organizational performance and skills; indeed, many of the organizations that have attempted to receive the kitemark cite the process itself, and the changes it precipitated, rather than winning or losing, as the ultimate benefit (Finegold 1997). To ensure that the kitemark has a high value and thus provides an incentive for organizations to attain it, governments must first ensure that all winners meet a rigorous 'best practice' set of standards (something which the IIP standard, and the TECs which oversee it, have been criticized for failing to do in some cases).

There can be both 'market' and 'voice and commitment' approaches to ensuring that standards are met. The former includes measures to improve the flow of information concerning best standards, and offering various incentives to improve. For example, as with ISO 9000, governments can use their substantial buying power to encourage the promulgation of the standard by giving preference to suppliers that attain it; or, as with IIP in the UK, access to various government grants can be restricted to firms achieving the standard. The 'voice and commitment' approach involves giving extended periods of advice and assistance to firms on how to improve their standards. For example, the Japanese Union of Scientists and Engineers, which makes the Deming Award, offers a process of up to two years' prior diagnosis and evaluation.

Identifying benchmarks for high-skill enterprises   To further facilitate the dissemination of information on high-skill enterprises, public and private sector benchmarking organizations can provide cross-company and cross-national comparisons of best practice. For example, the cross-national study of automobile assembly mentioned above found that in the mid-1980s newly hired assembly workers received 310 hours of training in Japan and 280 hours of training in Japanese-managed plants located in the USA, but only 48 hours of training at traditional American plants (Krafcik 1990). This simple fact was an alarm call for many US employers about the gap between typical US and best practice.

The National Institute for Economic and Social Research (NIESR) in London has been a pioneer in developing a firm-based methodology that could be extended to these different sectors (see studies cited in Chapter 3). The prime aims of the NIESR research programme have been, first, to examine in detail the important differences between countries in workforce education attainments and training provision; and, second, to seek to identify the mechanisms by which such inter-country differences in human capital formation contribute to relative levels of labour productivity. The main research method is distinguished by its emphasis on the collection and analysis of primary data from national samples of establishments which are both closely matched for product area and adequately representative of national populations of establishments in respect of other key criteria such as employment size. In addition, particular attention is paid to the effects of inter-country differences in the content of what is taught in schools, colleges, and work-based training programmes and in the standards of skill and knowledge attained by different sections of the workforce.

Extending comparative-policy benchmarking   Benchmarking can be extended to active labour-market, employment, and training policies. Identifying best practice in everything from computerized advertisements for training materials to training programmes can improve public policies. With the dramatic fall in the cost and time required to share information across continents, and the rising pressure to keep the workforce competitive, policy-makers should make these comparisons internationally—as well as evaluating the results of initiatives across multiple sites within their own borders. Policy-makers are already frequently looking to learn and apply lessons from other countries as they develop new labour-market, education, and training reforms (Finegold, McFarland, and Richardson 1993). Too often, however, these attempts at international policy borrowing are not accompanied by a careful evaluation of the original programme or a clear understanding of the differences in the surrounding institutional context that may affect the policy's effectiveness in another country. Policy-makers need to address the market and government failures that hinder efficient investment in human resources. One of the foremost barriers to raising this investment is good information about the supply and demand for skills and the effectiveness of current employment and training programmes.

Improving measurement of investments in human resources can have four benefits. First, it will permit companies to identify what works at work. Such knowledge can help companies improve their own management. Second, improved measurement will permit companies to benchmark themselves against their competitors. Third, it will permit governments better to understand what programmes are effective; this knowledge should improve public-sector investments. Finally, better measurement of investments in people will permit better measurement of budget deficits. These improvements, in turn, will improve government decision making and allocation of resources over time; ensure budget-deficit targets such as those for the EMU do not reduce valuable investments; and improve decision making for both financial and direct foreign investment.

CONCLUSION

Despite the scepticism about heavy reliance on skill creation to resolve social and economic problems that we have shown at a number of points in our analysis, we have ended with consideration of a number of practical measures for making a skills strategy work. This is consistent with the stance that we took at the beginning of the book: such a strategy comes into the awkward class of 'necessary but insufficient' policies. It is insufficient in that it is not feasible to expect that a majority of any country's workforce will be enabled by improved and more focused education to find useful, high-productivity employment to such an extent that unemployment, social integration, and poverty, and the social policies traditionally associated with their resolution, become residual. There is currently a strong desire among policy-makers to believe that such an outcome can be achieved, thereby reducing, if not solving, the pressing social problems of unemployment, income inequality, and poverty. As electorates become increasingly resistant to financing high public spending, and as political consensus over the respective role of markets and various forms of intervention becomes impossible to sustain, the skills-creation strategy becomes very attractive. It promises to minimize the need for welfare spending. And as an area of public policy that concentrates on improving the quality of labour supply, it has an appeal across the political spectrum (Cutler 1992). There is a danger of excessive expectations based more on fervent desire that an outcome might be possible than on a realistic evaluation of its chances—a phenomenon that could lead eventually to a serious bout of disillusion.

We must however also stress the necessity of a high-skill strategy. As we argued in Chapter 1, claims about the implications of competition in a globalized economy, and about the need to maximize the role of high-productivity labour if living standards in the advanced countries are to be sustained and improved, are realistic. For that reason we have considered the array of policy alternatives that are currently being attempted to facilitate higher levels of skill development, and have warned against certain contemporary tendencies (such as the disenabling of public policy instruments) which might undermine it.

Perhaps the most difficult type of conclusion to draw from a comparative study of different policy instruments is to assign an appropriate role to learning from experience elsewhere. On the one hand, and as we have seen at a number of points, imitation, in the sense of taking a set of policies from one country or firm and installing them in another, neglects questions of context. To disinter a few structural elements from the richly interlocked economic, political, and social institutions of, say, Germany and Japan is not well advised; and there are limits to the extent to which smaller countries can imitate ideas that seem to work in the vast economy of the USA, large parts of which are still not closely linked to the international economy. The contemporary tendency for governments and business management to be policy 'fashion victims' increases the risk of both inappropriate and superficial change, and an unwillingness to allow policy change time to take effect before a new change of direction is launched.

One can illustrate this by recalling an example that has appeared at several points in previous chapters. Until the early 1990s there was enthusiasm in a number of countries (among those covered by this study France, Italy, Sweden, and the UK) for imitations of German apprenticeship, though rarely did those advocating the imitation appreciate how the German institution was embedded in other elements of socio-economic structure. More recently, particularly following post-unification difficulties, Germany has become generally unfashionable. There is now less talk of the advantages of apprenticeship, and policy-makers, including in Germany itself, talk of the advantages of general academic education over vocational preparation. There is, however, little evidence that they are coming to grips with the implications of inviting all students to pursue academic courses when eventually most will fail to gain access to the kinds of occupations to which they believe such courses lead.

On the other hand it is absurd to argue that there can be no learning among economies, as they are not fully self-contained, separate structures. Attempts at copying successful ideas from elsewhere must be based on careful planning as to how the imported element may be grafted on to existing practices and structures; it can neither be expected to replace these nor to flourish without their support.

One consequence of this is that even if there is, for better or worse, convergence on some hoped-for 'one best way' for creating an appropriately skilled workforce, the outcome will not be convergence on a common set of institutions, as Regini (1996b) points out. The addition of a common set of new structures to some diverse past legacies is not an overall convergence, but a redefined diversity. At present it is not at all clear what the diversity of skill-creation institutions in the advanced countries will look like in, say, ten years' time, since current ideas about appropriate imitations embody a number of contradictions, as we have seen in this study. There are desires for more general, adaptable skills, but skills that are also relevant to employers' needs; the same sets of policies are often trying to help the unemployed but also to operate at the leading edge of advanced skills; there is a demand for vocational education and training to fulfil social policy goals, while it is also increasingly seen as a matter for private business to determine. It is unlikely that these contradictions will be resolved, but policy measures have to find means of accommodating them in addition to pursuing their ostensible task of creating the learning society.

APPENDIX

APPENDIX TABLE A.1. Exports of particular goods as proportions of total world trade in all goods, seven countries, 1976, 1989 and 1994

Product	Whole world			France			Germany		
	1976	1989	1994	1976	1989	1994	1976	1989	1994
Total	100.00	100.00	100.00						
Meat, skins (00, 01, 21)	1.76	1.58	1.37	0.175	0.172	0.158	0.091	0.115	0.071
Dairy (02)	0.75	0.76	0.61	0.112	0.098	0.100	0.100	0.125	0.101
Fish (03)	0.75	1.04	1.04	0.015	0.022	0.028	0.016	0.013	0.015
Grain (04)	2.80	1.71	1.13	0.275	0.207	0.153	0.068	0.071	0.074
Vegetables, fruit (05)	1.60	1.52	1.53	0.086	0.083	0.078	0.032		0.044
Other food (06–09)	3.51	1.40	1.83	0.135	0.096	0.149	0.120	0.158	0.146
Drink (11)	0.57	0.66	0.66	0.168	0.152	0.178	0.035	0.028	0.046
Tobacco (12)	0.49	0.50	0.54	0.008	0.005	0.006	0.016	0.033	0.035
Oil seeds (22)	0.67	0.36	0.44	0.007	0.050	0.011	0.001	0.006	0.005
Rubber (23)	0.52	0.35	0.26	0.028	0.023	0.016	0.020	0.017	0.014
Wood (24)	1.08	0.95	0.86	0.026	0.026	0.019	0.034	0.025	0.022
Paper (25)	0.69	0.72	0.41	0.010	0.012	0.009	0.009	0.008	0.009
Fibres (26)	1.19	0.81	0.55	0.054	0.026	0.014	0.065	0.047	0.035
Minerals (27)	0.59	0.36	0.29	0.022	0.020	0.015	0.033	0.030	0.024
Ores, scrap (28)	1.81	1.38	0.78	0.078	0.058	0.029	0.064	0.068	0.048
Animal and veg. mat., oils (29, 41–43)	0.92	0.92	0.90	0.045	0.034	0.030	0.077	0.055	0.050
Coal, etc. (32)	0.84	0.58	0.43	0.013	0.005	0.003	0.187	0.057	0.013
Petrol, crude (333)	14.07	5.09	4.01	0.000	0.000	0.000	0.000	0.000	0.000
Petrol refining, etc. (334, 335)	4.14	2.54	1.99	0.156	0.052	0.063	0.133	0.067	0.088
Gas (34)	0.74	0.74	0.65	0.011	0.007	0.006	0.004	0.008	0.010
Organic chemicals (51)	1.70	2.46	2.22	0.110	0.157	0.175	0.356	0.280	0.283
Inorganic chemicals (52)	0.75	0.89	2.74	0.092	0.074	0.063	0.120	0.105	0.082
Dyes, paints (53)	0.53	0.64	0.64	0.039	0.036	0.041	0.166	0.153	0.141
Drugs (54)	0.81	1.13	1.47	0.072	0.079	0.135	0.137	0.139	0.218
Cosmetics, etc. (55)	0.41	0.63	0.74	0.081	0.084	0.157	0.062	0.068	0.094
Fertilizers (56)	0.39	0.41	0.29	0.017	0.013	0.007	0.030	0.028	0.025
Plastics (58)	1.52	2.18	2.04	0.122	0.145	0.141	0.370	0.354	0.338

Misc. chemicals (59)	0.82	1.08	1.08	0.075	0.078	0.111	0.179	0.181	0.187
Ordnance (57, 951)	0.28	0.24	0.17	0.002	0.005	0.004	0.006	0.024	0.003
Leather (61)	0.35	0.45	0.47	0.026	0.019	0.012	0.045	0.032	0.027
Rubber goods (62)	0.68	0.79	0.77	0.106	0.095	0.085	0.106	0.106	0.093
Wood products (63)	0.54	0.55	0.63	0.028	0.015	0.026	0.045	0.041	0.035
Paper products (64)	1.55	2.07	1.81	0.080	0.097	0.122	0.151	0.223	0.232
Textiles (65)	3.32	3.20	3.25	0.239	0.153	0.163	0.446	0.319	0.319
Mineral products (66)	1.99	2.38	2.28	0.117	0.116	0.112	0.216	0.207	0.159
Iron and steel (67)	4.55	3.93	2.84	0.432	0.244	0.220	0.763	0.467	0.347
Non-ferrous metals (68)	2.25	2.52	1.71	0.094	0.087	0.096	0.219	0.187	0.178
Metal forms (69)	2.20	2.09	2.03	0.202	0.111	0.122	0.405	0.349	0.317
Engines (71)	2.24	2.64	2.53	0.212	0.193	0.218	0.244	0.300	0.306
Machine tools (72)	3.71	2.55	3.17	0.252	0.142	0.150	0.822	0.653	0.602
Metal machine tools (73)	0.96	0.97	0.70	0.060	0.022	0.024	0.325	0.154	0.137
Non-electrical machinery, etc. (74)	3.68	4.16	4.08	0.345	0.205	0.234	0.881	0.736	1.563
Office machinery (75)	1.20	4.28	4.59	0.098	0.169	0.169	0.188	0.165	0.245
TV, radio (76)	2.37	3.24	3.93	0.086	0.056	0.117	0.279	0.190	0.227
Electrical goods (77)	3.17	6.15	7.92	0.265	0.304	0.327	0.610	0.752	0.819
Cars (781)	3.63	5.59	5.13	0.448	0.415	0.344	0.846	1.380	1.052
Lorries, etc. (782, 783)	1.71	1.58	1.34	0.099	0.054	0.061	0.344	0.211	0.173
Motor vehicle parts (784)	2.06	2.59	2.60	0.184	0.232	0.232	0.376	0.541	0.439
Cycles, trailers (785, 786)	0.50	0.44	0.52	0.037	0.031	0.023	0.075	0.067	0.045
Railway vehicles (791)	0.20	0.11	0.20	0.048	0.015	0.031	0.029	0.016	0.052
Aircraft (792)	1.14	2.02	1.75	0.107	0.344	0.277	0.075	0.060	0.211
Ships, boats (793)	2.00	0.79	0.80	0.118	0.015	0.018	0.186	0.024	0.044
Furniture (82)	0.52	0.83	0.95	0.030	0.047	0.045	0.123	0.117	0.108
Travel goods, shoes (83, 85)	0.72	0.97	1.23	0.041	0.049	0.048	0.033	0.030	0.036
Clothing (84)	1.93	3.10	3.67	0.141	0.100	0.124	0.165	0.166	0.166
Instruments (87)	1.03	1.74	1.66	0.083	0.067	0.086	0.203	0.233	0.256
Precision goods (88)	1.20	1.33	1.26	0.072	0.057	0.052	0.181	0.114	0.107
Printed matter (892)	0.46	0.59	0.54	0.052	0.034	0.040	0.079	0.089	0.083
Other (812, 89)	1.44	2.73	3.99	0.143	0.168	0.201	0.285	0.390	0.372
Total	**100.00**	**100.00**	**100.00**	**6.279**	**5.471**	**5.676**	**11.274**	**10.582**	**10.968**

APPENDIX TABLE A.1. (Cont.)

Product	Italy			Japan			Sweden		
	1976	1989	1994	1976	1989	1994	1976	1989	1994
Meat, skins (00, 01, 21)	0.012	0.025	0.024	0.001	0.001	0.003	0.0126	0.0093	0.0038
Dairy (02)	0.011	0.017	0.019	0.000	0.000	0.000	0.0033	0.0022	0.0012
Fish (03)	0.004	0.006	0.014	0.069	0.015	0.048	0.0033	0.0046	0.0064
Grain (04)	0.033	0.049	0.056	0.002	0.004	0.007	0.0221	0.0069	0.0057
Vegetables, fruit (05)	0.162	0.123	0.105	0.009	0.004	0.001	0.0025		0.0009
Other food (06–09)	0.024	0.027	0.034	0.010	0.012	0.012	0.0249	0.0097	0.0109
Drink (11)	0.060	0.035	0.057	0.008	0.001	0.002	0.0002	0.0036	0.0054
Tobacco (12)	0.008	0.004	0.004	0.000	0.003	0.007	0.0017	0.0008	0.0006
Oil seeds (22)	0.000	0.000	0.000	0.000		0.000	0.0032	0.0003	0.0001
Rubber (23)	0.008	0.007	0.002	0.023	0.012	0.017	0.0013	0.0007	0.0012
Wood (24)	0.001	0.001	0.006	0.003	0.000	0.000	0.1030	0.0737	0.0627
Paper (25)	0.000	0.001	0.000	0.005	0.001	0.000	0.1445	0.0653	0.0336
Fibres (26)	0.024	0.026	0.007	0.057	0.031	0.026	0.0030	0.0013	0.0011
Minerals (27)	0.013	0.015	0.010	0.004	0.007	0.005	0.0034	0.0031	0.0020
Ores, scrap (28)	0.012	0.010	0.004	0.004	0.009	0.008	0.0628	0.0286	0.0175
Animal and veg. mat., oils (29, 41–43)	0.029	0.031	0.030	0.011	0.009	0.006	0.0066	0.0041	0.0037
Coal, etc. (32)	0.008	0.001	0.001	0.005	0.011	0.007	0.0007	0.0005	0.0004
Petrol, crude (333)	0.000	0.002	0.000	0.000	0.000	0.000	0.0000	0.0000	0.0000
Petrol refining, etc. (334, 335)	0.225	0.062	0.073	0.009	0.020	0.055	0.0262	0.0421	0.0345
Gas (34)	0.006	0.001	0.001	0.000	0.000	0.000	0.0003	0.0006	0.0007
Organic chemicals (51)	0.082	0.071	0.066	0.157	0.113	0.201	0.0147	0.0131	0.0155
Inorganic chemicals (52)	0.022	0.018	0.010	0.044	0.026	0.035	0.0112	0.0103	0.0070
Dyes, paints (53)	0.012	0.017	0.022	0.025	0.032	0.045	0.0049	0.0051	0.0071
Drugs (54)	0.048	0.037	0.069	0.017	0.029	0.039	0.0152	0.0219	0.0616
Cosmetics, etc. (55)	0.007	0.013	0.031	0.010	0.012	0.021	0.0051	0.0045	0.0059
Fertilizers (56)	0.011	0.008	0.001	0.018	0.002	0.002	0.0014	0.0024	0.0018
Plastics (58)	0.109	0.099	0.098	0.126	0.100	0.153	0.0321	0.0324	0.0296

Misc. chemicals (59)	0.027	0.029	0.043	0.031	0.047	0.076	0.0133	0.0112	0.0125
Ordnance (57, 951)	0.026	0.003	0.003	0.001	0.000	0.002	0.0075	0.0050	0.0042
Leather (61)	0.035	0.060	0.086	0.020	0.010	0.006	0.0065	0.0039	0.0017
Rubber goods (62)	0.055	0.052	0.050	0.087	0.113	0.111	0.0143	0.0106	0.0065
Wood products (63)	0.022	0.017	0.020	0.014	0.002	0.003	0.0211	0.0180	0.0174
Paper products (64)	0.040	0.051	0.070	0.049	0.042	0.054	0.1818	0.1893	0.1465
Textiles (65)	0.234	0.229	0.271	0.380	0.163	0.169	0.0299	0.0179	0.0156
Mineral products (66)	0.140	0.199	0.184	0.105	0.086	0.116	0.0176	0.0174	0.0145
Iron and steel (67)	0.246	0.305	0.169	1.203	0.347	0.370	0.1435	0.1074	0.0959
Non-ferrous metals (68)	0.036	0.040	0.048	0.070	0.054	0.073	0.0340	0.0325	0.0247
Metal forms (69)	0.166	0.138	0.182	0.239	0.155	0.160	0.0780	0.0576	0.0425
Engines (71)	0.083	0.065	0.090	0.168	0.295	0.433	0.0577	0.0456	0.0509
Machine tools (72)	0.258	0.270	0.333	0.265	0.430	0.491	0.1077	0.0674	0.0749
Metal machine tools (73)	0.063	0.058	0.061	0.149	0.193	0.153	0.0253	0.0128	0.0145
Non-electrical machinery, etc. (74)	0.255	0.314	0.376	0.315	0.457	0.621	0.1490	0.1020	0.1125
Office machinery (75)	0.065	0.125	0.109	0.155	0.931	0.878	0.0354	0.0459	0.0208
TV, radio (76)	0.069	0.044	0.049	0.790	1.021	0.751	0.0882	0.0512	0.1085
Electrical goods (77)	0.194	0.245	0.289	0.379	1.163	1.450	0.0837	0.0687	0.0742
Cars (781)	0.207	0.187	0.147	0.695	1.512	1.121	0.0778	0.1114	0.0850
Lorries, etc. (782, 783)	0.064	0.049	0.053	0.314	0.268	0.288	0.0700	0.0416	0.0373
Motor vehicle parts (784)	0.100	0.140	0.111	0.102	0.401	0.452	0.0660	0.0751	0.0762
Cycles, trailers (785, 786)	0.038	0.039	0.047	0.186	0.127	0.143	0.0077	0.0044	0.0031
Railway vehicles (791)	0.004	0.002	0.007	0.020	0.008	0.005	0.0033	0.0009	0.0025
Aircraft (792)	0.037	0.024	0.050	0.002	0.017	0.017	0.0035	0.0099	0.0108
Ships, boats (793)	0.018	0.005	0.018	0.809	0.036	0.290	0.1531	0.0079	0.0180
Furniture (82)	0.078	0.164	0.168	0.008	0.013	0.015	0.0268	0.0301	0.0253
Travel goods, shoes (83, 85)	0.216	0.245	0.192	0.011	0.003	0.003	0.0061	0.0016	0.0016
Clothing (84)	0.242	0.356	0.313	0.047	0.022	0.015	0.0229	0.0077	0.0064
Instruments (87)	0.029	0.038	0.051	0.000	0.199	0.233	0.0252	0.0238	0.0323
Precision goods (88)	0.032	0.038	0.039	0.227	0.341	0.269	0.0059	0.0040	0.0053
Printed matter (892)	0.000	0.000	0.030	0.009	0.019	0.013	0.0087	0.0075	0.0059
Other (812, 89)	0.223	0.287	0.303	0.161	0.319	0.208	0.0396	0.0359	0.0469
Total	**4.235**	**4.524**	**4.708**	**7.626**	**9.250**	**9.689**	**2.1209**	**1.5730**	**1.5161**

Appendix Table A.1. (Cont.)

Product	United Kingdom			United States		
	1976	1989	1994	1976	1989	1994
Meat, skins (00, 01, 21)	0.083	0.076	0.061	0.192	0.193	0.183
Dairy (02)	0.024	0.027	0.025	0.015	0.016	0.016
Fish (03)	0.017	0.026	0.029	0.044	0.085	0.082
Grain (04)	0.028	0.055	0.046	0.851	0.451	0.289
Vegetables, fruit (05)	0.017	0.017	0.014	0.183	0.151	0.178
Other food (06–09)	0.077	0.056	0.066	0.229	0.160	0.179
Drink (11)	0.108	0.054	0.107	0.008	0.010	0.032
Tobacco (12)	0.028	0.033	0.033	0.169	0.199	0.168
Oil seeds (22)	0.001	0.002	0.001	0.409	0.167	0.118
Rubber (23)	0.013	0.010	0.010	0.042	0.032	0.027
Wood (24)	0.002	0.002	0.001	0.164	0.156	0.139
Paper (25)	0.002	0.003	0.002	0.115	0.123	0.096
Fibres (26)	0.047	0.027	0.019	0.163	0.129	0.099
Minerals (27)	0.022	0.024	0.016	0.094	0.064	0.039
Ores, scrap (28)	0.021	0.045	0.025	0.165	0.213	0.094
Animal and veg. mat., oils (29, 41–43)	0.014	0.022	0.012	0.144	0.075	0.074
Coal, etc. (32)	0.015	0.007	0.003	0.343	0.171	0.074
Petrol, crude (333)	0.037	0.231	0.227	0.003	0.002	0.000
Petrol refining, etc. (334, 335)	0.205	0.084	0.095	0.120	0.156	0.140
Gas (34)	0.004	0.009	0.012	0.028	0.018	0.014
Organic chemicals (51)	0.145	0.157	0.176	0.255	0.312	0.326
Inorganic chemicals (52)	0.071	0.048	0.042	0.148	0.137	0.104
Dyes, paints (53)	0.058	0.052	0.055	0.036	0.047	0.058
Drugs (54)	0.093	0.108	0.150	0.116	0.119	0.154
Cosmetics, etc. (55)	0.049	0.042	0.074	0.053	0.041	0.091
Fertilizers (56)	0.011	0.006	0.003	0.070	0.075	0.068
Plastics (58)	0.109	0.085	0.093	0.192	0.242	0.287

Misc. chemicals (59)	0.127	0.074	0.092	0.158	0.174	0.183
Ordnance (57, 951)	0.033	0.021	0.018	0.150	0.031	0.096
Leather (61)	0.031	0.033	0.013	0.026	0.021	0.026
Rubber goods (62)	0.062	0.048	0.044	0.057	0.063	0.078
Wood products (63)	0.011	0.004	0.008	0.064	0.026	0.046
Paper products (64)	0.057	0.057	0.075	0.188	0.123	0.193
Textiles (65)	0.199	0.103	0.110	0.229	0.131	0.165
Mineral products (66)	0.356	0.194	0.166	0.308	0.131	0.154
Iron and steel (67)	0.170	0.136	0.140	0.221	0.080	0.106
Non-ferrous metals (68)	0.149	0.110	0.084	0.141	0.184	0.065
Metal forms (69)	0.167	0.086	0.095	0.247	0.169	0.220
Engines (71)	0.283	0.181	0.231	0.357	0.538	0.521
Machine tools (72)	0.327	0.175	0.167	0.865	0.424	0.492
Metal machine tools (73)	0.067	0.033	0.029	0.159	0.068	0.098
Non-electrical machinery, etc. (74)	0.270	0.204	0.219	0.778	0.403	0.588
Office machinery (75)	0.106	0.255	0.356	0.341	0.959	0.883
TV, radio (76)	0.129	0.064	0.180	0.265	0.221	0.427
Electrical goods (77)	0.192	0.267	0.365	0.552	0.951	1.317
Cars (781)	0.135	0.167	0.192	0.377	0.393	0.416
Lorries, etc. (782, 783)	0.110	0.023	0.031	0.322	0.134	0.149
Motor vehicle parts (784)	0.211	0.163	0.113	0.585	0.465	0.552
Cycles, trailers (785, 786)	0.033	0.015	0.026	0.037	0.025	0.039
Railway vehicles (791)	0.008	0.003	0.016	0.046	0.014	0.018
Aircraft (792)	0.089	0.142	0.141	0.703	0.620	0.759
Ships, boats (793)	0.061	0.019	0.019	0.055	0.027	0.031
Furniture (82)	0.029	0.015	0.027	0.028	0.048	0.093
Travel goods, shoes (83, 85)	0.016	0.011	0.021	0.010	0.010	0.021
Clothing (84)	0.085	0.076	0.098	0.057	0.042	0.150
Instruments (87)	0.098	0.112	0.138	0.282	0.351	0.429
Precision goods (88)	0.078	0.055	0.063	0.184	0.126	0.106
Printed matter (892)	0.057	0.062	0.069	0.070	0.080	0.102
Other (812, 89)	0.146	0.254	0.236	0.241	0.456	0.519
Total	**5.188**	**4.471**	**4.981**	**12.457**	**11.032**	**12.170**

REFERENCES

ABATTU, C. and BEL, M. (1996), 'Rhône-Alpes: la formazione fra Stato e impresa', in Regini (ed.), q.v.

ABEGGLEN, J. and STALK, G. (1985), *Kaisha: The Japanese Corporation* (New York: Basic Books).

ABRAHAMSSON, K., HULTINGER, E.-S. and SVENNINGSSON, L. (1990), *The Expanding Learning Enterprise in Sweden* (Stockholm: Swedish National Board of Education).

ABRAMOVITZ, M. (1982), 'Notes on International Differences in Productivity Growth Rates', in Mueller (ed.), q.v.

ADLER, N. J. (1997), *International Dimensions of Organizational Behavior*, third edition (Ohio: South-Western College Publishing).

AGLIETTA, M. (1979), *A Theory of Capitalist Regulation* (London: Verso-New Left Books).

AICPA [American Institute of Certified Public Accountants] (1995), *Improving Business Reporting—a Customer Focus* (Washington, DC: AICPA).

ALBERT, M. (1991), *Capitalisme contre capitalisme* (Paris: Seuil).

ALTMANN, N., KOHLER, C. and MEIL, P. (eds.) (1992), *Technology and Work in Germany* (London: Routledge).

ANDRESSEN, B.-J. (1994), Interview with Senior Vice President for Human Resources, Daimler-Benz, Santa Monica, Calif.

AOKI, M. (1988), *Information, Incentives and Bargaining in the Japanese Economy* (New York: Cambridge University Press).

—— and DORE, R. (eds.) (1994), *The Japanese Firm: Sources of Competitive Strength* (Oxford: Clarendon Press).

APPELBAUM, E. and BATT, R. (1994), *The New American Workplace: Transforming Work Systems in the United States* (Ithaca, New York: ILR Press).

ASANUMA, B. (1989), 'Manufacturer–Supplier Relationships in Japan and the Concept of Relation-Specific Skill', *Journal of the Japanese and International Economies*, 3, 1–30.

ATKINSON, J. and COLEMAN, W. (1989), 'Strong States and Weak States: Sectoral Policy Networks in Advanced Capitalist Economies', *British Journal of Political Science*, 19(1), 47–67.

AVENTUR, F. and BROCHIER, D. (1996), 'Continuing Vocational Training in France', in Brandsma *et al.* (eds.), q.v.

AXELSSON, R. (1989), *Upper Secondary School in Retrospect: the Views of Former Students*, doctoral thesis, University of Uppsala.

BACKES-GELLNER, U. (1995), 'Duale Ausbildung und/oder betriebliche Weiterbildung? Lehren aus einem internationalen Vergleich betrieblicher Qualifizierungsstrategien', *Berufsbildung*, 49.

—— (1996), *Betriebliche Bildungs- und Wettbewerbungsstrategien im deutsch-britischen Vergleich* (Munich: Rainer Ham).

BAGNASCO, A. (1977), *Tre Italie* (Bologna: Il Mulino).

—— (1986), 'Mercato e mercati del lavoro', in Cella, G. P. and Ceri, P. (eds.), *Lavoro e non-lavoro. Condizione sociale e spiegazione della società* (Milan: Angeli).

—— (1988), *La costruzione sociale del mercato* (Bologna: Il Mulino).

—— and TRIGILIA, C. (eds.) (1984), *Società e politica nelle aree di piccola impresa: Il caso della Valdelsa* (Milan: Angeli).

BAHNMÜLLER, R. (1996), 'Baden-Württemberg: il sistema duale in fronte alla crisi', in Regini (ed.), q.v.

BAILEY, T. (1993), 'The Mission of the TECs and Private Sector Involvement: Lessons from the PICs', in Finegold, McFarland, and Richardson (eds.), q.v.

BALL, S. J. and LARSSON, S. (1989), 'Education, Politics and Society in Sweden: an Introduction', in Ball and Larsson (eds.), *The Struggle for Democratic Education: Equality and Participation in Sweden* (Lewes: Falmer Press).

BANKE, P. (1991), *Gruppeorganisering. Fleksibel produktion og jobkvalitet i den syende industri* (Copenhagen: Dansk Teknologisk Institut).

BARTEL, A. (1995), 'Productivity Gains from the Implementation of Employee Training Programs', *Industrial Relations*.

BARTLETT, C. and GHOSHAL, S. (1992) *Managing Across Borders: The Transnational Solution*, fourth edition (Boston, MA: Harvard Business School Press).

BAUMOL, W. (1967), 'Macroeconomics of Unbalanced Growth', *American Economic Review*, 57, 3, 415–26.

BECATTINI, G. (1989), 'Riflessioni sul distretto industriale marshalliano come concetto socio-economico', *Stato e Mercato*, 25, 111–28.

—— (ed.) (1987), *Mercato e forze locali: il distretto industriale* (Bologna: Il Mulino).

BECHTLE, G. and DULL, K. (1992), 'Future of the Mass-Production Worker', in Altmann, Kohler and Meil (eds.), q.v.

BECKER, G. S. (1962, 1975), *Human Capital: A Theoretical and Empirical Analysis, with Special Reference to Education*, first edition 1962, second edition 1975 (New York: Columbia University Press).

BÉDUWÉ, C. and ESPINASSE, J.-M. (1995), 'France: politique éducative, amélioration des competences et absorption des diplômés par l'économie', *Sociologie du Travail*, 37(4), 527–54.

BENEDETTI, L. (ed.) (1991), *Quale investimento nella formazione delle risorse umane in Emilia Romagna* (Bologna: ACLI, CGIL, CISL, UIL, AECA, ECAP, ENAIP, ENFAP, IAL).

BENNETT, R. J. and McCOSHAN, A. (1993), *Enterprise and Human Resource Development* (London: Paul Chapman).

BERTOLA, G. (1990), 'Job Security, Employment and Wages', *European Economic Review*, 34, 851–86.

BEST, M. (1990), *The New Competition* (Oxford: Polity Press).

BIANCHI, P. (1985), 'Servizi reali: considerazioni analitiche e implicazioni di politica industriale', *L'Industria*, 6(2), 233–46.

—— (1990), 'Distribuzione spaziale dei servizi alla produzione', *Archivio di studi urbani e regionali*, 31(37), 125–41.

—— (1992), 'Levels of Policy and the Nature of Post-Fordist Competition', in Storper, M. and Scott, A. J. (eds.), *Pathways to Industrialization and Regional Development* (London: Routledge, 303–15).

—— and BELLINI, N. (1991), 'Public Policies for Local Networks of Innovators', *Research Policy*, 20, 487–97.

—— and GUALTIERI, G. (1990), 'Emilia-Romagna and its Industrial Districts: the Evolution of a Model', in Leonardi, R. and Nanetti, R. Y. (eds.), *The Regions and European Integration: The Case of Emilia-Romagna* (London: Pinter, 83–105).

BLANCHFLOWER, D. G. and LYNCH, L. M. (1992), 'Training at Work: A Comparison of U.S. and British Youths', in Lynch, L. M., *Training and the Private Sector: International Comparisons* (Chicago, IL.: University of Chicago Press).

BLINDER, A. S. and KRUEGER, A. B. (1991), *International Differences in Labor Turnover: A Comparative Study with Emphasis on the U.S. and Japan* (Washington, DC: Council on Competitiveness).

BLOSSFELD, H.-P. (1990), 'Changes in Educational Careers in the Federal Republic of Germany', *Sociology of Education*, 63, 165–77.

——, GIANNELLI, G. and MAYER, K.-U. (1993), 'Is there a New Service Proletariat? The Tertiary Sector and Social Inequality in Germany', in Esping-Andersen (ed.), q.v.

—— and HAKIM, C. (eds.) (1997), *Between Equalization and Marginalization*: *Women Working Part-Time in Europe and the United States of America* (Oxford: Oxford University Press).

BLUNDELL, R., DEARDEN, L. and MEGHIR, C. (1995), 'The Determinants and Effects of Training in Britain', mimeo. (London: Micro Labour Markets Group).

BOURDON, J. (1995), 'La Formation contre le chômage, une vision économique réévalué de l'investissment éducatif', *Sociologie du travail*, 37(4), 503–26.

BOYER, R. (1988), *The Search for Labour Market Flexibility* (Oxford: Clarendon Press).

—— (1991), *The Transformations of Modern Capitalism* (Paris: CEPREMAP).

—— and SAILLARD, Y. (eds.) (1995), *Théorie de la régulation: L'état des savoirs* (Paris: La Découverte).

BOYLE, N. (1992), 'The Politics of Recommodification: Labor Market Policy Change in Britain, 1979–90', Ph.D. thesis, Duke University.

BRANDSMA, J., KESSLER, F. and MÜNCH, J. (eds.) (1996), *Continuing Vocational Training: Europe, Japan and the US* (Utrecht: Uitgeverij Lemma).

BRESCIANI, P. G. (1987), 'Contrattazione/negozione della formazione professionale', *Prospettiva sindacale*, 53–67.

BRUSCO, S., REYNERI, E. and SERAVALLI, G. (1990), 'Gli interventi di politica del lavoro a livello locale', in Carinci (ed.), q.v., 181–250.

BÜCHTEMANN, C. F. (ed.) (1993), *Employment Security and Labor Market Behavior: Interdisciplinary Approaches and International Evidence*, Cornell International Industrial and Labor Relations Report No. 23 (Ithaca, NY: ILR Press).

—— and SOLOFF, D. (eds.) (1995), *Human Capital and Economic Performance: Theory and International Evidence* (New York: Russell Sage).

—— and VERDIER, E. (1998), 'Education and Training Regimes: Macro-Institutional Evidence', *Revue de l'économie politique*, 108(3), 291–320.

—— and VOGLER-LUDWIG, K. (1995), 'The "German Model" under Pressure: Education, Workforce Skills and Economic Performance in Germany', in Büchtemann and Soloff (eds.), q.v.

BUTTLER, F. and TESSARING, M. (1995), 'Allemagne: le capital humain, facteur d'implantation industrielle', *Sociologie du travail*, 37(4), 577–94.

BYNNER, J. and ROBERTS, K. (1991), *Youth and Work: Transition to Employment in England and Germany* (London: Anglo-German Foundation for the Study of Industrial Society).

CALLAGHAN, J. (1976), 'The Great Education Debate', speech given at Ruskin College, Oxford.

CAMPBELL, A. and WARNER, M. (1991), 'Training Strategies and Microelectronics in the Engineering Industries of the UK and Germany', in Ryan (ed.), q.v.

CAMPINOS-DUBERNET, M. and GRANDO, J.-M. (1988), 'Formation professionnelle ouvrière: trois modèles européens', *Formation Emploi*, 22, 5–29.

CAPECCHI, V. (1993), 'École et formation professionnelle en Italie', *Formation emploi*, 44 (Paris: La Documentation française).

CARINCI, F. (1990), 'Preistoria e storia: prima cronaca delle agenzie', in Carinci (ed.), q.v., 15–35.

—— (ed.) (1990), *L'agenzia regionale per l'impiego* (Naples: Jovene).

CARR, C. (1992), 'Productivity and Skills in Vehicle Component Manufacturers in Britain, Germany, the USA and Japan', *National Institute Economic Review*, 139, 79–87.

CASEY, B. (1990), *Recent Developments in West Germany's Apprenticeship Training System* (London: Policy Studies Institute).

CEDEFOP (1992), *Country Studies on the Financing for Vocational Training with Particular Reference to Continuing Training for the Gainfully Employed: Germany* (Berlin: CEDEFOP).

—— (1994), *Vocational Education and Training in France* (Berlin: CEDEFOP).

CENSIS (1994), *28° Rapporto sulla situazione sociale del paese 1992* (Milan: Franco Angeli).

CEVOLI, M., PALMIERI, S. and TAGLIAFERRO, C. (1992), 'Le dinamiche della domanda di professionalità', *Osservatorio isfol*, 14(5), 89–97.

CHAPMAN, B. and CHIA, T. (1989), 'Financing Higher Education', Centre for Economic Policy Research and Department of Economics Discussion Paper No. 213 (Canberra: Australian National University).

CLÉMENÇON, M. and COUTROT, L. (1995), 'La Relation formation-chômage. France: quelques résultats d'analyse secondaire et bilan bibliographique', *Sociologie du travail*, 37(4), 739–54.

COBALTI, A. and SCHIZZEROTTO, A. (1998), 'Education and Employment in Contemporary Italy', in Shavit and Müller (eds.), q.v.

COFFIELD, F. (1992), 'Training and Enterprise Councils: the Last Throw of Voluntarism', *Policy Studies*, 13(4), 11–32.

COLE, R. (1989), *Strategies for Learning* (Berkeley, CA: California University Press).

COLOMBO, A. and REGALIA, I. (1996), 'Lombardia: selettività e reattività degli interventi formativi', in Regini (ed.), q.v.

CRETICOS, P. A. and SHEETS, R. G. (1990), *Evaluating State-Financed, Workplace-Based Retraining Programs: A Report on the Feasibility of a Business Screening and Performance Outcome Evaluation System*, Research Report 89–08 (Washington, DC: National Commission for Employment Policy).

CROUCH, C. (1993), *Industrial Relations and European State Traditions* (Oxford: Clarendon Press).

—— (1995), 'Organized Interests as Resources or as Constraint: Rival Logics of Vocational Training Policy', in Crouch, C. and Traxler, F. (eds.), *Organized Industrial Relations in Europe: What Future?* (Aldershot: Avebury).

—— (1999), *The Structure of West European Societies: Post-Industrial Europe in an International Context* (Oxford: Oxford University Press).

—— and STREECK, W. (eds.) (1997), *Political Economy of Modern Capitalism* (London: Sage).

CROWLEY-BAINTON, T. (1993), *TECs and Employers: Developing Effective Links, Part 2* (London: Employment Department, Research Series No. 13).

CULPEPPER, P. (1998), 'Explaining Success and Failure in Training Reforms: Lessons from France and Eastern Germany', in Culpepper and Finegold (eds.), q.v.

CULPEPPER, P. and FINEGOLD, D. (eds.) (1998), *The German Skills Machine in Comparative Perspective* (Oxford: Berghahn Books).

CUTLER, T. (1992), 'Vocational Training and British Economic Performance: A Further Instalment of the British Labour Problem', *Work, Employment and Society*, 6(2), 161–83.

DAHLBERG, Å. and TUIJNMAN, A. (1991), 'Development of Human Resources in Internal Labour Markets: Implications of Swedish Labour Market Policy', *Economic and Industrial Democracy*, 12(2), 151–72.

DALY, A. (1986), 'Education and Productivity: A Comparison of Great Britain and the United States', *British Journal of Industrial Relations*, 2, 251–66.

——, HITCHENS, D. and WAGNER, K. (1985), 'Productivity, Machinery and Skills in a Sample of British and German Manufacturing Plants', *National Institute Economic Review*, 111, 48–61.

D'AVANZO, L. (1992), 'L'attività di formazione professionale nel governo dei processi di ristrutturazione', *Osservatorio isfol*, 14(5), 83–9.

DAVIS, N. (1996), 'Continuing Vocational Training in the United Kingdom', in Brandsma *et al.* (eds.), q.v.

DAVIS, S., HALTIWANGER, J. and SCHUH, S. (1996), *Job Creation and Destruction* (Cambridge, MA: MIT Press).

DELL'ARINGA, C. (1990), 'Industrial Relations and the Role of the State in EEC Countries', in Commission des Communautés Européennes, DG V, and London School of Economics and Political Science, *Salaires et intégration européenne* (Brussels: European Commission, V/908/90).

DERTOUZOS, M. L. *et al.* (1989), *Made in America: Regaining the Productive Edge* (Cambridge, MA.: MIT Press).

DEUTSCHES INSTITUT FÜR WIRTSCHAFTSFORSCHUNG (1996), *Employment and Social Policies under International Constraints* (The Hague: VUGA).

DORE, R. P. (1986), *Flexible Rigidities* (London: Athlone Press).

—— and SAKO, M. (1998) revised edition, *How the Japanese Learn to Work* (London: Routledge).

DRESSER, L. and ROGERS, J. (1997), 'Sectoral Strategies of Labor Market Reform: Emerging Evidence from the U.S.', European Union Seminar, 'Knowledge and Work', Amsterdam (Amsterdam: Max Goote Kenniscentrum).

DUE, J., MADSEN, J. S., JENSEN, C. S. and PETERSEN, L. K. (1994), *The Survival of the Danish Model* (Copenhagen: DJOF).

EISNER, R. (1994), *The Misunderstood Economy: what Counts and how to Count it* (Boston, MA.: Harvard Business School Press).

ELIASSON, G. (1994), *Markets for Learning and Educational Services: A Micro Explanation of the Role of Education and Development of Competence in Macroeconomic Growth* (Washington DC: Center for Educational Research and Innovation).

EMERSON, M. (1988), 'Regulation or Deregulation of the Labour Market?', *European Economic Review*, 32, 775–817.

EQW [The National Center on the Educational Quality of the Workforce] (1995), *The EQW National Employer Survey* (Washington, DC: The Center).

ERBÈS-SEGUIN, S. (1990), *Construction du marché de l'emploi pour les jeunes et politiques de formation en République Fédérale et en France* (Berlin: CEDEFOP).

—— GILAIN, C. and KIEFFER, A. (1990), 'Les Interventions de l'État en matière d'emploi: L'Exemple de la formation professionnelle en France et en République Fédérale d'Allemagne', *Sociétés Contemporarines*, 4 (Dec.), 25–51.

ESPING-ANDERSEN, G. (1996), 'Welfare States without Work: The Impasse of Labour Shedding and Familialism in Continental European Social Policy', in Esping-Andersen (ed.) (1996), q.v.

—— (ed.) (1993), *Changing Classes: Stratification and Mobility in Post-Industrial Societies* (London: Sage).

—— (ed.) (1996), *Welfare States in Transition: National Adaptations in Global Economies* (London: Sage).

ESSER, J. (1991), 'Does Industrial Policy Matter? *Land* Governments in Research and Technology Policy in Federal Germany', in Crouch, C. and Marquand, D. (eds.), *The New Centralism: Britain out of Step in Europe?* (Oxord: Blackwell), 94–108.

EYRAUD, F., MARSDEN, D. W. and SILVESTRE, J. J. (1996), 'Internal and Occupational Labour Markets in Britain and France', *International Labour Review*, 129(4), 501–17.

FELDHOFF, J. and JACKE, N. (1990), 'Qualifikationsprofile in den neugeordneten metallindustriellen Ausbildungsberufen', in Strikker, F. and Timmermann, D. (eds.), *Berufsausbildung und Arbeitsmarkt in den 90er Jahren* (Frankfurt am Main: Lang).

FELSTEAD, A. and GREEN, F. (1994), 'Training during the Recession', *Work, Employment and Society*, 8(2), 199–219.

FINEGOLD, D. (1991), 'Institutional Incentives and Skill Creation: Preconditions for a High-Skill Equilibrium', in Ryan (ed.), q.v.

—— (1992), 'The Low-Skill Equilibrium: an Institutional Analysis of Britain's Education and Training Failure', D.Phil. thesis, University of Oxford.

—— (1997), *Creating World-Class Standards: A Process for Relating US Skill Standards to International Quality and Skill Standards*, a draft report for the National Skills Standards Board (Washington DC: NSSB).

—— (1998), 'The New Learning Partnerships: Sharing Responsibility for Building Competence', in Mohrman, S., Galbraith, J. and Lawler, E. (eds.), *Tomorrow's Organization* (San Francisco, CA: Jossey-Bass).

——, BRENDLEY, K. W., LEMPERT, R., HENRY, D., CANNON, P., BOULTINGHOUSE, B. and NELSON, M. (1994a), *The Decline of the U.S. Machine-Tool Industry and Prospects for Its Sustainable Recovery*, Vol. 1, RAND MR-479/1-OSTP (Santa Monica, CA: RAND).

—— and KELTNER, B. (1996), *Institutional Supports for a High Performing Skills Standards System: Evidence from the UK, Australia and Germany* (Santa Monica, CA: RAND).

——. —— (1997), 'Institutional Effects on Skill Creation: A Comparison of Management Development in the US and Germany', mimeo.

——, KEYS, E., MILIBAND, D., ROBERTSON, D., SISSON, K. and ZIMAN, J. (1992), *Higher Education: Expansion and Reform* (London: Institute for Public Policy Research).

—— and LEVINE, D. (1997), 'Institutional Incentives for Employer Training', *Journal of Education and Work*, 10(2), 109–27.

——, MCFARLAND, L. and RICHARDSON, W. (eds.) (1993), *Something Borrowed, Something Learned? The Transatlantic Market in Education and Training Reform* (Washington, DC: The Brookings Institution).

——, SCHECHTER, S., *et al.* (1994b), *International Models of Management Development: Lessons for Australia*, RAND MR-481-IET, June (Santa Monica, CA: RAND).

—— and SOSKICE, D. (1988), 'The Failure of Training in Britain: Analysis and Prescription', *Oxford Review of Economic Policy*, 4(3), 21–53.

—— and WAGNER, K. (1997), 'When Lean Production Meets the German Model: Innovation Responses in the US and German Pump Industries', *Industry and Innovation*, 4(2), 207–32.

FLAMHOLTZ, E. G. (1985), *Human Resource Accounting* (San Francisco, CA: Jossey-Bass).

FRANCHI, M. and RIESER, V. (1991), 'Le categorie sociologiche nell'analisi del distretto industriale: tra communità e razionalizzazione', *Stato e mercato*, 33, 451–76.

FREEMAN, R., (1976), *The Overeducated American* (New York: Academic Press).

FREEMAN, R. B. (1991), *Crime and the Employment of Disadvantaged Youths*, Working Paper No. 3875 (Washington, DC: National Bureau of Economic Research).

—— (1994), *Working under Different Rules* (New York: Russell Sage Foundation).

FRESCHI, A. C. (1992), *I centri di servizi alle imprese in toscana* (Florence: Regione Toscana).

FRIEDMAN, D. (1988), *The Misunderstood Miracle: Industrial Development and Political Change in Japan* (Ithaca, NY: Cornell University Press).

FUKUYAMA, F. (1995), *Trust: The Social Virtues and the Creation of Prosperity* (London: Hamish Hamilton).

GAMBETTA, D. (1987), *Were They Pushed or Did They Jump?: Individual Decision Mechanisms in Education* (Cambridge: Cambridge University Press).

GAMBLE, A. (1994), *The Free Economy and the Strong State: The Politics of Thatcherism*, second edition (Basingstoke: Macmillan).

GANS, H. J. (1995), *The War against the Poor* (New York: Basic Books).

GARRAUD, P. (1995), 'La Mise en œuvre des politiques de lutte contre le chômage par la formation: les contraintes du service public en France', *Sociologie du travail*, 37(4), 675–96.

GATTER, J. (1998), 'Continuing Training in an Aging German Economy', in Culpepper and Finegold (eds.), q.v.

GEIßLER, K. A. (1991), 'Das duale system der industriellen berufsausbildung hat keine zukunft', *Leviathan*, 19, 68–77.

GOUX, D. and MAURIN, E. (1998), 'From Education to First Job: the French Case', in Shavit and Müller (eds.), q.v.

GRABHER, G. (1993), 'The Weakness of Strong Ties: The Lock-in of Regional Development in the Ruhr Area', in Grabher (ed.), q.v.

—— (ed.) (1993), *The Embedded Firm: On the Socioeconomics of Industrial Networks* (London: Routledge).

GRANOVETTER, M. (1985), 'Economic Action and Social Structure: The Problem of Embeddedness', *American Journal of Sociology*, 3, 481–510.

GRUBB, W. N. and STERN, D. (1989), *Separating the Wheat from the Chaff: The Role of Vocational Education in Economic Development*, MDS-040 (Berkeley, CA: National Center for Research in Vocational Education).

HALL, P. (1986), *Governing the Economy: the Politics of State Intervention in Britain and France* (Oxford: Polity Press).

HEALEY, M. J. and DUNHAM, P. J. (1994), 'Changing Competitive Advantage in a Local Economy: The Case of Coventry', *Urban Studies*, 31(8), 1279–1301.

HELPER, S. and SAKO, M. (1995), 'Supplier Relations in Japan and the United States: Are they Converging?', *Sloan Management Review*, 35, 3, Spring, 77–84.

HENNINGS, G. and KUNZMANN, K. R. (1990), 'Priority to Local Economic Development: Industrial Restructuring and Local Development Responses in the Ruhr Area—the Case of Dortmund', in Stöhr, W. (ed.), *Global Challenge and Local Response: Initiatives for Economic Regeneration in Contemporary Europe* (London: Mansell, 199–223).

HERRIGEL, G. B. (1993), 'Power and the Redefinition of Industrial Districts: The Case of Baden-Württemberg', in Grabher (ed.), q.v.

—— (1996), 'Crisis in German Decentralized Production', *European Urban and Regional Studies*, 3(1), 33–52.

—— (1998), 'Collective Regeneration and Cooperative Self-Blockage: Comparisons of the German, Japanese and American Steel Industries Since the Mid 1970s', in Culpepper and Finegold (eds.), q.v.

HIGUCHI, Y. (1987), *A Comparative Study of Japanese Plants Operating in the US and American Plants: Recruitment, Job Training, Wage Structure and Job Separation*, Working Paper No. 13 (New York: Columbia University Center on Japanese Economy and Business).

HINZ, T. (1998), 'Vocational Training and Occupational Mobility in Comparative Perspective', in Culpepper and Finegold (eds.), q.v.

HIPPEL, E. VON (1987), 'Cooperation between Rivals: Information Know-How Trading', *Research Policy*, 16, 291–302.

HIRSCHMAN, A. O. (1970), *Exit, Voice and Loyalty* (Cambridge, MA: Harvard University Press).

HIRST, P. and ZEITLIN, J. (eds.) (1989), *Reversing Industrial Decline?* (Oxford: Berg).

HJALAGAR, A.-M. (1990), *Det tekstilindustrielle kompleks i Herning* (Copenhagen: Nord-Refo 90(2)).

HJER, B. (1980), 'Performance in Manpower Training: the Swedish AMU Center Programme', mimeo. (Berlin: IIM).

HOLLINGSWORTH, J. R., SCHMITTER, P. and STREECK, W. (1994) (eds.), *Governing Capitalist Economies* (New York: Oxford University Press).

HOLZER, H. J., BLOCK, R. N., CHEATHAM, M. and KNOTT, J. H. (1993), 'Are Training Subsidies for Firms Effective? The Michigan Experience', *Industrial and Labor Relations Review*, 46(4), 625–36.

IANNELLI, C. (1999), 'Individual Decisions in Education: A Study of the Low Levels of Educational Attainment in Italy, with a Comparative Perspective', Ph.D. thesis, European University Institute, Florence.

IMANO, K. (1997), 'Internationalization of the Labour Market: Foreign Workers and Trainees', in Sako, M. and Sato, H. (eds.), *Japanese Labour and Management in Transition* (London: Routledge).

INFELISE, L. (1996), 'Continuing Vocational Training in Italy', in Brandsma *et al.* (eds.), q.v.

INTERNATIONAL ASSOCIATION FOR THE EVALUATION OF EDUCATIONAL ACHIEVEMENT (IAEA) (1987), *The Underachieving Curriculum: Assessing US School Mathematics from an International Perspective* (Champaign: Stipes Publishing).

ISFOL (1992), *Rapporto Isfol 1992* (Milan: Franco Angeli).

JACOBS, J., MCALINDEN, S. and TREADO, C. (1991), *The Impact of Programmable Automation on Employee Training and Occupational Change in American Manufacturing* (Michigan, IL.: Industrial Technology Institute).

JAPAN (Ministry of Labour) (1994), *Labour Management Communication Survey* (Tokyo: Ministry of Labour).

JARVIS, V. and PRAIS, S. J. (1989), 'Two Nations of Shopkeepers: Training for Retailing in France and Britain', *National Institute Economic Review*, 128, 58–74.

JOBERT, A. (1995), 'Italie: le chômage des jeunes diplômés', *Sociologie du travail*, 37(4), 697–714.

JOHANSSON, R. (1991), 'Counselling within the Employment Service and at Employment Institutes in Sweden', mimeo. (Solna: AMS).

KELTNER, B. (1995), 'Relationship-Banking as a Competitive Response to Dynamic Financial Service Markets: Evidence from the U.S. and Germany', *California Management Review*, 37(4), 45–72.

—— and FINEGOLD, D. (1996), 'Adding Value in Banking: An Innovative Human Resource Strategy', *Sloan Management Review*, 38(1), 57–68.

—— and MASON, G. (forthcoming), 'Customer Segmentation and Service Performance: Evidence from Commercial Banking in the US and Europe', *Sloan Management Review*.

KERN, H. and SCHUMANN, M. (1987), 'Limits of the Division of Labour. New Production and Employment Concepts in West German Industry', *Economic and Industrial Democracy*, 8, 151–70.

KING, D. (1993), 'The Conservatives and Training Policy: from a Tripartite to a Neoliberal Regime', *Political Studies,* 41, 214–35.

—— (1995), *Actively Seeking Work* (Chicago: University of Chicago Press).

—— and ROTHSTEIN, B. (1993), 'Institutional Choices and Labor Market Policy: a British–Swedish Comparison', *Comparative Political Studies*, 26(2), 147–77.

KING, R. and SCHNACK, K. (1990), 'The MSC's Area Management Boards: the Role of Employer and Union Representatives', in Crouch, C. and Dore, R. (eds.) *Corporatism and Accountability: Organized Interests in British Public Life* (Oxford: Clarendon Press).

KOCHAN, T. A., LANSBURY, R. D. and MACDUFFIE, J.-P. (eds.) (1997), *After Lean Production: Evolving Employment Practices in the World Auto Industry* (Ithaca, NY, and London: ILR Press).

KOIKE, K. (1994), *Skill Formation in Japanese Industry: Current Systems and Historical Development* (Washington: World Bank).

KÖNIG, W. and MÜLLER, W. (1986), 'Educational Systems and Labour Markets as Determinants of Worklife Mobility in France and West Germany: a Comparison of Men's Career Mobility 1965–70', *European Sociological Review*, 2(2), 73–96.

KRAFCIK, J. F. (1990), *Training and the Automobile Industry: International Comparisons*, Contractor report (Washington DC: Office of Technology Assessment).

KRÜGER, H. (1998), 'Gender and Skills: Distributional Ramification of the German Skill System', in Culpepper and Finegold (eds.), q.v.

KRUGMAN, P. (1994), 'Competitiveness: Does It Matter?', *Fortune*, 7 March, 109–15.

LABOUR PARTY (1997), *New Labour because Britain Deserves Better* (London: Labour Party).

LAM, A. and MARSDEN, D. (1992), 'Shortages of qualified labour in Britain: a problem of training or of skill utilisation?', *Vocational Training* (Spring), 10–32.

LANDELL, E. and VICTORSSON, J. (1991), *Långt kvar till kunskapssamhället*, SIND (1991) 2 (Stockholm: Statensindustriverk).

LAWLER, E. E., MOHRMAN, S. A. and LEDFORD, G. E. (1992), *Employee Involvement and Total Quality Management: Practices and Results in Fortune 1000 Companies* (San Francisco, CA: Jossey-Bass).

—— , —— , —— (1995), *Creating High Performance Organizations* (San Francisco, CA: Jossey-Bass).

LAWLESS, P. (1994), 'Partnership in Urban Regeneration in the UK: The Sheffield Central Area Study', *Urban Studies*, 31(8), 1303–24.

LEBORGNE, D. and LIPIETZ, A. (1988), 'L'après-fordisme et son espace', *Les Temps modernes*, 43(501), 75–114.

LEE, D. *et al.* (1990), *Schooling for Youth: A Study of YTS in the Enterprise Culture* (Milton Keynes: Open University Press).

LEVINE, D. I. (1995), *Reinventing the Workplace: How Business and Employees Can Both Win* (Washington, DC: Brookings Institution).

LEYDA, M., CAREY, M. and SCHAFFER, D. (1995), 'Calculating Return on Investment of Training Dollars', *American Society of Engineering Education College Industry Education Conference*, Conference Proceedings (New Orleans: the Society).

VAN LIESHOUT, H. (1997), 'Enhancing the Operation of Markets for Vocational Training and Education: A Governance Approach', Background Report to European Union Seminar 'Knowledge and Work', Amsterdam, April 1997 (Amsterdam: Max Goote Kenniscentrum, University of Amsterdam).

LOCKE, R. (1995), *Remaking the Italian Economy* (Ithaca, NY: Cornell University Press).

LUTZ, B. (1992), 'Education and Job Hierarchies: Contrasting Evidence from France and Germany', in Altmann, Kohler, and Meil (eds.), q.v.

LYNCH, R., PALMER, J. and GRUBB, W. N. (1991), *Community College Involvement in Contract Training and Other Economic Development Activities*, MDS-379 (Berkeley, CA: National Center for Research in Vocational Education).

McCALL, M. (1997), *High Fliers* (Boston, MA: Harvard Business School Press).

McDONNELL, L. and ZELLMAN, G. L. (1993), *Education and Training for Work in the Fifty States: A Compendium of State Policies*, N-3560-NCRVE/UCB (Santa Monica, CA: RAND).

MacDUFFIE, J. P. and KOCHAN, T. A. (1993), 'Do US Firms Underinvest in Human Resources? Determinants of Training in the World Auto Industry', mimeo.

MANPOWER SERVICES COMMISSION (1975), *Annual Report 1974–75* (London: Manpower Services Commission).

—— NATIONAL ECONOMIC DEVELOPMENT COUNCIL AND INSTITUTE OF MANPOWER STUDIES (1984), *Competence and Training: Germany, US and Japan* (London: HMSO).

MARAVALL, J. M. (1997), *Regimes, Politics and Markets: Democratization and Economic Change in Southern and Eastern Europe* (Oxford: Oxford University Press).

MARCH, J. G. and OLSEN, J. P. (1989), *Rediscovering Institutions: The Organizational Basis of Politics* (New York: Free Press).

MARIN, B. (1990), 'Generalized Political Exchange: Preliminary Considerations', in Marin, B. (ed.), *Generalized Political Exchange* (Frankfurt am Main: Campus).

MARKING, C. (ed.) (1992), *Kompetens i arbete: en antologi* (Stockholm: Publica).

MARSDEN, D. W. (1990), 'Institutions and Labour Mobility: Occupational and Internal Labour Markets in Britain, France, Italy and West Germany', in R. Brunetta and C. Dell'Aringa (eds.), *Labour Relations and Economic Performance* (London: Macmillan and International Economic Association).

MARSDEN, D. W. (1995), 'A phoenix from the ashes of apprenticeship? Vocational training in Britain', *International Contributions to Labour Studies*, 5, 87–114.

—— and RYAN, P. (1991), 'The Structuring of Youth Pay and Employment in Six European Economies', in Ryan (ed.), q.v.

MARSHALL, A. (1912), *Industry and Trade* (London: Macmillan).

MASON, G. and FINEGOLD, D. (1995), *Skills, Machinery and Productivity in Precision Metalworking and Food Processing: A Pilot Study of Matched Establishments in the U.S. and Europe* (London: National Institute of Economic and Social Research).

MASON, G. and WAGNER, K. (1994), 'High-level Skills and Industrial Competitiveness: Post-Graduate Engineers and Scientists in Britain and Germany', NIESR Report Series No. 6, 1–53 (London: NIESR).

MAYER, K. U. and BLOSSFELD, H.-P. (1990), 'Die gesellschaftliche Konstruktion sozialer Ungleichheit im Lebensverlauf', in P. A. Berger and S. Hradil (eds.), *Lebenslagen, Lebensläufe, Lebensstile*, special edition, *Die Sozialen Welt*, 7.

MAYNTZ, R. and SCHARPF, F. (eds.) (1995), *Gesellschaftliche Selbstregelung und politische Steuerung* (Frankfurt am Main: Campus).

MEGHNAGI, S. (1989), 'Technical and Vocational Education in Italy: the State and the Regions', *European Journal of Education*, 24(2), 159–65.

—— (1991), 'Mutamenti del lavoro e processi di conoscenza', in Bondioli, Meghnagi and Pagnocelli (eds.), *La formazione in Italia* (Milan: Angeli), 67–104.

MILLER, R. (1996), *Measuring What People Know: Human Capital Accounting for the Knowledge Economy* (Paris: OECD).

MINGIONE, E. (1991), *Fragmented Societies: A Sociology of Economic Life beyond the Market Paradigm* (Oxford: Blackwell).

MOHRMAN, S. A., COHEN, S. G. and MOHRMAN, A. M. (1995), *Designing Team-based Organizations: New Forms for Knowledge Work* (San Francisco, CA: Jossey-Bass).

MORGENSON, C. (1992), 'The Rise of The Corporate Business School', *Target Management Development Review*, 5(6), 13–17.

MUELLER, D. C. (ed.) (1982), *The Political Economy of Growth* (New Haven, CT: Yale University Press).

MÜLLER, W. (1994), 'Bildung und soziale Plazierung in Deutschland, England und Frankreich', in Peisert, H., and Zapf, W. (eds.), *Gesellschaft, Demokratie und Lebenschancen: Festschrift für Ralf Dahrendorf* (Stuttgart: Deutsche Verlagsanstalt)

MYRDAL, H.-J. (1991), 'The hard way from a centralized to a decentralized industrial relations system: The case of Sweden and SAF' (Stockholm: SAF).

NAPOLI, M. (1984), *Occupazione e Politica del Lavoro in Italia: Profili della Legislazione 1974–1983* (Milan: Vita e Pensiero).

NIESR (1990), *Education, Training and Productivity* (London: NIESR).

NILSSON, L. (1981) 'Yrkesutbildning i nutidshistoriskt perspektiv', doctoral thesis, University of Göteborg.

NISHIGUCHI, T. (1994), *Strategic Industrial Sourcing: The Japanese Advantage* (New York: Oxford University Press).

NORTH, D. C. (1981), *Structure and Change in Economic History* (New York: Norton).

NORTH, D. S. (1995), *Soothing the Establishment: Impact of Foreign Born Scientists and Engineers on America* (Lanham, MD: University Press of America).

OECD (1993), *Employment Outlook* (Paris: OECD).

OECD (1994*a*), *The OECD Jobs Study: Evidence and Explanations. Part I: Labour Market Trends and Underlying Forces of Change* (Paris: OECD).

OECD (1994*b*), *The OECD Jobs Study: Evidence and Explanations. Part II: The Adjustment Potential of the Labour Market* (Paris: OECD).

OECD (1996*a*), *Employment Outlook* (Paris: OECD).

OECD (1996*b*), *The OECD Jobs Study: Technology, Productivity and Job Creation, Volume 2, Analytical Report* (Paris: OECD).

OECD (1996*c*), *Education at a Glance 1996* (Paris: OECD).

OECD (1997*a*), *Economic Outlook* (Paris: OECD).

OECD (1997*b*), *Employment Outlook* (Paris: OECD).

OECD and STATISTICS CANADA (1995), *Literacy, Economy and Society* (Paris: OECD).

OHLIN, B. (1967), *Interregional and International Trade*, revised edition (Cambridge MA: Harvard University Press).

OKUDA, H. (1996), 'Continuing Vocational Training in Japan', in Brandsma *et al.* (eds.), q.v.

OLSON, M. (1965), *The Logic of Collective Action: Public Goods and the Theory of Groups* (Cambridge, MA: Harvard University Press).

—— (1982), *The Rise and Decline of Nations: Economic Growth, Stagflation and Social Rigidities* (New Haven, CT: Yale University Press).

OSBORNE, D. and GAEBLER, T. (1992), *Reinventing Government: How the Entrepreneurial Spirit is Transforming the Public Sector from Schoolhouse to Statehouse, City Hall to the Pentagon* (Reading, MA: Addison-Wesley).

OSTERMAN, P. (1994), 'How Common is Workplace Transformation and Who Adopts It?', *Industrial and Labor Relations Review*, 47(2), 173–88.

OULTON, N. (1996), 'Workforce Skills and Export Competitiveness', in A. L. Booth and D. J. Snower (eds.), *Acquiring Skills: Market Failures, Their Symptoms, and Policy Responses* (Cambridge: Cambridge University Press).

PARKER, E. and ROGERS, J. (1998), 'Sectoral Training Initiatives in the U.S.: Building Blocks of a New Workforce Preparation System?', in Culpepper and Finegold (eds.), q.v.

PARKER, K. T. and VICKERSTAFF, S. (1996), 'TECs, LECs, and Small Firms: Differences in Provision and Performance', *Environment and Planning C: Government and Policy*, 14, 251–67.

PESTOFF, V. (1991), *The Demise of the Swedish Model and the Resurgence of Organized Business as a Major Political Actor* (Stockholm: Department of Business Administration, University of Stockholm).

PITTON, L. (1991), 'L'esperienza dell'agenzia del lavoro di Trento nel campo della formazione professionale', *Osservatorio isfol*, 13(5), 111–18.

PORTER, M. E. (1990), *The Competitive Advantage of Nations* (London: Macmillan).

—— (1992), *Capital Choices: Changing the Way America Invests in Industry* (Washington, DC: Council on Competitiveness).

POTERBA, J. M. and SUMMERS, L. H. (1991), *Time Horizons of American Firms: New Evidence from a Survey of CEOs* (Washington, DC: Council on Competitiveness).

POWELL, W. W. and DiMAGGIO, P. (eds.) (1991), *The New Institutionalism in Organizational Analysis* (Chicago, IL: University of Chicago Press).

PRAHALAD, C. K. and HAMEL, G. (1990), 'The Core Competence of the Corporation', *Harvard Business Review*, May–June, 79–91.

PRAIS, S. J. (1981), 'Vocational Qualifications of the Labour Force in Britain and Germany', *National Institute Economic Review*, 98.

—— (1989), 'How Europe Would See the New British Initiative for Standardising Vocational Qualifications', *National Institute Economic Review*, 129.

—— (1991), 'Vocational Qualifications in Britain and Europe: Theory and Practice', *National Institute Economic Review*, 136.

—— and WAGNER, K. (1983), 'Schooling Standards in Britain and Germany: Some Summary Comparisons Bearing on Economic Performance', *National Institute Economic Review*, 112.

——, —— (1985), 'Some Practical Aspects of Human Capital Training: Training Standards in Five Occupations in Britain and Germany', *National Institute Economic Review*, 105.

PRAIS, S. J. and WAGNER, K. (1988), 'Productivity and Management: the Training of Foremen in Britain and Germany', *National Institute Economic Review*, 123.

PRIETO and HOMS (1995), 'Formation, emploi et compétivité en Espagne', *Sociologie du travail*, 37(4), 557–75.

QUACK, S., O'REILLY, J. and HILDERBRANDT, S. (1995), 'Structuring Change: Recruitment and Training in Retail Banking in Germany, Britain and France', *International Journal of Human Resource Management*, 6(4), 759–94.

RASELL, M. E. and MISHEL, L. (no date), 'Shortchanging Education: How U.S. Spending on Grades K–12 Lags behind Other Industrial Nations', Briefing Paper (Washington, DC: Economic Policy Institute).

RAULT, C. (1994), *La Formation professionelle initiale* (Paris: La documentation française).

REGINI, M. (1996a), 'Le imprese e le istituzioni: domanda e produzione sociale di risorse umane nelle regioni europee', in Regini (ed.), q.v.

—— (1996b), 'Conclusioni', in Regini (ed.), q.v.

—— (ed.) (1996), *La produzione sociale delle risorse humane* (Bologna: Il Mulino).

REICH, R. B. (1992), *The Work of Nations: Preparing Ourselves for 21st Century Capitalism* (New York: Vintage Books).

RICHARDSON, W. (1993), 'Employers as an Instrument of School Reform? Education–Business "compacts" in Britain and America', in Finegold, D., McFarland, L. and Richardson, W. (eds.), *Something Borrowed, Something Blue? A Study of the Thatcher Government's Appropriation of American Education and Training Policy*, Part 2, *Oxford Studies in Comparative Education*, 3(1).

ROACH, S. S. (1994), *The Perils of America's Productivity-Led Recovery*, Special Economic Study (New York: Morgan Stanley & Co. Inc.).

ROBINSON, P. and STEEDMAN, H. (1996), 'Rhetoric and Reality: Britain's New Vocational Qualifications', mimeo. (London: Centre for Economic Performance).

ROGERS, J. and STREECK, W. (1991), *Skill Needs and Training Strategies in the Wisconsin Metal Working Industry* (Madison, WI: University of Wisconsin-Madison: La Follette Institute of Public Affairs).

ROSE, R. (1991), 'Youth Training in a Time-Space Perspective', in Ryan (ed.), q.v.

—— and PAGE, E. C. (1990), 'Action in Adversity: Responses to Unemployment in Britain and Germany', *West European Politics*, 13(4), 66–84.

ROTHSTEIN, B. (1985), 'The Success of the Swedish Labour Market Policy: the Organizational Connection to Policy', *European Journal of Political Research*, 13, 153–65.

ROUSSEAU, D. (1995), *Psychological Contracts in Organizations: Understanding Written and Unwritten Agreements* (Thousand Oaks, CA: Sage).

RYAN, P. (1995), 'The Institutional Setting of Investment in Human Resources in the UK', in Büchtemann and Soloff (eds.), q.v.

—— (ed.) (1991), *International Comparisons of Vocational Education and Training for Intermediate Skills* (London: Falmer Press).

SABEL, C. F., HERRIGEL, G. B., DEEG, R. and KAZIS, R. (1989), 'Regional Prosperities Compared: Massachusetts and Baden-Württemberg in the 1980s', *Economy and Society*, 18(4), 374–405.

SADOWSKI, D. and DECKER, S. (1993), *Vertragliche Regelungen zur beruflichen Weiterbildung in Deutschland* (Berlin/Bonn: Bundesinstitut für Berufsbildung).

SAKO, M. (1988), *Partnership between Small and Large Firms: The Case of Japan* (Luxembourg: Commission of the European Communities, Directorate for Enterprise).

—— (1992), *Prices, Quality and Trust: Inter-Firm Relations in Britain and Japan* (Cambridge: Cambridge University Press).

—— (1994), 'Training, Productivity and Quality Control in Japanese Multinational Companies', in Aoki and Dore (eds.), q.v.

—— (1995), *Skill Testing and Certification in Japan* (Washington DC: World Bank).

—— (1996), 'Suppliers' Associations in the Japanese Automobile Industry: Collective Action for Technology Diffusion', *Cambridge Journal of Economics*, 20, 651–71.

—— (1997), 'Introduction: Forces for Homogeneity and Diversity in the Japanese Industrial Relations System', in Sako and Sato (eds.), *Japanese Labour and Management in Transition* (London: Routledge).

SAKO, M. and HELPER, S. (1998), 'Determinants of Trust in Supplier Relations: Evidence from the Automotive Industry in Japan and the United States', *Journal of Economic Behaviour and Organization*, 34, 387–417.

SANDBERG, Å. (ed.) (1995), *Enriching Production: Perspectives on Volvo's Uddevalla Plant as an Alternative to Lean Production* (Aldershot: Avebury).

SANDLER, T. (1992), *Collective Action: Theory and Applications* (New York: Harvester Wheatsheaf).

SAUTER, E. (1996), 'Continuing Vocational Training in Germany', in Brandsma *et al.* (eds.), q.v.

SAXENIAN, A. (1994), *Regional Advantage: Culture and Competition in Silicon Valley and Route 128* (Cambridge, MA: Harvard University Press).

SCHLESINGER, L. A. and HESKETT, J. L. (1991), 'The Service-Driven Company', *Harvard Business Review*, Sept.–Oct., 71–81.

SCHMID, G. (1990), 'Institutions Regulating the Labour Market: Support or Impediments for Structural Change?', in Appelbaum, E. and Schettkat, R. (eds.), *Labor Market Adjustments to Structural Change and Technological Progress* (New York: Praeger).

SEAVEY, D. and KAZIS, R. (1994), *Skills Assessment, Job Placement, and Training: What Can Be Learned from the Temporary Help/Staffing Industry?* (Boston, MA: Jobs for the Future).

SENKER, P. (1990), 'Policy Implications of the EITB's History' (University of Sussex: Social Science Policy Unit).

SHAVIT, Y. and WESTERBEEK, K. (1995), *Educational Reforms and Educational Stratification in Italy*, Working Paper (Florence: European University Institute).

—— and MÜLLER, W. (eds.) (1998), *From School to Work* (Oxford: Clarendon Press).

SINGELMANN, J. (1978), *From Agriculture to Services: The Transformation of Industrial Employment* (Beverly Hills: Sage).

SMEA (1994, 1995), *Chusho Kigyo Hakusho* (White Paper on Small and Medium-sized Enterprises), annual publication (Tokyo: SMEA).

SMITKA, M. (1991), *Competitive Ties: Subcontracting in the Japanese Automotive Industry* (New York: Columbia University Press).

SOSKICE, D. (1991*a*), 'Skill Mismatch, Training Systems and Equilibrium Unemployment: A Comparative Institutional Analysis', in Abraham, K. and Padoa-Schioa, F. (eds.), *Mismatch and Equilibrium Unemployment* (Cambridge, Mass.: Harvard University Press).

—— (1991*b*), 'The Institutional Infrastructure for International Competitiveness: a Comparative Analysis of the UK and Germany', in Atkinson, A. B. and Brunetta, R. (eds.), *The Economics of the New Europe* (London: International Economic Association and Macmillan).

Soskice, D. (1994), 'Reconciling Markets and Institutions: The German Apprenticeship System', in Lynch, L. M. (ed.), *Training and the Private Sector: International Comparison* (Chicago: Chicago University Press).

Standing, G. (1988), 'Training, Flexibility and Swedish Full Employment', *Oxford Review of Economic Policy*, 4(3), 94–107.

Steedman, H. (1987), 'Training in France and Britain: Office Work', *National Institute Economic Review*, 120, 58–70.

—— (1988), 'Vocational Training in France and Britain: Mechanical and Electrical Craftsmen', *National Institute Economic Review*, 126, 57–70.

—— Mason, G. and Wagner, K. (1991), 'Intermediate Skills in the Workplace: Deployment, Standards and Supply in Britain, France and Germany', *National Institute Economic Review*, 136, 60–76.

—— and Wagner, K. (1987), 'A Second Look at Productivity, Machinery and Skills in Britain and Germany', *National Institute Economic Review*, 122, 84–95.

——, —— (1989), 'Productivity, Machinery and Skills: Clothing Manufacture in Britain and Germany', *National Institute Economic Review*, 128, 40–57.

Stevens, M. (1995), 'Transferable Training and Poaching Externalities', in Cambridge Centre for Economic Policy Research, *Acquiring Skills: Market Failures, Their Symptoms and Policy Responses* (Cambridge: The Centre).

Streeck, W. (1985), 'Industrial Relations and Industrial Change in the Motor Industry', Public Lecture, University of Warwick (Coventry: University of Warwick).

—— (1989), 'Skills and the Limits of Neo-Liberalism: the Enterprise of the Future as a Place of Learning', *Work, Employment and Society*, 3, 90–104.

—— (1992), *Social Institutions and Economic Performance: Industrial Relations in Advanced Capitalist Economies* (London: Sage).

—— Hilbert, J., van Kevelaer, K. H., Maier, F. and Weber, H. (1987), *The Role of the Social Partners in Vocational Training and Further Training in the Federal Republic of Germany* (Berlin: CEDEFOP).

Sweden (1966), (Ecklesiastikdepartementet): *Yrkesutbildningen*, SOU: 1966: 3 (Lund: SOU).

—— (1976), Reg. Prop. 1975/76: 39 (Stockholm: Riksdagen).

—— (1979), Reg. Prop. 1978/79: 180 (Stockholm: Riksdagen).

—— (1980), Reg. Prop. 1979/80: 145 (Stockholm: Riksdagen).

—— (1983), SOU, 1983: 22 (Stockholm: SOU).

—— (1984a), Reg. Prop. 1983/84: 116 (Stockholm: Riksdagen).

—— (1984b), SOU, 1984: 31 (Stockholm: SOU).

—— (1986a), SOU, 1986: 2 (Stockholm: SOU).

—— (1986b), SOU, 1986: 3 (Stockholm: SOU).

—— (1989a), (Utbildningsdepartementet): *6000 platser och 10000 platser för försök i gymnasieskolan. Hur, var och varför?*, SOU 1989: 106 (Stockholm: SOU).

—— (1989b), (Utbildningsdepartementet): *Ungdomars kompetens. Vägar in i framtidens kunskapssamhälle*, SOU 1989: 113 (Stockholm: SOU).

—— (1989c), (Utbildningsdepartementet): *Ut värdering av försöksverksamheten med treårig yrkesinriktadutbildning i gymnasieskolan. Första året*, SOU 1990: 90 (Stockholm: SOU).

—— (1991a), (Arbetsmarknadsdepartementet): *Kompetensutveckling—en Utmaning*, SOU 1991: 56. Interim report of Kompetensutredningen (Stockholm: SOU).

—— (1991b), *Växa med kunskaper—om gymnasieskolan och vuxen-utbildningen*, Reg. Prop. 1990/91: 85 (Stockholm: Riksdagen).

—— (1992*a*), (Finansdepartement): *Långtidsutredningen 1992*, SOU 1992: 19 (Stockholm: SOU).

—— (1992*b*), (Arbetsmarknadsdepartementet): *Kompetensutveckling*, SOU 1992: 7. Final report of Kompetensutredningen (Stockholm: SOU).

—— (1992*c*), *Vissa gymnasie- och vuxenutbildningsfrågor m.m.* Reg. Prop. 1991/92: 157 (Stockholm: Riksdagen).

TAN, H. and PETERSON, C. (1992), 'Post-School Training of British and American Youth', in Finegold *et al.* (eds.), q.v.

TAN, H. W. and BATRA, G. (1995), *Enterprise Training in Developing Countries* (Washington, DC: The World Bank).

THALÉN, I. (1988), *Swedish Labour Market Policy* (Stockholm: Arbetsmarknadsdepartementet).

THURLEY, K. and LAM, A. (1989), 'Utilisation and Development of Skills of Engineers in Electronics and Information Technology Industries: UK versus Japan', Fourth World Conference of Continuing Engineering Education (Beijing: The Conference).

TRIGILIA, C. (1986), 'Small-Firm Development and Political Sub-Cultures in Italy', *European Sociological Review*, 2(3), 161–75.

—— (1989), 'Economia dei costi di transazione e sociologia: cooperazione o conflitto?', *Stato e mercato*, 25, 129–58.

—— (1991), 'The Paradox of the Region: Economic Regulation and the Representation of Interests', *Economy and Society*, 20(3), 306–27.

TUIJNMAN, A. (1989), *Recurrent Education, Earnings and Well-Being. A Fifty-Year Longitudinal Study of a Cohort of Swedish Men* (Stockholm: Almquist and Wiksell).

UEDA, H. *et al.* (1996), 'Higashi Osaka no Chusho seizogyo ni kansuru Jittaichosa no shukei kekka ni tsuite' (Results of the Survey of Small and Medium Manufacturing Firms in East Osaka), *Kikan Keizai Kenkyu*, 19(2), 27–66.

UNITED NATIONS (annual), *UN International Trade Statistics Yearbook* (New York: UN).

USA (Bureau of Labor Statistics) (1994), *How Workers Get Their Training: A 1994 Update* (Washington, DC: US Government Printing Office).

—— (1995*a*), *Economic Report of the President 1995* (Washington, DC: US Government Publisher).

—— (Department of Labor) (1995*b*), *What Works (and What Doesn't)* (Washington, DC: US Government Publisher).

—— (Department of Labor) (1997), Department Web Page.

—— (National Center on Education and the Economy (NCEE)) (1990), *America's Choice: High Skills or Low Wages!*, Rochester. Report of the Commission on the Skills of the American Workforce (New York: The Commission).

—— (NCEE) and National Alliance of Business (NAB) (1994), *A Guide for Benchmarking International Skill Standards*, Draft Guidelines (Washington DC: US Department of Labor).

VAUGHAN, P. (1993), *TECs and Employers: Developing Effective Links, Part 1* (London: Employment Department, Research Series No. 12).

VERDIER, E. (1995), 'Education and the Youth Labor Market in France: The Increasing Cost of Adjustment in the 1980s', in Büchtemann and Soloff (eds.), q.v.

—— (1996), 'L'Insertion des jeunes "à la française": vers un ajustement structurel?', *Travail et emploi*, 4, 37–54.

VICKERSTAFF, S. and PARKER, K. T. (1995), 'Helping Small Firms: The Contribution of TECs and LECs', *International Small Business Journal*, 13(4): 56–72.

VICKERSTAFF, S. and PARKER, K. T. (1996) 'Evaluating TECs: An Analysis of Differences between TECs and their Possible Implications for the Delivery of Policy', mimeo.

VISSER, J. and HEMERIJCK, A. (1997), *A Dutch 'Miracle'* (Amsterdam: Amsterdam University Press).

VOELZKOW, H. (1990), *Mehr Technik in die Region: Neue Ansätze zur regionalen Technikförderung in Nordrhein-Westfalen* (Wiesbaden: DUV).

WAGNER, K. (1998), 'Costs and Other Challenges to the Dual System', in Culpepper and Finegold (eds.), q.v.

WALTON, R. (1985), 'From Control to Commitment in the Workplace', *Harvard Business Review*, 63(2), 76–84.

WATANABE, Y. (1995), 'Sangyo kudoka? Nihon no kikai kogyo ni nani ga shojite iruka: oosaka no baai' (Hollowing out? What is happening to the machinery industry in Japan: the Case of Osaka), *Chusho Kigyo Kiho*, 2, 1–8.

WHITTAKER, D. H. (1997), *Small Firms in the Japanese Economy* (Cambridge: Cambridge University Press).

WILLIAMSON, O. (1975), *Markets and Hierarchies* (New York: The Free Press).

—— (1985), *The Economic Institutions of Capitalism* (New York: The Free Press).

WOLF, A. (1995), *Competence-Based Assessment* (Buckingham: Open University Press).

WOMACK, J. P., JONES, D. T. and ROOS, D. (1990), *The Machine That Changed the World* (New York: Rawson Associates).

WOOD, A. (1994), *North–South Trade, Employment and Inequality* (Oxford: Clarendon Press).

WOOD, S. (1998), 'Building a Governance Structure for Vocational Training? Employers, the State and the TEC Experiment in Britain', in Culpepper and Finegold (eds.), q.v.

ZEMSKY, R. and SHAPIRO, D. (1994), *On Measuring a Mirage: Why U.S. Training Numbers Don't Add Up* (Philadelphia: The National Center on the Educational Quality of the Workforce).

ZUCCON, G. C. (1992), 'La formazione post-secondaria nel progetto della Commissione Brocca', *Osservatorio isfol*, 14(5), 137–46.

INDEX